LEARNING TO CHANGE LIVES

The Strategies and Skills Learning and
Development System

The Strategies and Skills Learning and Development (SSLD) system is an action-oriented model that enables clients in social work, health, mental health, and human services settings to address their needs and life goals. In *Learning to Change Lives*, author A. Ka Tat Tsang introduces SSLD's powerful framework and practice, which has been developed based on three decades of experience in psychotherapy, counselling, education, training, consultation, and community service.

Learning to Change Lives provides detailed, step-by-step guidelines for SSLD intervention – starting with engagement with the client, assessment, translating problems into intervention plans, systematic learning, and development of appropriate strategies and skills. Key practice procedures are described clearly and illustrated by case examples, specific instructions, and sample worksheets. Aimed at clinical practitioners, mental health professionals, social workers, and other human service professionals, this book can be used as a manual by practitioners and as a textbook for courses and training programs.

A. KA TAT TSANG is a professor in the Factor-Inwentash Faculty of Social Work at the University of Toronto.

Learning to Change Lives

The Strategies and Skills Learning and Development System

A. KA TAT TSANG

UNIVERSITY OF TORONTO PRESS
Toronto Buffalo London

© University of Toronto Press 2013
Toronto Buffalo London
www.utppublishing.com
Printed in Canada

ISBN 978-1-4426-4581-3 (cloth)
ISBN 978-1-4426-1401-7 (paper)

Printed on acid-free, 100% post-consumer recycled paper with vegetable-based inks.

Library and Archives Canada Cataloguing in Publication

Tsang, Adolf Ka Tat, 1954–
Learning to change lives : The Strategies and Skills Learning and Development System / A. Ka Tat Tsang.

Includes bibliographical references and index.
ISBN 978-1-4426-4581-3 (bound)   ISBN 978-1-4426-1401-7 (pbk.)

1. Social skills – Study and teaching.   2. Human services personnel.
I. Title.

HM691.T72 2013   302'.14   C2012-907222-2

University of Toronto Press acknowledges the financial assistance to its publishing program of the Canada Council for the Arts and the Ontario Arts Council.

 Canada Council   Conseil des Arts
for the Arts   du Canada

University of Toronto Press acknowledges the financial support of the Government of Canada through the Canada Book Fund for its publishing activities.

Contents

List of Figures, Tables, Boxes, and Worksheets vii

Preface ix

Acknowledgments xiii

Part One: The SSLD Idea   3

1 Introduction   5

2 Social and Interpersonal Strategies and Skills as Human Action   20

3 Basic Principles of Strategies and Skills Learning and Development   44

Part Two: Basic SSLD Procedure   59

4 Problem Translation   61

5 Review of Current Strategies   95

6 Formulating and Designing Relevant Strategies and Skills   109

7 The Learning Process   126

Part Three: Building Blocks   137

8 Reception   141

9 Expression   151

10 Engagement 174

11 Managing Relationships 187

12 Instrumental Tasks 218

Part Four: SSLD Practice and Related Issues 233

13 Learning and Applying SSLD 235

14 Issues Related to SSLD: A Personal Note 284

References 297

Index 321

Figures, Tables, Boxes, and Worksheets

Figures

- 2.1: Human Action and the Environment   23
- 2.2: Reciprocal Influence between Two Interacting Individuals   31
- 2.3: SSLD Analysis of Problem Behaviour   39
- 3.1: Effective Performance of Learned Strategies and Skills to Meet Client Needs   52
- 4.1: Behaviour-Oriented Functional Analysis of Presenting Problems   64
- 4.2: Inferring Needs   68
- 4.3: Client Needs Profile   73
- 5.1: Strategies, Composite Skills, and Micro-processes   105
- 6.1: Example of Learning Program Organization   114
- 13.1: SSLD in Community Development and Anti-oppressive Practice   256

Tables

- 3.1: Preplanned or Prepackaged Program versus Contingency-Based Skills Learning   46
- 5.1: Strategies and Skills   103
- P3.1: Basic Components of Strategies and Skills   138
- 8.1: Selective Statement of Facts   143

Boxes

- 1.1: Features of SSLD   15

2.1: Basic Tenets of the SSLD Model   37
4.1: Problem Translation Procedure   87
4.2: Behaviour-Focused Interviewing   91
5.1: Setting Up the In-Session Role-Play   99
6.1: Designing a Learning Module   118
6.2: Generating New Skills through Collaborative Creation   123
8.1: What Does a Person Want?   149
9.1: Ingredients for Interpersonal Attraction   157
9.2: Positive Reframing   158
9.3: Friar Lawrence: The Natural Positive Reframer   160
9.4: Emotional Work in SSLD   169
10.1: Strategies and Skills Facilitating Engagement   177
10.2: The Case of Eugene   183
11.1: Relationship Building   202
13.1: Community Participation Scale   259
13.2: The Case of Suna   280

Worksheets

4.1: Needs Profile   86
4.2: Behavioural Diary   93
11.1: 3-D Appreciation Exercise   199

Preface

This book is written for practitioners in the human service professions, including social work, psychology, education, nursing, health and mental health, human resources, and training and development. It is the result of more than thirty years of experience in the application of social skills training (SST) procedures and psychology-of-learning principles to a wide range of human service contexts. I was first exposed to social skills training in the seventies. As a graduate student in clinical psychology, I participated in an assertiveness training program at the Student Counselling Unit of the University of Hong Kong. The experience did raise some issues for me with regards to the cultural appropriateness and relevance of the idea of assertiveness, as well as the role of assertiveness in long-term relationships. I did, nonetheless, find the experience helpful and subsequently started exploring the possible application of similar training procedures to other practice situations. As a novice, I was helped by the pioneering work of Michael Argyle (1972) and his colleagues (Trower, Bryant, & Argyle, 1978) in SST.

Since then I have adopted the SST method in my work with a diverse range of clients – including individuals, couples, groups, organizations, and communities. Some authors, especially in social work, refer to them as clients and client systems; in this book I will use the term client to include client systems. My clients are from a wide variety of settings, including children with infantile autism as well as their parents and family caregivers; adults with long histories of schizophrenic disorder; volunteers working in the social services; youth with emotional and behavioural problems and the social workers who work with them; adolescents and adults with relationship problems; residents living in public housing projects seeking to improve their environment and community; couples wanting to improve their relationships; executives learning to coach their staff; human resource professionals; and new immigrants trying to adjust to life in North America. I have delivered courses and conducted many training and professional development workshops on the method. This work has been done in Canada, China, Hong Kong, South Korea, New Zealand, and Thailand, and has involved clients and practitioners from many cultures.

Before 2005, these programs were called social skills training (SST). Apart from Argyle's (1967, 1972) pioneering work, I developed the programs with reference to the work by leaders in the field such as Singleton, Spurgeon, and Stammers (1979), Curran and Monti (1982), Trower (1984), L'Abate and Milan (1985), Hollin and Trower (1986), and Liberman, DeRisi, and Mueser (1989). In the process, I tried to stay attuned to the performance of my clients and students, as well as the feedback they gave and made ongoing modifications to my methods. This process gradually transformed the content and structure of my programs, as well as the process and style of delivery. Over the last few years, I have shifted towards a language of skills learning instead of training, and I am increasingly talking about strategies in addition to skills. The word "social" is probably appropriate in most contexts, although there are situations in which people are talking about strategies and skills for a broader scope, such as in managing their emotions, or even in reconstructing their life-world; and there are people interested in more specific domains such as intimate relationships, career development, or performance within an organization.

While I am indebted to the practitioners and scholars who contributed to the development of social skills training both in the UK and North America, I am most thankful for the invaluable feedback given to me by my clients, students, and professional colleagues over the years. Their feedback, which includes comments, questions, challenges, and sharing of personal and practice experience, has supported the ongoing revision and refinement of my practice. In the last few years, I have systematically reviewed the method, its theoretical premise, and its application and development in different contexts, and I have come to realize that a number of modifications and special features have evolved in the process. I have since then decided to give this modified method a name that will more accurately reflect its nature and its scope: strategies and skills learning and development (SSLD). This book is an attempt to summarize my experience, observation, and reflection over this period.

My main goal is to present a system of practice that will be useful to colleagues in social work, counselling, psychotherapy, education, and related human service and health care professions. Ideally, this book will be used in connection with a professional development program on SSLD, but experienced colleagues can probably benefit from just reading this book.

Consistent with the SSLD perspective, which will be detailed later, the structure of this book is designed to support professional skills development. Theoretical and conceptual content is presented in a way that facilitates application. Recognizing that there are different learning styles among readers, the book is organized to enhance systematic learning in an incremental manner. In the mastery of skills, certain key procedures and their underlying principles may need to be repeated. I imagine that most readers will go through a spiralling process – moving forward through revisiting earlier learning every now and then. My hope is that most readers will find the apparent repetition helpful in consolidating conceptual understanding and mastery of the key procedures. Readers are encouraged to apply what is learned in the book in an incremental manner. A dialogue with the content of the book involving reference to your own direct practice experience and particular case examples will be most valuable.

More experienced colleagues may selectively read sections of the book that appear relevant. I am looking forward to ongoing feedback and exchange with clients, students, and colleagues. I am prepared to review and revise this document in a few years' time, making it more current and relevant to the changing practice context. Readers are encouraged to visit the website at http://ssld.kttsang.com and get in touch with me to share their comments, and for this I wish to thank all of you in advance.

Acknowledgments

The development of SSLD as a system would not be possible without the foundation laid by pioneers in social skills training such as Michael Argyle. I started reading Argyle in 1971, when I was still in high school. Although I later moved beyond the paradigm of experimental social psychology, my exposure to this body of research and scholarship was eye-opening. My early curiosity about interpersonal behaviour and interest in psychosocial intervention found their translation into actual practice thanks to the invitation by Kwong-yuen Liu to work with experiential learning groups in Hong Kong in the 1970s. His self-directed learning and readiness for modification, change, and innovation remain valuable lessons till this day.

Since then, many people have contributed to my learning and exploration. The late Erik Kvan of the University of Hong Kong taught me how to question, and showed me multiple paths to take in our attempt to understand human reality. At around the same time, David Y.F. Ho showed me how psychological and political realities intersect, and has remained a source of inspiration to my own thinking about culture and cross-cultural practice. While I am most thankful to my teachers and mentors, I have to say that I am equally indebted to my students, who have shared their experience, questions, learning, and insights with me. In the 1980s, students and colleagues like Cecilia Man-Sze Cheung, Roxco Chun, Florence Chu, Terence Chan, and Debbie Lam gave me invaluable support in introducing social skills training to different areas of human service. When I moved to Canada in 1989, I asked Cecilia Man-Sze Cheung to coordinate a social skills training study group to keep the practice and learning going. Over more than two decades, Cecilia and her group have maintained close collaboration in direct practice, held countless learning sessions, reviewed hundreds of hours of recorded practice, designed and delivered innovative programs, and created many valuable opportunities for learning and professional development both for themselves and their students and mentees. The group remains an energetic and vibrant network for professional learning and development to date. Timothy Leung, Kit-lin Au, Frederick Yeung, William Chu, Ivan Yau, and Edward Chan have all made significant contributions to the group process. Timothy Leung has offered invaluable insights and feedback towards the conceptual development of SSLD. Kit-lin Au has been instrumental in bringing SSLD to diverse fields of application, especially in the area of community development. She is a rare role model who integrates clinical practice seamlessly into her community activism and development work. Ivan Yau has been a wonderful supporter and collaborator throughout, and is my co-editor of the first Chinese book on SSLD, published in 2011. He is also the person who most persistently encouraged me to get started on writing this book when I allowed myself to be distracted by the many projects that appeared less daunting at the time.

During my time in Canada, my students and colleagues have infused valuable experience and insights into the development of SSLD, together with immense positive energy. Hanna Kim has been coordinating the Toronto SSLD study group since 2010, and co-authored the first SSLD paper in Korean. She has also participated in SSLD teaching and coordinated the production of video and online instruction materials. Members of the Toronto study group have made various contributions to the SSLD system, such as developing programs, practice manuals, and website content. Sam Wong first built the SSLD website in 2008, and ongoing website development has benefited from the input of Willie Lo, Cindy Choi, and Renee Xu. Aicha Benayoune introduced the system to Algeria in 2011 through an intensive training program, the first of its kind in the Arabic-speaking world. She has also helped to produce demonstration and instruction videos for SSLD practice. Linus Ip has been very active in introducing SSLD to the health area, and has helped develop programs for insomnia, chronic pain, palliative care, weight management, caregiver support, and integrating SSLD with yoga and bodywork. Xiaoting Wang, Sophia Kim, Theresa Peng, and Jane Wu have contributed to different SSLD applications ranging from insomnia to immigration and settlement. Sherlyn Hu, a former student, has offered invaluable support in terms of background research and content development in various SSLD programs. She has also played a pivotal role in the entire writing and revision process of this book. Her professionalism and the high-quality research assistance she provided have made the writing of this book a most gratifying experience.

Finally, I have to emphasize that the development of SSLD is a result of our collaboration with clients who share their problems and issues with us, and who have in the process helped us learn new strategies and skills, gain new insights, and develop new perspectives and conceptual tools. Practitioner colleagues who have participated in SSLD programs and consultation sessions in different parts of the world have also enriched our experience and understanding by generously sharing theirs. This book is, in a sense, my way of saying thank you.

LEARNING TO CHANGE LIVES

The Strategies and Skills Learning and
Development System

PART ONE

The SSLD Idea

Chapter One

Introduction

Life is full of challenges. As we engage in our quest for well-being, happiness, or cherished goals in life, we often find that we are not adequately equipped to deal with the demands of a rapidly changing world. More often than not, the challenges we face involve other people, who are either related to us in a personal way or are performing a role that has an impact on our lives. In order to achieve what we desire, we have to interact with these people and hopefully we can get them to respond in ways that are favourable to whatever we wish to accomplish. Ever since infancy, we have learned to express our needs, seek help, communicate feelings and ideas, listen, understand, negotiate, argue, support, assist, care, fight, cooperate, share, or simply have fun with others. The list can go on and on. All these actions involve skills that are central to our survival and well-being, and these are sometimes called *life skills*. As many of them involve other people and are usually performed within a social context, they are also called interpersonal skills or social skills. People can be more or less skilful in this regard, and their competence or skilfulness has direct implications for how effective they are in achieving their desired goals and how satisfied they are with their lives. Simply put, our quality of life is contingent upon our skill level in managing life situations and relationships.

This book introduces a system of learning and developing strategies and skills for a more gratifying life. I believe that effective social and interpersonal strategies and skills will increase one's likelihood of attaining personal goals and achieving well-being. I also believe that such strategies and skills can be mastered through active and systematic learning. Within the human services, there are a number of practice models and programs that utilize a skills-training approach. They are usually called social skills training (SST). In mental health practice, the term social skills therapy has also been used. When working with children – especially those with developmental issues – and other vulnerable groups, the term life skills training is often used. There are other training programs with more specific titles, such as assertiveness training and parent effectiveness training. A number of training modules in the corporate and human resources sectors have been delivered as coaching, communications and presentation skills training, leadership training, and so on.

A common feature across this wide array of professional activities is the emphasis on the acquisition of skills, rather than teaching conceptual or theoretical content. The training usually involves hands-on experience by the learners, with emphasis on procedures such as demonstration, role play, simulation, feedback, homework assignments, and the like, often supported by video recording and playback. Most of these modules follow an expert trainer model, in which the trainer is supposed to have mastered the skills to be taught, and quite often there are well-structured training programs complete with manuals, exercises, worksheets, and other program material.

Social Skills Training: A Brief Review

According to Goldstein (1981), social skills training is a planned, systematic teaching of behaviours required and consciously desired by a person for the purpose of functioning in an effective and satisfactory manner over a prolonged period of time. Social skills are situation-specific and they are learned. Interpersonal effectiveness is determined by the acquisition of verbal and non-verbal responses that constitute one's social repertoire (Pope, 1986).

The theory and practice of SST can be traced back to a number of origins: Salter's (1949) social learning theory, Wolpe's (1958) reciprocal inhibition intervention, Zigler and Phillips' (1961) linking between social competency and mental health, Schofield's (1964) highlighting of SST as a necessary alternative to interventions that have a social class bias, and Bandura's social learning theory (1969, 1977a) and social cognitive theory (1986). The early work of Argyle (1967, 1972) outlined a practice system based on his integration of research findings in experimental social psychology.

Given its foundation in the learning theory tradition, SST probably fits the broad category of cognitive behavioural therapies (CBT). Hayes (2004b) identified three generations in the development of cognitive behavioural therapy. The first wave was seen as a rebellion against existing clinical traditions such as psychodynamic therapies, which were not empirically based and were therefore considered scientifically weak by the early behavioural therapists. These therapists tried to apply empirically studied change efforts based on conditioning theories and behavioural principles. Behavioural therapies focused directly on problematic behaviour and emotion, and were generally designed to solve fundamental issues of human living such as anxiety, phobias, and obsessive-compulsive behaviours (e.g., Ayllon, Haughton, & Hughes, 1965; Wolpe & Rachman, 1960). Whereas the first generation was mainly based on classical and operant conditioning theories, the second wave of therapies was guided by cognitive and social learning theories. They focused on empirically based direct change efforts, but also included cognitive change targets and social learning in addition to conditioning procedures (Beck, Rush, Shaw, & Emery, 1979; Mahoney, 1974; Meichenbaum, 1977).

Synthesizing elements from the first and second waves, the third-wave interventions are characterized by: (1) grounding in an empirical, principle-focused approach; (2) focus on contextual and experiential change strategies in addition to more instructive ones; (3) building of broad, flexible, and effective repertoires of responses instead of the mere elimination of narrowly defined problems; and (4) emphasis on the relevance of the issues examined for both the clinician and the clients (Hayes, 2004b). Acceptance and commitment therapy (ACT; Hayes, Strosahl, & Wilson, 1999), mindfulness-based cognitive therapy (MBCT; Segal, Williams, & Teasdale, 2002), and dialectical behavioural therapy (DBT; Linehan, 1993) are examples of the third-wave intervention modalities.

Application of SST

Social skills training has been widely applied as a core intervention in mental health and education for a variety of populations throughout the years, including those living with mental illnesses, adolescents who are involved with the criminal justice system, students who are rejected or neglected, those with disabilities, and more broadly for individuals who are living with emotional and behavioural disorders and lack social competence (Forness, Kavale, Blum, & Lloyd, 1997; Kauffman,

2005; Nanyang & Hughes, 2002; Parker & Asher, 1987; Trower, Bryant, & Argyle, 1978).

Throughout the years, SST as an intervention has been studied extensively. A computerized bibliographical search in the summer of 2011 using the keyword "social skills training" returned 8,465 results on the Scholars Portal (a digital repository of over 20 million scholarly articles included in databases hand-selected by subject specialists at the twenty-one university libraries of the Ontario Council of University Libraries). The following section provides a brief summary of the key findings.

Effectiveness

Many authors have studied the relevance and effectiveness of SST across a spectrum of client groups, such as students with emotional and behavioural disorders (e.g., Gresham, 1997, 1998; Mathur & Rutherford, 1996; Smith & Travis, 2001; Strain, 2001), and individuals living with schizophrenia and related disorders (Heinssen, Liberman, & Kopelowicz, 2000; Kopelowicz, Liberman, & Zarate, 2006). SST did receive considerable support from empirical studies and has been recommended as an evidence-based practice in official guidelines for the treatment of schizophrenia (American Psychiatric Association, 2004).

Critique

Reviewers of the research evidence, however, have raised a number of issues with SST, such as the lack of generalization, the lack of appropriate assessment to reflect individual uniqueness, and treatment fidelity.

1. LACK OF GENERALIZATION

The lack of generalization has been a prominent finding in reviews of behavioural treatment modalities, including SST, since the seminal article by Stokes and Baer (1977). Rutherford and Nelson (1988) reviewed 5,300 behavioural treatment studies and found that less than 2 per cent addressed generalization and maintenance of treatment effects. The review on treatment for students with emotional and behavioural disorders by Landrum and Lloyd (1992) reached a similar conclusion. The flexible use of learned social skills in natural environments continues to be a challenge (Williams White, Keonig, & Scahill, 2007). As described by Maag (2006), promoting generalization has been a thorny issue for basic behavioural treatment studies, let alone interventions as complicated as social skills training. A number of strategies have been proposed to address the generalization issue: (1) selecting socially valid behaviours, or those behaviours that will enhance the quality of the subjects' lives in their social context; (2) focusing the intervention on peer group; (3) promoting entrapment – that is, recruiting natural communities to reinforce socially appropriate behaviours; and (4) embedding the client in a social system that supports learned behaviours (Farmer, Van Acker, Pearl, & Rodkin, 1999; Maag, 2006). Such reviews highlighted the issue of learning transfer, when the in-session structure and procedures do not correspond to *bon vivo* realities.

2. ASSESSMENT AND DEFINITION OF OUTCOME

Apart from generalization, two frequently cited issues related to SST are: (1) that it is not tailored to individuals' issues; and (2) its lack of socially valid outcome measures. These two issues have been raised by many authors for more than two decades but still remain unresolved to this day (Maag, 2006; Quinn, Kavale, Mathur, Rutherford, & Forness, 1999). Assessing individual uniqueness prior to SST intervention is rarely undertaken (Maag, 2006).

3. TREATMENT FIDELITY

The measurement of intervention implementation is of particular challenge to most practitioners (DiGennaro Reed, Hyman, & Hirst, 2011). Although most recognize the importance of documenting treatment integrity, practitioners expressed that time and work demands frequently deter them from collecting such important data in practice settings (Hagermoser Sanetti & DiGennaro Reed, 2011; Perepletchikova, Hilt, Chereji, & Kazdin, 2009).

4. INADEQUATE RESPONSE TO CLIENT HETEROGENEITY AND INDIVIDUAL UNIQUENESS

Models and related techniques have been developed to guide assessment, but the preoccupation with standardization and psychometric conventions places limits on flexibility and the capacity to accommodate individual differences and diversity. For example, Gresham and Elliott (1984) categorized social skills problems into four general categories: skill deficits, performance deficits, self-control deficits, and self-control performance deficits. Similarly, Hughes and Hall (1987) described a model that combined correct and incorrect social perceptions with strategic repertories of no error, behavioural skill deficit, cognitive deficit, and cognitive-behavioural deficit. These models assume a normative standard of what is adequate and what is deficient. The strict categorization they use cannot handle the heterogeneity and changing needs, circumstances, characteristics, and capacities of individual clients.

5. SOCIAL VALIDITY

Another methodological challenge found in many of the SST interventions is the lack of social validity (Gresham, 1998; Gresham, Cook, Crews, & Kern, 2004). This has been raised by many scholars for over two decades but has remained an open question (Maag, 2006). Social validity can be defined in terms of (1) the social significance of the intervention goals – whether the goals are what society wants; (2) the social acceptability of the intervention procedures; and (3) the social importance of the intervention's effects (Gresham & Lopez, 1996; Kazdin, 1977; Wolf, 1978). Various authors have provided specific, practical recommendations for conducting socially valid assessments and interventions. Gresham and Lopez (1996) summarized a representative sample of procedures that could be used to socially validate an intervention: (1) development norms, or the use of normative information to make a decision about the outcome; (2) functional analysis of behaviour; (3) semi-structured interviews to gather information for fine-tuning an intervention, in addition to rating scales; (4) relevant judges of the social acceptability of an intervention; (5) archival data; (6) behavioural markers; (7) concurrent choices – the alternatives that the client rejects in contrast to the socially valid option; (8) integrity assessment; and (9) combined social validation procedures.

Addressing the Challenges

SST researchers have suggested strategies to address the challenges listed above. Hughes and Sullivan (1988), for example, provided a few general recommendations for infusing outcome assessment into SST studies: (1) the observation system used to measure performance should correspond to skills taught during the intervention; (2) the outcome measures used should correspond to the individual's uniqueness; and (3) the outcome assessment should take place over an extended period of time. Some recommended the use of standardized social skills assessment scales that explicitly assess social skills for early screening, determining specific areas of deficit to design individualized interventions and standardize measures of progress (Merrell, 2001). The use of a standardized measure will hopefully determine the individual client's skills deficit, allowing the researcher to link this assessment to a corresponding treatment, while the same standardized measure can be used to track and monitor progress (Merrell, 2001).

The Limits of Standardization

The attempt to develop standardized measures of social skills that can give adequate coverage of deficits to be addressed and yet remain relevant to the specific needs and circumstances of the client has proved to be too challenging. The wide range of skills that different clients may need to master usually exceeds what can be covered by a single measure. Moreover, what constitutes skilful behaviour is contingent upon a spectrum of factors such as age, social norm, culture, specific context, and purpose of interpersonal and social engagement; and some of these factors do change over time and across social contexts. It is not surprising that a recent review shows a relative paucity of standardized social skills assessment instruments that are satisfactory, while almost every intervention has used direct observation and measurement of operationalized social skills (DiGennaro Reed, Hyman, & Hirst, 2011). The trade-off between standardized measures with wide applicability and individualized assessment that targets specific client needs has emerged as a key issue in the research literature on social skills assessment. For instance, practitioners working with children have noted that a detailed understanding of children's social interactions cannot be attained using conventional rating scales or questionnaires but instead requires direct observation in a variety of contexts (Yeates et al., 2007).

The tension between standardization and personalized assessment in defining outcome raises a related question regarding the issue of social conformity in SST. Rigid adherence to what is perceived as socially valid and acceptable may reinforce conformity to prevailing social norms, which is not necessarily the best thing. Clients coming from different social situations or locations may have to deal with social conventions in a variety of ways. There is a fine line between conforming to social norms and adapting to them effectively. My own work with immigrants and minorities who find themselves in racist or otherwise discriminatory social contexts highlights the significance of critical engagement with dominant social values and norms instead of unques-

12   The SSLD Idea

tioned conformity to them. Intervention goal-setting should give due consideration to the client's needs and circumstances as well as social reality. It is important to recognize that interventions do not only help clients to conform to social norms but can also support clients in taking actions that lead to changes in social realities. In reviewing SST studies, it is important to see if outcomes are defined on the basis of unquestioned social norms and conventions, or on reciprocal consideration of social reality and the client's needs and circumstances.

From SST to SSLD

Strategies and skills learning and development (SSLD), building on previous work on SST, is a learning system that helps people expand their repertoire of strategies and skills through systematic learning so that they become more effective in addressing their own needs and achieving their goals in life. Problems and challenges that people face are often framed as disease or pathology in conventional mental health and social service practice. In contrast, SSLD conceives such problems and challenges as manifestations of human needs that are unmet because the strategies and skills employed are misguided or ineffective. In most situations, the learning and development of the appropriate strategies and skills will result in effective gratification of those needs. The newly learned strategies and skills will free people from old practices that are inappropriate or ineffective.

The SSLD system takes advantage of the extensive range of experience, knowledge, research, skills, and expertise cumulated by SST practitioners and researchers. The review of SST presented above has highlighted some challenging issues in the development of SSLD. In a sense, the issues of generalization or learning transfer and that of assessment are both reflective of characteristics of the empirical behavioural tradition that many SST practitioners and researchers adhere to. In this tradition, emphasis is placed on theoretical formulations that can be empirically validated, and data are conceived in terms of objectively observable behaviour, which can preferably be measured and quantified reliably. Standardization and implied universal applicability and relevance are highly valued in this tradition. Ideally, social skills as a construct can be conceptualized as relevant to all people – pretty much like the construct of intelligence – and a comprehensive measure can be developed. If this construct can be operationalized, then we should have a reliable measure of the adequacy or deficiency of the client's repertoire of skills. The measure can then indicate a standard set of social skills that practitioners can train people to acquire through a systematic procedure, which should ideally be standardized and manualized. It follows that the effective implementation of SST in a standardized manner should almost uniformly raise the social competence of clients. In this model, individual difference is supposedly measurable on some standardized scales.

This is the model I more or less followed in my earlier SST practice. The idea of a parsimonious set of social skills that is relevant for all, with everything being measurable and quantifiable, was pretty attractive. When I first worked with autistic children back in 1980, for example, I developed a standardized behaviour rating scale that was applied to all of them. The scale covered different domains of auto-stimulation, learning, social behaviour, and communicative behaviour, and these items were arranged in an ordinal scale. The scale worked reasonably well as a clinical tool to help my colleagues and me monitor the progress of each child, but we also discovered that these children had individual learning styles, preferred modes of interaction, and differential aptitudes for various learning tasks. When we started working with parent-child dyads and ran simultaneous parent and children groups, we found ourselves working with an increasingly complex set of behaviours and processes, including parenting styles, attachment patterns, and family dynamics.

At around the same time, I started an SST group for adults with schizophrenic disorder. The diversity of their needs, circumstances, characteristics, and capacity made it almost impossible to get them to go through a standardized program. I allowed myself to focus on what they needed to learn in order to address their particular needs instead of prescribing standard skills for each of them to master. It later struck me that learning transfer was almost never an issue when using this approach. What we did most of the time was ask these clients to bring in challenging situations they faced in real life, and then we would try to figure out effective strategies and skills for dealing with them. The fact that I was practising within a Chinese cultural context in Hong Kong probably facilitated this flexibility. Some of the more standardized practice based on Western social behaviours or skills, ranging from how to greet a stranger to being assertive with one's family members, were modified to suit individual circumstances. What I experienced as a practitioner was that the SST procedure was very effective when I used observation learning, review, feedback, refinement, rehearsal, and real-life application procedures, but did not insist on using any standardized measure of social skills. When positive outcome was realized in terms of observable behaviour or facts, such as moving out of seclusion, socializing, making friends, finding and keeping a job, and completing graduate school, I was adequately encouraged to continue my application and refinement of the procedure.

Looking back, I realize that my preference for engaging with the client's reality in all its complexity over standardization and measurement probably led me to the adoption of a more flexible (or what some SST colleagues may call less disciplined) practice. Such practice orientation gradually transported me from a linear categorical mode of thinking and practice to a multiple-contingencies mode, which I will explain in more detail later. At this point, it is perhaps sufficient to say that my practice was guided by attempts to develop strategies and skills to address the client's specific needs and circumstances. Standardization, measurement, and quantification were pursued when they were helpful to the process. I soon found myself developing many innovative procedures with my clients, and the positive results have kept me actively involved in such processes till this day. The development of SSLD as a distinct system was probably primed three decades ago through a goal-oriented, client-need-driven, flexible, and open practice that privileged development and innovation over compliance and model fidelity.

Apart from the objectives that we have already discussed – emphasis on the particular needs, circumstances, characteristics, and capacity of the client; readiness to respond to real-life challenges; flexibility in procedure and assessment; and adapting to the specific social and cultural context – the development of SSLD has been concentrated on observable behavioural change and careful documentation of the learning process. After decades of gradual modification and incorporation of new elements, SSLD distinguishes itself from other SST procedures by its focus on the underlying mechanism of learning and development, an emphasis on multiple-contingencies thinking, and a broader scope that covers not only skills for specific situations but also strategies for more effective personal, interpersonal, and social functioning in the long term. SSLD has a much wider range of application than SST, including clinical and non-clinical populations; the capacity to engage with intersecting diversities related to ethnicity, culture, gender, sexual orientation, and so on; and an awareness of the rapidly changing social realities in an increasingly globalized environment. The model has

> **Box 1.1. Features of SSLD**
>
> - Emphasis on the particular needs, circumstances, characteristics, and capacity of the client.
> - Goal-oriented: addresses client needs.
> - Addresses real-life complexities.
> - Flexible and open system, not insistent on compliance and model fidelity.
> - Emphasis on observable change or outcome.
> - Learning and development rather than training.
> - Multiple-contingencies thinking.
> - Not just skills for specific situations, but also strategies for longer-range goals.
> - Engages with intersecting diversity and globalized context.
> - Wider range of application, educational frame, non-clinical population.

been used in individual counselling, couple and marital counselling, group work, organizational development, corporate training, as well as community organizing and development (please see Box 1.1).

The focus on the mechanism of learning and development means that the program is oriented towards the learner's needs and circumstances instead of what the trainer is prepared to offer. It therefore emphasizes learning rather than training, although the role of training is duly recognized. Special attention is also given to learning *how* to learn, on top of *what* to learn. The SSLD model draws on learning principles derived from social psychology and the psychology of learning, especially social-cognitive and social-learning theories (Bandura, 1977a, 1986). Moving beyond the operant conditioning paradigm, which remains a conceptual component in some versions of social skills training, these theories conceptualize the individual as an active agent and an active learner. They also document how individuals learn without a trainer's deliberate efforts. Learning principles derived from these research-based theories will be applied to help learners develop an expanded repertoire of strategies and skills that can enable them to become more effective in attaining their desired goals in life. Using these methods, the learner's expanded repertoire can exceed that of the trainer – which is usually not the case in traditional applications of social skills training. The role of the trainer in SSLD therefore encompasses not only direct training and instruction but also coaching through careful observation and feedback, facilitation of active and independent learning, and nourishing a space for creativity, innovation, experimentation, and discovery. This allows the SSLD practitioner to be helpful without necessarily being an expert in a specific problem area, and supports the collaborative creation of new strategies and skills by the client and the practitioner to manage unfamiliar situations and address new challenges.

Another key feature of SSLD is multiple-contingencies thinking. What is contingent is not fixed, but variable; it changes in relation to the factors and processes that condition it. Whether someone experiencing difficulties in relationships will seek professional help is, for instance, contingent upon many factors such as the availability of information and services, whether such help-seeking is socially acceptable or stigmatized in the community, previous experience of receiving help, ability to pay, expectancy regarding such help, and a host of other considerations. While many people need to maintain a sense of order in their lives, and imagine people, events, relationships, and so on to be stable and predictable, they often do not appreciate that such stability is often sustained by a large number of variables, factors, and processes that do change across time and situations. In everyday life, many aspects of human reality are contingent; and these multiple contingencies interact with each other to produce complex situations, which often challenge the neat and tidy theories that helping professionals espouse. Many theoretical systems in the helping professions are articulated in linear, logical statements, often dealing with a limited number of specific variables. Instead of thinking in terms of multiple contingencies, broad, generic categories are used and simple, linear relationships are imagined. Some of these theories make sweeping generalizations with the assumption that everyone is the same. For instance, some authors think that it is possible to argue whether cognition or emotion is more primary and whether one therefore determines the other. This question is of limited value in multiple-contingencies analysis. The reality is that the relationship between cognition and emotion is never the same for everyone across all situations, and it does not remain constant over time. The precise relationship has to be considered with reference to the multiple contingencies of personal characteristics, current needs and circumstances, the goals to be attained by the individual concerned, and contextual variables. For any given individual, it is possible for emotion to take over and condition or even distort the way one perceives, remembers, and thinks in some situations, while the same person can exercise highly effective cognitive moderation and regulation of emotion under other circumstances. A graduate student in pharmacology I once worked with, for instance, can exercise very rational management over her behaviour, performance, and relationships in the workplace, but experiences a very different balance of power between emotion and cognition when she is dealing with her friends, her husband, and her son.

Apart from a learning-focused orientation, multiple-contingencies thinking sets SSLD apart from many social skills training procedures that are based on standardized, pre-designed programs. Pre-packaged programs assume that the participants have similar needs and will therefore go through a similar learning process and learn the same skill set. While packaged programs do work well in a wide range of situations, their effectiveness can be enhanced by multiple-contingencies thinking – the acknowledgment that learners can have varying needs, learning styles, learning histories, personal strengths and limitations, and compatibility levels with the trainer, and that the actual learning process is contingent upon these variables. SSLD recognizes the advantage of pre-designed programs – they are relatively easy to master and deliver, and therefore more cost-effective. Taking a learning-process focus and a contingencies orientation, SSLD builds upon existing skills training programs to design courses of learning that can respond to the learners' specific needs, characteristics, circumstances, and capacity.

Development of strategies on top of the mastery of particular skills is another point emphasized by SSLD. In interpersonal and social situations, people need to learn specific skills to deal with particular circumstances, such as handling the unreasonable demands of a supervisor or a parent in an assertive manner. In these circumstances, they can apply the appropriate skill and make the right move, and their problem will be solved or their immediate goal will be realized. In many of these cases, however, people are not dealing with an isolated, one-off situation, but have longer-term goals such as career advancement or maintaining a stable, gratifying relationship with one's parent or partner. These longer-term life goals require the development of a strategy, which involve multiple moves and the coordinated application of a series of skills. In the social and interpersonal world, we sometimes see people who are very skilful but pursue ineffective strategies. An assertive move, for example, may help us attain an immediate goal, but may also damage a longer-term relationship. This is like comparing the winning of a battle with the winning of a war. It is important, therefore, to consider the overall relational or social context as well as the individual's long-term objective in the design of procedures for learning and developing strategies and skills.

As strategies and skills are closely tied to people's needs, goals, or aspirations, the SSLD system pays special attention to human motivation. Human actions are understood in terms of their functions with reference to human needs, instead of being taken at face value. When presented with a problem, be it a mental health issue or an interpersonal problem, SSLD will first attempt to understand what motivates the current behaviour and which needs remain unmet. For instance, if someone is behaving aggressively towards other people, an SSLD practitioner will try to find out what function this aggression serves. It may serve instrumental functions such as protecting one's territory. It may be motivated by a strong need for domination and control. Upon closer analysis, we may find that the aggressive person has other needs that are unmet, such as the need for intimacy. In a situation like this, SSLD practice does not deal with aggressive behaviour by trying to reduce it but examines the person's overall needs in order to develop effective strategies for meeting them.

Given the diversity of human experience, needs, and circumstances, there exists a huge variety of strategies and skills for people to acquire. It is not realistic to expect the practitioner to be able to come up with all the necessary strategies and skills for every client situation. Instead, SSLD practice emphasizes understanding the client's needs and goals, with the practitioner's key role being to assist the client in exploring, learning, and developing the relevant strategies and skills in a goal-directed manner. Whereas the practitioner can often offer valuable knowledge and skills in a given client situation, it is important to realize that SSLD practice can also lead to new learning for the practitioner. When confronted with challenging situations that are unfamiliar or beyond the practitioner's experience, the SSLD system enables the creation of new strategies and skills through client-practitioner collaboration. The procedure for such collaborative creation will be described in Chapter 6.

The SSLD system has broad application in many fields of human service, including social work, mental health, health care, education, community development, organization development, human resources, cross-cultural work, service business, media, public relations, and so on. Professionals from these sectors can all benefit from SSLD training and use it to develop useful practice programs for their clients.

The extensive scope of human services is increasingly characterized by diversity among both the clients and the practitioners. Differences in ethnocultural background, gender, sexual orientation, age, ability, religious orientation, and so on, can bring productive challenges to the practitioner. Adopting multiple-contingencies thinking, the SSLD system can respond with sensitivity and flexibility to intersecting diversities, with a firm focus on the particular needs and circumstances of each client. SSLD practice is supported by an integrated approach to working with diversity (Tsang, Bogo, & Lee, 2010; Tsang & George, 1998). In this approach, we do not assume that people belonging to a particular ethnocultural group all share the same characteristics, beliefs, and behavioural patterns. Instead, individuals may have internalized different elements drawn from their native culture as well as other cultural sources (Ho, 1995). A person from Korea or Hong Kong, for example, may have internalized more elements from Fundamentalist Christianity than from Buddhism. A lesbian woman from a Muslim community may have a very different understanding of her culture than a heterosexual woman. Case examples and illustrations used in this book will reflect such an approach to diversity.

Contemporary practitioners are situated in an increasingly globalized environment, with ever-increasing opportunities to work with unfamiliar situations presented by clients coming from distant parts of the world. They need a system of knowledge and practice that can respond to this increasing complexity with a parsimonious set of analytic concepts and practice principles. The SSLD system provides a robust and yet flexible tool to support practitioners in the human services. Some colleagues may choose to use SSLD as their primary practice method, while others might combine SSLD with other intervention procedures. SSLD can easily be adopted as an adjunct or a complementary procedure to enhance most intervention systems. The distinctive features of the SSLD system will hopefully emerge with more clarity as readers go through this book.

Chapter Two

Social and Interpersonal Strategies and Skills as Human Action

An Action- and Performance-Oriented Approach

Strategies and skills learning and development (SSLD) is a procedure focusing on action and performance. Professionals in education and training know too well that there is a huge gap between cognitive knowledge and action. In health education, for example, the knowledge that cigarette smoking is hazardous to one's health is a necessary but grossly insufficient factor in stopping smoking. In the battle against HIV/AIDS, sexual health educators are distressed by how often knowledge about safe sex does not translate into action. This knowledge-action gap is widely noted in other areas of human service, although it is not always candidly acknowledged. Many trainers, consultants, therapists, counsellors, and educators would prefer to protect the space and funding allowing them to deliver programs and services that only result in cognitive or intellectual knowledge without being required to demonstrate their effectiveness in terms of learner action and performance.

The SSLD model specifically targets behaviour and actual performance that are directly observable, with demonstrable interpersonal and social effects. The learning procedure is consistently anchored in human action, not only thoughts and ideas. Unlike the old-school behaviourists, SSLD practitioners do not deny the role played by cognition. As a matter of fact, the SSLD model recognizes the significance of the interplay among many psychological and social forces.

Structure of Our Life-World

The life-world that human beings live in is constituted in a complex manner. Different factors, events, and processes interact with each other to produce a rich array of phenomena. Most people are only aware of a small portion of the events taking place in their world; it is almost impossible for anyone to have complete knowledge and understanding of them, let alone control and mastery. SSLD recognizes the inherent limitation of our knowledge, understanding, mastery, and control of our life-world, but nonetheless believes that they can be increased or improved through learning and development.

Using a multiple-contingencies model, SSLD regards the interaction among factors, events, and processes in the human life-world as contingent upon each other. We are suspicious of linear categorical formulations with assumed universal validity or applicability. For example, we do not believe that cognition always determines emotional experience or that emotions always conditions cognition. What we experience emotionally is contingent upon multiple factors and processes including cognition, environmental circumstances, bodily state, needs and motivation, and the activity we are pursuing. Using the six broad domains of environment, biology, motivation, emotion, cognition, and behaviour to capture the complexities of the life-world, we are hoping to construct a parsimonious framework that can facilitate our conceptualization and formulation for practice. We recognize that factors and processes are not necessarily located entirely within a specific domain, but can move across their nebulous boundaries and interact with each other.

The environment, for example, has its own objective properties or characteristics, and these can have variable effects on people and can carry different meaning and significance for them. At the same time, the individual's physical condition, motivation, thoughts, emotions, and actions can have direct impacts on both the objective properties of the environment as well as the way external reality is experienced. On the one hand, people can build cities, consume natural resources, transform raw material into products, produce pollutants, make laws, develop communities, create identities, wage wars, censor ideas, oppress other human beings, and so on. On the other hand, external realities can affect human lives physically (e.g., natural disasters, food supply, climate), psychologically (e.g., natural events construed as acts of gods, biological functions such as menstruation or childbirth experienced as magical), and socially (e.g., collaboration and division of labour in order to survive).

Human thought and action can transform social reality in significant ways. The process of social construction has been explored by sociologists and psychologists (e.g., Berger & Luckmann, 1966; Gergen, 1999,

2001; Potter, 1996). In this sense, the environment is simultaneously constructed internally and experienced as something external. In social cognitive theory (Bandura, 1977a, 1986), the environment and the individual are in a reciprocal determination relationship; the individual acts on the environment and changes it while the environment also influences the individual's physical condition, motivation, emotional experience, thought, and action.

Imagine the case of a boy who was abused (environment) and uses excessive eating (action) to deal with his psychological pain and unexpressed anger (emotion, motivation), leading to diagnosable medical conditions (biology, environment) and a poor self-image (cognition, emotion), which is reinforced by social stereotypes about people who are obese (environment). One could certainly pursue more in-depth analyses of each of these domains – for example, the internal conflicts regarding food and its association with shame and guilt (emotion); the physiological, metabolic, and neurological implications of obesity (biology); or a critical discourse analysis on how society deals with food and weight (environment). Figure 2.1 below summarizes the major domains of our life-world. It should be emphasized that the domains are conceptual tools to facilitate understanding of people's circumstances, and that our analysis focuses on the contingent relationships among the factors and processes in different domains. The small number of domains can hopefully help us to map out major factors and processes and their interactions in each case.

Human Action as Purposive and Goal-Directed

Given the complex interaction among these factors and processes, any starting point chosen in any given analysis can be regarded as arbitrary. Any event we focus on is likely the result of some other antecedent factors and processes. In SSLD, we take the pragmatic approach of tracing human action or behaviour back to its motivational origin as a convenient first step. Most human behaviour – with rare exceptions such as reflexes – is motivated, purposeful, or goal-directed. Social and interpersonal behaviours are linked to personal needs, goals, wants, and desires. Recognizing the motivational forces behind a particular action is the primary step in SSLD. A person who is always behaving in an aggressive manner towards others, for instance, is often seen as an aggressive person, and many people (professionals included) will try to do things to stop her or his aggressive behaviour. From an SSLD

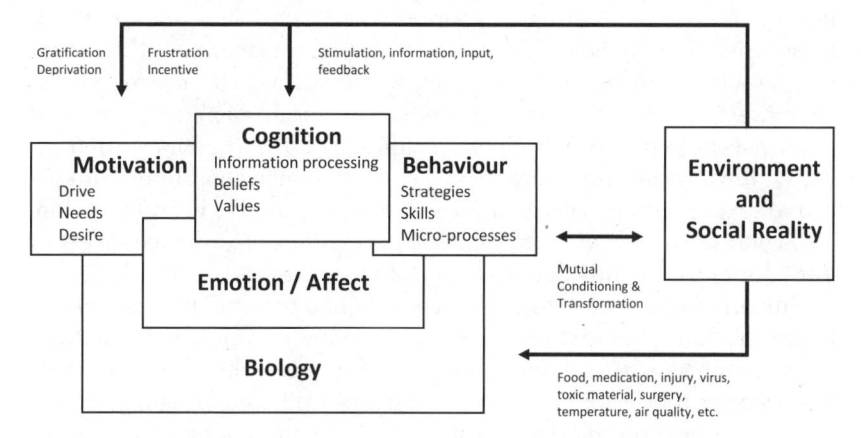

Figure 2.1. Human Action and the Environment

Motivation	Cognition	Behaviour	Environment
Drive	Information processing	Strategies	and
Needs	Beliefs	Skills	Social Reality
Desire	Values	Micro-processes	

Gratification / Deprivation
Frustration / Incentive
Stimulation, information, input, feedback

Emotion / Affect

Biology

Mutual Conditioning & Transformation

Food, medication, injury, virus, toxic material, surgery, temperature, air quality, etc.

perspective, however, the most important point is to understand what this individual is trying to do or achieve – in other words, her or his needs and desired goal. We do not assume that aggressive behaviour always means the same thing. A person may use aggression to express anger and frustration. Aggression may also be the only means the person knows for attaining personal goals or getting what she or he needs, be it money, food, attention, or personal space. The same person may also use aggressive means to express affection or even erotic desire. It is possible that the person has only developed a very narrow repertoire of social skills with aggressive behaviour being one of their limited options, and this may be why it is used across a variety of social settings. Understanding the individual's motivational background is essential for helping them to develop an expanded set of strategies and skills for achieving personal goals without resorting to aggression.

Some of the human motivational forces are grounded in biological conditions, such as hunger or the need for sensory stimulation and pleasure. It can be argued that many of the "social" motivations can be traced back to biological needs of some sort, such as survival, protection from the elements, food, sex, procreation, and so on. The fact that a motivational force is biologically grounded does not, however, mean that it cannot be socially conditioned. Sex drive, for example, can be seen as biologically based, but different individuals pursue sex for different purposes. There are people who have sex in order to reproduce, and there are people whose drive for procreation is so strong that they will try non-sexual or technology-assisted reproduction (e.g., donor insemination). There are also people whose sex drives are specifically non-procreative. Some people have sex for pleasure, and there are people who do it for financial gain. Some people use sex to express gratitude, care, hostility, trust, domination, submission, and a host of other psychological or emotional realities. These expressions often occur within a social and interpersonal context, which conditions both the actual sexual performance and the meaning ascribed to it, and therefore also conditions the extent to which a particular performance meets or does not meet the individual's expectations or needs.

Human motivation is, therefore, conditioned by a combination of factors, including ones that are biological, social-environmental, emotional, and cognitive. If we take food as another example, we can say that the need for food is biological in origin, but understanding contemporary human action related to food is a very complex task. Just focusing on the motivational aspects of obtaining and consuming food, we can clearly see how people manifest different responses when they are hungry. Some people seek immediate gratification; some people overeat; and some people refrain from eating for various reasons, which are usually cognitively mediated – they may be observing a religious ritual, going on hunger strike for a political cause, or attempting to punish their parents by not eating. The very concept of food itself is subject to cultural conditioning. Most people in the West, for example, do not usually think of termites, dogs, or scorpions as food, but they are enjoyed by a large number of people around the world.

Human motivation to eat, or to have sex, is influenced by emotional factors as well. It is well known that when people feel depressed, their interest in both food and in sex may decline. Emotional processes always interfere with motivational processes. Imagine a student who is very motivated to excel in her academic studies because she wants to prove to her critical parents that she is not stupid and worthless. She might be preparing for an exam when her parents comment that no matter how hard she tries, she is going to fail. This criticism can lead to anger or frustration, and may interfere with her motivation to do well. She may become even more determined or she may feel undermined and defeated.

Motivation is a key psychological domain for SSLD, as the main point of the intervention is to enhance the learner's capacity for need gratification and goal attainment. Successful SSLD results in the mastery of functional strategies and skills, and therefore leads to a more gratifying life. An analysis of the relationship between motivation and action reveals its complexity; and one simply cannot assume that the same behaviour is always motivated by the same drive, need, or purpose. This conceptual dissociation between motivation and behaviour opens up the space for exploring the varied patterns of connection. In practice, it is important to recognize the underlying motivation and needs of an individual's behaviour. As will be illustrated later, understanding the motivational substrate of behaviour is the most important starting point for SSLD.

The interaction between human motivation and social reality is a fascinating drama. Certain human needs, wants, or desires are socially supported and facilitated whereas others are subject to tight control or even suppression. In the West, for example, most people are led to believe that they need to spend a lot of money in order to experience romance (Illouz, 1997) and need to follow certain patterns of consumption with their wedding (Geller, 2001). On the other hand, expressions of sexual feelings and erotic desires are heavily regulated (Foucault, 1990; Segal, 1994). Driving, as another example, is widely seen as a natural need by people in North America, but there is a highly controversial political-economy surrounding this practice. The dynamics of how human needs are socially legitimized raise challenging questions for scholars, researchers, and professionals working with human and social issues.

Human Action and Biology

As mentioned above, our biology often plays a role in our motivational processes. Biological needs for air, nutrients, water, sensory stimulation, safety, comfort, tactile contact, and so on remain powerful forces that drive human action, although these motivational and action sequences are heavily conditioned by social and cultural forces as well as being mediated by cognitive and emotional processes. In SSLD, understanding the biological domain is important in many ways. First of all, our biological program, which includes our neurological or nervous system, may facilitate or limit our learning and our physical abilities. Certain behaviours or response patterns, for instance, are inherited. There is some evidence that general intelligence and certain aspects of social skill or social sensitivity may be affected by genetic factors (Buck, 1991; Scarr & McCartney, 1983; Vernon, Petrides, Bratko, & Schermer, 2008). Another aspect of our biological domain that requires attention is how it correlates with psychological processes. Our endocrine and neurophysiological processes, for example, are important correlates of major experiences such as arousal, emotional states, and information processing. Anatomical or structural damage to our biological program, especially to the brain, can have significant psychological and behavioural consequences. Factors and processes in other domains can also lead to human actions that alter the person's neurophysiological condition. The ingestion of psychotropic drugs, which includes addiction as well as psycho-pharmacotherapy, is a distinct example.

There are other examples of how our biological condition can have an impact on our social and interpersonal conduct. Gender, for example, can be seen as a primarily biological reality, but its social and psychological implications are tremendous. Depending on the social and cultural context, height, body build and figure, agility, motor dexterity, or even skin colour or complexion can take on social and psychological meanings that materially affect a person's self-image, perspective, thoughts and actions, as well as the life chances made available to them.

Human Action as Cognitively Mediated

The idea that human action is mediated by cognition has a very long history. Many traditional philosophies, religions, and teachings have attempted to modify human action by changing how people think. More recently, cognitive therapy has become increasingly popular as a strategy for changing people's behaviour (Chambless & Ollendick, 2001; Deffenbacher, Dahlen, Lynch, Morris, & Gowensmith, 2000; Goode, 2000). The belief that cognitive processes can mediate human behaviour is probably not to be disputed, but human service professionals and educators have long recognized the knowledge-action gap. Thinking straight and knowing the right thing to do are inadequate guarantees of corresponding action. Many therapists have included behavioural interventions and skills training as an adjunct to cognitive therapy. The development of cognitive behavioural therapy (CBT) can be seen as supplementing the limitations of purely cognitive interventions (Cooper, 2008).

Instead of seeing cognitive procedures and behavioural learning as two separate and discrete processes, the SSLD model recognizes the role of cognitive mediation in the learning of skills and the development of strategies for more effective personal, interpersonal, and social functioning. According to social cognitive theory (Bandura, 1986), most human behaviour or action is learned through modelling or observation learning. Observation learning always involves cognitive representation of the observed behaviour to be learned. This cognitive representation can be a direct visual and auditory copy of an act performed by a model, but very often it also involves symbolic or linguistic representation. A common, everyday example is learning how to cook from a recipe. Another example is following do-it-yourself manuals. Reading this book is yet another example of cognitively mediated learning through symbolic or linguistic representation. Such cognitive mediation, however, has to be translated into actual behavioural practice for the learning to be consolidated.

Besides its role in observation learning, cognitive representation is also important in mediating feedback to enable refinement of the learning of skills and the development of strategies. In real-life social situations, the ability to receive verbal feedback and assimilate verbal and linguistic information is a central building block for effective social and interpersonal performance. To have an uninterrupted process of assimilating feedback, one needs to be relatively free from emotional interference. A person with a fragile sense of self (or what some psychologists consider an internal cognitive representation of self), for instance, will have more difficulty understanding and accepting corrective feedback from others, and is more likely to interpret the feedback as criticism and respond with anger, defensiveness, cynicism, or withdrawal. In contrast, a person with a more positive self-image, which includes a constellation of positively valued cognitions regarding oneself, is more likely to get the information and value contained in the same feedback, and more ready to translate that understanding into appropriate action.

A critical role of our cognitive and information processing facilities is, therefore, the way we make sense of interpersonal and social realities. In SSLD, we do focus on actual behavioural performance, and we are also mindful of the pervasiveness of our sense-making and meaning-giving acts as human beings and social agents. How we make sense of a particular personal or social situation often shapes our course of action and the social consequences of those actions. For example, a high school student experiencing boredom may think that he is isolated and unwanted, and thus interpret his boredom as a result of his failure as a friend, or as a member of the family or community. In contrast, the same person can see the boredom he experiences as a sign of the need for novel stimulation and experience, and will start exploring activities which could be interesting and pleasurable. Cognitive processing of bodily states, for example, has been found to affect emotional response and social behaviour (Dutton & Aron, 1974; Schachter & Singer, 1962). To give another example, a young girl who experiences erotic attraction to another girl may think that she is sick or sinful, thus feel intense guilt and shame and then actively avoid the other girl. Alternatively, she can accept same-sex attraction as a totally legitimate personal option and can then explore ways to engage with the girl she is interested in.

Similarly, how we make sense of interpersonal and social realities often plays a role in how we respond as social agents. For example, a woman who is abused by her spouse may believe that it is "natural" for women to submit to men, and that it is her duty to appease her spouse. This woman may then change her behaviour to become even more subservient. She may also feel resentful but not believe that the situation can be changed, given the long history of oppression of women in her immediate community. In this case, she might try to endure the situation for as long as she is capable. If she thinks that she is too weak or disempowered to do anything but can call on members of her community who are in a better position to intervene, she may attempt to seek help from these individuals. Alternatively, it is possible for her to interpret the situation as one that requires learning to be more autonomous, independent, and assertive. Another possibility is for her to think of the situation as a systemic social issue, and therefore one requiring collective action in addition to individual coping and resistance. In this case, the woman may pursue the behavioural strategies of reaching out to other women, learning more about social action and change, and accessing social resources and support systems.

Cognitive approaches or strategies are themselves contingent upon other factors and processes. Dominant social discourses, norms, or conventions play a significant role in conditioning how people think and make sense of the world (O'Gorman, Wilson, & Miller, 2008; Richerson & Boyd, 2005). In social cognitive theory (Bandura, 1986, 1991), the process of internalizing social norms and values is understood in terms of social learning. The internalized values are mediated by self-regulatory mechanisms that involve factors and processes in other domains such as interpersonal relationships and external environmental inducement.

In sum, sense-making and meaning-giving are key components of our social responses. These cognitive processes are central to our understanding of our own needs, regulation of our emotional responses, assessment of our social reality, and imagination of possible strategies or courses of action – all of which mediate our learning and performance of tasks in a skilful and effective manner. As an intervention model, SSLD acknowledges the pivotal role of such cognitive functions and the way they can be translated into action – learning the requisite strategies and skills – and it sees them through to actual performance in real life.

Human Emotion and Human Action

As mentioned above, emotional processes can interfere with our behavioural strategies and skills. Whereas cognitive therapy theories usually emphasize how cognitive processes can shape emotional responses (Alford & Beck, 1997; Beck, 1976), psychotherapists and counsellors who focus on emotional processes in their work usually recognize the intimate relationship between human emotion and motivation. In a very practical way, emotions are strong motivational forces. One obvious example is fear, which is recognized as a primary human emotion (Greenberg, 2002). It can drive the human being into extreme fight-or-flight responses. It can also colour the individual's perception of reality, focusing attention on aspects of the situation that might threaten her or his safety or well-being. For example, an employee notices that her boss did not greet her when they met in the photocopying room. If she is not fearful of losing her job or of negative evaluation, she might interpret the situation in terms of the boss being in a rush or preoccupied with his own thoughts. Another employee facing a similar situation with a fear of losing his job would have a higher probability of reading that as rejection or a sign of the boss's negative evaluation. Similarly, a young child who does not have a reason to fear domestic violence will interpret and respond to parental criticism in a different way than a child who does. We can easily imagine other emotions such as jealousy, anxiety, erotic arousal, or depression playing a role in affecting our motivation, the way we make sense of social reality, and the way we respond to specific situations.

Human Action and External Reality – Mutual Conditioning and Transformation

Earlier learning psychologists and behavioural theorists such as Pavlov (1927), Skinner (1938, 1953), and Watson (1925) tended to emphasize the influence of external environmental forces on human action. In these theories, the individual is conceptualized as a passive recipient of the effects of external events presented as stimuli or experienced as behavioural consequences. Classical conditioning theory understands human action primarily as organismic responses to external stimuli. Operant conditioning theory considers human conduct as a product of different reinforcement and punishment contingencies. A major contribution of Bandura's social cognitive theory (1986), which was articulated in his earlier version of social learning theory (1977a), is the idea of reciprocal determination. Human beings are conceived as active agents who interact with the environment. The impact of human action on social reality is duly recognized. This model, when applied to interpersonal situations, tracks the interactional sequence between two or more social agents.

The recognition of reciprocal determination is closely tied to the idea of the individual as an active, autonomous agent; this has been further elaborated by Bandura (1977b, 2001). When analysing interpersonal and social realities, determination, which implies a deterministic causal paradigm, may not be the most appropriate concept. In the development of contemporary social theory, scholars have become increasingly aware of the fluidity and contingent nature of social realities. The recognition that reality is socially constructed (Berger & Luckmann, 1966) challenges a deterministic model based on positivist-empiricist assumptions. Constructivist frameworks are increasingly being applied to a wide range of social analyses (Frueh, 2003; Katzenstein, 1996; Palincsar, 1998; Truan, 1993). Mutual conditioning and transformation, therefore, may be a more accurate description of the relationship between the individual and the environment.

Within the SSLD framework for understanding human action, environmental events can certainly function as stimuli as conceived by respondent conditioning theorists, but they are more likely to be cognitively processed by the individual before a human response is produced. For example, people living in urban centres in the West may be conditioned to be alert and vigilant upon hearing a buzzing sound or an alarm, but it is the interpretation that plays a more important role in determining the specific reaction. Let us imagine how a reaction is produced. If an individual determined that there was a fire, upon hearing the alarm she would likely be looking for a safety exit. She would be extra-vigilant for signs, which she had socially learned to be associated with safety-exit directions. Let us further imagine that on her way she came across a man travelling from the opposite direction and holding a wet towel to his nose; this scenario would provide her with addi-

Figure 2.2. Reciprocal Influence between Two Interacting Individuals

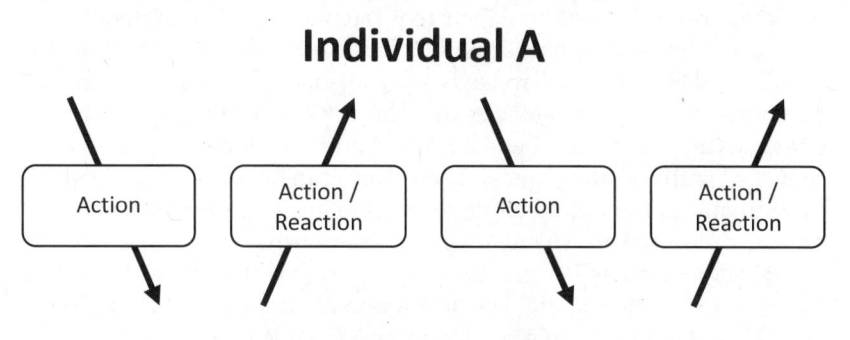

Individual A

| Action | Action / Reaction | Action | Action / Reaction |

Individual A

Source: Adopted from Bandura (1986), 27.

tional information, which might alter the direction of her escape. Had the man said, "the stairwell is filled with smoke," then she would more likely change her escape route. This new information, or feedback, is an important part in the cycle of interaction between the individual and the environment. When applied to the interpersonal context (see Figure 2.2), a person's reaction is experienced as feedback by the other person in the interaction.

Within the SSLD model, the individual is seen as an active agent who is autonomous and goal-directed, but actions and effects are not understood within a deterministic model. When the individual's action is effective, it has a higher chance of bringing about the desired outcome in the person's social reality. For example, if a person feels erotically attracted to another person and wishes to set up a date, she or he needs to perform a particular behavioural sequence which may involve calling the other person on the phone, face-to-face conversation, email, note writing, text messaging, or engaging an intermediary. Any of these will involve a certain level of skilfulness, which will in turn affect the probability of success. Interpersonal attraction, however, does not work in a simple, mechanistic manner. It is possible to imagine that even the most socially effective person can still get rejected for a date, because the other person might not be interested or could have her or his own issues, such as social phobia or fear of intimacy.

The recognition of contingencies in interpersonal and social realities takes SSLD beyond a rigid preoccupation with a singular goal – and beyond the naïve assumption that all goals can be realized simply through improving one's social skills. It encourages the learner to adopt a pragmatic appraisal of reality, which requires reciprocal consideration of means and ends. The learner will have to first come to a good understanding of her or his own needs and personal circumstances as well as environmental contingencies in order to set realistic goals. Relevant strategies and skills can then be learned and developed to increase the chance of realizing these goals. These goals can be adjusted in the process of their attainment when there are changes in personal or environmental circumstances (feedback). The relationship between goals and the strategies and skills that are supposedly directed towards them is dynamic rather than static. The development and learning of strategies and skills are pursued in a pragmatic and flexible manner.

Basic Premise of SSLD

The SSLD model is based on a number of theoretical tenets. The first is that most human behaviours are purposeful or goal-directed. Human purposes or goals can be understood in terms of motivating drives which are related to basic human needs. Following from this position, human beings are conceived as self-directed, proactive agents rather than passive recipients of external environmental influence. Closely linked to this position is the recognition of the interaction among motivational, cognitive, emotional, and biological processes.

This second tenet conceives human beings as embodied. Instead of committing to a dualistic conceptualization of body and mind, human thought and action are seen as embodied realities always involving biological correlates. The model emphasizes that the motivational, cognitive, emotional, biological, and environmental processes interact in a complex but concerted manner. It is recognized that processes in these different domains can take on different roles and varying levels of significance across situations. In some cases, emotional processes might be more salient; in others, the cognitive processes might be more influential. Similarly, environmental realities as well as biological and motivational processes can have very different effects. The model does not make generic assumptions regarding whether cognitive or emotional processes are primary and therefore more important, as respectively asserted by cognitive therapists (Alford & Beck, 1997; Beck, 1999; Beck, 1995) and emotion-focused therapists (Greenberg, 2002; Greenberg & Safran, 1987). Individual and situational variations are recognized as significant contingencies to be considered in the actual practice situation.

The third is a related concept of mutual conditioning and transformation, which is built on Bandura's (1977a, 1986) idea of reciprocal determinism. Human agents engage in a process of mutual influence and transformation with the environment. Within the social and interpersonal world, human beings came to mutually influence and transform each other through their interactions. The same can be said about human beings and social systems and structures. In other words, while individuals are subject to the influence and conditioning forces of social systems, including ideology, discourses, organizations, and institutions, their agentive actions also impact on these social systems and structures, and can lead to their creation, transformation, or destruction. An important concept in this formulation is power, for although in theory the influence and transformation can be mutual and reciprocal, the actual processes of change are heavily conditioned by the reality of power. In an abusive parent-child relationship, for example, the unequal distribution of power will put serious limits on what the child can accomplish within that context. In the human services, especially in social work, an important consideration is the possibility of empowerment. The child can be supported, for instance, in accessing child protection services, and can learn a new set of coping strategies and life skills to either resist, change, or exit from the abusive reality. This analysis can also be applied on a collective level. In social contexts where groups of individuals are marginalized or oppressed – be they women, older people, sexual minorities, individuals with disabilities, refugees, displaced peasants, homeless people, unemployed workers, and so on – it is possible for these groups to collectively develop strategies and learn skills that can bring about changes in their social and personal circumstances, leading to an improvement in their overall quality of life.

This leads us to the fourth key idea in SSLD – that most human behaviours are learned. According to Bandura (1977a, 1986), human beings learn mainly through observation learning or modelling, although respondent conditioning and operant conditioning can also play a role. Observation or imitative learning can occur through direct real-life exposure, but can also be mediated through symbols, images, or language. Whereas a lot of learning takes place in everyday life without deliberate instruction, training, or coaching, very often individuals need a more systematically designed program of learning in order to meet their specific needs. Young immigrants growing up in a socio-economically disadvantaged context, for example, may not have adequate opportunities to acquire the social and interpersonal strategies and skills needed for job-hunting and career advancement in their natural environment.

SSLD programs specifically designed to address their disadvantages will increase their chance of success in terms of labour market participation and career advancement.

The fifth point is that human behaviours vary in their effectiveness in relation to the attainment of goals. Although most human behaviours are purposeful, not all of them are equally effective. When a particular behaviour is ineffective, the individual's chance of goal attainment or personal fulfilment is compromised. In some cases the person will simply give up, such as in the case of learned helplessness, which is found to be linked to depression (Seligman, 1974, 1991). In some other cases, the individual may persist in the use of an ineffective means, such as someone who uses alcohol or drugs to manage stress or emotional pain originating from interpersonal problems. This leads to the sixth key formulation in SSLD: many behaviours that are considered problematic are actually attempts to address human needs by ineffective or socially inappropriate means.

Reconceptualizing problematic behaviours as ineffective strategies or skill deficits opens up a perspective that is less pathologizing or stigmatizing and more proactive and empowering. Using the substance use example again, if we take the individual as someone who has needs and the drug or alcohol intake as a strategy for meeting those needs (e.g., pain relief, pleasure, acceptance into a particular social group, etc.), we can pay attention to the person's needs and how to meet them, and not only to how problematic the person's behaviours are. Many years ago, I worked with a group of children diagnosed with infantile autism, and many of these children manifested the "symptom" of spinning on their own. Instead of seeing that only as a problem, I took the spinning as their attempt to achieve pleasurable sensory stimulation. In my play sessions with them, I tried spinning with one of them held in my arms and found that quite a few of them actually liked that. They even approached me afterwards for more. Through this simple process, these children learned an important social skill (approaching an adult for interactive play) to meet a personal need (pleasurable sensory experience) and broke through the interpersonal isolation that is supposed to define their pathology.

In the SSLD model, problems presented by individuals experiencing difficulties in their life are understood in terms of their underlying needs and the current behavioural strategies they are employing to meet them. Their current behaviours are assessed in terms of their relevance and effectiveness with regard to the individual's needs and goals. The problem is usually translated into an understanding of the person's needs, helping the individual to articulate personal goals, and collaboration with the individual in developing relevant strategies and skills that are more likely to be effective in meeting her or his needs. It should be emphasized here that in this translation process, the individual's needs (e.g., pain relief, security, physical comfort or pleasure) are often not problematic in themselves, while the goals (e.g., gaining acceptance by friends, career advancement, maintaining an intimate relationship) are quite legitimate in most cases as well. It is usually the behavioural strategy they have adopted (e.g., drug use, violence, embezzlement of funds) that is considered problematic. It is nonetheless possible that an inappropriate interim goal is set (e.g., getting a friend to be an accomplice) in relation to a behavioural strategy that is misdirected overall (e.g., stealing a car to take a date out for a ride), but even in this case, the need (to develop an intimate relationship) itself is not the problem.

It should be pointed out that some of the "problematic" strategies can be quite effective in achieving the intended goal, and sometimes they are only problematic because they are deemed inappropriate in the given social context. Using marijuana to achieve sensory pleasure and as a shared activity to facilitate social interaction, for example, or engaging the service of sex workers to address one's sexual need, can be effective strategies if these behaviours are not criminalized and heavily stigmatized. In societies where they are outlawed, they become problematic because they can invite interventions that would disrupt the person's life and her or his pursuits in other areas (e.g., keeping a job, going to school). From a global perspective, much human behaviour that is motivated by very legitimate needs and goals (e.g., a young woman wanting to realize her potential by becoming a political leader; a gay man wanting to have sex with his partner) have been prohibited or restricted. When engaging in SSLD practice, we have to be mindful of the political implications of our intervention both in terms of our assessment and the direction of the strategies and skills we are developing with our clients. We do not simply assist learners to conform to prevailing social norms, but are committed to personal and collective empowerment. The expansion of an individual's or a group's repertoire of strategies and skills is believed to be inherently empowering, for the people concerned will then have a wider range of options and will be capable of actions that were previously not possible. Later in Chapter 13 of this book, we will explore the application of SSLD in collective and community interventions with reference to ideas of empowerment and bringing about social change.

Finally, the SSLD model maintains that when a person learns new behavioural strategies and skills that are more effective in attaining personal goals, previously learned ones which are less effective can be replaced. This proactive orientation channels time and energy away from exploring the etiology or genealogy of the client's "problem," which is the preoccupation of many psychotherapists and counsellors. It focuses our attention on the person's need and goals, and on possible behavioural strategies to address them effectively. A man who is emotionally needy, and who feels insecure and unworthy as a person, may try to control his partner's activities (linked to a deep fear of losing the partner), express strong jealousy, utilize dominating and bullying strategies, and may even resort to verbal and physical violence. Trying to punish or suppress his responses and behaviours is probably not the best approach. When he can come to an understanding of his needs and learn appropriate strategies to address them, he will be performing interpersonal and social skills that enhance his self-efficacy, strengthen his impulse control, facilitate effective communication of his emotional needs, and improve intimacy with his partner based on mutual understanding, respect, and trust. At that stage, it would not be necessary for him to resort to those less effective, and socially more costly, strategies that he previously employed.

The emphasis on developing new alternative strategies instead of stopping or suppressing problematic behaviour is congruent with a nonjudgmental and empowering orientation. The strengthening of a person's self-efficacy, or "beliefs in one's capability to organize and execute the courses of action required to manage prospective situations" (Bandura, 1977b, p. 2), has been found to be related to more effective goal attainment as well as better health, both mental and physical (Pajares, 1997). The collaborative learning process also enhances our engagement and working alliance with the client, which is recognized as a key contributing factor to positive client change (Bogo, 2006; Grencavage & Norcross, 1990; Lambert, 1992; Lambert & Barley, 2002; Martin, Garske, & Davis, 2000; Norcross, 2010). A summary of the basic tenets of the SSLD Model is given in Box 2.1.

Case Illustration

To illustrate how SSLD approaches a problem situation, we can use the example of a man who is having multiple problems (see Figure 2.3

Interpersonal Strategies and Skills   37

Box 2.1. Basic Tenets of the SSLD Model

1. Most human behaviours are motivated and goal-directed; the individual is conceived as an active agent.
2. Human action is embodied and mediated by biological, cognitive, and emotional processes.
3. Human action and external environmental realities interact with each other, and there is a process of mutual conditioning and transformation.
4. Most human behaviours are learned. Some are learned in informal, everyday situations, while some are learned through structured programs.
5. Human behaviours vary in their effectiveness with regard to the attainment of goals.
6. Problematic behaviours are attempts to attain goals by misguided or ineffective means.
7. The mastery of new strategies and skills that are effective can lead to displacement of formerly learned ones that are ineffective or inappropriate.

---

below). He drinks heavily and as a result he cannot hold on to his job, nor can he be counted on to take care of his children. He usually refuses to engage with people and rejects demands for help. He is easily agitated and can become very hostile and aggressive even with very minor provocation.

The typical SSLD approach to this case is to analyse the person's needs. This is done by inferring motivations from his current behaviour, a procedure called problem translation, which will be described Chapter 4. Usually we will find that his current behaviours – which include drinking, avoidance of social role demands, and aggression towards his family members – are all functional, in that these behaviours are driven by a set of needs and serve related functions. This man may be experiencing immense anxiety for he feels that he cannot cope with the demands in his life. He may also feel a lot of emotional pain and be seeking relief from that. Feeling inadequate inside and overwhelmed by external events, he may be desperately trying to gain mastery and control over his external world, his internal emotional experiences, and his own behaviours, which are judged to be problematic by others. Given all the pressure and unpleasant circumstances he has to put up with, he has a strong desire for pleasurable experiences, which he can only find in drinking. The drinking may also serve as his pain relief and anxiety reduction strategy. His aggression towards his family is a desperate, and ineffective, means to gain control and mastery over his environment, especially his interpersonal and social world.

In order to help this man, an SSLD formulation will suggest that trying to reduce or suppress his problematic behaviours usually do not work well, for without them his needs will remain unmet. A more thorough treatment shall involve the learning and development of strategies and skills which will be effective in meeting his needs. These can include better interpersonal skills so that he can obtain the responses he desires from others, such as empathic understanding, care, collaboration, emotional support, and intimacy. He may have to learn alternative ways to reduce pain and attain pleasure, which can be anything ranging from developing a hobby to learning yoga, enjoying socializing with others, listening to or playing music, or participating in team sports. In order to establish a different lifestyle, he needs to be able to solve his current problems, such as unemployment and tension with his family. The learning of social skills and life skills such as job-searching, interviewing, and conflict-resolution skills can be very relevant. He may also need to learn to manage his sources and level of stress, and to develop effective coping strategies.

These strategies and skills can be learned and developed systematically through an SSLD program. It is expected that when he has mastered these strategies and skills, he will become more effective in meeting his own needs and achieving his desired goals in life. He will then have little need for his original behaviours such as drinking and aggression, which are therefore likely to be replaced by the newly learned strategies and skills.

Advantages of the SSLD Model

SSLD has several advantages as a practice model for facilitating change in human action. It offers a conceptual model based on an educational and learning paradigm instead of a medical model, making it a less stigmatizing and more empowering approach. It is proactive and client-centred. It offers a systematic procedure for both clients and practitioners to follow, and has an extremely wide range of applicability. It is a cost-effective intervention method and can be adapted easily to most

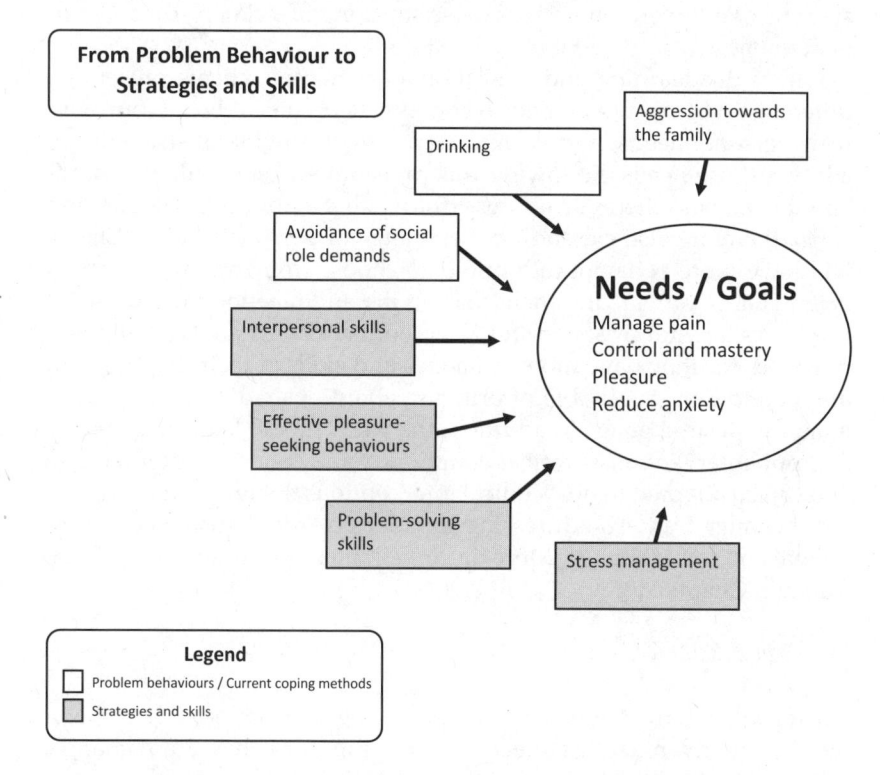

Figure 2.3. SSLD Analysis of Problem Behaviour

From Problem Behaviour to Strategies and Skills

- Aggression towards the family
- Drinking
- Avoidance of social role demands
- Interpersonal skills
- Effective pleasure-seeking behaviours
- Problem-solving skills
- Stress management

Needs / Goals
Manage pain
Control and mastery
Pleasure
Reduce anxiety

Legend
☐ Problem behaviours / Current coping methods
▨ Strategies and skills

practice settings. It can be used in personal, family, group, organizational, and community contexts. The following section will document the many advantages experienced in my own practice.

Conceptual Advantages: Theory and Value

SSLD has several advantages as a system for facilitating change in human action. First of all, it is not based on a medical model that conceptualizes human experience and action as pathology and subscribes to a deterministic understanding of etiology and treatment. Instead, it takes on a learning and educational orientation. SSLD understands the problems presented by clients in terms of unmet needs, and seeks to translate them into goals and courses of learning. It recognizes the human needs underlying behaviours that are considered problematic and does not carry the value judgment or stigmatization implied by other systems of intervention such as those speaking of sickness, disorder, or delinquency.

Within this learning and educational orientation, clients presenting different problems are helped to connect their current behaviour with their personal needs, and then to learn new behavioural strategies to address those needs. Following this procedure, clients will almost invariably expand their current repertoire of behaviour or strategies and skills, therefore also expanding their range of personal choice. Clients will have more behavioural options to choose from, and thus stand a better chance of realizing their goals in life and meeting their personal needs. As a result of successful intervention, clients are typically empowered, for they have more strategies and skills at their disposal and are therefore more capable of bringing about desired changes and/or attaining desired goals. In addition, the SSLD model lends itself easily to group intervention as well as community and collective intervention, and can be adopted in non-clinical interventions not only targeting personal change but also addressing broader objectives such as environmental and social change. More discussion on these applications can be found in Chapter 13.

Technical Advantages

On top of its educational and empowering orientation, SSLD has a number of advantages as a technical program for behavioural change. With SSLD, the client participates in defining the intervention objectives and in articulating her or his personal goals. The motivation comes directly from the client's conscious effort to attain such goals. This approach in defining intervention objectives is very conducive to client-practitioner engagement as well as the development of a working or therapeutic alliance. Client resistance, which usually arises out of the perceived discrepancy between the trainer's objectives and those of the client, is minimized.

Another technical advantage of SSLD lies in its behavioural focus. This focus on observable behaviour, as will be shown in Chapter 4 on problem translation, does not deny the significance of subjective sense-making, personal meaning, and social construction of reality, but instead provides a firm anchorage on concrete, observable change. Both the theory and the practice procedure are very concrete and systematic.

It therefore allows clients to experience progress made in a very tangible manner, namely observable changes in their own behaviour as well as the behaviour of others. This enhances motivation and facilitates monitoring of progress. The measurement of outcomes for practice effectiveness, service evaluation, quality assurance, and research purposes is thus facilitated. SSLD actually draws on the extensive body of empirical research associated with the development of social cognitive theory and with service programs using social skills learning and training procedures.

SSLD is a well-structured method supported by systematic procedures. The practice principles are concrete and specific, and can easily be organized and presented in practice manuals and learning materials. Compared to other systems of interventions, it is relatively easy for practitioners to learn and master. Within a service context demanding high cost effectiveness and demonstrable results, SSLD offers an attractive option. It is particularly useful in settings requiring time-limited interventions. Compared to other time-limited procedures, it has the added advantage of being cumulative, for it is essentially a program of incremental learning – subsequent intervention can be built upon earlier learning by the client.

Practical Advantages

Besides its advantages with regard to theoretical orientation and technical features, SSLD has additional practical advantages. It articulates an action- and result-oriented approach with its clear focus on goal attainment and relevant behavioural strategies. In human service settings requiring active input from the practitioner, such as educational or training institutions, residential care settings, outreach programs, and community work, SSLD can be the intervention model of choice. The model's learning and educational orientation reduces the risk of pathologization and stigmatization, and is likely to decrease possible client resistance. This feature fits in nicely with the expectations of helping professionals to be more active in providing direction and guidance held by clients in some cultural communities (Chu, 1999; Exum & Lau, 1988; Lin, 2002; Miller, Yang, & Chen, 1997), and it actually encourages active learning and self-direction, leading to empowering outcomes for clients.

The learning and development of behavioural strategies and skills has an extremely wide range of applications. Varieties of this practice have been applied to children with pervasive developmental disorders, psychiatric patients, adults with developmental challenges, couples trying to improve their relationships, university students learning to be more assertive, women struggling with depression, men who need to control their anger, new immigrants adjusting to their host country, community members advocating for social change, executives who need to develop leadership skills, managers coaching their employees, businesspeople working internationally or cross-culturally, and many other groups of people. In a way, almost anyone can benefit from further learning and development of behavioural strategies and skills to enrich their lives.

As mentioned above, SSLD is conducted in an incremental manner with cumulative results. Apart from being highly compatible with time-limited service arrangements, the adoption of SSLD as an intervention within a service unit can also minimize the potential negative effects of staff turnover. Should a course of intervention be terminated prematurely, the benefits of cumulative learning are probably more transferable than therapeutic gains made through other intervention approaches. In the case of transfer, the new practitioner may quickly establish a working relationship with the learner in order to continue with, and build upon, the learning previously completed.

Apart from being applied independently as a system of intervention, SSLD can also be used in connection with other intervention modalities. Cognitive behavioural therapists have long been employing social skills training to complement cognitive procedures. In my own experience, some clients have presented an issue that is highly amenable to SSLD (e.g., social phobia or sexual dysfunction), worked on it, and then moved on to more emotionally focused or insight-oriented work. Other clients have started off with more conventional talk therapy. After having achieved some cognitive reconstruction and resolved their emotional issues, some of these clients then need to learn specific strategies and skills to enhance their functioning (e.g., strengthening intimacy with their partner; learning presentation and negotiation skills for more effective performance at work). Its behavioural focus and its performance and result orientation usually make it easy for clients to understand the relevance of SSLD to their situation and their needs and goals. Depending on the specific service context, the SSLD program can be delivered by the same practitioner, or the client can work with another colleague specializing in this intervention procedure.

Given all these advantages, SSLD has tremendous potential for being adopted as a key intervention method across a wide range of human service settings. The next section will introduce the basic principles of SSLD practice, to be followed by more detailed descriptions of practice procedures.

Chapter Three

Basic Principles of Strategies and Skills Learning and Development

SSLD builds on earlier developments in social skills training and shares some of the same basic principles and procedures. This section introduces these principles and procedures, highlighting features that are characteristic of the SSLD approach. The first critical point is determining the objective of the intervention, and here lies the difference between a preplanned or prepackaged program and a contingency-based approach. In conventional social skills training or similar practice, it is not unusual to have a preplanned program with specific content targeting a given group of clients, such as an assertiveness training program designed for women, or a life-skills training program designed for children with developmental challenges. Such programs are designed around the common needs of a relatively homogenous group, and certain content components are believed to be relevant to most participants. A contingency-based program does not assume that the practitioner has a prior knowledge of the client's needs, and finding out about the client's specific circumstances and learning needs becomes the first step in the intervention.

I am, however, not suggesting that all preplanned programs disregard the client's needs and specific circumstances. In a preplanned program, clients are typically assessed to determine if they are likely to benefit from the program. In individual interventions, clients' circumstances will be matched with available programs. In group interventions, a set of eligibility criteria will be established to screen clients for the group program to be delivered. A possible limitation here is that clients are selected according to the offerings of pre-set programs. A contingency-based approach puts the emphasis on the client's particular circumstances and needs, and the intervention program is contingent upon client situations. The program design allows for ongoing monitoring to inform the development of specific intervention procedures corresponding to client needs and progress.

In a preplanned or pre-packaged program, the first step is client selection or matching. In a contingency-based approach, the first step is problem translation – a procedure that translates the client's presenting issues into a set of learning objectives through careful analysis of the client's current behaviours and their underlying motivation. The specific procedures involved in problem translation will be detailed in the next chapter. At this point, it should perhaps be emphasized that the presenting issue is first understood by connecting it to possible client needs. For example, a person who feels depressed after breaking up an intimate relationship may present emotional difficulties such as anger, confusion, depression, negativity, and so on; and behavioural manifestations may include refusal to eat, social withdrawal, temper tantrums, and other acts that may lead to self-injury. It is not easy to imagine what a preplanned program for such an individual may look like. In a contingency-based intervention, however, we will be exploring the needs underlying such emotional responses. The needs supposedly met by the partner in the terminated relationship, such as affiliation, intimacy, companionship, emotional nurturance, sexual pleasure, self-esteem, social approval, and the like, are not to be overlooked. There can be an issue of adjusting to a different routine for one's personal and social life. Very often, a relationship that does not work out may also threaten an individual's sense of self, including self-esteem and the sense of control and mastery over one's life. The need for emotional ventilation can also be important in maintaining homeostasis and well-being. Practitioners of a contingency-based approach will try to engage with the client and establish a shared understanding of the client's needs. This understanding is critical as a first step and can release the client from being obsessed with unhelpful ideas such as getting back together with the ex-partner, which in some cases can be misconstrued as the client's goal. Once a shared understanding of the client's needs is established, we can then work with the client to set realistic goals that are functionally related to these needs, such as effective emotional ventilation and management of emotional responses, courses of action that will increase self-efficacy and self-esteem, and the design of activities that would lead to pleasure and personal fulfilment.

Table 3.1 summarizes the differences between preplanned intervention and contingency-based intervention. It should be emphasized that

Table 3.1. Preplanned or Prepackaged Program versus Contingency-Based Skills Learning

Preplanned or Prepackaged Intervention	Contingency-Based Intervention
▪ Preplanned, fixed; same program for everyone (e.g., assertiveness training) ▪ Assumes similar problems or common needs ▪ Structured or manualized; easier to learn and deliver	▪ Common skill set to be learned ▪ Contingent upon the needs and specific circumstances of the client(s) ▪ Emphasizes individual needs and characteristics ▪ Demands individualized problem translation ▪ Both common and individualized skills

the two approaches are not incompatible, and they can share similar practice procedures such as observation learning, rehearsal and feedback, real-life practice, and so on. Preplanned programs have certain advantages in terms of standardization, ease of mastery, and delivery. By contrast, contingency-based practice is an open system allowing for the creation of new strategies and methods in response to the specific needs and circumstances of the client. It has the advantage of being amenable to a much wider range of situations, but is more demanding to learn and master as a system. In actual practice, some components of preplanned programs can be used to build an intervention program while allowing the practitioner to remain open and flexible to the client's presenting issues as well as the client's unique but variable needs and circumstances.

Multiple-Contingencies Thinking

Contingency-based intervention is derived from multiple-contingencies thinking or modelling (Tsang, 2008). Multiple-contingencies thinking focuses on the multiple and interacting processes in life. The word "contingency" refers to an event that has the possibility to occur but is not necessarily probable or intended. It also refers to a possibility that one has to be prepared for. The adjective form of the word also carries the meaning of a possible event that is incidental to something else, or the condition of being dependent on chance. What is contingent is not fixed or stable, and is conditioned by other factors or processes. Colleagues in mental health and human service practice are often exposed to linear categorical thinking, and to intervention models based on the assumption that people go through more or less the same steps in achieving positive outcomes. For instance, a categorical understanding of people's conditions, such as depression or anxiety disorder, is matched with a standardized practice such as cognitive therapy. Multiple-contingencies thinking recognizes that human experiences and outcomes are contingent upon a host of ever-changing variables and processes. An issue that is apparently similar among all clients, such as substance abuse, sometimes requires very different professional responses contingent upon specific client needs, characteristics, and circumstances, including social and cultural context or situational variables.

Closely related to the idea of multiple contingencies is the notion of equifinality, which means that people can arrive at the same destination through different pathways. In practice, it means that clients can achieve the same outcome by using different methods or following different trajectories of change. Subscribing to contingency-based thinking and program design means that we do not assume that every client with the same problem – be it insomnia, social phobia, or depression – has to go through exactly the same procedures in order to get better. The actual process for each client can be different, and this again is contingent upon personal as well as environmental factors and processes, including the dynamics or chemistry between the client and practitioner dyad or group. The intervention program has to be flexible enough to respond to the diverse needs and circumstances of the clients, and to allow sufficient space for them to pursue different trajectories towards realizing their goals.

The Motor-Skill Metaphor

Before describing the actual procedure of SSLD, it is instructive to consider the motor-skill-learning metaphor used by Michael Argyle, a pioneer in social skills training. Argyle (1983) suggested that motor-skills learning offers a useful metaphor for understanding the learning of social skills, which should be very different from academic training. In the learning and mastery of motor skills such as rollerblading, dressmaking, carpentry, or playing the cello, people usually recognize a few important facts. One of them is that people with different aptitudes and prior learning will learn with different speed and proficiency. Another fact is that verbal or written instruction, while important or even indispensable, is often not sufficient in getting the person to master the skill.

The learning is usually experiential, involving demonstration, hands-on or direct imitation, coaching, and on-site feedback. A third point is that repeated practice is critical to the mastery of motor skills, and this takes a lot of time. One example I often use is learning to play a musical instrument; the key point that I try to make is that most skills learning should be like this: there is a lot of practice involving countless incidents of specific feedback on almost every aspect of the performance. A few recent bestsellers (e.g., Colvin, 2008; Gladwell, 2008; Taleb, 2005) have recommended the 10,000-hour rule, suggesting that most forms of outstanding performance require long hours of practice. Unfortunately, in most academic and professional training settings, there is simply not enough time and opportunity for similar rigour and attention to details, especially factoring in individual differences in terms of endowment, talent, and learning style. Finally, in motor-skills learning, people are often aware that mastery of a skill is a necessary but not sufficient factor for good performance.

Applying the motor-skill-learning metaphor to the learning and development of strategies and skills for personal and social lives will help focus our attention on a few issues. The first is the recognition of individual variations in learner aptitude and endowment. This is where contingency thinking is important in addressing individual differences. The emphasis on experiential learning takes us beyond the confines of instructions and interventions focusing on cognitive learning. Recognition of the importance of practice in achieving proficiency helps to address the knowledge-action gap found in a lot of academic and professional training situations. Finally, the focus on performance establishes the ultimate outcome measure in the learning process. Learning is not complete when the learner can tell people what should or can be done; it requires the actual performance of the action resulting in the attainment of the desired goal. The next section will describe the general procedures in the systematic learning of strategies and skills based on these principles.

1. **Problem Translation: Reformulate Problems and Issues into Learning Objectives**

The first step in contingency-based strategies and skills learning and development is problem translation, a procedure that translates the client's presenting issues or problems into specific learning objectives. First, a client's situation is analysed in terms of needs and current strategies. After exploring what the client thinks the problem is, we move on to examine what the client's needs are and what the client is doing with regard to those needs. Assessment of the client's needs has to be a collaborative process, and the practitioner cannot impose her or his appraisal or analysis on the client. SSLD emphasizes good engagement and building of a strong working alliance in the beginning phase of the intervention – a recommendation based on extensive research in the field of psychotherapy (Barrett-Lennard, 1962; Bogo, 2006; Gomes-Schwartz, 1978; Hartley & Strupp, 1983; Luborsky & Crits-Christoph, 1988).

Following the break-up example given previously, once a shared understanding of the client's needs has been established (e.g., self-esteem, affiliation and intimacy, emotional healing), we will move on to set up relevant goals (e.g., improved self-efficacy, establishing an intimate relationship). We will then examine the client's current coping strategies (e.g., self-injurious behaviour, temper tantrums) and then assess their relative effectiveness. The process will help us identify new strategies and skills to be learned or developed (e.g., intimate emotional communication, reciprocation, expression of care and concern, creating pleasurable experiences).

2. Generating and Designing Goal-Directed Strategies and Skills

Once a set of learning objectives has been established, we will move on to design the strategies and skills to be learned or developed by the client in order to achieve those objectives. In standardized preplanned programs, the practitioner will choose from a set repertoire of skills and try to match them with the client's needs and situation. In contingency-based practice, we can draw from the trainer's own repertoire of strategies and skills, and from documented skills in preplanned programs, as well as creating new strategies and skills collaboratively with clients through a systematic procedure. This collaborative creation of new skills has tremendous potential for expanding the capacity of the client.

At this point, the meanings of a number of terms should be clarified. Traditionally, professional intervention based on social learning principles has talked about skills or social skills. A skill can be defined as a set of behaviours that is instrumental in bringing about a certain desired outcome. Using an analogy from sports, a set of behaviours that is instrumental in landing the ball at the desired spot is a skill. In cooking, a set of behaviours that will slice a carrot to the desired thickness and shape is a skill. In one's personal and social life, a set of behaviours that draws desired attention to oneself is a skill. Similarly, a set of behaviours that distracts undesired attention from oneself, which is a goal in itself, is another skill. A social skill is a skill that is relevant to an individual's social situation.

A strategy can be seen as more a complex sequence of behaviour, and this is also instrumental or goal-directed. For example, in a job interview situation, the job applicant will need skills that draw attention to her or his favourable qualities, such as the skill of connecting: "Speaking of teamwork, I had this experience of working with my team in this challenging project ..." The skill of answering challenging questions may be another example. A successful job search, however, does not only depend on sophisticated skills but also on an effective overall strategy, which requires relevant skills to support it and yet goes beyond the specific skills themselves. An effective strategy may, for example, involve broadening one's information sources to include personal networks, web-based information, and active, unsolicited searching. Each of these courses of action requires its own set of skills, such as interpersonal skills, computer skills, and assertiveness and presentation skills. Strategy, therefore, is a more extensive and inclusive concept than skill. In this book, we will sometimes use the term "strategy" to include both the strategy and its relevant skills.

On top of the conceptual difference between the two terms, it should also be pointed out that when thinking of strategies and skills instead of just skills, we are also recognizing an important reality in personal lives and interpersonal relationships; that is the relational context. In some of the social skills training practices, attention is focused on the given situation and on achieving one's goal within that situation. In social and interpersonal relationships, achieving one's goal or having one's way in a specific situation may require one to be very skilful, but it can nonetheless be a poor move strategically, especially when we are thinking of the relationship over the long term. For instance, a salesperson who upstages her or his colleague might gain a new client or a new account, but the damaged relationship and its demonstration effect – if it is witnessed by other colleagues or team members – may backfire and undermine the salesperson's original goal. To borrow an analogy from chess, a move can be very skilful and effective, such as a move that protects a piece, but may be a bad one in the overall scheme of things if it does not increase one's chance of winning the game. Strategic thinking is an important feature of contingency-based SSLD, for it is recognized that the value of a skill is to be assessed within the overall context of the person's needs and goals, and the relevant strategies employed to attain them.

A third concept that needs to be introduced and clarified is that of performance. Whereas both the trainer and the learner are often focused on learning the right strategies and skills, it is the ultimate performance in real life that counts. A number of factors are known to have an impact on the performance of even highly skilled players, including anxiety, fatigue, or situational variables such as noise and distraction. Good trainers and coaches usually anticipate situational factors that may affect performance. In theory, however, we need to accept the fact that performance is never completely consistent, and that personal and environmental fluctuations are part of real life. In SSLD, we try to help learners understand that mastering a strategy and attaining a skill do not always guarantee optimal performance, and that interfering factors need to be anticipated and managed. This due consideration of the actual context for performance facilitates the smooth transfer of learning from the consultation room to real life.

In formulating and designing strategies and skills, an SSLD practitioner is mindful of the ultimate performance to be produced by the learner. It is not only necessary to see a clear, functional connection between the goal and the strategies and skills to be learned and developed; one must also see how the learner can master these strategies and skills with sufficient proficiency to reliably produce an adequate and effective performance. Figure 3.1 shows how a person experiencing abuse is understood with regard to her or his needs, as well as the alternative strategies and skills this person can learn in order to address such needs more effectively.

3. Systematic Learning and Development

Once objectives are determined and the relevant strategies and skills have been identified, we will move on to the actual learning and development phase. The procedure involved has been developed and well documented by practitioners of social skills training. The first step is to help the learner develop a sense of the skill that will eventually be performed. According to social cognitive theory, the major mechanism of human learning functions through modelling or observation learning, which involves the learner observing another agent, known as the model, in the actual performance of the skill to be learned. In social

52   The SSLD Idea

Figure 3.1. Effective Performance of Learned Strategies and Skills to Meet Client Needs

Needs / Goals
Safety
Order
Self-esteem / efficacy
Relationship
Income

Current coping methods: Submission; Putting up; Avoiding provocation

Strategies and skills: Appease; Social networking; Interpersonal skills; Accessing / utilizing services; Occupational / financial competence; Managing emotions

Legend
- Current coping methods
- Strategies and skills

skills training, this is turned into a procedure called demonstration. In SSLD, we have a slightly broader conceptualization of this process.

Modelling, Demonstration, Observation, and Symbolic Mediation

Extensive research has been done to demonstrate how people learn by observing models (Bandura, 1986). In adult learning and educational settings, however, we have also noticed that a lot of learning can take place without direct observation. Very often the process is substituted by what can be called **symbolic mediation** – the performance of the model is mediated or represented by symbolic systems such as language, diagrams, or pictures. The best example is perhaps the cookbook. Many people are able to produce the same dish by reading a cookbook and following the instructions without actually observing an expert chef. Many DIY (do-it-yourself) manuals are based on the same principles of symbolically mediated observation learning. Symbolic mediation can also include audio-visual aids used in education and training.

The use of symbolic mediation, in verbal or other forms, greatly increases the possible range of observation learning. In everyday life, however, verbal or other forms of instruction are often given but not always followed. Understanding verbal instructions does not always translate into action, and this is the knowledge-action gap we mentioned above. In SSLD, one of the contingencies we need to consider is the learner's current competence, learning history, and aptitude. Some learners are very efficient in looking at manuals and then mastering the skills, whereas others need a lot of observation learning as well as systematic coaching, or hand-holding. Just take the example of learning to use a new computer software application. Some people need minimum instruction, some people only need the online tutorial, some people need to take courses, and other people need ongoing instruction and coaching as they start to use the application. It should also be pointed out that people needing minimum instruction in learning one kind of skill (e.g., computer) may need extensive instruction, modelling, and systematic coaching with another kind of skill (e.g., developing intimacy in a relationship). This is another reason why preplanned programs that assume people have the same aptitude and learning style may not always meet the needs of all the learners. In a contingency-based SSLD program, attention is always paid to the learner's capacity and circumstances. In certain situations, learning how to learn may be a critical step in the program. For instance, when helping children suffering from autism to learn interpersonal skills, it is important to help them to learn how to imitate first; and in order to learn to imitate, they need to learn how to pay attention to the behaviour of others. As many of these children tend to avoid interpersonal contact, getting them to attend, observe, and learn to imitate will become a program objective in itself. In my experience, even children with the same diagnosis differ in their initial readiness to learn these very basic interpersonal skills, and the program has to adjust to their individual circumstances.

In traditional social skills training, the trainer will typically model the target performance, and the learners will observe and then reproduce the skill. In some situations, the practitioner may bring in models who are particularly skilled in what is to be learned. In my own experience, learning can take place without an external model or explicit demonstration, especially when we are trying to improve upon existing skills. For example, in the learning of communication skills, learners can have the opportunity to watch video recordings of their baseline performance – their regular performance before exposure to SSLD. They will then imagine how their performance can be improved, with or without input from the practitioner. In a group-learning context, the other group participants can offer extremely valuable feedback and input as well. In most cases, the learner is capable of processing such input symbolically and then applying it to their subsequent performance. Such learning without demonstration by the practitioner or an expert is more empowering, in that the raw material for learning and refinement comes mainly from the clients.

Learning and Mastering the Skill: Imitation, Enactment, Simulation, and Feedback

SSLD is predicated on the belief that conceptual knowledge, which can result from cognitive instructional processes, does not always translate into action automatically. Even with learners who are more proficient in enacting instructions that are conceptually learned, they still need a process through which their enactment can be refined. In traditional social skills training, learners usually go through a systematic learning procedure involving imitation or enactment, simulation, and feedback.

Imitation or enactment is the process of cognitively translating what is learned through observation and/or instruction into action. Novices in learning a given skill typically have varying levels of success with the initial enactment. In my many years of experience training professional counsellors and psychotherapists, for example, I see people struggling to put the complex system of instructions they learn from lectures and textbooks into practice. What my students have found to be most helpful is a systematic learning laboratory in which they can try out the composite skills such as listening, empathic communication, engagement, handling resistance, and so on in a safe and structured environment, wherein they can learn from their mistakes or less-than-perfect performances, receive constructive feedback, and make specific adjustments. In this kind of learning, the use of video recording, playback, and review is usually extremely helpful.

In SSLD, it is important to set up a safe learning environment in which the learner is rarely judged, criticized, or ridiculed. Instead, the learner is briefed to expect mistakes and less-than-perfect performances during the learning process. In a one-on-one learning context such as individual counselling, the practitioner will encourage the learner to participate actively in the process through producing or reproducing behavioural sequences that they use or plan to use in real-life situations, to experiment with new behaviours, and sometimes to deliberately make mistakes or fail. Feedback given to the learner should be constructive and empowering. In a group-work context, members of the group can be specifically trained to give such feedback. Positive feedback, especially in the context of a group of peers, is very helpful for strengthening self-efficacy. It has been found that self-efficacy is positively correlated with performance (Bandura, 1997; Maddux, 1995; Stajkovic & Luthans, 1998). Other than being constructive and empowering, feedback should be concrete and specific as well. Video recording and playback is a powerful procedure in improving performance. The opportunity to see oneself on video, and to receive concrete and constructive feedback, helps the learner to focus on aspects needing improvement and to fine-tune their performance.

Another factor affecting the transfer of learning from the classroom to real-life situations is the similarity of the two situations. A general principle is to set up the learning and rehearsal situation to be as similar to the real-life performance situation as possible. If circumstances permit, it is ideal to rehearse in the actual performance site. This is what people in theatrical and similar performance work do with their dress rehearsal. Simulation and role-playing are often employed in SSLD programs. Again, aspects of the simulation and role-play should be managed to resemble real-life situations as much as possible. Many years ago, a client of mine who was an engineer at a public utilities organization needed to rehearse a presentation that was to be given in front of his board of directors – a situation for which a real-life rehearsal is difficult to set up. With his consent, I invited a number of my colleagues to role-play as his directors and had him present a new initiative to them. The physical setting was also set up as close to his description of the real-life setting as possible. My colleagues were given some prior briefing and asked to come up with difficult and challenging questions, which the client was apprehensive about. The rehearsal went well – and the actual board meeting later turned out to be less difficult than the one we had rehearsed.

The experiential learning process in SSLD provides a safe environment for experimentation, innovation, repetition, and incremental refinement. Eventually, the learner has to apply the newly mastered strategies and skills in real life. In setting the performance expectations or standards during the learning program, it is therefore important to assess the risk of sending the learner out to a potentially challenging or disempowering situation. A key principle here is incremental learning, with complex strategies or tasks broken down into more manageable incremental steps. Although creativity and risk-taking is often encouraged, care is usually taken to help learners avoid difficult experiences that will tax them beyond their coping capacity.

Expectation management is another strategy that can help to protect the client from a disempowering disappointment when the performance does not bring about the expected outcome. The general principle is to adjust the expectation a little below the anticipated performance and outcome, so as to reduce the client's chance of experiencing failure and defeat. Many of our clients have faced repeated negative experiences before, and it is helpful for them to see how their new performance has improved over previous ones even when the ultimate goal is yet to be realized. Combining incrementalism and expectation management will allow clients to experience small, successful steps, which in my experience tend to add up and facilitate more significant progress later on.

Real-Life Practice, Report Back, Review, and Refinement – The 4Rs

Whenever learners are ready to try out new behaviours in real life, they are encouraged to do so. Very often, this real-life practice is a result of a process of in-session classroom learning aiming at difficult tasks, such as dealing with mean and undermining criticisms coming from one's spouse, parent, or boss. Another example could be for an individual with a long history of severe mental illness and social isolation to start developing intimate relationships. It is, however, also possible for learners to experience changes in real-life behaviours even when they have only received minimal input from the program. One prominent example is the use of homework exercises, which has been found to be very useful by practitioners of cognitive behavioural interventions and social skills training (Kazantzis, Deane, Ronan, & L'Abate, 2005). Certain homework exercises are well-tested and involve very low risk, such as recording a behaviour targeted to be changed, or simple exercises such as communicating positive feedback to a family member or trying to initiate a conversation with a colleague at work.

Regardless of the complexity, level of difficulty, and timing of the real-life practice, it is always important for the learner to have an opportunity to report back and obtain further feedback through review with the trainer and/or fellow learners in a group. This process will lead to incremental improvement of the skill to be mastered, and sometimes may even generate innovative strategies and skills as a result of the interactive learning process.

4. Evaluation

The final step in the learning of strategies and skills is the confirmation of successful completion. This final evaluation is made with reference to the needs of the learner, which have been identified earlier in the learning process, and the goals set collaboratively between learner and practitioner. Such evaluation with concrete and observable outcome markers makes the procedure explicit to both the client and the service provider, and therefore facilitates accountability and service quality assurance. The evaluation process itself is process-oriented, emphasizing the lessons learned and *how* the learner has come to master the new sets of strategies and skills. This is a deliberately empowering process aiming at increasing the learner's self-efficacy or the belief in one's capacity in managing situations in one's personal and social life. This focus on learning will also allow the learner to adopt a similar approach to problem solving in the future. Problems experienced by the learner will hopefully be translated into an understanding of one's needs, and then into goal-directed learning and development.

PART TWO

Basic SSLD Procedure

Chapter Four

Problem Translation

Problem translation is the first step in contingency-based SSLD. It is a feature of SSLD that allows the practitioner to respond to the unique circumstances, needs, characteristics, and capacities of specific clients or client groups, including families, special purpose groups, organizations, and communities. Presented problems are analysed in terms of the client's needs and goals as well as the current skills and/or strategies used to attain them. The "problem" is eventually translated into learning objectives. The procedure therefore involves (1) engaging with the client through establishing a shared understanding of the client's needs and circumstances; (2) behaviour-oriented functional analysis of the presenting problem or situation; (3) needs assessment and documenting of the client's needs profile; and (4) (re)articulation of goals. This procedure roughly corresponds to what is commonly referred to in clinical practice as engagement and relationship building, assessment (and/or diagnosis), clinical formulation, and contracting phases. It should be emphasized that these four tasks do not have to be conducted in a rigid sequence. Experienced practitioners are often able to achieve these smoothly and somewhat simultaneously without tightly controlling the therapy agenda, allowing clients ample space and freedom to present their issues, concerns, and experiences.

Engagement and Working Alliance

In practice, problem translation is not a mechanical process, but a dynamic one involving collaboration with the client. Recognizing the significance of engagement and the establishment of working or therapeutic alliances in bringing about positive client change (Barrett-

Lennard, 1962; Gomes-Schwartz, 1978; Hartley & Strupp, 1983; Luborsky & Crits-Christoph, 1988), the problem translation process in SSLD is conducted with the distinct purpose of engagement and alliance building. It takes place within the context of a dialogue between the client and the practitioner. This dialogue targets the three key components of the working alliance (Bordin, 1979): (1) agreement on the goals of therapy; (2) agreement on the tasks needed to achieve the agreed-upon goals; and (3) the development of an interpersonal bond.

Through problem translation, an SSLD practitioner first tries to gain an accurate understanding of the client's thoughts and actions, especially with reference to the client's needs and goals. The purpose is to establish a shared understanding. The goals of the intervention have to be set and owned by the client. Such a shared understanding of goals will minimize subsequent client resistance. The second task in the engagement process is to get the client to appreciate how SSLD procedures are related to the agreed-upon goals. Given the clear goal-directed nature of SSLD procedures, this should not be too difficult. One should nonetheless take special care to ensure that the client understands and is comfortable with the proposed procedure. Sometimes clients come with the expectation of extensive talk therapy, and we have to make sure that there is sufficient narrative space for clients to tell their stories. We can then articulate our understanding of their needs and goals and then connect them to SSLD procedures. In practice, it is better to spend more time at the beginning on establishing a good engagement than to renegotiate fundamental issues later in the process.

The third aspect of the engagement and alliance-building process is the interpersonal bond between the client and the practitioner. This is usually achieved through the communication of empathic understanding of the client's experience, emotional attunement to the client, accurate understanding of the client's subjective meanings, an accepting and nonjudgmental attitude, emotional support, collaboration, and cultivation of positive expectancy with regard to the outcome of the intervention. The structure of SSLD lends itself readily to the accomplishment of these engagement tasks. The problem translation process is a deliberate attempt to gain an accurate understanding of the client's experiences and needs. The contingency-based orientation respects the client's unique circumstances. The SSLD problem translation process is inherently nonjudgmental as it reframes problems into needs, goals, and learning tasks. Recognizing the client's needs and strivings is in itself emotionally supportive and empowering. The problem translation procedure and subsequent SSLD tasks all emphasize client-practitioner collaboration. Finally, the action-orientated style, and the extensive research and clinical experience that support the development of SSLD procedures, will facilitate the development of positive expectancy with regard to intervention outcomes.

Behaviour-Oriented Functional Analysis (BOFA)

Before getting into the specific procedures of needs assessment, a number of related conceptual issues have to be clarified. First of all, problem translation involves functional analysis and is behaviour or action oriented. Functional analysis refers to the analysis of human actions with reference to the functions they are supposed to serve, and a behaviour-oriented approach grounds the analysis on observable behaviour instead of relying solely on abstract constructs. For instance, a person reporting paranoid delusional thoughts is usually considered sick, and the experience reported is seen as symptomatic of schizophrenic disorder. The delusion is not thought of as something functional but something dysfunctional. From a functional analysis perspective, reporting delusional thoughts is a behaviour that serves a function (Figure 4.1). Verbalization may serve to release some anxiety. Reporting or sharing the experience with others can be construed as a form of help-seeking. The construction of the delusional idea itself can be understood as a cognitive attempt to make sense of overwhelming stressors and threats to one's sense of mastery and control – and hence a first step towards managing them.

Such functional analysis focuses the practitioner's attention on the client's needs, and on what the client is trying to achieve through behaviours that are sometimes considered problematic or dysfunctional. The client is seen as an active agent pursuing goals. The behavioural orientation anchors our analysis on specific, observable actions taken by the client, instead of extensive conversations about nonspecific experiences or thoughts. SSLD practice typically does not involve lengthy conversations between the client and the practitioner, but this does not preclude the exploration of subjective experiences and personal meanings. When the client presents subjective experiences and provides personal meanings, such narratives are taken into account in the analysis, leading to an understanding of the client's needs and goals as well as how the client employs different strategies to address them. When abstract constructs are used instead of behavioural indicators or markers,

64 Basic SSLD Procedure

Figure 4.1. Behaviour-Oriented Functional Analysis of Presenting Problems

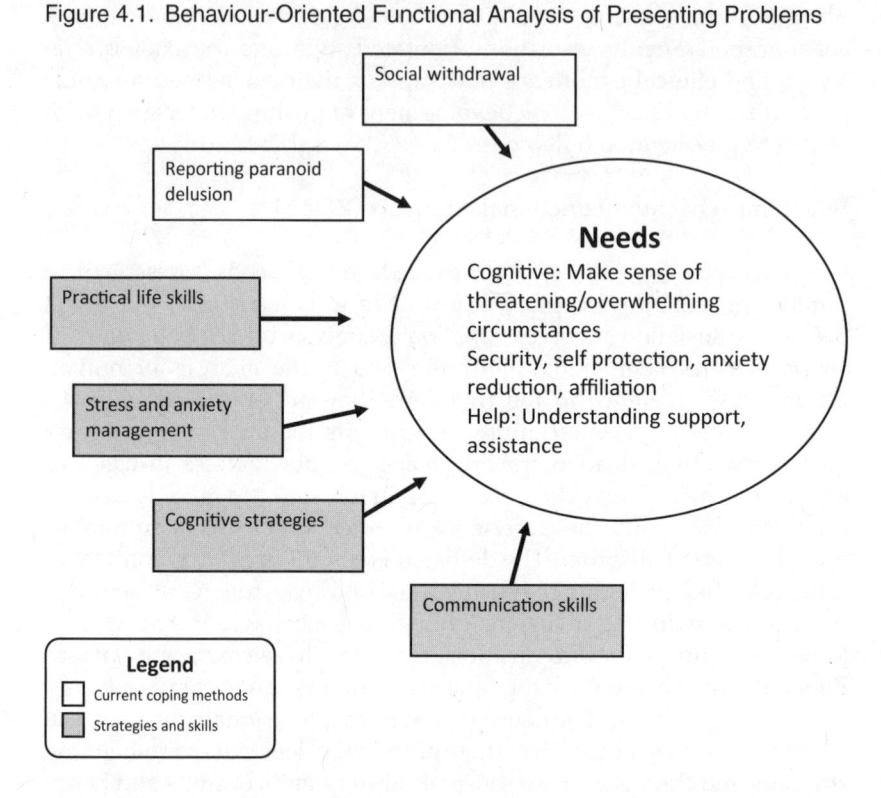

```
                    Social withdrawal
                            │
                            ▼
  Reporting paranoid                ╭─────────────────────────╮
  delusion ─────────────────▶       │         Needs           │
                                    │ Cognitive: Make sense of│
  Practical life skills ──────▶     │ threatening/overwhelming│
                                    │ circumstances           │
                                    │ Security, self protection, anxiety
  Stress and anxiety ─────────▶     │ reduction, affiliation  │
  management                        │ Help: Understanding support,
                                    │ assistance              │
  Cognitive strategies ───────▶     ╰─────────────────────────╯
                                            ▲
                    Communication skills ───┘

  ┌─────────────────────────────┐
  │         Legend              │
  │ ☐ Current coping methods    │
  │ ▨ Strategies and skills     │
  └─────────────────────────────┘
```

we try to clarify the meaning by requesting that the client provide such markers or indicators. For instance, if a client says that she wants her partner to understand her better, we would like to know what observable behaviour from the partner will indicate or mark good understanding for the client. If another client wants to have a good relationship with his partner, we would again ask what a good relationship might look like and what behaviours by each party would mark this relationship. If a client wants to become more independent, we will ask for behavioural markers of independence.

Subjective Experience and Meaning

It should be emphasized that such behaviour-oriented functional analysis does not restrict the client's exploration of her or his personal needs, subjective experiences, and meanings. Nor does the practitioner impose fixed or pre-set behavioural markers onto ideas presented by the client. The client remains in charge of where he or she wants to go, and has the final say in determining what actions or behaviours will mark a particular idea. For example, independence for one client may mean getting a job. For another client, independence may mean being able to make decisions without consulting one's parents or spouse. Yet another client may see independence as being able to take care of oneself physically and being able to use public transportation without assistance. Similarly, for one client a good relationship may mean that one can spend two evenings per week on one's own without worrying about the needs of one's partner, while for another client it may mean having dinners together with the partner every evening.

Awareness of the variability of the relationship between an idea and its behavioural markers can actually improve communication and reduce misunderstanding. When behavioural markers are not specified, it is possible for two parties in a relationship – including practitioner and client – to use the same word to mean very different things. For instance, when someone comes in and says that he wants to be more assertive, we do not automatically assume that he wants to be trained in the set of assertive skills we have handy in a preplanned program. We need to understand what the client means by assertive. We may ask the client to tell us what he imagines he will be doing when he becomes more assertive. Similarly, if another client wants to be less self-defeating or self-undermining, we do not automatically assume that we know what self-defeating or self-undermining means. The client has to specify the markers.

The relationship between a word (sign) and its meanings (what is signified) is not fixed, but contingent upon personal, social, cultural, linguistic, and situational variations (Derrida, 1973, 1978). We will always let the client define or specify the concept. A behaviour-oriented functional analysis respects the subjective, agentive, and meaning-giving roles of the client, and helps to establish shared understanding. It prevents practitioners from imposing their assumed meanings on the client, and reduces the chance of talking across each other by using the same word to mean different things.

Client-Centred Orientation

Functional analysis focuses on functions, needs, and goals. It takes behaviours as purposeful and meaningful. It supports client-centred thinking and practice in that the intervention is firmly grounded in what the client needs and what the client wishes to attain. The practitioner does not decide for the client what is good and desirable, but instead supports the client in identifying and articulating her or his needs, and then subsequently assists the client in learning and developing effective strategies and skills to meet those needs in ways that the client considers desirable. Ultimately, it is always the client who takes action to achieve the desired goals.

Identifying Behavioural Markers

Problem translation in SSLD requires the problem presented by clients to be understood in terms of their behavioural patterns and interactions. When the presenting problem is stated in terms of abstract conceptualizations, the first step is to translate them into observable action or behavioural events. For example, a couple seeking counselling may state that they have a very poor relationship. An SSLD practitioner will seek to describe the relationship first and may ask questions such as: What are they doing with each other? What are they doing to each other? How do they communicate factual messages? How do they communicate emotional messages?

Similarly, clients are requested to translate key non-behavioural descriptions into observable behaviour. When a client feels lonely, we are interested in when, how often, and under what circumstances. We are also interested in what the client does when she or he feels lonely. Does the client just sit there idly, watch TV, lie on the bed, listen to music, become restless and pace up and down the room, surf the Internet, smoke, drink, or take drugs? When clients uses adjectives such as dominating, mean, spiritual, or naïve, we want to translate them into explorations leading to concrete and specific behavioural markers, such as: "You said that your mother is very dominating, in what ways is she dominating? You feel that your husband is a very mean/spiritual person, what are the things he has done to make you think so? You said you were very naïve at the time, what did you do?

Specifying and Quantifying

Sometimes clients may actually refer to behaviour, but the meaning can still be imprecise. For example, when parents say they punish or discipline their children, we want to know what exactly is being done. Are the parents talking about time-outs, spanking, gentle verbal reprimands, depriving the child of food, or hitting the child with a belt? And even when the behaviour is specified, it sometimes makes a huge difference to know the extent, duration, frequency, or quantity. Some practitioners are skeptical regarding the value of such specification and quantification, but in practice we can easily imagine a wide range of situations in which they can make a huge difference. Examples include playing with one's children, volunteering in the community, family violence, substance (ab)use, experience of hallucinations, telling lies, sexual activity, sharing housework, visiting one's aging parents, stuttering, washing hands, and so on.

Multiple Markers

Translating abstract concepts, descriptors, adjectives, or even verbs into specific behaviour markers is not always a simple, linear process. Very often the concept or the action the client is describing may be polythetic, or consisting of multiple elements. For example, good performance at work may refer to multiple behaviour markers such as productivity, which can be measured in terms of number of items produced, sales volume, or total area cleaned; absence rate, which can be measured in terms of hours, days, or shifts; frequency of rule violations or quarrels with coworkers and/or supervisors; efficiency as measured in the number of hours taken to complete a task; a specific number of difficult client situations successfully handled; and the like. We can easily think of other polythetic constructs such as a good parent-child relationship, which likely involves behaviour markers of effective communication, amount of pleasurable time shared together, attending to needs of the parent/child, and so on.

Context and Frame

Behaviours are performed within contexts. These may be situational, relational, cultural, historical, or otherwise. Within particular contexts, different people may also bring in different frames for meaning-making. These frames are conditioned by the individual's history of socialization and social learning, espoused ideology or belief systems such as religion or political philosophy, internalized values and attitudes, world view, cognitive style or preferences, social location, identifica-

Figure 4.2. Inferring Needs

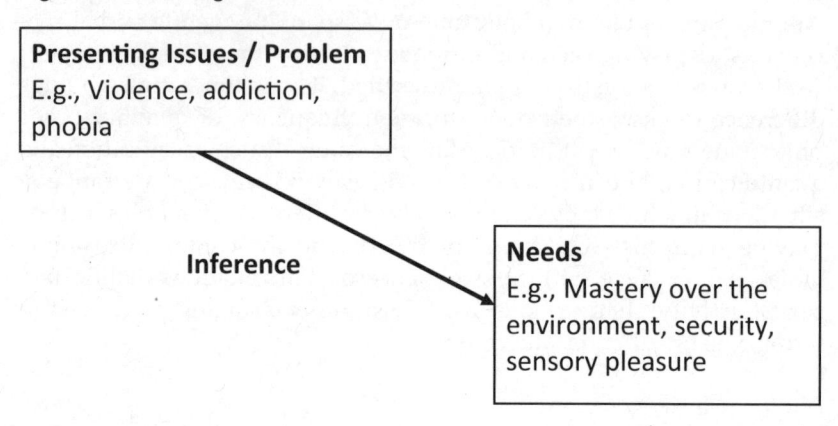

```
┌─────────────────────────────┐
│ Presenting Issues / Problem │
│ E.g., Violence, addiction,  │
│ phobia                      │
└─────────────────────────────┘
            ↘
              ↘                ┌──────────────────────────┐
    Inference  ↘               │ Needs                    │
                ↘─────────────▶│ E.g., Mastery over the   │
                               │ environment, security,   │
                               │ sensory pleasure         │
                               └──────────────────────────┘
```

tion, and so on. For example, when a male client says that he is seeing a male friend a lot, one has to know what "seeing" means (what they actually do together) and what is meant by "a lot" (frequency), as well as what the relationship means to the client (e.g., socializing, getting/giving support, intimate sexual relationship). Similarly, when a parent says her child is "out of control," the meaning is not fixed but is contingent upon several factors, including sociocultural and personal ones.

The critical role of framing can be illustrated by two cases. In the first case, a young girl describing how her mother is being "good" to her provides behavioural markers such as giving her pocket money, driving her home from school, taking her out shopping, and so on. Another girl describes similar behaviours from her mother but frames them in a negative sense. She complains that her mother discourages her from doing part-time work to earn her own pocket money, and uses her mother taking her home from school and accompanying her on shopping trips as examples of the mother's restrictive control.

Inference

Whereas we often try to translate experiences, perceptions, and descriptions into behavioural markers in SSLD, sometimes we work in the opposite direction as well – we infer meaning, needs, and intentions from the client's behaviour (Figure 4.2). For example, a person who keeps complaining that he got pushed over and ripped off by his friends, yet keeps on allowing such things to happen, may be harbouring a strong need to please others and feel accepted by them. This is an inference that can and should be tested. In SSLD practice, the practitioner's inference has to be tested against the client's perception and behaviour. When a client rejects an inference, the general principle is to avoid arguing with the client, but to consider the client's alternative explanation carefully. The client may, for instance, say that he does not have a strong need to please these friends or to gain their acceptance; it is simply his belief that one should be generous towards friends. Instead of arguing with the client, we may invite the client to examine his interpretation in juxtaposition with the complains he has made against his friends, or to explore what will be a more desirable pattern of interaction and reciprocation between him and his friends, including how his friends are responding to his own needs and expectations.

When an inference is made, the result is a conceptual construct. The practitioner may use constructs such as need for domination, ambivalence, or even psychopathological or diagnostic constructs such as passive aggression, symbiosis, borderline personality, enmeshed family relationships, and the like. In SSLD, the value of a construct is assessed with regard to how it helps the learner to make sense of, and attain mastery over, the behaviour(s) this construct refers to. If we infer that the client has a specific psychological need, a behaviour pattern or tendency, or a personality type, the value of these constructs is assessed in terms of whether they will facilitate the client's cognitive processing of information and lead to positive behavioural change. The client's agreement with the trainer's inference does not constitute a positive clinical outcome and is not sought in SSLD practice. It is only useful if the construct is recognized by the client, and when it helps to produce actions that will bring about change in the client's behaviour and her or his social or interpersonal reality.

Needs Assessment: The Psychology of Needs and the Politics of Desire

When trying to make sense of the client's behaviour, the psychological concept of need is the most frequently made inference in SSLD. As mentioned above, the concept of need, as an inference, is based on observable behaviour. Issues and problems presented by clients are analysed in terms of behaviours, and behaviours are functionally analysed with regard to needs. As explained above, client problems otherwise described as violence, addiction, or psychopathology are seen as behaviours that are ineffective in meeting the client's needs or that are socially inappropriate, which usually means that such behaviour will lead to negative social consequences for the client, thus compromising her or his chance of need gratification and goal attainment.

The concept of need is valuable in SSLD to the extent that it is helpful in understanding and changing the client's situation. For instance, Mary, a fifty-year-old woman, needs to be in control in interpersonal situations, and she is aware of this need. Her goal is to feel in control, which in her case includes the ability to negotiate and maintain a stable and mutually gratifying relationship with her boyfriend of fourteen years. SSLD intervention then focuses on helping her to learn and develop effective strategies for achieving her goal.

In another example, John, a forty-year-old man, believes that he has very spiritual needs that are not being met. He has inferred this from his sense of futility despite his material and social success, low energy level, and a generally lousy mood. In an SSLD exploration, we seek to understand the behavioural markers of spiritual fulfilment, which John describes as: (1) having more energy to start new initiatives, which includes going to work on time, less procrastination or missing deadlines, and regularly attending an early morning yoga class; (2) being more connected with others, which translates into maintaining better relationships that go beyond superficial exchanges – meaning more intimate sharing of emotional experience and putting more time and resources into those relationships both by himself and others; and (3) liberating himself from his materialistic and consumption-oriented lifestyle, which translates into selling his luxurious SUV, significantly reducing his spending on clothing and fine dining, financial contributions to an international development agency, and signing up for four weeks of volunteer work in South America.

Needs Assessment

In the assessment of needs, it is tempting for the practitioner to resort to a simple, universal theory of needs. One of the most widely known models is Maslow's (1943) hierarchy of needs. Argyle (1983) also listed major motivational drives for human social behaviour. Maslow (1943) himself did warn against the simple listing of human drives; he recognized that the same human motivation or goal can be pursued through different behavioural strategies, and that social, cultural, and situational factors all play a role together with motivation in determining human behaviour. He nonetheless proposed a model with a hierarchical structure which he believed to be relevant to all human beings.

The contingency thinking used in SSLD privileges attention to individual differences, although certain needs are shared by the vast majority of human beings. In SSLD, needs are inferred from client narratives and behaviours. Practitioners and clients can in theory make whatever inference makes sense to them; and whenever there is a shared understanding between client and practitioner, the need inferred will likely have practical value. Following this thinking, it is not necessary to have a list of needs, for different constructs or labels can be used for the same set of behaviours. Using spiritual needs as an example once again, what one calls "spiritual needs" may be labelled differently by another person, who might say that she just needs to have a direction or purpose in life, while another person may say that he has a need to organize his current life into a coherent intellectual framework.

In the same vein, we can also imagine that people using the same need label may refer to very different goals. A client claiming to have a strong need for achievement may be thinking of leaving the small town he is living in to go to a bigger city and work as a mechanic. Another client using the same need label may be thinking of becoming the CEO of her company. Yet another client may be trying to get married and become a parent. Someone else could be thinking of writing a novel for publication.

I have, therefore, suggested to practitioners that they freely explore these issues with their clients to discover their clients' needs and how they can be described or labelled. During training programs, however, many colleagues have said that even though they realize that this is an open-ended process – and while they appreciate the individual variation among clients with regard to the way needs are conceptualized and connected to actual behaviours, personal goals, and life events – they will still find a list of needs to be helpful as a reference. Some colleagues have suggested that a list may help to alert them to possibilities that they might otherwise overlook. I am therefore providing a tentative list here. This list is based on Argyle's (1983) list and my own experience in practice and training.

It should first be pointed out that since needs are inferred, and they are inferred in different ways by different people, there are obvious overlaps among the need categories. Moreover, a number of different needs can be addressed simultaneously by a specific behaviour. A good example is sex. Some people see sex as a discrete and independent need, while other people partialize or compartmentalize it into a need for sensory stimulation and/or physical pleasure, a need for affiliation and/or connection, a need for self-expression or identity, and so on. Eating can be another example. In affluent societies, desire for food is often related to more than just hunger or physical need. Sharing food can take on tremendous social and interpersonal meaning. A family dinner, a dinner on a date, a quick bite between meetings, fine dining with business associates, dining at a fundraiser, and so on – all of these carry different meanings, and in some of these eating situations, food may actually be of marginal significance. In disadvantaged communities, in contrast, food may be connected with survival, power and social status, or a significant basis for social bonding.

For the practitioner, common needs can be seen across different clients, even though they may use different labels. It is, however, important to remember that the common needs we see constitute our reality, but not necessarily the reality of our clients, who may still see their own needs as special or even unique. Clients' experience of their own needs is contingent upon a host of factors, including personal history, individual sense-making and/or meaning-giving, identity, social location, social and cultural context, specific situations and circumstances, and so on. Instead of assuming a universal list of needs that applies to all clients, or organizing these needs in terms of a hierarchical structure with the assumption that certain needs are universally more basic than others. In SSLD we talk about needs profiles, which can be different for each client or client system (e.g., group, family, organization, community). A needs profile (Figure 4.3) documents the needs that are most relevant for a particular client and looks at how these needs relate to one another. It is the result of needs assessment and it forms the basis for the formulation of goals and the development of corresponding strategies and skills.

A Tentative List of Needs for Reference

This section will list a number of needs commonly found among clients. As clarified above, these needs are not conceptualized as objective realities applicable to all human beings. Instead, the list is intended to help practitioners make sense of the client's specific circumstances and to document the client's needs profile. The list is not intended to be comprehensive or exhaustive. The items are not discrete, but can overlap with each other and relate to each other functionally. They are not listed

Figure 4.3. Client Needs Profile

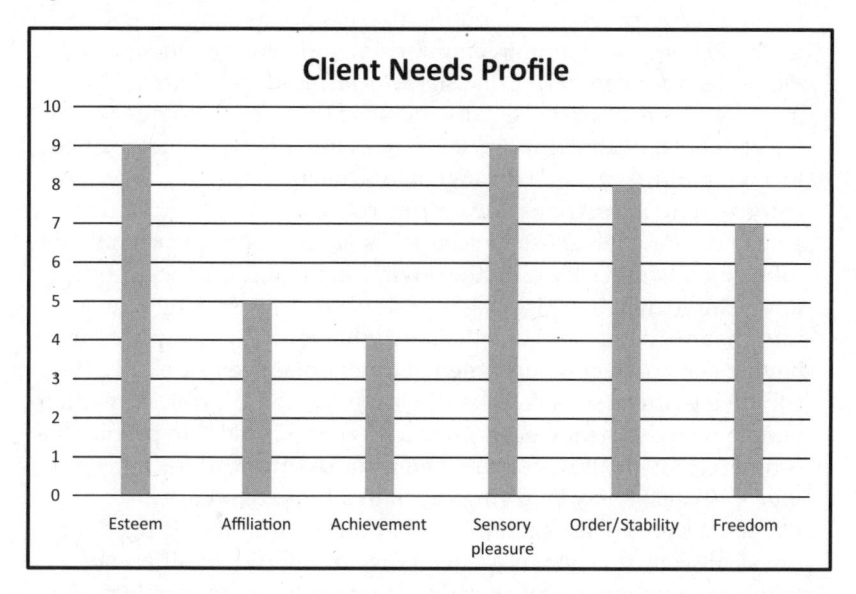

Client Needs Profile

Esteem	9
Affiliation	5
Achievement	4
Sensory pleasure	9
Order/Stability	8
Freedom	7

in order of priority or hierarchical significance, although the biological needs are listed before the psychological and the social. Some individuals can forgo items on the top of this list in pursuit of those listed below. Other people can do without certain items for a long period. It should also be added that needs can interact and transform each other, that they are dynamic and fluid, and that they do change over time. In SSLD practice, clients' needs and/or their perception of their own needs can often change in the course of the intervention.

1. *Biological needs for survival and subsistence.* This refers to material and energy needed for biological survival, including nutrients, oxygen, water, sensory stimulation (e.g., light, sound, tactile), rest, and sleep. Most people understand the need for air, water, and food, but sensory stimulation is also needed by our bodies for them to maintain normal functioning. It is important to recognize that for human beings, such biological needs are usually gratified within a social and interpersonal context – arguably with the exception of breathing, though it can be argued that air quality is a function of socio-economic development. Rest and sleep are also important

biological needs critical to the normal functioning of our bodies. Physical activity can be added to this category as something that the body needs to maintain equilibrium and healthy functioning.
2. *Physical safety, sense of security, stability, predictability, control.* The need for physical safety usually includes the need for shelter from the elements. In contemporary urban living, physical safety is tied to a wide range of social arrangements, including food safety, law enforcement, industrial safety, traffic rules, building regulations, and so on. People's sense of security is often related to psychological factors. Familiarity with the environment and the social context, for example, will increase one's sense of security. Having relevant information, being able to anticipate what is about to happen, and having control over environmental or external events can all contribute towards a sense of security, mastery, and control. Very often people who think they need information or who seek to predict the future (e.g., consulting fortune tellers, tarot card readers, or *fengshui* specialists) may be trying to attain a sense of security.
3. *Physical comfort.* This is related to, but different from, the need for physical security. There is a huge range of individual difference with regard to what is physically comfortable. Some people prefer ergonomically designed furniture; some people require air conditioning; some people crave tactile comfort; and some people emphasize a well-designed and coordinated environment.
4. *Pleasure: sensation, desire (including sexual desire), ecstasy.* Aesthetic and musical pursuits can be seen as related to this need, as can the "high" sought by people who use psychedelic substances. In East Asia, people are said to be after a specific "feel." This set of needs may also include people in search of new experiences, adventure, and excitement. The need for pleasurable experience is, on the one hand, highly regulated, such as in sexual or drug-induced pleasure. On the other hand, certain types of pleasurable experience are socially facilitated and turned into major industries, such as music, entertainment, and tourism.
5. *Self: identity, esteem, autonomy, agency, action, expression, efficacy.* To develop, maintain, or protect a sense of self is an extremely strong human need. Some people will pay a high price, or even risk their life, for this requirement. In classical psychoanalytic theory, Freud (1936, 1966) observed that the ego will try to defend itself from potential threats and/or damages. The concept of the ego defence mechanism has since become part of everyday language in the

West. This highlights the need to maintain a sense of self whose coherence and integrity are usually seen as essential to personal and social life. It should be emphasized that the development and maintenance of a healthy sense of self usually take place within an interpersonal context. The need for identity and esteem is often contingent upon the need for affiliation and acceptance by others. This also includes the need to be known, understood, and recognized by others as the person who one is.

6. *Achievement: mastery, control, fulfilment.* The self usually seeks to express itself, realize its potentials, or simply perform what it does well. This can stem from an intrinsic drive to achieve, or it can be the result of doing something for its own sake, as with someone who has an aptitude for dancing and enjoys doing it well. The drive for achievement can be instrumental as well, as in the case of someone using one's talents to achieve material reward. It should be emphasized that the intrinsic and the extrinsic are not necessarily mutually exclusive; they can often coexist and even complement each other. In order to achieve, whether with an intrinsic or extrinsic aim, people need to gain mastery over their bodies, like in the case of dancing or yoga, or over some external object, as in the case of cycling or playing a musical instrument. Sometimes it also requires gaining control over environmental events and even other people's reactions, like in the case of running a political campaign. In pursuing what might seem like the same goal, some people put more emphasis on the attainment of external markers of success, whereas others may focus on a more subjective sense of fulfilment.

7. *Actualization, transcendence, spiritual quest.* Some people see self-actualization as an extension of self-expression. It can be further extended to include the need to transcend – going beyond the common-sense world, or what is mundane or mediocre. Some people place this kind of quest within the domain of the spiritual. This can include the realization of political, social, artistic, or religious ideals.

8. *Connection: affiliation, intimacy, belonging, community, identity.* The need to feel connected can be manifested in a very physical manner, such as an infant's clinging and need for tactile contact with a parent or caregiver (Koester, Brooks, & Traci, 2000). It is also expressed as a need for some kind of psychological or emotional connection or bond with other human beings. There is a large psychological literature on attachment (e.g., Ainsworth, 1982; Ainsworth, Blehar,

Waters, & Wall, 1978; Ainsworth & Bowlby, 1965; Bowlby, 1958, 1969, 1988, 1999; Cassidy & Shaver, 1999). People negotiate relationships with others that have different levels of intimacy, ranging from a good rapport in one-time encounters to long-term committed relationships. This also includes erotic and sexual relationships.

Another important aspect of human connection is that we build relationships with groups and communities, not only with individuals. To some people, membership in a certain group (e.g., a prestigious social group, profession, or a noble class) or connection to a community (ethnic, religious, political, or cultural) is essential to their sense of identity and experience of well-being. The need to belong or to be accepted can sometimes override other needs, including the need to survive. This set of needs include constructs such as loyalty, commitment, comradeship, or martyrdom. This particular connection can also be extended to explain altruistic behaviour, civic participation, volunteerism, and the like.

9. *Cognitive need for meaning and order*. The need to make sense of and ascribe meaning to one's experience is arguably the most powerful human drive for cultural and intellectual development. On a personal level, most people need to maintain a cognitive structure that allows them to experience their life in the world as meaningful, orderly, and coherent. Some people have an almost compulsive need for this experience and can become cognitively very rigid. In practice, clients having a need for cognitive order may ask questions like: Why was I the person to be paralysed after this car accident? Why did my lover leave me? How can my parents do this to me? Taking these questions as denial is not the best way to work with the client. In a sense, we need to recognize cognitive needs as legitimate. This can also include the need for information, which has been recognized as a civil right in liberal-democratic societies. The need for information, as mentioned in point 2 above, can play an important role in an individual's sense of security; information or knowledge can be empowering in that it increases an individual's probability of acquiring control over the situation to be dealt with.

10. *Emotional needs*. Emotional needs can come in many forms. Very often, practitioners think of emotional needs in terms of the need for emotional caring or support from others, which is closely

related to the need for connection. Another way to think of emotional needs is in terms of equilibrium and homeostasis – emotional processes play themselves out in phases and interact with each other, with the individual always tending towards a state of balance. In this view, an aroused emotion – be it fear, joy, or anger – will seek to express or discharge itself, after which the individual will return to a state of quiescence. In emotion-focused therapy (Greenberg & Paivio, 1997), individuals need to identify and get in touch with their own emotions, and to own them. The expression and ventilation of emotions, which are often socially regulated, discouraged, or prohibited, are encouraged and facilitated. The power of emotional work in psychotherapy highlights how much emotional expression has been controlled or inhibited in everyday life, and how emotional needs are often not met.

11. *Token*: Tokens are not what we actually need, but things that we have to attain and then exchange for what we need. The most obvious example is money. In a sense, money is not what we really need, but an instrument for accessing other things that we do. In reality, however, many people have experienced goal displacement and come to pursue money even when they have no idea what they wish to exchange it for. As a token, money has been hyper-associated with socially valued meanings such as achievement, power, status, and so on. A concept related to the need for tokens is that of the transitional object, and there is much literature on the topic (e.g., Greenacre, 1969; Applegate, 1989; Leiman, 1992; Winnicott, 1971). Simply put, a transitional object is an object that acquires meaning and value within the context of an interpersonal relationship. The acquisition of the transitional object will bring symbolic gratification related to one's connection with a significant other. Helping a client to recognize that a certain object is only transitional will facilitate more direct and effective client action towards improving the interpersonal relationship itself.

A similar analysis can be applied to power. Whereas many people do talk about a need for power or a drive for power, power is in fact something we need in order to do or get something else. Like money, power can also take over as an aim in itself, and a lot of people believe they need to have more power. It is sometimes helpful to clarify with the client why the power is necessary and how it will improve the client's life and well-being.

78 Basic SSLD Procedure

The Politics of Desire: Needs and Social Regulation

Needs, as we can now see, are rarely purely biological. The way needs are experienced, articulated, and met are almost always conditioned by social forces; and most needs-driven human behaviour takes place within a social and interpersonal context. The very idea of needs is a result of social construction, and as such it is shaped by ideology and social discourses. There is a regulatory system that names, legitimizes, and prioritizes human needs. As mentioned above, certain needs, such as sex, are more heavily regulated, whereas others, such as the need for more attractive looks or fashionable clothing, are socially facilitated and encouraged (although the latter can also be sexually motivated). Intimately tied to the social regulatory system is a political economy, which pervades into what we consider the most private domains of life, such as intimate romantic relationships (Illouz, 1997). Human needs and desires are simultaneously aroused and disciplined; these complex and sometimes contradictory measures are often combined with market forces. The prevailing social discourses of body shape, food, and health, for example, are articulated in a complex network of messages involving books, audio-visual materials, workshops, courses, clinics, hospitals, media, advertising campaigns, marketing strategies, and an overwhelming array of products. Parallel to the market economy is a similar process in public policy and social programs, which deploy public resources according to dominant values, or the values of those in power. In America, for example, public funding for certain programs, such as abortion services for women, is contingent upon the political and religious values espoused by the administration. An inquiry into the mechanism of social regulation of human needs and desires and the associated political economy is beyond the scope of this book, but a number of related issues are fundamental to the practice of SSLD.

The most critical question, in my opinion, is the role of the SSLD practitioner as a social agent. SSLD practitioners are supposed to help clients to develop strategies and skills that are effective within their social contexts. This can easily be read as getting clients to behave in ways that are socially appropriate and therefore conform to prevailing social conventions and values. Following this line of reasoning, SSLD practitioners can be seen as agents of social control, trying to substitute behaviours that are deviant with more conformist ones. It should be emphasized that SSLD practice is not confined to changing the individual. Based on the idea of mutual conditioning and transformation, SSLD practice recognizes the individual's autonomy and the inevitability of the individual's action having an impact on society. Through learning, education, and personal development, individuals can become empowered and therefore more capable of bringing about changes in the social environment that they desire (IIisley, 1992; Merriam & Brockett, 1997). SSLD can also be applied to client systems such as social groups, organizations, and communities to support the development of collective action. Individual and/or collective empowerment, therefore, is an important objective in SSLD practice. Positive social change is brought about by human action. By recognizing and respecting the clients' needs and desires, the learning and development of strategies and skills target both individual and social change.

Whereas SSLD may have empowering and emancipatory potential, it is important to recognize that it is inevitable that clients and practitioners will have internalized elements of the dominant social discourses. The power of social forces in constructing, legitimizing, and naturalizing specific discourses and practices (Berger & Luckmann, 1966) cannot be underestimated. Various social practices that we now find objectionable, such as slavery, feudalism, racism, and the like, were widely supported and taken for granted across various historical and social contexts. It took a lot of people a lot of courage, effort, and time to change them. Once society has constructed something as natural, most people will just accept it as an everyday reality and not question it. Gender roles, for instance, are experienced as natural by a lot of people and are therefore not questioned. Another example is the socially scripted life-course of going to school, entering the labour force, getting married, and raising a family. Even when some people are aware of the problems of a naturalized social practice, it does not follow that they will choose to deviate from it or change it. For example, many people are aware of the commercialization of romance and weddings, and yet they still desire and pay for a lavish wedding (Geller, 2001; Otnes & Pleck, 2002).

Unconscious Needs

This leads to a question often asked by practitioners learning to do SSLD – the question of unconscious needs. Some practitioners have come across situations in which the client does not recognize their own needs. It is important to remember that with SSLD, clients do not have to gain insight into their unconscious to achieve positive change. The ultimate outcome measure is that clients develop effective behavioural strategies for meeting their needs and attaining personal goals. SSLD practice, however, does not exclude cognitive interventions that will help clients develop an overall understanding of their situation, including their needs. Whereas practitioners do not have to impose their own inferences or interpretations on clients, or to get clients to agree with them, they can present to the client the pattern of behaviour they have noticed based on the client's presentation and report. For instance, a practitioner can re-present to the client the incidents of her or his attempts to please others at the expense of her or his own needs or convenience. If the client has an alternative interpretation, which is not unusual, the general principle is not to argue with the learner but to work on specific behavioural goals, such as becoming more assertive, and developing strategies and skills that will address the client's own needs while causing the least negative impact to her or his relationship with the other person.

The following case can serve as an example of unconscious needs: a young woman who had a developmentally challenged younger sister resented the fact that she was always the person in the family left to take care of this younger sister, and it appeared that everyone in the family – sometimes including the young woman herself – would put the younger sister's needs before hers. She had been in therapy before and the therapist had suggested to her that she was unsure of her parents' love and was trying desperately to win and maintain it. The young woman was not sure about that interpretation. In her SSLD program, when the pattern was presented to her, she related her previous therapy experience and added that it did not change her behaviour or situation at home. She was then asked to describe her desired pattern of sharing responsibilities around her younger sister as well as what could be done to bring this about. She then learned to raise this issue openly with her family and negotiated an arrangement that she found satisfactory.

Socialization and Internalization

The sociological inquiry into socialization and the psychological theories of internalization both try to understand how individuals exposed to ideas and values in their social contexts come to take these ideas and values as their own. Social cognitive theory (Bandura, 1986, 1989, 1991) recognizes the role played by social institutions including educational, political, and legal systems, as well as religion, media, and cultural products. The role of socializing agents who are significant others in a child's life is given special emphasis, for Bandura believes that direct exposure to a model's behaviour is more important than verbal instruction. In the process of growing up and being socialized, children form cognitive representations of the behaviours of people they are exposed to, including appreciation of their underlying rules and principles. Such cognitive representations play an important role in children's modelling and reproduction of behaviours they have observed. Children exposed to the same models and behaviours, however, selectively internalize different elements, and what is internalized is contingent upon a number of factors. These factors include the extent to which the model is similar to the child, how nurturing the model is to the child, the functional relevance and value of the model's behaviour, the effectiveness or success of the model's behaviour, and the child's locus of control, or the extent to which one perceives oneself as having control over one's behaviour and/or the external environment. The internalized content will constitute a self-regulatory system, which will then become operative in monitoring future behaviour and learning.

The idea of the unconscious is related to that of internalization. In a way, the unconscious is a result of internalized social values and standards. The internalized self-regulatory system prevents the experience, processing, and expression of needs and wishes that are prohibited, or perceived to be prohibited, by society. As such, the unconscious is not only a product of psychology, but also a product of socio-political processes. The dominant social discourses and the disciplinary practices of society render many human thoughts and actions unacceptable, unspeakable, or unthinkable. What is not conscious is not known, not articulated, and not examined. In psychotherapy, counselling, education, and human service work, practitioners often assist clients to negotiate an expanded space in which to examine their needs and wishes, thoughts and ideas, feelings, and actions, leading to reformulation and reconstruction of thoughts and ideas as well as the generation of new actions. In the process, many of the experiences, emotions, and ideas that were originally inaccessible to clients will be discovered, articulated, expressed, and realized or performed. What has been unthinkable is now thinkable, and what has been unspeakable is now speakable. In SSLD, although the focus is not on exploring the unconscious, what can happen through the examination of patterns of behaviour, the exploration of needs, and the articulation of wishes, desires, and goals, is that clients become more aware of their own needs and what they desire in life. The intervention usually increases their autonomy and self-efficacy, and it fosters positive expectancy with regard to the realization of personal and/or collective goals. Instead of being restricted by what one is not conscious of, the intervention expands the client's awareness and self-understanding as well as fostering a better appreciation of the relationship between social reality and her or his own thoughts and actions. This will then be supported by an increased capacity for goal attainment, fulfilment, and self-actualization.

SSLD practice therefore encourages a critical awareness of prevailing ideologies and social discourses, and aims at opening up maximum space for clients to articulate their needs, desires, and goals in life. Our role is to help clients achieve what they desire, and not to impose our own ideological preferences or commitments on them. For example, if a couple desires to have a lavish wedding and their goal is to get jobs with better pay, we may help them to explore the psychological needs that they are aiming to meet with the lavish wedding, but we will not turn the intervention into a social analysis class on consumerism and the institution of marriage. Similarly, if clients have internalized religious or cultural values that are different than our own, it is important for us to respect that. For instance, a newly immigrated taxi driver believes that his eldest child should give up going to university and help support his ever-growing family – his wife is pregnant with their sixth child. He is valuing a big family over educational attainment for his children, and contraception is not an option given the religious values shared by him and his wife. In this case, we do not seek to change his religious commitments but will instead explore what he, his wife, and his family believe to be important needs and what they imagine as a more desirable state for the family and its members.

This, however, does not mean that we simply go along with our clients' values and ideas even when they can be damaging to the clients and/or their significant others. By focusing on their needs and desires, and remaining open and flexible with our own thoughts and ideas, we can often arrive at workable solutions. A student of mine working in the child protection service once came across a young girl whose parents were arranging for her to be sent back to Africa to be circumcised, as the procedure was illegal in Canada. My student approached this case by first recognizing the parents' wish for a happy life for the daughter – establishing a shared understanding of their goal as the first step of engagement. She then got the parents to imagine their daughter's life in Canada and what role female circumcision might play in her life as she grows up in this country. She then realized that the parents believed that if their daughter were not circumcised, no one in their community would marry her. My student, after listening to their negative experience of the immigration and settlement process, was able to re-present the parents' observations of how young people from their country had changed after coming to Canada. She then invited the couple to imagine how many of the young people in their culture would grow up not following their parents' teachings and instructions. The couple claimed that the majority of the young people were becoming Westernized, less traditional, and less obedient. She then asked them to imagine what would happen twenty years from now. The conversation then led to estimating the percentage of young men from their culture who would insist on marrying a circumcised bride twenty years later in Canada. The father estimated it to be less than half. At that point, the student found common ground with this couple.

Needs Assessment: Profile and Priority

Needs assessment during the problem translation phase of SSLD practice usually results in a needs profile of the client or client system. In the example of the new immigrant couple given above, the client system needs to feel that they are in control of their lives, including the future well-being of their daughter. They need a sense of connection with their own ethno-cultural community, which is related to a need for identity, especially when one is in a new country where social practices, values, and standards are very different. Reading their behaviour (making arrangements to send their daughter to Africa for circumcision) as physical abuse that violates child protection legislation and not appreciating its purpose is not likely to be very helpful. Functional analysis ensures that we try to explore the clients' motivations, needs, wishes, desires, or aspirations, and not just make an assessment based on *prima facie* evidence. Engaging with clients by sharing in their own understanding of their needs constitutes a solid starting point for effective intervention.

Needs assessment is a dynamic process that takes multiple contingencies into account. In most cases, clients have a diverse range of needs, which can be overwhelming. Ineffective attempts at meeting them can be frustrating and disempowering, leading to compromised self-efficacy. The needs themselves can sometimes be perceived or experienced as confusing, conflicting, or simply impossible to meet. In the problem translation process, the identification of needs is not done in a mechanical manner, but is always performed with reference to the client's response, capacity, and unique circumstances. A number of principles can guide the needs assessment task. The first consideration is significance – the need has to be experienced as significant and personally relevant by the client. For example, a teenager from a South Asian immigrant family is experiencing tremendous pressure from his parents to excel academically. He is also trying very hard to gain acceptance by his peers in junior high, where academically strong students are often thought of as geeks and run the risk of being ridiculed or isolated. It is not that the teenager does not see the value of academic achievement. It is only that he does not feel a pressing need for it now, and he does not need cognitive persuasion to the contrary. Intervention is more likely to be effective through first joining with the client in addressing his need for affiliation and acceptance by his peers, which is also functionally related to his sense of identity and esteem.

Related to significance is the consideration of urgency. It is not unusual that we come across crises or situations requiring urgent responses. Professional colleagues working with family violence or child protection, for instance, know too well that although the "root problem" of the situation may be related to the unmet psychological needs of the perpetrator, it is often necessary to first attend to the victim's urgent need for safety and/or subsistence. Another example is a fifteen-year-old girl who comes to a school social worker reporting an unwanted pregnancy for the third time in two years. The social worker knows that this is a behavioural pattern suggesting a host of underlying needs that are unmet, but has to deal with the current pregnancy situation nonetheless. Experienced colleagues will sometimes be able to help the client to review her behavioural and relationship patterns while assisting her in managing the crisis, but a focus on resolving the pressing issues has to be maintained.

Sometimes practitioners are confronted with clients with multiple problems and a long history of ineffective coping, usually associated with experience of oppression and marginalization. Aboriginal peoples in North America, for example, are overrepresented in a host of difficulties and problems, including poverty, homelessness, substance use, trouble with the law, family violence, mental health problems, and various traumatic experiences (Correctional Services Canada, 2008; Health Canada, 2002; Human Resources Development Canada, 2003; Ontario Aboriginal Health Advocacy Initiative, 2003). A needs assessment with a homeless Aboriginal man in a major urban centre may generate a needs profile with a long list of needs. The list can be overwhelming, and it is often not practical to address all of these needs at once. An incremental approach is most likely to be effective. Apart from considering the personal significance that the client assigns to these needs as well as their relative urgency, a third factor to be considered is their manageability. Needs that are entangled in a long and complex history of trauma or dysfunctional experience, though significant, may not be effectively addressed in the short run. Given the usually disempowering experiences the client may have had, including negative experiences with helping professionals, service providers, and programs, it is probably advisable to work on a manageable task first. The need for a successful and empowering first experience with the practitioner is often critical for engagement as well as fostering positive expectancy and self-efficacy, which will become extremely valuable over the long run.

Needs Profile

In documenting a client's needs profile, the first step is to list all the needs identified (see Worksheet 4.1). Each item entered has to be clearly indicated by specific behaviour markers. It is also important that each item is recognized by the client. In case agreement has not been achieved, separate entries can be made specifying which is the client's inference or label and which is the practitioner's. After a list has been prepared, each item can be assessed with regard to its significance and/or relevance as perceived by the client, its urgency, and its manageability. This assessment will enable the client and the practitioner to jointly determine which need or needs should be worked on first.

Articulation of Goals

Once the needs to be addressed have been prioritized, they can be further translated into goals. The translation of needs into goals allows the client to imagine possible gratification, and as such it is an empowering process that helps to foster positive expectancy. The practitioner, however, has to be careful in facilitating realistic formulation of goals. Goals that appear unrealistic to the client may lead to skepticism or cynicism and can be alienating. Clients who have repeatedly experienced failure and frustration need to feel connected to goals that are attainable. In case the client has a much more pessimistic assessment regarding the

Worksheet 4.1. Needs Profile

Name of Client: Date:
Presenting Issues:
List of Needs:

Need	Behaviour Markers	Priority*

* Priority assessed with regard to (1) perceived significance by the client; (2) urgency; and (3) manageability.
   1. The need(s) to be first addressed:
   2. Specific goals (with outcome markers):

Goal	Outcome Markers

feasibility of a goal, the general principle is, again, not to argue with the client. It is usually more helpful to resort to incrementalism – getting the client to see how an incremental step towards a larger goal can realistically be achieved. For example, a bi-ethnic lesbian with severe mental illness who has been out of work and living a relatively isolated life for over a decade may have difficulty imagining how she can be gainfully employed, develop a fulfilling intimate relationship, and reconnect with her family and community, even though she is clear that these are exactly what she needs and desires. She can be invited to think in terms of what needs have to be accomplished first for one of these goals to be achieved. In this case, the client identifies that not worrying about the return of major psychotic symptoms and being able to keep a healthy daily routine will be a helpful first step.

The principle of incrementalism is also relevant in the reverse situa-

> **Box 4.1. Problem Translation Procedure**
>
> 1. Listening to the presenting issues and/or problems; engaging with the client.
> 2. Behaviour-oriented functional analysis (BOFA):
>   - Translate issues/problems into behavioural markers;
>   - Client behaviours are analysed functionally – with reference to their purpose or the needs they are supposed to address.
> 3. Needs assessment: map out the client's needs profile.
> 4. Articulation of goals.

tion of the client having an overly optimistic, ambitious, or unrealistic goal. When asked about her goals, a teenage girl who had left home and was involved in sex work stated that she would only give up sex work if she could make a bigger income doing something else. When asked about what kind of work would give her that income, she expressed the wish to own and operate a video-equipment store, which she thought would bring her the income she wanted while also being something that she would really enjoy doing. The girl had very limited education and did not speak English well, which was the language she would need in the area where she wanted to run the store. She also did not have the start-up capital for the store. When the "what is the first step" question was explored, she said that she could start by improving her English.

Getting the client to work on a small, manageable first step can sometimes break a longstanding vicious cycle of setting self-defeating goals, having frustrating experiences, and encountering negativity. An incremental strategy allows the practitioner and client to build on small, successful experiences to gradually establish positive expectancy, nourish self-efficacy, and develop the client's trust in both the practitioner and the intervention program.

Behaviour-Focused Interviewing: Problem Translation in Action

The problem translation procedure described above (summarized in Box 4.1) has to take place within the context of an interview. The first interview or two in SSLD practice shares very similar objectives with other models of practice. The major tasks are: (1) engagement with the client towards building a working alliance; (2) gaining a good understanding of the client's problems or issues and their underlying needs; (3) assessment and clinical formulation according to the intervention model. The behaviour focus of SSLD, however, means that the interviewing is also done in a slightly different way. This section will highlight the key features of behaviour-focused interviewing.

As the name suggests, this kind of interviewing is focused on behaviour. This behavioural focus is supposed to help the client, and therefore should not be allowed to turn into an obstacle for clients in their presentation of issues, articulation of their experiences, and description of their circumstances. In inviting the client to become behaviour-focused, we are not trying to substitute the client's language with behavioural language, but rather to let behavioural language facilitate clarity in articulation and expression. The client's initial presentation of problems and issues typically includes both behavioural and non-behavioural elements. For example, when asked about her situation in the first session of counselling, a woman with a diagnosis of anorexia described herself as "a complicated person" who is "sneaky and devious" – these are non-behavioural descriptions. Her narrative also contained behavioural descriptions, such as how much and what she ate every day as well as what medication she was taking.

A behaviour-focused interviewer may be interested in translating "a complicated person" and "sneaky and devious" into behaviour markers. This can be done by asking the client questions such as: you said you're a complicated person, how does this show in what you do, what you think, or the way you experience things? Alternatively, we can ask: what are the things you do that make you think you are sneaky and devious? This is usually not difficult to do, but it should be emphasized that we should not translate every non-behavioural component of the client's narrative into behaviour markers; we should focus only on those parts that are seen as related to the key issues that the client may want to work on. When we are about to zoom in and get a behavioural focus, we need to first determine if defining "a complicated person," or developing behaviour markers for "sneaky and devious," should be a focus of attention with this client. In this particular case, the client was not too concerned with herself being complicated; the sneaky and devious part was most relevant in terms of her attempts to hide her anorexia and binge eating from her family. As a general principle, when we want to focus on a non-behavioural description or construct, we have to know why we are focusing on that piece and how it is possibly related to the overall picture of the client's needs and goals.

In the first session, we usually want to provide the client with maximum narrative space to tell her or his story. It is usually not helpful to fire off too many specific questions during the first session, for that might interrupt the client's narrative flow and set a question-and-answer pattern that puts the client in a relatively passive position. It also reinforces a power difference between the client and the practitioner. Narrative space can be opened up for the client by asking generic, broadly focused types of questions such as: What brings you here today? What are the things you want to talk about? Do you want to tell me about your situation? Active listening and empathic responses are helpful in the beginning phase. The behaviour-focused explorations can come later in the session when we have developed a tentative idea of what the client's key issues may be.

In behaviour-focused explorations, the SSLD model privileges the client's needs, wishes, or desires. When we are listening to the client's narrative, we will try to find anchors to these constructs. For example, when a client complains, "It's so frustrating talking to my husband, he never gets the point," we may explore what she expects from her husband or what will make her feel better. We can re-present this to the client by saying something like, "You want to be understood by your husband, don't you?" Or, "What you would like to see happening is your husband understanding what you're trying to say to him." In another example, a man states that life is pointless and futile. We may explore his possible needs by testing a hypothesis: "Would you feel better if you had a clearer sense of purpose and meaning in life?" As a third example, a teenager says, "As soon as I walked into the party, I knew it was a f------ mistake, a total waste of my f------ time." We can respond by saying something like, "So, the party turned out to be not what you expected, you were expecting something different." That would allow us to explore the client's needs, wishes, or desires.

Understanding the client's needs is central to the formulation of an overall picture of the client's situation. Based on this overall picture, we may then strategically focus on key needs and goals, and the current strategies that the client is using to address them. The common structure for most behaviour-focused questions is to first connect to something the client has said or presented, like: You said you're sneaky and devious, you said your partner is mean, you said your mother is manipulative, or you said you have been a loser all your life. Then we add the specific questions, like: What are the things you/she/he do(es) that make you think so? What do you do when you're angry? The following vignette with a client with clinical depression can illustrate how we can get on to behaviour markers.

PRACTITIONER: You said you feel depressed all the time, so what do you do when you feel depressed?
CLIENT: Nothing. I just do nothing.
PRACTITIONER: So when you're depressed and doing nothing, where are you?
CLIENT: Home, I just stay in my room.
PRACTITIONER: Where in your room would you be? Bed, sitting on a chair somewhere?
CLIENT: *I spend quite a bit of time lying on my bed, not sleeping, though, and I sometimes sit on my bed as well, not doing anything, I don't really have a lot of space in my room, it's kind of small.* [Note: there may be a wish for more space]
PRACTITIONER: How much time would you say you spent lying in bed yesterday, not counting the time you were sleeping at night?

When we are establishing behaviour markers, it is important to bear in mind that we have to be collaborating with the client. It will be disengaging if we let the client feel that we are just doing our task by trying to translate concepts into behaviour markers. It is always good practice to keep checking in with the client. One of the process markers of good engagement is an increase in the content and depth of the client's self-disclosure. Clients who are engaged will provide more information, elaborate on points, and sometimes volunteer "free information" – things that we did not ask for. For example:

PRACTITIONER: You said you do not feel comfortable going out of your own room when your family is there.
CLIENT: Yes, they want to watch shows that I do not like, and I don't feel like asking them to change channels or whatever, but I end up listening to their programs even when I stay in my room, so I sometimes play music with my headset on, even when I'm not really listening, and that's the time when I feel most miserable, thinking about the past, and the friends and activities that I used to enjoy.

We have to watch out for repeated one-word answers and passive yes-no answers. When this happens, we may want to leave the behav-

> **Box 4.2. Behaviour-Focused Interviewing**
>
> 1. Listening and emotional engagement.
> 2. Allowing narrative space and getting a general picture first, but subsequently focusing on specifics.
> 3. Listening for needs, wishes, and desires.
> 4. Shifting to behavioural mode when a shared understanding of needs and goals has been attained.
> 5. Collaborating with the client in developing behaviour markers.
> 6. Ensuring that the translation process enhances shared understanding.
> 7. Attending to the significance and effectiveness of the client's behaviour.

iour focus for a while and reopen the narrative space for the client to talk more about things that are of interest to him or her.

It is usually helpful for us to provide a summary, connecting behaviour-focused translations to the client's presenting issues. For example, we might say:

> Earlier in the session you said you have been a loser all your life. You said that you are now thirty-five and you feel you have not accomplished a thing. You are not happy with the fact that you did not finish college, and you believe you have a problem holding on to a job, although you have actually worked in this one for over a year and a half. It appears that you really want to see yourself getting some kind of further training and education so that you can move ahead in your career. You also feel that you might be able to do better if you were able to deal with authority figures who are critical of you.

The key point that we need to remember in the interview is that the behaviour-focused translation is geared towards a shared understanding between the client and the practitioner. The process should help clients to see the connection between their needs and wishes and the actions they are taking to address them. While we are focusing on behaviour markers in order to gain clarity and specificity, we must remain mindful of the significance of the client's behaviours, what they mean to the client, and their current and/or potential effectiveness with regard to the goals that the client desires. A summary of the behaviour-focused interviewing procedures is given in Box 4.2.

Charting Target Behaviour Using the Behavioural Diary

The behavioural diary is a very helpful aid for supplementing behaviour-focused interviewing and assessment. It can be easily understood and filled out by most clients. First, we specify the behaviour or the type of behaviour to be assessed. For instance, a divorced woman can chart all of her actions and activities intended to help her meet men. This will give the client a clear visual representation of the variety and level of her activity. In my own work, I have used the behavioural diary with a wide variety of clients. Some people with severe mental illnesses, for example, can simply record all of their daily activities, for they often report that they spend most of the day doing "nothing." The behavioural diary will show exactly how much time they spend in the washroom, lying on their bed, sitting on the couch, watching television, or listening to voices. Clients whose functional capacity is severely compromised – sometimes because they are in inpatient or alternative forms of residential care – may need help to fill out the form on a daily basis. This, however, usually takes only a few minutes, and most of them will learn to do it themselves after a few days. Sometimes I will ask clients to colour their behavioural diaries. Choosing their own colour codes, they can indicate what they enjoy doing the most and when they feel bad. Alternatively, they can use their colours to indicate which activities they wish to increase in the future and which ones they wish to decrease. Even clients with a long history of withdrawal and seclusion are able to indicate certain activities they find pleasurable, giving us valuable clues for designing strategies to increase their social activities. It is, however, important to always include a positive spin in the development of the colouring scheme so that it is not all negative. When a client with a history of schizophrenic disorder was using dark green to indicate when she was feeling "most down," and brown to indicate when she felt "really bad," I suggested that she choose a colour to cover those times when she was not feeling that bad. She chose the colour yellow, and that later became a focus of intervention and a useful marker of progress.

The behavioural diary has been used to chart a wide range of behaviour, including alcohol consumption, violence, obsessive-compulsive behaviour, insomnia and disturbed sleep, attempts to initiate relationships, bed-wetting, Internet utilization, or simply time spent interacting with others. I have also used the behavioural diary with amazing

Worksheet 4.2. Behavioural Diary

Name: _____
Week Starting: _____
Target Behaviour: _____

Hour Starting	Monday	Tuesday	Wednesday	Thursday	Friday	Saturday	Sunday
4:00 a.m.							
5:00							
6:00							
7:00							
8:00							
9:00							
10:00							
11:00							
12:00 p.m.							
1:00							
2:00							
3:00							
4:00							
5:00							
6:00							
7:00							
8:00							
9:00							
10:00							
11:00							
12:00 a.m.							
1:00							
2:00							
3:00							

results in couple counselling. I often ask both partners to chart the time they spend together, specify the activity, and colour-code it with regard to the extent they find these times enjoyable or pleasurable. For example, a man thinks that he is spending time with his wife when he is watching TV at home, although she is somewhere else in the house, and codes that as pleasurable. The wife does not include that as time spent together. In another example, almost all the pleasurable time slots for one partner involve other family members, whereas the other partner only colours the time when they are on their own as pleasurable.

Reactivity Effect and Behavioural Assessment

A feature related to the behavioural diary that is worth mentioning is the *reactivity effect*. When a given behaviour is observed, it *reacts* to the observation and changes. When asked to chart a particular behaviour that is seen as undesirable, such as smoking, fighting with one's partner, or staying up late, clients will become more aware of its occurrence, and this may interfere with the mechanism that produces the behaviour. The frequency of the behaviour to be measured will sometimes decrease. Similarly, behaviour perceived as desirable by the client, such as helping out with housework, calling up a family member needing care, or completing work-related tasks, will sometimes increase due to the reactivity effect. The occurrence of the reactivity effect in behaviour charting or assessment can add to the client's positive expectancy and motivation to change. At the very least, it demonstrates that the target behaviour is malleable.

Apart from frequency, the reactivity effect can have an impact on performance as well. A typical, everyday-life example is stage fright or performance anxiety. When social attention is focused on a given behaviour, its actual performance can be affected. Sometimes the performance can be enhanced by a moderate increase in arousal level or anxiety, while in other cases the performance may be negatively affected. In SSLD practice, we always try to optimize the possible reactivity effect to facilitate client learning and behavioural change. Precaution has to be taken if a negative impact is anticipated. Warning the client in advance of possible negative interference usually helps.

Chapter Five

Review of Current Strategies

In practice, the needs assessment and goal-setting tasks in problem translation may come as a significant cognitive reconstruction for some clients, but can be quite expected and unsurprising for others. The time needed to achieve this also varies. Many client-practitioner dyads can come to a shared understanding within the first session, whereas others may take two to three sessions, or sometimes more, to get to this point. In any case, when needs have been identified and goals have been articulated, it is time to look at the actions taken by the client to address them. In most cases, we will find that clients are already doing something that is functionally related to the goals. The immigrant parents mentioned above, who have tried to make arrangement to send their daughter back to Africa to be circumcised, are doing something about their daughter's happiness. The key questions here are: (1) What is the client doing to address her or his needs? (2) Is what the client is doing functionally relevant? (3) To what extent are these strategies effective? and (4) What do these behaviours tell us about the client and how will this inform our intervention?

Identifying Relevant Behaviours and Their Function

As discussed in Chapter 4, SSLD practitioners always try to help clients examine their current behaviour, such as heavy drinking and infrequent eating. In a way, the review of current behavioural strategies will have already started during the problem translation phase. It is only that in problem translation, the focus is on *inferring needs* from current behaviour; and in the current phase of reviewing behavioural strategies, we may be looking at the same behaviours with a focus on their relevance and effectiveness with regard to these underlying needs.

Every client who comes to us is doing something with regard to her or his needs. As discussed above, clients may or may not see the connection between behaviour and needs. For example, a young woman with anorexia may or may not see her refusal to eat as related to her need to gain autonomy and independence from her parents, to gain peer acceptance by looking "the right weight," or to preserve a particular self-image related to purity, sexuality, or aesthetic appeal. Similarly, a middle-aged man who drinks heavily may or may not see his drinking as a way to reduce social anxiety, a means for easing psychological pain related to being abused as a child, or a way to project a particular self-image among his peers.

Very often clients do not see the connection, and may see themselves as pursuing goals that are not related to their needs in a functional way. For example, a young man who works as a salesperson in a hardware store has been spending an inordinate amount of money on photographic equipment, running up a significant credit card debt. He is preoccupied with getting the latest and most expensive models. He believes this is what he needs to be a good photographer. Through problem translation, it is noticed that his major satisfaction comes from showing people his new gear and what it can do and that he is actually beginning to experience difficulty in getting people's interest. Getting him to see his need for affiliation, appreciation, and esteem opens up the space for assessing the value of his current strategy of purchasing expensive equipment.

In other situations, the clients may be aware of their needs and taking functionally relevant steps to address them. For example, a divorced woman wants to meet a man. She goes out with her friends, goes clubbing, uses online dating sites, and puts out personal ads. She has gotten a few dates this way. Such activities can be captured quite well by the behavioural diary introduced before; and it can give the client a clear picture of her current activities, their respective frequencies, and their distribution. Let us say that the client is now moving in a potentially beneficial direction and pursuing appropriate strategies, but she is still having difficulty making a connection or developing a relationship. We may then want to look at what she is actually doing in those interpersonal contexts when she is interacting with a man. It is possible that her skills in expressing herself, projecting a positive self-image, emotional engagement, and so on could be improved. The review of her current skills can sometimes be based on self-report or indirect observation (e.g., her own account of the encounters, personal ad entries written by the client, pictures of what she wears to the dates), but it is usually more effective to observe the client's actual behaviour directly.

In-Session Role-Play

In-session role-play with video recording and playback is a frequently used procedure in SSLD. In individual sessions, we can either invite the client to bring a friend or family member to do the simulation role-play, or we can get a colleague or a volunteer to role-play with the client. We refer to people who role-play with clients as *collaborators*, and some authors in experimental social psychology and social skills training have used the term "confederate" instead. In SSLD groups, the typical arrangement is to have group members role-play with each other, and this usually works very well. In all cases, prior informed consent and the protection of the client's privacy have to be clearly established. In settings where SSLD procedure is routinely employed, clients can be briefed during the intake process, and informed consent can be obtained then.

In-session simulation is an effective way to review current behavioural strategies and assess the client's skill level. It is also used extensively later in the actual skills learning and development phase. The use of video-recorded role-play facilitates direct observation of the client's behaviour, which is usually better than self-report or immediate in-session observation by the practitioner, colleagues, collaborators, or other participants, because a lot of details may not be picked up or remembered by the observers. Clients may also have difficulty in interpreting feedback such as, "it would be helpful if you change the way you smile or nod." It is so much easier to see it on video. Clients who need to improve their social and interpersonal skills are not always sensitive to the relevant details of their interactions. Interpersonal and social sensitivity, sharp observation of interaction processes, and self-monitoring of social performance can, however, be learning objectives in SSLD programs. Careful self-observation and reporting on one's actions and the responses of others in an organized manner is a skill that a lot of people need to learn.

When introducing in-session role-play to the client, it is important to provide them with specific details regarding the purpose and the process of the role-play and video recording. In my experience, most clients like seeing themselves on video and can benefit tremendously from it. In learning groups, members usually have fun with the recording and review, and there is usually quite a bit of positive energy generated. It is rare that clients refuse to be videotaped, but I have also come across exceptions. Once there was a woman in a group-learning situation who told me that she had been sexually abused, and the abuse had involved video recording. Her special circumstances obviously needed to be accommodated, and in similar situations we also need to be mindful of whether the client is likely to benefit from the given group arrangement or individual work might be more appropriate. When video recording cannot be taken for whatever reason, audio recording should be considered as an alternative. Audio recording still captures a rich range of information which cannot be easily retained otherwise. When all forms of electronic recording are not viable, we will have to resort to careful observation, note-taking, and thick feedback.

With informed consent by clients, video recordings are invaluable for research and teaching. In practice, recordings of earlier sessions can be used in later sessions to highlight progress made by clients. The role of video recording, however, should not be overplayed. I have seen practitioners in settings who are preoccupied with aesthetics and visual effects, to the extent that they get in the way of the actual intervention program. There are service units that take pride in their heavy investment in expensive, state-of-the-art video equipment, which is nice, but not really necessary. In most situations, a basic home video camera is sufficient, as long as clients and participants can have a clear picture of their behaviour and the soundtrack is clearly audible. A colleague of mine uses an inexpensive video camera on his laptop and is quite satisfied with the way it works. Regardless of the technical sophistication of our equipment, it is more important to ensure that they are in working order before each session, for we do not want to waste valuable in-session time to set up or fix the equipment, or to regret afterwards that we failed to record critical processes. Box 5.1 summarizes how in-session role-play can be set up.

When the session is properly set up, the actual role-play can begin. In assessing the client's baseline skill level, the client will be instructed to behave as is. The role-play simulation should be as close to real life as possible to facilitate the transfer of in-session learning to *in vivo* or real-life situations. The client will be the key person in identifying the salient features of the real-life situation. Every effort should be made to make the simulated situation relevant. In some settings, it is even possible to do on-location simulation role-play. For example, in in-patient, residential, correctional, or school settings, much of the client's every-

> **Box 5.1. Setting Up the In-Session Role-Play**
>
> 1. Obtain informed consent from all participants involved in the role-plays, clearly specifying the protection of the client's privacy.
> 2. Clearly define the goals and objectives of the role-play, specifying what is to be reviewed/assessed, and/or what is to be learned and developed.
> 3. Whenever possible, try to use video recording. If not, audio recording and/or immediate observation and feedback can be used.
> 4. Do not spend too much time on the aesthetics and visual effects; the main purpose is to capture the client's performance and to provide specific feedback.
> 5. Expensive, sophisticated equipment is usually unnecessary.
> 6. Always remember to check and make sure that the recording equipment is in order.

day life is within the same physical premises, and it may sometimes make sense to use the actual location.

In addition to the physical setting, the interpersonal and social features are important dimensions of the simulation. In many cases, they can be more important than the physical features. For example, a client having difficulty with authority figures needs to role-play with collaborators who can convincingly play the role of an overbearing and intimidating authority character. In individual work, the practitioner can usually do an adequate job; however, there are some situations where the client may bring in people she or he knows to be collaborators. Colleagues of the practitioner can sometimes be invited to be collaborators as well. There are also settings where professional simulators are hired to do the role-plays. The advantages of professional collaborators include convincing acting, more effective improvisation, sensitivity and responsiveness to the client's needs, and consistent performance. They do, of course, incur additional cost. In group work, members can usually provide an adequate pool of talent, but external collaborators can also be invited – again, with the fully informed consent of all the group members involved.

During a simulation, clients can sometimes be asked to reverse roles and play the person that they are dealing with in real life. People who are learning to prepare for job interviews, for example, can benefit by literally sitting on the other side of the table. Reverse role-play can sometimes be done with the practitioner or a collaborator taking on the client's role, but it is possible to let the client play both roles, very much like the two-chair method in gestalt therapy (Yontef & Simkin, 1993), only that the focus here is on behaviour instead of emotional responses. This does not mean that we totally disregard emotional processes. It is helpful, and in some cases even necessary, to let the client process her or his feelings and emotions before focusing on her or his behaviour. The playing of both sides can be very helpful in expanding the client's perspective. It can reduce anxiety, if that happens to be an interfering factor in the client's interpersonal or social performance. One of the beneficial side effects of this role-play is an increase in the client's sense of mastery, and therefore self-efficacy, for in playing the role of the other person, clients will be taken out of a habitual mode of emotional response, which can be overwhelming and immobilizing for some of them.

If the client feels prepared for it, this dual role-play can be a useful assessment tool. For example, a teenager complaining about how he is having a problem with his father who is described as sadistically critical and undermining can be asked to role-play a recent conversation with his father. The advantage of this procedure is that the client will be working with the character he presented in session, and that represents his reality. It can be more effective than a simulation role-play by a collaborator who might not necessarily deliver a convincing enactment of the father's behavioural patterns.

Our focus, however, stays with the client, rather than the other character the client role-plays. Our assessment is firmly anchored in the functionality and effectiveness of the client's behaviour. The client is constantly reminded to think in terms of the function of her or his specific responses: "What were you trying to accomplish by doing/saying that?" and, "To what extent did you achieve your objective by doing/saying that?" To answer the second question, we obviously have to take into account the reaction of the other party. Helping the client to see the connection between her or his behaviour and the reaction of other people helps to develop interpersonal sensitivity, which is an essential component of interpersonal effectiveness. We can reinforce this perspective by saying something like, "Your goal was to pacify him, and reduce the tension, and then you said ... and we then see him becoming even more hostile and critical." This can be followed by a prompt such as, "Now that you have a chance to look at what you did and how other people responded, would you think of doing anything differently?"

This articulates the principle of positively reframing the assessment into a future-oriented and action-oriented formulation, instead of just an appraisal of the client's performance.

Assessment of Effectiveness

In assessing the effectiveness of the current strategies of clients, the desired goal is always the major criteria. In a contingency-based intervention, there is no universal schema or bell curve for assessing a client's skill level, as what is effective is contingent upon many factors, including personal circumstances, social environment, cultural context, and specific situational variations. It is sometimes tempting for trainers and learners to think of a universal social effectiveness measure that can be applied to all situations, but we always have to consider the client's goals. For example, a college student who does not want to be in the limelight or in a leadership position, but who enjoys warm and cozy interactions with peers, will need a different set of skills than someone who has high aspirations in student politics. The two sets of skills are different, but do not necessarily have to be compared in terms of their value or status.

Strategies and Composite Skills

In a goal-oriented assessment of strategies and skills, the major question is the extent to which the current skills are effective. If the current strategies and skills are completely effective, the client does not need our service. SSLD practice therefore assumes that improvement is needed at least in some aspects of the client's strategies and skills. Our analysis has to cover strategies, skills, and performance. Let us use life insurance sales as an example. Salespersons of life insurance usually want to maximize their sales of policies, which is their goal. Some of them are very skilful presenters of information, especially in clarifying the different features of different insurance products. Others are skilful in persuading prospective clients to accept the need to invest money into insurance policies. Yet others are very skilful in obtaining new contacts and referrals. In this case, obtaining contacts, presenting products, and persuasion are all important skills for life insurance sales. Mastering these skills is obviously important, but success in this industry requires effective strategies on top of them. A strategy articulates a coordinated sequence of actions – with each of them potentially requiring specific skills – in order to attain the ultimate goal. In the insurance example, we can talk about an overall marketing or sales strategy. For example, a salesperson who notices that a particular ethnic group is immigrating to her or his part of the country in big numbers may strategically establish relationships with key people in that emerging community, study the culture, history, demographics, and life-insurance purchase patterns in their country of origin, and the like. The salesperson may even try to learn their language. Each of these strategic moves involves a number of skills, such as making cold calls, researching the background of the community leaders, accessing community-based publications and information, and doing Internet or library searches on the particular ethnic group and their culture and practice.

Skills that are necessary components for building an effective strategy are called *composite skills* of that strategy. We can go back to the divorced woman example mentioned above. Her goal is to meet a man, with the view of developing a serious relationship. She has adopted a few active outreach strategies such as Internet dating and using personal ads. She might have mastered the composite skills for these outreaching strategies; she has actually been successful in that she has got a few dates. Yet her current strategies, though functionally relevant, appropriate, and even effective in their own right, are nonetheless insufficient given her ultimate goal. She needs to develop a complementary strategy of improving her interpersonal effectiveness in a dating situation, which includes the composite skills of self-presentation, self-expression, reciprocal self-disclosure, emotional engagement, and the like. Table 5.1 lists some more examples of goal-directed strategies and their composite skills.

Specifying the functionally relevant strategies and their composite skills is a way to locate where specific learning and development are needed. In a sense, the formulation of strategies is a more conceptual or cognitive process, but the actual development of strategies often involves the learning and mastery of specific skills, which are mostly behavioural. When executed, a strategy is almost always a sequence of skilful performance within an interpersonal or social context. In practice, it is usually easier for clients to appreciate the connection between specific behavioural strategies and the goals they desire if the composite skills and the way they actually operate are clearly represented to them. For clients whose functioning has been more severely compromised, such as in the case of long-term schizophrenic disorder, overall strategies (e.g., developing social competence to deal with dif-

Table 5.1. Strategies and Skills

Goal	Strategies	Composite Skills
Woman wanting to leave abusive relationship	• Ensuring personal safety • Building financial self-sufficiency	• Communication • Access to community services • Vocational • Job interviewing • Financial management
Gay man in a rural area wanting to meet other gay men	• Online communities • Frequenting nearby hangout spots	• Self-presentation • Writing • Computer • Grooming • Pick-up • Engagement
Immigrant woman wanting to communicate with teenage children who identify strongly with North American culture	• Learn more about North American teenage culture • Direct communication with children	• Language • Internet • Research • Listening • Expression and presentation • Engagement
Older man wanting to be accepted by peers in seniors' home	• Be a good citizen • Become interesting	• Providing physical assistance • Giving emotional support • Telling jokes • Access to health information • Ballroom dancing
Adult client with a long history of schizophrenic disorder wanting to improve relationship with family members	• More assertive with regard to own needs and preferences • Building mutually gratifying and supportive relationships	• Direct communication of emotional needs and personal preferences • Refusal of unreasonable demands/requests • Dealing with criticism • Increasing emotional sensitivity • Communicating emotional support • Self-disclosure • Building commonalities and connection

ficult personalities) can be difficult to imagine, but more concrete and demonstrable skills (e.g., learning to refuse unreasonable requests) may be a good starting point.

Finally, it has to be emphasized that strategies and skills are conceptualizations of client behaviour at different levels of abstraction. The boundary between them is not rigid, but is quite nebulous. The differentiation is offered as an aid in conceptualizing client behaviour, and the concepts are intended for pragmatic purposes – they are useful only when they are helpful in the intervention process. It is possible that practitioners and clients can conceptualize the same behaviour sequences either as strategies or skills. The most important points are: whether the conceptualization helps clients get a clearer understanding of their situation; what the connection is between behaviour and goals; and what can be done to become more effective in terms of their agentive, interpersonal, and social functioning.

Micro-processes and Performance

Following from the above analysis, a skill can also be conceptualized into different component units, and each unit can also be considered a distinct skill. For example, we can say that building good relationships with as many people as possible in your school is a good strategy to get elected into student council. Other strategies may include a poster and email campaign, volunteering for a high-profile school event, and the like. The personal relationship strategy requires skills such as meeting strangers and developing a rapport with them quickly. That can involve approaching a person at the right time (perceptiveness and sensitivity, not interrupting something important to the other person); introducing oneself; making a connection (starting with what the other person might be interested in, for example); making an impression (something positive that the other person is likely to remember); and so on.

Each skill, therefore, can be further broken down into smaller component units. We call these smaller units "micro-processes." Again, like the boundary between strategies and skills, the separation between skills and micro-processes is not rigidly fixed. In pragmatic terms, a micro-process is a component of a skill that can be identified as a meaningful unit by the client, and it can be further divided into components (see Figure 5.1 for example). The key point here is that we should not get caught up with defining and differentiating among strategies, composite skills, and micro-processes. These labels are created to help clients and practitioners make sense of the complex sets of behaviour sequences to be learned, and to guide their learning and development.

In the assessment of skills, attention should be paid to the micro-processes. Identification of these micro-processes and how they contribute to the overall effectiveness of the skill is helpful in providing

Figure 5.1. Strategies, Composite Skills, and Micro-processes

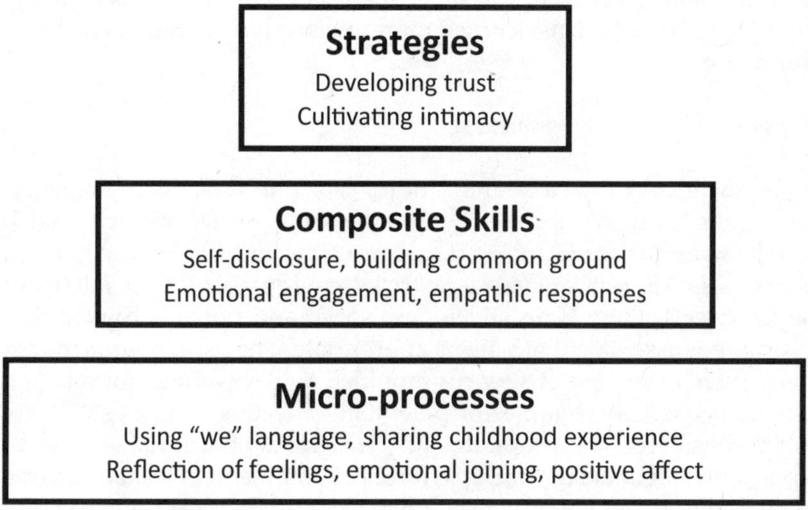

Strategies
Developing trust
Cultivating intimacy

Composite Skills
Self-disclosure, building common ground
Emotional engagement, empathic responses

Micro-processes
Using "we" language, sharing childhood experience
Reflection of feelings, emotional joining, positive affect

feedback to the client, and in informing subsequent learning and training tasks. In a couple-counselling situation, for example, the two partners are asked to role-play an everyday conversation as part of the assessment. The role-play is videotaped. We find that both partners do not listen to each other, change the topic quite frequently, give negative or critical feedback, and express very little spontaneous affection. These micro-processes can become major items in assessment feedback and in subsequent interventions.

Another factor to be considered is performance. Sometimes clients may have been exposed to particular skills and even coached in the micro-processes; it may be only in the real-life situation requiring the effective performance of the skill that the client for some reason just cannot deliver. This could be due to simple performance anxiety or more deeply rooted emotional blockages. It is therefore important to recognize compromised performance in the review and assessment of current skills so that we do not confuse lack of skill with fluctuation in performance level. For example, in a couple-counselling workshop, participants were asked to learn to listen for emotional content in other participants' narratives. Everyone learned this smoothly when they were working in small groups with participants who were not their partners. Once they were put in the same small groups with their partners, the emotional interference began to operate. It was the previous learning and the presence of other members that helped each couple apply what they had just learned more effectively, facilitating good performance.

Effectiveness and Appropriateness

The practitioner has to be mindful that the effectiveness of strategies and skills is always assessed within particular social contexts; and it can be tempting for us to resort to our own terms of reference in these situations. Appropriateness is a tricky concept, and as pointed out in Chapter 4, there is an enveloping social and political context that shapes our assessment of what is appropriate. The use of marijuana for relaxation, or the use of services provided by sex workers for meeting sexual needs, are examples of potentially effective strategies that are often considered inappropriate and problematic. Practitioners have to constantly negotiate the multiple forces of dominant social and cultural values, the client's specific position, the legal and professional codes of conduct that bind us, and our own values and ethical commitments. The tension among these forces often calls for creative and innovative solutions, and it is important for us to maintain an open and flexible approach in our practice instead of sticking to fixed or rigid principles and procedures.

Understanding the Client as a Learner

After finding out what the client is doing to address her or his needs, determining whether those actions and behaviours are functionally relevant, and assessing the effectiveness of the client's current skills, a review of the current strategy process should help us learn something about the client's behavioural inclinations and learning style. Some clients refer to principles a lot, some are spontaneous in their responses, some demand structure and systematic instructions, some show a lot of initiative, some are hesitant to participate in role-plays, and some are thrilled by them. Attending to particular patterns and learning styles can facilitate engagement with clients and help to motivate them in the learning process. This is consistent with the contingency-based thinking of SSLD in that we do not assume a similar response pattern and learning style for every client, and in that we allow for individual differences.

Given the extremely wide range of possible applications for SSLD procedures, the clients we work with can include children with pervasive developmental disorders, politicians running for office, adults with a long history of severe and debilitating mental health issues, senior executives coaching their staff, people who have suffered severe trauma or social deprivation, high school students who want to improve their interpersonal effectiveness, new immigrants who are trying to settle in a new country, marketing personnel trying to boost their sales, or couples who wish to improve their relationship. As learners, our clients come with diverse backgrounds, experiences, and life histories. They have very different personal endowments, current resources, and limitations, including intelligence, aptitude, education, financial resources, family support, social networks, community resources, and so on. It is important to recognize all of these diversities and how they may affect the client's learning process. In my own experience of working with people from different cultures, for example, I understand that clients may bring very different expectations to the practice situation, and the way they perform their roles as clients and learners can also be different. The maintenance of an open, flexible, and engaging style is most likely to be beneficial. It is also important for us to be prepared to learn from clients regarding the cultures or subcultures they come from and what they have adopted or internalized, instead of making assumptions about them, or relying on over-simplified, stereotypic characterizations of their culture (Tsang & Bogo, 1997; Tsang, Bogo, & Lee, 2010; Tsang & George, 1998).

Focusing on Strength and Potential

As SSLD assessment emphasizes a learning and educational instead of a medico-pathological approach, our understanding of the client's needs and goals is always complemented by an assessment of the client's current functioning, which will include both the strategies and skills to be learned and those the client has already mastered. Whereas we tend to believe that almost everyone needs to learn something new, we also recognize that even people who are considered very dysfunctional by mental health and helping professionals often possess tremendous strength and potential for growth. People who have struggled with a long history of mental illness, for example, often demonstrate remarkable resilience as they go through a seemingly endless sequence of frustrating, hurtful, or humiliating experiences in life. People challenged by physical conditions and developmental disorders often show an amazing capacity for learning and change. We are actually very privileged when we have the opportunity to accompany people when they overcome challenges in life such as abuse, discrimination, unemployment, divorce or break-up, loss of a loved one, war, violent crime, torture, natural disaster, chronic illness, imprisonment, substance dependence, and so on. There are moments when I wonder if I could hold up as gracefully as my clients had I faced the same challenges in life. In my decades of practice, I have learned so much from the experience and insight of my clients. SSLD, therefore, emphasizes the process of learning together with our clients, and seeks to create and maintain a space for clients to realize their strengths and potentials.

Endnotes

The review of current strategies involves a scan of the various attempts made by the client with regard to their identified goals. This covers a horizontal plane and can be quite extensive. Once the key strategies have been mapped out, we get on to a vertical exploration: we will move into the specific composite skills and a more in-depth assessment of the micro-processes. We pay attention both to what people have to learn and to what they have already mastered. A good review will prepare us for the next phase – the design and implementation of learning procedures.

The problem translation and assessment procedures described in these two chapters involve quite a few component steps. In SSLD training programs, practitioners sometimes want to have a relatively more concise conceptualization; I have suggested the N3C formulation to them. N3C stands for needs, circumstances, characteristics, and capacity. The acronym prompts the practitioner to explore these aspects of the client's situation. Apart from exploring the client's needs in depth, the practitioner has to pay attention to the circumstances that the client is in (e.g., being unemployed, divorced, or having just lost a loved one). The assessment will also include the client's characteristics, such as gender, age, sexual orientation, religion, ethnicity, cultural orientation, personality, value orientation, learning style, and other qualities. Capacity includes the client's existing repertoire of strategies and skills, resilience, strength, social and symbolic capital, economic and financial resources, and so on. Many practitioners have found the N3C formulation helpful in their practice and professional exchange with each other.

Chapter Six

Formulating and Designing Relevant Strategies and Skills

After problem translation and current strategies review, we come to the formulation and design of strategies and skills. Unlike packaged programs that offer a standard training program for all participants, contingency-based SSLD custom-designs a learning program for each client. In group-work settings, the actual learning procedure is contingent upon the particular needs and circumstances of individual group members. Collective needs of groups, organizations, and communities are similarly addressed with regard to their specific circumstances.

Following the hierarchical structure of goals, strategies, composite skills, and micro-processes described in the last chapter, the first step in the formulation and design of learning procedures can usually start with strategies – with the assumption that the client's goals are reasonably well-defined, at least for the time being. Articulation of overall strategies will then be followed by specification of composite skills, many of which the client may have already mastered, and others that the client may need to acquire or refine through SSLD. As mentioned above, the attention to micro-processes will be helpful in the learning and development of a given skill.

Agreeing on Strategies and Learning Objectives

After the engagement, problem translation, and current strategies-review procedures, most clients and practitioners would have come to a shared understanding of the client's goals and possible strategy options. In some cases, this shared understanding is either not feasible or is incomplete, such as in the case of helping children with autism to learn social skills, or when working with clients who have a more circumscribed view on their needs and goals than we do, which is not uncommon when working in psychiatric and mental health settings. In such situations, the general principle is to establish and work on the highest common factor. Given the incremental character of SSLD practice, we can work whenever there is common ground, and shared understanding will generally be expanded upon successful completion of shared tasks.

For instance, when we are working with clients with serious mental health issues who are returning to community living after an extended period of hospital and residential care, the idea of an overall set of strategies that addresses their housing, employment, social, personal, and emotional needs can appear unrealistic, remote, or even overwhelming or threatening to them. It would probably be better if we work with them to first identify priority areas and then to develop a simple, manageable strategy. Successful completion of the first task – say, for instance, finding housing – will break a pattern of passivity and negative expectancy, empower the client, enhance the client's self-efficacy, and set up a tentative positive expectancy for developing subsequent tasks.

When working with clients who are not in the position to make decisions, such as in the cases of young children, seniors with dementia, or clients with developmental challenges, it is important to work with their caregivers or legal custodians. We should, nonetheless, try to understand as much as possible what the client's own preference may be and give it due consideration in our formulation of an intervention plan. As well, whenever it makes sense, we will try to explain our formulation and plan to the best of the client's understanding.

Formulation of the Learning Program

The more we can translate the ultimate goal (e.g., improved couple relationship, social integration) into specific tasks (e.g., learning to listen to each other and understand each other's needs, overcoming social phobia, and initiating interpersonal contact), the easier it is for clients to understand the process of the SSLD intervention and develop positive expectancy regarding the eventual outcome. The composite tasks can be organized into a list of learning objectives. Each learning objective is to be achieved through a number of specific learning modules. In SSLD, a learning module is a self-contained unit of learning activity with specified objectives, procedures, and learning outcome.

Structure of the SSLD Program

When clients go through the SSLD process by learning strategies and skills one-by-one, one session after another, it is helpful for the practitioner to have a conceptual map of how the different learning activities are connected to each other. This understanding can be shared with the client as much as possible whenever the client is interested and has the capacity to comprehend. Programs for learning and development can be understood as hierarchically organized, down from the generic overall statement of goals to very specific learning activities.

For instance, a client with social phobia may have an overall goal of social integration, which means an active social life within the context of gratifying interpersonal and social relationships. As shown in Figure 6.1, this overall goal can be broken down into more specific *composite tasks*, or *learning objectives*, such as initiating social contact, relationship building, cognitive reframing, emotional regulation, and managing negative responses. Any one of these tasks or objectives has to be achieved through a sequence of *learning modules*. Whereas learning objectives are useful in conceptualizing and designing an SSLD program, the learning modules are the actual program units that clients go through. Learning to initiate social contact, for instance, requires composite strategies and skills that can be structured into specific learning modules such as identifying or creating a social space for meeting people, managing the physical aspects of self-presentation, mastering a repertoire of opening lines for initiating contact, practising responsiveness and interactivity in social conversation, strategic self-disclosure, and so on.

Each learning module can cover all three levels of strategies, skills, and micro-processes mentioned earlier. To avoid confusion, it should be clarified here that the strategy/skill/micro-process schema is helpful for analysing units of human action or behaviour. The goal/objective/module/activity schema is to be used for learning program design. The two schemas do not correspond in a neat and tidy manner, although both schemas ultimately target an identified goal or a desired outcome. In practice, we are using the program design structure (goal/objective/module/activity) to help clients to develop the necessary strategies and skills.

A learning module on self-presentation, for example, can include learning activities targeting grooming, posturing, facial expression, engaging in eye contact, location-context management, and so on. Location-context management, for instance, can be regarded as a strategy, for it is a design to increase the probability of successful interpersonal engagement. In a way, it can be seen as a strategic way of staging and presenting oneself. What it means in real-life practice is for clients to choose a specific location or social context in which they feel most comfortable initiating social contact. A student, for example, may choose the cafeteria. Another young person may choose the local temple, church, or mosque. Some clients enjoy restaurants while some dread them. Bars are preferred by some, but many may find them too challenging or risky. Following the principles of contingency and incrementalism, we let the client start with a location that is least anxiety-provoking. The context is closely associated with the physical location, but can be quite variable. The classroom, for instance, is a well-defined physical location, but the context can be before class, during class, or after class. The restaurant is a location while the social context can be a one-on-one or a group date, a birthday party, or a company celebration. Realizing the strategy would include other composite skills such as making a reservation, getting invited to a party, or getting supportive buddies to attend. Each of these will involve their own respective micro-processes.

Learning activities can address strategies, skills, or micro-processes, and can be in the form of instructions, group discussions, in-session exercises, simulation or role-play, homework assignments, and so on. Learning to improve on grooming and posturing, for instance, can often be achieved in a learning-group context by asking members to give each other feedback and to focus on aspects of grooming or posturing that would be most engaging. Visual aids such as photographs of people belonging to that population sector (high school students, young executives, medical supplies salespeople) can also be used as a stimulus for discussion and obtaining feedback. A homework exercise to make oneself over can also be assigned. Following the principle of contingency-based intervention, the specific design of the module and the learning activities to be included do not have to be the same for every client situation. For clients who are particularly challenged with regard to social efficacy, for example, a buddy system can be set up to facilitate the completion of homework assignments, which would not be necessary for clients who feel comfortable doing this on their own. The example given above deals with grooming and posturing simultaneously, but they also can be dealt with separately if that would make learning easier for the clients. Again, we can illustrate how the behaviour analysis schema and the learning program schema are integrated in an actual SSLD program using these examples: grooming and makeovers can be seen as a strategy, picking the right shirt as a skill, and deciding how many buttons one should do up (or not do up) as a micro-process.

It should be emphasized that the purpose of this section is not to reinforce a rigid understanding of what constitutes a goal, a composite task or learning objective, a learning module, or a learning activity. These labels can be used with flexibility. The key points are: (1) the learning and development process is organized logically; (2) each learning objective has to be translated into specific activities involving experiential learning and behavioural change, not just conceptual understanding; and (3) the design of the learning program is contingent upon client circumstances and characteristics, including learning capacity and learning style.

Designing Learning Activities

Once the learning tasks are mapped out with reference to the final goal or outcome desired by the client, we can move into action. The selection and sequencing of specific learning objectives and the modules to address them have to be informed by a good assessment of the client's strategies and skills; the procedure for this assessment has been presented in the preceding chapter. Most clients would have already mastered some of the relevant composite skills required for their specific strategies. Our task now is to clearly identify the necessary strategies and skills to be learned and developed. For example, if we are working with a couple trying to improve their relationship, the composite tasks or learning objectives may include (1) improving the communication pattern; (2) creating more shared experiences that are pleasurable for both partners; and (3) helping the partners to support each other in their personal growth and development.

Couple communication has been studied extensively, and many programs for improving couple relationships have already been developed (e.g., Chee & Conger, 1989; Gurman & Jacobson, 1986; Jacobson & Margolin, 1979; Jakubowski, Milne, Brunner, & Miller, 2004; Lee, 1991; Perez, 1996; Reardon-Anderson, Stagner, Macomber, & Murray, 2005). It is obviously possible that many couples can benefit from preplanned programs that are available, and these programs and/or components can be used when they are appropriate. The SSLD approach does not seek to reinvent the wheel, but simply tries to get the best program for

Figure 6.1. Example of Learning Program Organization

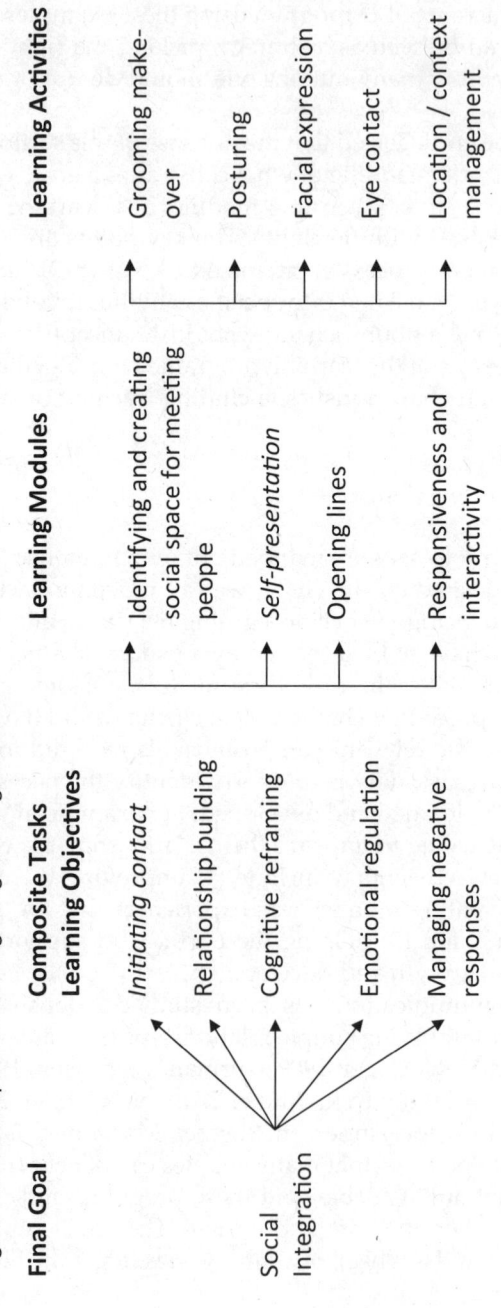

Final Goal	Composite Tasks Learning Objectives	Learning Modules	Learning Activities
Social Integration	*Initiating contact*	Identifying and creating social space for meeting people	Grooming make-over
	Relationship building	*Self-presentation*	Posturing
	Cognitive reframing	Opening lines	Facial expression
	Emotional regulation	Responsiveness and interactivity	Eye contact
	Managing negative responses		Location / context management

each couple by responding to their specific needs and circumstances. Following the procedure described above, the design of a learning program entails the specification of composite tasks, setting them up as learning objectives. Once these objectives are specified, we will have to come up with learning modules in the actual in-session work with clients. Knowing that some of the strategies and skills needed by a given client couple may have already been documented, the design of the learning program and of specific learning modules will involve: (1) the identification of procedures in existing preplanned programs that are relevant to the clients' needs and learning objectives; (2) reciprocal consideration of the strategies and skills needed to achieve the clients' goals with respect to the clients' current skill levels; and (3) specifying strategies and skills to be learned and developed that are not currently available.

What this means in actual practice is that not all couples will need to learn the same things, and their sessions can be quite different. There are many existing procedures, both in-session and in the form of take-home exercises, that are designed to facilitate better couple communication or to enhance relationship quality, but their application is contingent upon the particular needs and goals of each couple as well as their current repertoire of skills. For instance, with a highly educated, high-income, and high-conflict couple, the design of pleasurable activities to be shared may not be too challenging for them intellectually, and they may not really need to learn this. They may, however, need to learn to be emotionally attuned to each other, while at the same time regulating or containing their own emotional responses. An intercultural couple, as another example, may need to learn to appreciate how growing up in a different cultural context may affect a person's perception of certain social realities such as racism, values such as the role one's aging parents should play in one's life, and everyday life habits such as diet or dental hygiene. I have developed specific exercises to help couples move incrementally through less challenging or risky sharing of difference and ultimately towards significant childhood or developmental events that shape their current thought and action.

Reciprocal consideration of skills to be learned and the client's current repertoire of skills is another key feature of contingency-based intervention. Clients start with very different experience and skill sets, and our intervention should take their unique circumstances into account. Not only do we need to plan or design specific strategies and skills with regard to the goals desired by the client but the very process of learning itself has to be adjusted as well. Clients have different endowments and aptitudes with regard to the strategies and skills to be learned. Some clients are very good at conceptual understanding and following instructions systematically. Some clients learn more effectively through an intuitive grasp of the essential dynamics of interpersonal processes they observe. Some clients need a lot of structure and reassurance, while some others are excited by new experiences or challenges. As suggested earlier, SSLD assessment pays attention both to what people need to learn and to their characteristics, including their learning style, strengths, and potential. In training programs for practitioners, I sometimes use the N3C acronym mentioned at the end of the last chapter to help them ensure that they have given due attention to the client's needs, circumstances, characteristics, and capacity.

Designing Specific Learning Modules

When it comes to the actual in-session work with clients, the design of specific learning modules is the centrepiece of SSLD intervention. There are a number of building blocks for the design of specific learning modules for SSLD programs. The first is the selective application of learning modules that are currently available.

Ready-Made Modules

These ready-made modules include those that have been documented in the published professional literature and the undocumented ones that are used by practitioners. In my own experience, there are many ingenious learning modules designed by practitioners targeting a wide spectrum of learning objectives. There are also numerous documented procedures, and it is not possible to catalogue all of them exhaustively. Even with the enhanced capacity of online search engines, many of these procedures are not readily accessible. Some of them are published in books and manuals that are not part of a digitized database. It appears that practitioners tend to have developed their own repertoire of preferred procedures or modules, and very often at least a good proportion of them have not been documented and are therefore not readily available.

A major advantage of using ready-made procedures or learning modules is convenience, as you can apply them right away instead of spending time and resources on developing new ones. Sometimes there is the added advantage of empirical or clinical evidence if the procedure has been used extensively or is part of an outcome study. A contingency-based innovative procedure or module is by definition untested, and its efficacy is based on our favourable predictions, which are based on knowledge, experience, and judgment. Ready-made modules, however, can be limited in terms of their direct relevance to particular client situations, for they are not always designed to address the very case that a practitioner happens to be working with. Empirical evidence can also be a problem, especially when the evidence is collected in situations and among client groups that are not similar to what the practitioner is dealing with. The experienced practitioner usually weighs professional opinion, practice experience, and empirical evidence in a complex formula to derive the best intervention for the client. In SSLD, we give particular emphasis to the client's needs, circumstances, learning styles, and personal preferences, and encourage practitioner colleagues to give these factors more weight than their own preferences in the design of learning programs. Another important principle is to keep expanding our own repertoire of learning modules and procedures by reading, participating in learning programs, professional development, supervision, consultation, and exchange with colleagues.

Apart from tapping into existing knowledge, SSLD practitioners are encouraged to be creative. Over the years, I have created many learning modules, and most of them have been applied beyond the original context within which they were created. There are two ways for creating or generating new strategies and skills that can then be organized into a learning module. One of them is practitioner design, in which the SSLD practitioner designs a procedure to address a specific learning objective. The other is collaborative creation, in which the practitioner works together with the client or clients to generate new strategies and skills to address a specific learning need.

New Learning Modules Created by the Practitioner

Following the example of couple counselling used above, practitioners often need to bring together learning modules to address specific learning objectives such as improving communication, increasing shared pleasurable moments, or fostering mutual support for growth and development. Let us assume that after considering a couple's current behaviour and interaction pattern, we come to an agreement with them

> **Box 6.1. Designing a Learning Module**
>
> 1. Specify the learning objective, with the outcome stated in terms of observable action or behaviour.
> 2. List the conditions of possibility. What needs to have happened for the desired outcome to emerge?
> 3. Translate the list into incremental steps.
> 4. Describe each step in specific detail, preferably giving behavioural instructions.

that they need to improve their communication in order to deal with their perceived incompatibility in value orientation. One of the partners may believe that this is a world in which only the fittest survive, and that it is therefore necessary to be competitive and successful. Children, according to this partner, have to be prepared for fierce competition in order to achieve and excel. The other partner, in contrast, believes that compassion and interpersonal connection are more important, and that it is more important for children to develop a capacity for empathy, a sense of justice, and the readiness to give or to share. This couple could be experiencing a lot of tension and conflict, especially when it comes to their own career development, social relationships, and child-rearing practice. There may not be a lot of documented procedures for dealing with this specific issue. To design a procedure that may work, we need to specify the learning objective, then analyse its components and the incremental steps that our clients need to take in order to realize it (Box 6.1 summarizes these steps).

1. Analysing the Composite Elements

The first question we ask in the creation of a new learning module is what it is supposed to accomplish. In the example given above, the desired outcome is for the couple to come to some kind of shared understanding with regard to significant issues in their lives. In SSLD, the focus is on action and behaviour; it is probably all right if the couple maintains different value orientations as long as they can find ways to conduct the life they share without causing undue tension, conflict, and subjective discomfort. For instance, if they can agree on their respective career plan, how their shared and individual social spaces are organized and managed, and how they can interact with their children, then the purpose of improved communication will be considered achieved. This is consistent with the behaviour-oriented character of SSLD.

The second question we ask is what needs to have happened for the couple to be able to come to such an agreement and shared understanding. This will likely lead to a list of conditions such as (1) they are willing to talk to each other; (2) they can listen to each other; (3) they can understand where the other party is coming from even if they do not agree; (4) they see how the other party's value is related to her or his earlier life experiences, including cultural and family exposure; (5) they understand how the expressed value is often driven by underlying needs, such as a need for security, affiliation, esteem, and the like; (6) they appreciate that although their expressed values are different, they are similarly espousing values that are functionally related to their respective needs; (7) they recognize that there are usually more ways than one to address these needs; (8) they accept that different values do not always dictate completely incompatible actions, and that compromise and concession are possible; (9) they try to imagine that the values people espouse do not have to be rigidly adhered to; (10) they appreciate that they do not uphold these values with the same valence in all situations, and they do make concessions and modifications with regard to the purpose of each situation; (11) they believe that when there is increased understanding, trust, mutual respect, and appreciation between two individuals, it is easier to negotiate common purposes even when underlying values may vary; (12) they are willing to explore ways to improve understanding, trust, mutual respect, and appreciation; and (13) they believe that the above is achievable through SSLD procedure and by working with their current practitioner.

This list may appear a bit long when it is written out, but most experienced practitioners actually go through a very similar internal process when they respond to complex client situations. Having an anticipated list of necessary steps to take will make it possible for us to begin to put a program together. There are, for example, specific learning modules to help get people who have opposite or incompatible positions with regard to attitude, opinion, positions, and assumptions to listen to each other and come to some form of concession or compromise. The Listening Triad Exercise (Pfeiffer & Jones, 1974), which was designed for this purpose, will be described in more detail in the chapter on reception (Chapter 8, p. 145). In the case where such ready-made modules are not available, which is the focus of this section, having more small steps specified will allow the practitioner to at least try to tackle the composite tasks one by one.

2. Incrementalism and the Art of the Possible

Incrementalism is a key concept in the creation of new learning procedures. The ability to see how small steps take place in sequence to lead to the desired outcome is very helpful. This ability usually increases with experience in SSLD practice; it may also help to study process research procedures such as task analysis (e.g., Berlin, Mann, & Grossman, 1991; Greenberg, 2007; Schwartz & Gottman, 1976) and interpersonal process recall (Henretty, Levitt, & Mathews, 2008; Larsen, Flesaker, & Stege, 2008). These clinical research procedures sharpen our sensitivity to the clinical change process and may increase our capacity to conceptualize how micro-processes are arranged in sequences to bring about more significant client change.

In trying to help couples understand the differences between them, I have used a module for sharing early life experiences by asking them to reflect on what experience in their early lives might have contributed to a particular value they now espouse. By shifting the focus onto the sharing of experience instead of arguing over a value or principle, the emotional tension usually goes down, allowing more space for mutuality. Seeing how values are shaped by one's life experience will usually loosen the rigidity with which people hold on to them, permitting people to see those values as contingent and variable rather than fixed.

Experienced practitioners sometimes feel that procedures like these "just come" to them, but it is helpful to describe the process through which such creativity emerges. The first key ingredient usually includes a clear goal-directedness, focusing our attention on how to achieve that specific small step. The second involves turning what is fixed and unchangeable into what is contingent and variable. The third principle is to avoid the area that is most difficult to change, or invested with the most defensive energy. This can be aided by a quick review using the framework on human action and the external world proposed in Chapter 2, which covered the various domains including motivation, cognition, biology, emotion, action, and external environment. The fourth is to imagine what is possible with the client and the client system, or what they are capable of doing and willing to try, such as talking to each other with a view to mutual understanding. In the case of couple counselling, the additional principle of mutuality is key. When planning modules for other clients, however, different considerations will become more salient. When working with clients with severe social phobia, which sometimes includes clients who have had episodes of severe mental illness, the issue of emotional safety is often prioritized. We do not subject these clients to the risk of further damage to their already feeble sense of self efficacy, but instead plan modules that will not expose them to failure, or take care of anticipated negative consequences by building them into the design as an expected outcome, thus protecting them through psychological immunization.

Manageability and a Successful First Step

Another important note on incrementalism is that tasks do not have to be learned in the sequence that they will ultimately be performed, but rather in the order of manageability from the client's perspective. This is a lesson I learned in the earlier phase of my career when I consulted with institutions for men with severe developmental delays. In one of those situations, we were dealing with the task of helping some of these clients learn to put on their pants. The staff found it quite challenging, and the principle of modelling or observation learning did not seem to work. During consultation, I asked them to break the process down into incremental steps, and they did. Then I asked them which was the easiest thing for the clients to learn. They realized that it was pulling up the pants once they had already passed over the ankles and the knees, and then pulling up the zipper. This led the group to realize that the sequence could be learned almost backwards. When staff had assisted the clients to put their pants over their ankles and knees, pulling them up from there was not a huge problem. Doing up the zipper required fine motor coordination which was a challenge, but most clients could learn to do it in time, with some of them actually showing a sense of accomplishment and joy when praised by the staff upon completion. Working backwards in an incremental manner helped many of these clients to master the task. A key principle in SSLD practice, therefore, is to start the learning process with a successful step, however small. This principle can be applied to the learning of other sequences. It is always important for clients to experience success in new learning, as this contributes to positive expectancy, to the working alliance between client and practitioner, and most importantly to an empowering sense of self-efficacy.

Generating New Strategies and Skills through Collaborative Creation

The principles of contingency-based thinking and incrementalism are fundamental to the design and implementation of SSLD learning programs. Another important element is innovation. SSLD practitioners will often find it necessary to modify existing procedures or create new ones in the process of working with clients who present unfamiliar situations and issues. It is sometimes possible for clients to present an issue or situation for which the practitioner does not have a ready solution. Even experienced practitioners will come across situations that they have not worked with before, and they do not always have a handy response that effectively addresses the client's needs. Under such circumstances, we may turn to collaborative creation and development of new strategies and skills.

The collaborative creation procedure in SSLD originated from a procedure known as *evocation*, which I learned as a participant in a group-training program back in the 1980s that was conducted by Yaro Starak, an academic and group trainer based in Brisbane, Australia.

Evocation was a procedure used to help group members to explore new experiences or new behaviour through brainstorming. I subsequently developed the evocation procedure along SSLD lines and specified the component steps. In this modified procedure – which I now call "Collaborative Creation of New Strategies and Skills," or simply "collaborative creation" – suggestions for new solutions are generated through the responses evoked from the participants. These suggestions are then processed systematically according to SSLD principles. The procedure, which was originally used in group contexts, has also been adapted to work with clients in individual consultation (Box 6.2).

1. Defining the Desired Outcome

The first step in collaborative creation is to define the desired outcome. In SSLD practice, the need for collaborative creation usually comes after problem translation, when the goals for intervention have been set. The particular outcome that is desired, however, can sometimes be more specific. For example, in a group program for women with depression, one of the goals is for them to learn to become more assertive in their interpersonal relationships; thus a specific objective could be saying no to requests from family members. Many of these women may have a strong need to maintain a harmonious relationship with

> **Box 6.2. Generating New Skills through Collaborative Creation**
>
> - Define desired outcome.
> - Brainstorming:
>   - Specify criteria/conditions;
>   - Identify useful ideas and elements;
>   - Incrementalism.
> - Simulation and rehearsal.
> - Modification and refinement.
> - Real-life practice.

these family members, even when their demands are sometimes excessive. They need to develop and learn assertive responses which will not damage their relationships. The desired outcome in this particular case is to be able to say no in a nice way so that the relationship is not negatively affected.

2. Brainstorming

In a typical situation requiring collaborative creation, the client(s) and the practitioner do not have a handy strategy or skill for achieving the desired outcome. In order to generate that, a brainstorming or open evocation of input from the client (in individual consultation) or the members (in groups) is the usual next step. It is best for the brainstorming process to be as open as possible. When proposed strategies, no matter how wildly imagined, do not seem to work, asking clients or members to explain why they might not work will help to *define a set of criteria* of what may work. In the group for women with depression, for example, a member suggested that using the depressive condition as an excuse could be an effective way to say no. Another member countered that she would not want to reinforce a sick role for herself. Another member commented that not everyone would want family members to know about their depression. This input helped the group to define a criterion for success, which was not having to refer to or reinforce a sick role.

In most cases, clients will come up with suggestions for strategies that are partially effective or contain elements that may work. Back to the same example, a member suggested that getting her husband to talk to family members might remove her burden. This solution obviously does not work for people who do not have husbands. We can, however, pursue how the husband might say no to others, and see if that can be adopted to become part of what the women can say. The idea of getting help and support from a significant other can also be elaborated in other ways, such as getting a trusted person to help a client to rehearse assertive expressions or actions.

Extracting potentially useful ideas or elements from clients will contribute towards the generation of strategies and skills. This process of building from components also feeds well into an incremental learning procedure. When a number of strategies and skills finally emerge from collaborative creation, we will go through the same process of breaking them down into incremental steps to be learned, which has been discussed above.

3. Simulation and Rehearsal

Once the strategies and skills to be learned have been spelled out, clients can then go through the process of learning through in-session observation learning, simulation, role-plays, and rehearsal, which will be described in more detail in the next chapter. With collaborative creation, the outcome definition and brainstorming segments serve the purpose of instruction and provide a good cognitive template for the strategies and skills to be learned. As elements or components are suggested by the clients themselves, it is usually easier for them to participate in the in-session learning activities. Clients often feel empowered and excited that they have contributed to the creation of a solution for their own problems, which can also be used later by people experiencing similar difficulties.

4. Modification and Refinement

When the strategies and skills are simulated and rehearsed in-session, there is always an opportunity to make modifications and refinements. As real-life conditions and circumstances are represented in-session, clients will learn to deal with those specific contingencies, such as a family member responding negatively to an assertive statement made by a client. Getting members to work on the spot to deal with such contingencies and challenges is usually an energizing and interesting process. The positive side effects of this process are most valuable in strengthening client self-efficacy.

5. *Real-Life Practice*

The ultimate testing ground for the effectiveness of a newly learned strategy or skill is in real life. The spirit of innovation and experimentation prepares clients to take risks. Many clients who have had negative interpersonal or social experiences in the past are risk-avoidant and reluctant to try new things. They are usually more ready to try things that they have participated in developing than things they are simply instructed to do. In any case, we must always help clients to prepare for potential failure and frame the real-life practice as part of the experimentation and innovation process. In my many years of experience in getting clients to go out and experiment with new behaviour, I have almost never come across situations in which clients are harmed and severely set back in their learning. Adequate simulation and rehearsal as well as psychological immunization are key safety measures to take before asking clients to experiment with new strategies and skills.

Endnotes

Whereas the SSLD model emphasizes the learner's direct, hands-on learning and actual performance in real life, formulating and designing relevant strategies and skills is central to the practitioner's input. From my own experience in training practitioners, I have found that most practitioners can learn to follow a well-written manual with relative ease, especially when sufficient details have been given. More seasoned practitioners can sometimes learn to deliver a program skilfully just by reading and understanding the manual. This speaks to the advantage of preplanned or pre-packaged learning programs. From the practitioner's perspective, learning to do a good appraisal of the client's circumstances and needs, and then coming up with a well-formulated and well-designed learning program, is usually more challenging; many practitioners need to learn to do this through a process of repeated consultation, coaching, and apprenticeship. The current design of programs for training practitioners recognizes this learning process, and practitioners can go through stages or levels of training in an incremental manner. The basic level of training introduces the basic tenets and major components of SSLD, with the more advanced training focusing more on managing contingencies and on formulation and design.

Chapter Seven

The Learning Process

Multiple Domains of Learning

In an SSLD program, client learning can occur in different domains. Whereas the key focus is on action or behaviour, we recognize that clients often go through cognitive and emotional learning as well. Given the fact that almost all human behaviours are embodied acts, in that they are all mediated by the body, one can say that learning occurs in the biological domain as well. Motivational patterns can also change as a result of learning or behavioural change, and the process may involve cognitive input (e.g., recognizing that certain expectations are not realistic), physiological change (e.g., thirst being quenched, pain being inflicted or relieved), or even anatomical alteration (e.g., a transsexual individual after a sex change) or action affecting the body (e.g., intake of psychotropic substances, addiction, self-injury, exercise, physical training, etc.). As mentioned in Chapter 2, these domains are intricately connected to each other and are in constant interaction. Behaviour is chosen as a focus in SSLD because its aim is that concrete actions will lead to desired change in people's life-worlds, ultimately gratifying their needs and realizing their aspirations. It should be emphasized that learning, though focused on action and behaviour, can be directed at realizing personal goals involving changes in the other domains, as in cases where people wish to get rid of their feelings of guilt or depression, modify their poor self-image, overcome fear of intimacy or fear of driving, or find a purpose in life.

Learning to change one's actions or behaviour often requires multiple input and change sequences that involve the other domains. The process of engagement and relationship building between clients and practitioners, for example, involves a distinct emotional dimension. For effective learning to take place, positive expectancy, confidence and trust in the practitioner, motivation to change, and a generally positive emotional bond with the practitioner and the other members (in the case of groups) are all helpful conditions. This chapter will describe the learning process in SSLD with a focus on action, or strategies and skills – while the role of associated changes in the other domains will be described along the way.

Making Sense by Adopting the SSLD Framework

For the practitioner, it appears that actual learning and development of strategies and skills will only take place after problem translation and the formulation of the learning program. From the client's perspective, looking at one's problems through the lens of SSLD implies a learning process. With a skilful SSLD practitioner, the problem translation process will take place smoothly as the client presents her or his problems, concerns, and circumstances. Within the first couple of sessions, the client will begin to acquire a new way of making sense of her or his situation, which typically reveals the connection between the client's experience and the client's needs, wishes, and concerns. The client will come to view the problem situation differently, with newly discovered connections among needs, goals, and the strategies and skills required to address them. In other words, the client will learn a new way to make sense of her or his experience, circumstances, and action.

This learning can be seen as largely cognitive, but in practice, this reconstruction takes place within the context of a professional relationship. As mentioned above, the first couple of sessions with the practitioner are focused on engagement, which means that the client is learning to relate to a stranger and to play the role of a client while at the same time figuring out what the SSLD intervention is about. Understanding that the client is going through multiple learning tasks right from the beginning phase of the professional contact should draw our attention to the need for providing assistance and facilitation in the client's learning process. The practitioner may want to, for example, create an open and safe space for learning and exploration, reinforce active learning behaviours, provide helpful feedback, give clear and concise information regarding SSLD ideas and formulations, offer explanations and rationales for the actual procedure, and model positive interpersonal behaviour.

Adopting an SSLD framework is, therefore, not simply a cognitive learning task for the client. For instance, a man who has gotten into trouble with the law for abusing his wife may view his problem as an occasional loss of control over his anger. The initial exploration and the problem translation process may reveal other issues that might be difficult to process, such as a deep sense of insecurity or feelings of inferiority, isolation, shame, and embarrassment. An open, non-judgmental, and emotionally attuned stance on the part of the practitioner is essential in enabling the client to embrace a new way to look at his own needs and circumstances.

Learning and Developing New Strategies and Skills

After gaining a new understanding of their situation, clients can move on to learning and developing new strategies and skills. As mentioned in Chapter 3, the learning process first involves developing a cognitive representation of the skills to be mastered through observation learning or modelling, followed by experiential learning of skills in session and then practising the newly acquired skills in real life through the 4Rs process. This learning process will then be reviewed and evaluated, and further learning and follow-up activities can be added on when necessary.

Imagining the Strategies and Skills To Be Mastered

The problem translation process enables clients to form a new understanding of the issues they want to deal with. This new understanding can then be extended to include a cognitive representation of the pathways clients can pursue to address their needs and attain their desired goals in real life. In traditional social skills training, the focus is on specific skills to be learned. In SSLD, the pathways include the skills and their strategic combinations. In theory, people should have an overall strategic view of what needs to be mastered in order to realize their desired outcomes before starting their skills learning. In practice, there can be some flexibility. For instance, with clients who are not prepared for a comprehensive cognitive understanding of their overall situation due to compromised cognitive capacity or severe emotional challenges like grief or trauma, an incremental approach starting with small, manageable steps may be pursued first. The strategic overview can be established later.

When helping clients to imagine their overall strategic pathways, it is usually helpful to have them present their view to make sure that the client and practitioner have a shared understanding. Having clients write out the step-by-step learning plan often enhances self-direction, ownership, and self-efficacy. Some clients may work better with visual representations such as diagrams. In SSLD practice, the strategic plan can be reviewed and revised from time to time with client progress and changes in circumstances.

Once this has been done, the client will then be ready for learning and developing the necessary skills. This can be done through observation of a model or through symbolic mediation such as written instructions and guidelines, pictures, animation, and audio or video instructions. In social skills training, more emphasis is put on the demonstration of the required skills by the trainer. The learners are supposed to observe and then model the trainer's skilful performance. In SSLD, we emphasize active learning by the client, and attempt to minimize the power difference between the client and the practitioner. Whenever possible, we try not to emphasize the expert role and authority of the practitioner. One of the best ways to start the learning process is to have people observe their own video-recorded performance and identify aspects that they can improve upon. In group work, we can use suggestions, demonstrations, observations, and feedback from other members.

When it appears necessary or desirable to have some demonstration by the practitioner – such as when clients really need the input to help them imagine the possibility of change, or when there is a technical part that they do not understand – we will still try to get maximum client involvement in the process. For example, we can demonstrate a part of the skill to be acquired, and then stop to invite the client to give feedback and/or continue in our place. We can also demonstrate more than one version of the same skill to indicate that there is not a single perfect version to be learned by everyone. This also conveys the idea of contingency – what is a good performance is contingent upon a number of factors. Clients can then be asked to comment on the different versions to identify elements that are more helpful to them. They can also be encouraged to think of ways to modify or improve upon the demonstrated version so that it will work better in their own situation.

Learning by Doing

The best way to master a skill is to learn it experientially. The cognitive imagination that clients have formed has to be enacted, both in-session and in real life. The in-session learning process is most valuable for clients in terms of the opportunity to experiment and improvise, to obtain feedback, to learn from mistakes in a safe environment, and to be their own judge with regard to what is the most helpful way of doing something. As mentioned before, video recordings allow for detailed review and feedback, and they can be kept for future use. The most valuable learning opportunity they afford is for clients to be reviewers of their own performance, and they therefore reinforce self-directed learning. In my own practice, it is not uncommon for clients to discover aspects of their performance that surprise them, and to identify aspects and patterns that the practitioner does not pick up.

A key process in experiential learning is feedback. The most helpful feedback tends to be specific and concrete, providing information for clients to improve upon their current performance. Careful attention to details and micro-processes is usually necessary. For example, clients learning to indicate attention and interest to another person have to be able to differentiate between an attentive gaze and staring. When learning to facilitate verbal flow and disclosure, clients may need to learn to utilize "free information" volunteered by the other party. Helpful feedback may include indicating the various items of free information offered by the other party that clients did not pursue. In offering feedback, both practitioners and other clients (such as the other partner in couple counselling or members in an SSLD group) have to make sure that it is framed positively, usually in terms of what learners can do to improve their performance. Critical comments that only focus on the learner's weakness can be reframed to be positive feedback. For example, instead of saying, "You missed the free information when your partner mentioned her cousin, her trip to Mexico, and how she hated driving," we can say, "There are a few leads your partner has given you that you could have pursued, such as her cousin …" Instead of saying, "You completely missed the emotional content presented by your partner," we can ask clients to identify the emotional content and think of ways of communicating their empathic understanding of such content.

In SSLD practice, learning to frame and deliver positive feedback can itself be a skill to be learned. In couple counselling, for instance, giving positively framed feedback can be an important component of the counselling process in its own right. Couples can learn to systematically reframe criticisms, complaints, and accusatory remarks into positive feedback such as, "You may want to …" or, "If you do that, I will feel better." Sometimes, people are capable of making cynical comments using positively framed words just by altering their tone of voice. This is when attention to nonverbal micro-processes can be helpful. One of the exercises we can use in an SSLD program is to ask clients to say the same words in different tones, and let the receiver of feedback indicate which version is most helpful. Giving the receiver of feedback the option to comment on and choose among multiple articulations and presentations is often used in SSLD programs. Finally, it should be emphasized that we are not ruling out critical observations in the client's learning process. It is only that critical observations are to be repackaged into a form that will be conducive to client learning and self-efficacy.

Homework

Homework assignments are an important component of SSLD learning, and they help to bridge in-session learning and actual performance in real life. For the practitioner, homework assignments have to be understood in terms of their role in the client's learning. We should have a good idea of the purpose and intended effect of homework assignments, and of how they relate to the overall processes of change. In designing and assigning homework to clients, we again emphasize the significance of client participation. Homework is never imposed on clients in SSLD. Clients are supported in taking on the role of an active learner, and they have to appreciate the purpose and meaning of their homework assignments. We may also want to make the homework a fun thing to do whenever possible. Whereas many SSLD homework assignments are structured and standardized, such as the behavioural diary, we always encourage client input, such as identifying and labelling the target behaviour to be charted or colour-coding their emotional experience. In other instances, clients can plan their own assignments, such as designing a new pleasurable experience for themselves, challenging themselves to get into an unfamiliar social situation, or finding a new way to show appreciation to a family member.

The 4Rs

When clients are ready, they are encouraged to apply their learning in their real lives. The 4Rs of real-life practice, report back, review, and refinement are crucial steps in establishing the newly acquired strategies and skills in the lives of clients. In SSLD practice, the 4Rs have to be concrete and specific. For example, when clients say that they had a good conversation with their boss or partner or customer, we need to have specific behavioural indicators of what a "good" conversation means. Our understanding will be clearer when specific verbalization and/or behavioural outcomes (e.g., changing my work shifts, helping out with the dishes, purchasing my product) are reported. Learning to report real-life practice experiences and illustrating them with behavioural markers and/or factual indicators is also a communication skill that many clients need to learn.

Following a similar line of thought, review and refinement can only be done effectively when there is either detailed reporting or recording. When it is advisable and when privacy rights are duly respected, electronic recording of real-life performance will form the best basis for review and refinement. This is what we do in training psychotherapists. Another good example is when parents bring back a video recording of how they engage their child in reading. Such recordings enable specific and concrete feedback that would otherwise be impossible.

Incrementalism

Incrementalism is a key principle in SSLD practice. When clients are trying to acquire and master new ways of thinking about their problems and issues, and the new strategies and skills to deal with them, they may sometimes feel challenged or even overwhelmed by these tasks. Practitioners who are eager to help their clients to make progress often wish to complete these tasks efficiently. The most efficient pathway sometimes involves breaking the task at hand into smaller components that are more manageable from the client's perspective. A task that is perceived as beyond one's capacity can be intimidating, and may cause client anxiety or resistance. Incrementalism can be applied both in in-session learning and in homework assignments. Whenever clients indicate that a task may be too difficult or challenging, we have to work with them to come up with a modified task that they think they can manage. It should be noted that this does not mean that clients never take up challenging tasks. It only means that the challenge and risk they take is calculated. After all, SSLD is about expanding client options and repertoires of strategies and skills. When clients see how an apparently daunting task can be broken down into smaller, more manageable steps, not only do they find it easier to perform but they can also be learning incrementalism as a way of strategic thinking that can be valuable in the long run. Learning to reconstruct an extremely challenging or impossible task into a set of steps that one can start taking in the direction of attaining one's goal is an extremely useful cognitive skill in its own right.

Notes on Setting Up

In Chapter 3, we emphasized the advantage of setting up the learning situation as similar to the real-life situation as possible. Clients should play an active role in this process. They should be able to participate in designing and directing simulation or role-play exercises, and in indicating the significant aspects of the actual practice situation. Clients can often offer the best input with regard to the physical set-up, the implicit social or cultural rules, the people present and their personal characteristics, and so on. Active client participation and enhanced self-direction are likely to bring about positive expectancy.

Simulation of real-life situations works particularly well in group-work contexts when we have established a trusting environment. When group members show enthusiasm in the simulation and role-play exercise, the person who is using the simulation to learn usually feels valued and supported. The person can also experience mastery and control in scripting the simulation, choosing members for the role-play, and assigning roles. Group members participating in the simulation can offer valuable feedback on the interpersonal effect of the learner's performance. SSLD practitioners usually need to have a good sense of how an experiential learning or simulation procedure will play out when setting it up collaboratively with clients, especially with regard to the anticipated outcome and the change processes that may take place.

Another issue related to setting up is how new strategies and skills are introduced by the practitioner, or how they are to be generated through collaborative creation. Ideally, SSLD practitioners should be able to move smoothly between these procedures. When clients are ready to acquire the strategies and skills they need, they should have a sense that not all the answers need to come from the practitioner. They can feel free to make suggestions and comments and to participate actively and freely when collaborative creation is needed. As mentioned earlier, SSLD encourages client agency and autonomy, and the intervention process is set up to facilitate this. Whereas practitioners have different personalities and styles, the general recommendation is that we do not emphasize practitioner power and authority. We therefore try to refrain from dictating the set-up and the process, and we provide structure and give directions with due consideration of the learning needs and styles of our clients.

Follow-Up and Maintaining Positive Outcome

Based on the social cognitive conceptualization of learning, the SSLD model aims at developing strategies and skills that are intrinsically reinforcing and therefore do not need external reinforcement to be maintained. In theory, the newly learned and developed strategies and skills, to the extent that they are effective in bringing about the desired changes in the learner's life, will be maintained and strengthened automatically. In actual practice, people will sometimes run into more complicated or challenging situations, and may overlook or forget some of the principles they think they have mastered during the program, thus follow-up or booster sessions can be very helpful. Whereas there is no fixed and fast rule regarding the number and frequency of booster sessions needed, three months and six months are intervals that most people feel comfortable with. Sometimes a request for consultation can come even years after the initial program – however, this is usually not the result of a loss of previous learning, but rather the emergence of new challenges in the person's life. In these cases, the previous successful experience and the resulting positive expectancy are usually helpful in the new phase of learning.

Termination

The ultimate goal of SSLD intervention is client independence and autonomy. When clients have mastered the necessary strategies and skills and are therefore capable of living a more gratifying life, they are ready to leave their SSLD practitioner. Termination is usually a smooth process, with clients feeling positive and appreciative and practitioners experiencing satisfaction. In a way, we are constantly preparing for termination in SSLD practice. We may be an important support for the clients in the beginning phase of our intervention, and we may even play a key role in helping them find direction and meaning in their lives, but clients have to become increasingly independent of us. For instance, we are careful not to remain a major source of support for our clients. We must assist them to develop the support they need in their own lives. Given the heavy emphasis on needs in SSLD practice, we want to ensure that we do not use our professional work with our clients to address unmet personal needs in our own lives. The structure and design of SSLD practice facilitate a clear understanding of goals and how they are to be accomplished within the context of a professional relationship, which is shared by both the client and the practitioner. As clients and practitioners make progress together, clients are increasingly empowered with an enhanced sense of self-efficacy. Reluctance to leave the SSLD program and/or the practitioner is rare. When it happens, a review of the progress should be performed to identify unmet or unaddressed needs, both of the practitioner and of the client. These needs should then be addressed through a program with an explicit emphasis on movement towards client independence and autonomy.

Summary

A contingency-based understanding of learning pays attention to the particular circumstances and needs of the individual. It also pays attention to the interconnection and interaction among the various domains of human experience: biological, motivational, emotional, cognitive, behavioural, and environmental. It follows the principles of goal-directed learning and incrementalism, as well as the clear target of actual performance in real life. These principles of learning, apart from being very useful in SSLD programs, can actually be applied in other learning contexts.

PART THREE

Building Blocks

In this section, we will introduce basic building blocks for SSLD practice, covering (1) receptive skills such as attentive listening, recognizing emotional content, attitudes and positions, and sensitivity to underlying needs; (2) expressive skills involving articulation, presentation, and/or disclosure of factual data, opinions, needs, and goals, as well as emotional content; (3) interactive skills like engagement and intimacy building, which involve processes such as building common ground, maintaining an open and safe narrative space, communicating positive emotions, expanding mutual understanding, and creating a shared private space; and (4) instrumental skills that usually target a particular functional task or accomplishment, such as selling something to a customer, borrowing money from a banker, or getting someone from another department to agree with your proposed work plan. Such task-oriented instrumental strategies often involve complex skills, such as getting the other person to see things from your perspective, making your proposition look attractive, invoking a sense of obligation, or negotiating common ground.

As shown in Table P3.1, each of the sets can involve a wide spectrum of strategies, skills, and corresponding micro-processes. No one can actually give an exhaustive list of all the possible strategies and skills, and there are often unusual circumstances that call for creativity and innovation. The table gives an example of a template that supports a better conceptualization and organization of skills components that we might want to include in the learning plan. Again, we emphasize that we do not believe that everyone should learn the same sets of skills; rather, they should learn the skills that are called for in their given circumstances.

Table P3.1. Basic Components of Strategies and Skills

Skills Set	Examples of Skills and Micro-processes
Reception	Listening and Observing • Factual content • Attitude, opinion, position • Emotional content • Needs, wishes
Expression	Articulation, Presentation, and Disclosure • Factual information • Opinion • Emotion • Needs, wishes, intention
Relationship	Engagement • Building common ground (agreement, sharing, inclusive language) • Maintaining an open and safe narrative space (meshing, not interrupting, not changing topics, recognition, nonjudgmental and nonviolent responses) • Positive emotion (empathic understanding, acknowledgment, appreciation, support)
Relationship Management	Relationship building • Relationship building • Improvement and enhancement • Transformation • Termination
Instrumental	Focusing on performance • Not getting personal • Research, knowledge, and power • Staying goal-oriented • Instrumental tasks in a complex project • Developing a game plan • Preparing for action: learning the specific skills

A case involving an inter-cultural, same-sex couple will be used to illustrate how SSLD might work. One partner was of South Asian heritage and the other partner was Anglo-Saxon. The South Asian partner, Arun, believed that he was not understood and valued by his partner, Mike. He felt that Mike, who comes from the mainstream culture, always took for granted that whenever there were differences between them, it was Arun who needed to make the adjustment. Mike believed that he was respectful of Arun and his culture, that he has done his best to accommodate Arun's needs, and that Arun was oversensitive and had a propensity to attribute differences to racism. In an in-session review of communication patterns, Arun and Mike were invited to look at a videotaped conversation of theirs. They used the video to attend to micro-processes such as the share of airtime, who changed the topic and how, the frequency of interruption, and who interrupted his partner more. The partners found that they used different strategies to control or manage their conversations, most of them resulting in restricting the narrative space for sharing and building mutuality. More specifically, Arun tended to change topics when he did not feel comfortable, and showed more periods of silence, while Mike took up more air time. Mike tended to use expressions like "you did" or "you said," whereas Arun more often used "we." Such micro-process analysis allowed the couple to modify specific behaviours in their interaction by learning new patterns, and it did not require debate over inferred concepts such as racism or oversensitivity, which are not particularly helpful in facilitating behavioural change.

Given the high proportion of clients who need to improve their communication and interpersonal effectiveness, we are devoting more space to how this area of human experience and activity can be improved through SSLD. This section highlights the contingent nature of SSLD and is not an attempt to propose a prescriptive syllabus for all clients. It is probably more appropriate to regard the scheme to be introduced below as a road map. Each client may have a different destination and may desire a different path. The map shows the major coordinates and landmarks so as to facilitate route planning by clients and practitioners.

As indicated above, the basic strategies and skills can be conceptualized into four major components: receptive, expressive, interactive, and instrumental. They are obviously not completely discrete and mutually exclusive. In real life, they are often closely connected with each other, and there are also skills that can achieve more than one of the four functions. Self-disclosure of personal experience, for example, is expressive in nature, but if appropriately timed and articulated, it can be a powerful sign of good receptive skill. For example, if someone shares an experience of humiliation and her or his partner in the interaction self-discloses a similar experience of humiliation, it evidences attentive listening and good understanding of both factual information and emotional significance. It is also conducive to the development of common ground and mutuality. Again, depending on the purpose of engagement, good communicative and relationship-building strategies may be directed towards intrinsic goals, such as developing intimacy or trust. Alternatively, such strategies and skills can be employed for an instrumental purpose, such as managing a crisis or conflict situation, getting a job, or selling a product. The four components are therefore offered to facilitate the conceptualization and formulation of intervention plans, which will involve different combinations of them.

Chapter Eight

Reception

The most important first step in communication and social interaction is reception. The ability to "get" what the other party is trying to communicate is very basic, but counsellors or therapists are often surprised by how often clients do not listen, or do not get or understand even very clear and straightforward messages in their everyday lives. The ability to receive and accurately interpret interpersonal and social messages is a function of general intelligence, but emotional and interpersonal sensitivity, or what many people have come to call emotional intelligence (Goleman, 1995), can be equally or even more important. Such emotional and interpersonal sensitivity can be improved through systematic learning.

Listening and observation skills can be learned efficiently through simulation role-play and video review. The typical procedure involves the learner having a brief conversation with a collaborator and then reporting on what she or he has heard. The collaborator can sometimes be a person in the learner's real life. In couple counselling, for instance, the couple can be role-playing with each other. The learner will have the opportunity to receive feedback from the collaborator and the trainer. Video playback is very effective in helping the learner to attend to what has been missed. The content can be separated into factual, attitudinal, emotional, and motivational dimensions. Factual content is usually easier to learn, and some people may not need to spend a lot of time learning it. Attention to emotional content and inferring needs and personal goals are more challenging by comparison. People with specific mental health issues, such as Asperger's syndrome or schizophrenic disorder, may need more intensive coaching in these areas.

Factual Content

Factual content includes objective data like statistics, weather forecasts, or historical information. It also includes information regarding objects, like the location of the supermarket or the colour of the paint on the walls of the bedroom. Whereas it is recognized that such information can very often carry emotional and interpersonal significance, like the yellow roses that a person got on her or his first date, we selectively focus on the factual aspect in the early phase of learning. Apart from physical objects, information about people is another important part of factual content. In interpersonal communication, the speaker's characterization of other people tells the listener a lot about the speaker himself or herself. For example, when a man describes his friends, he always refers to the cars they drive, which university they went to, or how much money they make. This gives the listener an idea of this man's perspective regarding friends. The third aspect of factual content is events, such as a grandmother's birthday, a car accident, a fight with one's spouse, or life in a refugee camp. Again, the report of events usually carries personal meaning and significance, and it is often emotionally charged. The selective attention on factual content is an incremental step towards better interpersonal communication. In designing the role-play and review, we can break down the learning process into smaller steps, starting with objective information, then information regarding people, and then information about events. Depending on the sophistication level and learning capacity of the client, we may sometimes ask clients to attend to more than one of these factual aspects simultaneously, or even all aspects together.

Attitude, Opinion, Positions, Assumptions

When clients have mastered basic competence in listening to factual content, or when they come to us with that ability, we can then focus on the other aspects. Speakers often express attitudes, opinions, positions, and assumptions in their utterances, sometimes explicitly, sometimes implicitly. These attitudes can be harmless personal preferences, such as, "I prefer dry wines to fruity ones," but they can also be prejudiced, such as, "Our economy would be much better if we stopped allowing all those immigrants to come to this country." This statement implies that immigrants are a negative economic force and do not contribute to economic growth. Sensitivity to such attitudes, even when they are not

Table 8.1. Selective Statement of Facts

Social Situation	Selective Statement of Facts
A friend emphasizing the benefits of organically grown and non-genetically modified food.	1. Less than 20 per cent of residents in this city can afford that. 2. A friend of mine had breast cancer, and she got better just by eating organic and non-genetically modified food, attending alternative therapy, and drinking a lot of water.
Upon hearing the news of a friend's child dropping out of university.	1. Young people without a degree are much more likely to be unemployed. 2. Bill Gates did not finish his undergrad.
A colleague just bought a new house.	1. That neighbourhood has a huge problem with drugs in its high schools. 2. A news magazine reported the highest property appreciation rate for that area.

explicitly stated, can be very helpful in interpersonal communication. In everyday life, people make statements based on many assumptions. Very often these assumptions are unquestioned; they pass as natural and are therefore not noticed. Being able to recognize underlying assumptions in other people's utterances can enhance our capacity to understand their values and attitudes, and inform our communicative and interactive strategies with them. Applying the same process reflexively to oneself is extremely valuable in developing better self-understanding. This ability can be learned and developed by a systematic process of deciphering the attitudes, opinions, values, or assumptions contained in people's utterances.

Expression of attitudes can be direct and explicit, like in the case of someone saying that she does not support the invasion of Iraq by the U.S.; this is probably the easiest type of expression to pick up. Sometimes people make a comment or statement of facts that also conveys an attitude. For instance, upon hearing the news of a friend getting married, a man says, "Well, fifty per cent of marriages end up in divorce." He is reporting a statistical fact, but he may also be expressing a negative opinion regarding this particular marriage. The selective statement of facts in relation to a social situation is a common way for people to express their opinions and attitudes. Table 8.1 gives some examples of different factual statements that can be made to convey different attitudes in the same social situation. Statements of facts in relation to a social situation are usually selective; paying attention to what factual statements are selectively made is a useful step in learning to identify attitudes.

Attitudes and opinions can also be expressed by the social position one assumes. For example, when the government decides to increase minimum wage, someone who says, "Isn't running a business difficult enough in this country?" is speaking from the position of an employer, even when she or he may not necessarily be running a business. In contrast, when someone says, "This can hardly catch up with the increase in cost of living," the speaker is taking the position of a minimum-wage earner. Taking a position, or identifying with particular individuals or groups, is widely used by people to express attitudes and opinions in everyday life.

Another way to read other people's attitudes and opinions is to pay attention to their attribution frame, or the perspective from which they offer explanations and make sense of social reality. For instance, if someone tells her friends that her aging aunt is not happy with her life, one of her friends may say, "Her life would be much better if she were married," while another friend may say, "Life is more difficult for women than for men." Both individuals, through offering their explanation for the aunt's unhappiness, bring in very different perspectives on the life of women and its relationship with social reality. One of them believes that marriage is essential to a woman's happiness or well-being, whereas the other believes that gender difference puts women in a disadvantageous position. The different attribution frames employed by individuals are often related to their internalized values or ideologies. In the example above, the first comment may be related to a pro-marriage and pro-family ideology, whereas the second comment is more likely to be associated with a feminist gender-analysis perspective.

In everyday social situations, simple statements or comments can often contain multiple assumptions and attitudes. Some individuals are able to identify these assumptions readily, while others may take some time to learn to do so. For example, once I heard a graduate student say, "I'll stop working when I have a baby, I could not stand another woman taking care of my child." This student was making many assumptions: (1) the mother or a woman (not the father or a man) will take care of the baby; (2) taking care of the baby will have priority over work and career; (3) she will be able to afford to stop working when she has a baby; and (4) she will be a better caregiver for her baby than any other woman.

The ability to identify and decipher attitudes and opinions can be learned through systematic exposure to social situations and a variety of statements coming from different perspectives and positions. This learning can be facilitated by simulated or role-played conversation as mentioned above. During the simulation of specific social situations, the learner can be asked to recognize attitudes, opinions, and assumptions contained in specific utterances. Electronic recording and playback, together with feedback from the collaborator and the practitioner, can usually help to improve the learner's ability to recognize attitudes and assumptions.

The Listening Triad Exercise (Pfeiffer & Jones, 1974) is a procedure often used in interpersonal relationship training programs to help people learn to listen to the views of others and respond effectively in everyday conversations, especially in the case of argument or a difference in opinion. The exercise is usually done in a group context, where members break into smaller groups of three. Two of the members will engage in a conversation involving an argument or difference in opinion. For example, they can take different views on abortion and start a debate. The third member will serve as the umpire to enforce the rules of the exercise. The rules are quite simple: one member can start the conversation or argument, and it does not matter who starts first, but if agreement is not readily reached, coin-flipping or drawing lots should easily resolve the situation. To begin the exercise, the first speaker will present her or his view. Then the other person can respond. The only thing is that before the second person can present her or his views, she or he has to first repeat all the points made by the first speaker to the satisfaction of both the first speaker and the umpire. After the second speaker has accurately repeated the first speaker's points and then presented her or his own points, the first speaker can respond. Again, the first speaker has to repeat all the points made by the second speaker before he or she can add new points. The umpire will ensure that each speaker's arguments are both listened to and repeated before new arguments can be made. This exercise, through ensuring careful and accurate listening to other people's attitudes, opinions, positions, and assumptions, is a very effective procedure for resolving differences and enhancing mutual understanding. I have used it extensively in couple counselling with very good results.

Emotional Content

Most human utterances and action have an emotional dimension. In interpersonal and social interactions, emotional messages are very important, and in some situations they can be more important than the factual content. Recognizing and deciphering emotional messages are relatively easy tasks when the messages are expressed explicitly. In a society where free and spontaneous emotional expression is often discouraged and heavily regulated, however, emotional messages are frequently expressed in subtle ways that are not easily picked up by other people. Emotions like anger, resentment, or jealousy are usually considered socially undesirable, and individuals tend to be more cautious in expressing them. Feelings like sexual or erotic desires are so heavily regulated and conditioned that their expression is often regarded as inappropriate, thus their open and explicit communication is not always easy. Added to this is the fact that the socialization that many people receive does not prepare them to articulate or express their emotions effectively. Later in this book (Chapter 9), we will explore how effective expression of emotions can be learned. In this section, we will focus on emotional reception.

Emotional messages can be expressed in at least four modes. The first is direct verbal expression of labelled emotions, such as someone saying, "I'm mad," "I'm very depressed," or "I'm disappointed." The other mode is also verbal, but in this mode the emotional content has to be deduced or inferred. For example, when someone says, "I never imagined that he would do that to me," the person may be expressing shock, disappointment, or both. The third mode of emotional communication is nonverbal, such as facial expressions, gestures, posture, and tone of voice. These nonverbal expressions are very powerful – sometimes they can be more powerful than the verbal content (Argyle, 1983, 1988; Knapp & Hall, 2007). The fourth mode is what I will call signifying acts.

Signifying acts are a special class of human action that should be mentioned here. As the name implies, these acts are performed by people to signify specific feelings, attitudes, and/or other meanings. Slamming the door during a fight between a couple is a good example, as is sending flowers on someone's special day. There are, however, more subtle performances. In my own culture, for example, a typical family dinner is a social space saturated by numerous signifying acts. Chinese people usually sit around a table with dishes to share. The table setting and seating arrangement are obviously signifying acts in such communal dining. During dinner, it is not unusual for family members to use their chopsticks to pick up food for each other; what they pick up, for whom, and in what order is a complex dance reflecting intra-familial dynamics. For instance, in Northern China, the belly is the most valued part of a fish; a parent may thus pick up that part and give it to the favoured child. Alternatively, the belly can also be the part reserved for the grandparents, the mother, or the father. Each pattern tells a different story about the family. If you are from the southern parts of China, however, the meaning of the belly of the fish is reversed. The same thing can happen when a chicken is served. The way that different parts of the bird are picked up and given to other members of the family can be equally revealing, and the rules regarding which part of the bird is most prized also vary. Being socially competent in a culturally appropriate manner requires effective management of multiple contingencies. Western psychologists and researchers often think that Chinese people are not emotionally expressive (Hsu, 1971; Kleinman, 1982, 1986; Potter, 1988), as they take verbalization as the primary mode of expression. There is actually a complex set of cultural rules governing emotional expression through signifying acts.

An entire book could be written on this subject alone, but I will give one more example here to illustrate the point. In 1984, Chinese director Chen Kaige completed the movie *Yellow Earth*. It was a movie with very few lines, but the emotional content was extremely heavy. The protagonist was a girl living in rural China. She was illiterate and due to economic necessity was forced to marry someone she did not like. She fell in love instead with a young Communist cultural worker who was visiting her village, yet she knew there was no prospect for that relationship. She thus planned to take her life after the wedding. Before her wedding day, she walked twenty kilometres to the Yellow River to bring back two buckets of water for her father – water was a precious commodity as they were living in the mountains. She also spent time weaving a pair of sandals out of dried grass and grinding wheat to make bread for the man she loved. All these tasks were done with very few words spoken, but the emotional intensity was profound.

In the learning and development of interpersonal skills, the ability to pay attention to signifying acts in everyday life and to read their meanings accurately is extremely valuable. This is especially true in intimate and significant relationships. In couple counselling work, I often help clients to develop this sensitivity through paying attention to their partners' small acts (as well as their variation), such as the clothes and accessories they wear, the dishes they prepare, the things they bring home, or the items they rearrange or move around the house. Clients will also learn to appreciate the little things their partners do with or for their parents, friends, business associates, and the like. Among family members, there are routines that often become invisible and unappreciated. We can think of the countless trips parents take when driving their children to various activities, the copious loads of laundry done over the years, and the many meals prepared. In the musical *Fiddler on the Roof*, the question "What is love?" is answered by reference to these apparently humdrum, repetitive acts.

Needs, Wishes, and Goals

Apart from an accurate reading of expressed emotions and meanings, the most critical task in interpersonal and social interaction is to appreciate the motivation behind other people's utterances and actions. The way to infer needs in the context of professional SSLD practice has been covered in the chapter on problem translation. This section describes the inference process for clients or learners. In everyday life, people do try to make sense of other people's behaviour with reference to motivation. Very often, attention is paid to people's motives or "agenda," and negative connotations are sometimes ascribed to them. People may guard against other people's attempts to take advantage of them, and may try to make sure they are not "losing out" in the interaction. Within the SSLD approach, however, we take a slightly different position. Assuming that human actions are always motivated, we believe that an adequate understanding of a person's action includes an appreciation of its underlying needs. As discussed before, behaviours judged to be socially problematic are simply ineffective attempts to address basic, legitimate human needs. In SSLD, therefore, we suspend value judgment and try to understand the human needs that are functionally related to the client's manifest behaviour. In a way, we adopt a humanistic orientation, assuming that as human beings we all have similar kinds of needs, although the emphasis or priority given to different needs and their specific manifestations can vary from person to person and from situation to situation.

The process of inferring needs, wishes, and goals can therefore be seen as a pathway to the core of our being – the forces that get us going as human beings and the striving that fills and marks our lives. In

> **Box 8.1. What Does a Person Want?**
>
> - What is the person trying to achieve?
> - What do you think will make the person feel better?
> - What does the person feel unhappy or complain about?
> - What do the person's fears or concerns tell us?
> - What is the person trying to avoid?

social and interpersonal relations, an accurate reading of other people's needs and motives is helpful in guiding the process of interaction. In the learning of receptive skills, the client is usually exposed to other people's expressions and/or statements through in-session role-play or electronically recorded samples (see Box 8.1). As in the development of the reception of facts, attitudes, and emotions, the learner will come to recognize needs and motives through repeated trials and by receiving feedback.

As this process of inferring needs and concerns requires us to move from the concrete observables to the abstract, a few questions can serve as useful catalysts when helping clients learn how to infer needs. One of these questions is: what is the person trying to achieve? For example, a person who is always going out of his way to respond to the requests or demands of others might be motivated by a strong affiliation need in that he wants other people to like him and stay connected to him as friends, or he could be doing this to confirm a self-image of being nice and helpful – or both. Another question we can ask is: what will make this person feel better? For example, a woman complains that she often gets stood up by her dates and sometimes by her friends. What will make her feel better is if people take her seriously and actually show up at the appointed time. In other words, she needs to feel valued and respected by other people.

Sometimes a person's needs can be inferred from negative statements such as complaints. An older person complaining that it is awful that she has been trapped inside the house in an especially snowy week of the winter wants to be able to go out and have some activity. A younger person saying that he is neglected by his family is expressing a need for attention and care. Similarly, a person's fears and concerns can be very informative. A working woman who is afraid of losing her job may need job security and the independence and autonomy it affords.

A teenaged boy who is concerned about whether his newly acquired outfit looks cool may be expressing a need for approval by his peers. Following the same reasoning, what a person is trying to avoid can also communicate the person's needs. The connection between avoidance and what is needed is sometimes explicit; for example, someone in a financially tight situation may avoid unnecessary expenditure to ensure that there will be enough money for high-priority items. The connection, however, can also be less explicit or even appear to be paradoxical. A common example is found in the way people manage their interpersonal relationships. When we see someone repeatedly avoiding intimate relationships, we do not automatically infer that the person does not need intimacy and is seeking solitude. Instead, it is quite possible that what the person is avoiding is potential rejection and the emotional damage it entails. If this reading is correct, then the person needs to learn to negotiate relationships, while at the same time learning strategies and skills that can lead to improved self-efficacy.

Chapter Nine

Expression

Communication involves both reception and expression. Expression includes the presentation of self and the expression of ideas and feelings. It is considered effective when it achieves the desired goals within a given social context. The purpose of specific social or interpersonal engagement, therefore, should guide the mode of self-expression.

Self-Expression Is Purposeful

Being purposeful and goal-directed in self-expression seems a very simple and logical position to take, but a careful analysis of actual social behaviour reveals how this domain of human life has been heavily conditioned by extremely powerful social, cultural, and economic forces. In some parts of the world, there are salient political and religious regulations on how people dress, talk, and behave, and what aspects of their self can be expressed. The expression of the sexual aspects of oneself, for example, is heavily regulated in most social contexts. Self-expression and the presentation of self in social contexts is, therefore, an area attended by significant economic and political interest. The fashion and cosmetic industries, for instance, are grounded on many people's desire to present a certain image of themselves, and their belief in the efficacy of the products they consume and utilize. Political regimes and religious organizations, on the other hand, wish to maintain stability and order by putting limits on the way people actually express themselves. We are, therefore, touching on an exciting area where multiple disciplines including psychology, sociology, political science, economics, cultural studies, anthropology, and many others have to be integrated to offer an adequate understanding. Without trying to pretend that a simple intellectual synopsis can be presented within the limited space of this section, our discussion will start with the disclaimer that we are only taking a pragmatic focus on how individual action, through learning new strategies and skills, can help us achieve our personal and social goals more effectively.

Is Purchasing a Product All That We Need?

Many people wish to present themselves positively for various purposes. Some people are trying to look good in order to sell things, be they products or ideas. Some people wish to gain a good impression that can increase their chances of being hired, or being loved. Some people desire to look attractive; this can be central to their sense of identity. The amount of money and time people invest into managing how they look is phenomenal. The fashion industry, as reported in the *New York Times* (Horyn, 2007), is a $300-billion business consisting of public companies and private fashion houses. According to the January 2008 report by Datamonitor on European, Asian, and American consumers, approximately 20 to 30 per cent of women have considered plastic surgery, albeit those who actually pursued it only amounted to about 3 per cent. However, 73 per cent of women who completed the survey indicated body shape as their "major concern" – and, meanwhile, men are also taking more time to look after their physical appearance (Datamonitor, 2008). Most women desire to be slimmer across their lifespan (Field et al., 1999; Hurd Clarke, 2002), including those who are not overweight (Allaz, Bernstein, Rouget, Archinard, & Morabia, 1998; Cash & Henry, 1995). Women are also more likely than their male counterparts to adopt drastic weight-loss measures (e.g., laxatives and surgery) in addition to dieting to shed the extra pounds (Berg, 1995; Grogan, 1999). The related industries have been very successful in selling the idea that their products will deliver what people want, and can be effective in helping them to achieve their personal and social goals. This process includes advertising, which is ubiquitous in the cultural world. Movies and TV shows reinforce the value of products ranging from cars to shoes. Skincare products, health supplements, facial treatments, Botox, and plastic surgery are in huge and growing demand. Only a much smaller number of people are interested in finding out whether these products actually bring the good relationships, career advancements, or emotional happiness that consumers are hoping to attain. Consumers' brains are conditioned to work actively in the selection of one brand over another, to keep up with which Hollywood celebrity is wearing what at the Oscars, or even researching into the percentage of a particular ingredient in a cosmetic product – but not to ask the question of the statistical connection between the use of particular products and the attainment of personal goals that these products are supposed to help deliver. Research in psychology and other social science disciplines with regard to happiness, interpersonal attraction, gratifying intimate relationships, good sex, career success, and the like – despite its regular appearance in TV shows and columns of popular magazines – is often given relatively little attention and not taken too seriously by the consuming public.

SSLD: A Pragmatic Approach

A pragmatic approach to self-presentation and expression recognizes such social realities, including the powers of the market. Professional counsellors, therapists, consultants, and trainers helping their clients to attain more effective self-presentation and better relationships can take the consumption of fashion, cosmetics, plastic surgery, and related products as part of their clients' repertoire of strategies to achieve what they want in life, and can assess the effectiveness of such strategies accordingly. From an SSLD perspective, systematic learning of effective strategies and skills always takes place within a social context. We do not need to dispute our clients' faith in such products if it is already deeply entrenched in their belief system. Some of our clients may actually need to hold on to this belief in order to avoid feeling totally helpless. We also need to acknowledge that these products sometimes do help a little. Our focus is on the bigger picture of helping people develop a more effective overall strategy, which may include the methodical purchase and utilization of some of these products.

As mentioned above, individuals are driven by different motivations when they are expressing or presenting themselves socially. In SSLD, we focus on the particular needs and circumstances of individual clients. Over the last three decades, I have worked with people who are running for public office, executives who want to be more effective managers, front-desk receptionists, couples experiencing relationship issues, and individuals suffering from social phobias. These people obviously have very different needs and circumstances, but they all need to learn to express and present themselves effectively. In this section, we will explore procedures for learning and developing these relevant strategies and skills.

Self-Presentation

People are usually motivated to present themselves positively in particular ways. Even people who do not think they spend much time and energy on it usually care about other people's views and reactions. Trying to look casual or trying to project an I-don't-care attitude can both be considered modes of self-presentation with particular desired effects. What happens is that many people do not have an accurate understanding or assessment of their interpersonal or social contexts, nor do they often have a clear sense of the goals they wish to accomplish in them. People who wish to become physically attractive, for instance, sometimes assume that those attracted to good-looking people are also going to be caring and loving partners for life. The individuals who put on an off-putting presentation may secretly desire attention and appreciation – and when they do not get that, their disappointment and resentment will feed into further staging of negativistic presentations.

With SSLD, we can help people to manage the way they present themselves and therefore help them to achieve their personal and social goals. Depending on various contingent combinations of personality, culture, social circumstances, and specific goals, self-presentation takes on a variety of forms. Goffman's (1959) classic on the presentation of self in everyday life provides a good metaphor taken from drama, making enhanced use of concepts such as performance, front, persona, identity, role, and script. His work also gives a good introduction to the complex process of symbolic interaction. Goffman rightly focused on the "desired goal of the actor" (p. 17), and even talked about "impression management" (p. 208), but he did not get into the specific details of how people, including the marginalized and stigmatized groups he seemed to care about, can actually develop strategies and skills to empower themselves and effectively achieve their desired goals. Building on insights from both sociology and social psychology, SSLD procedures start with a good assessment and understanding of people's needs and goals, as well as the particular circumstances under which their goals are to be realized.

In a recent SSLD group for individuals with various forms of difficulty in their interpersonal and social lives, there was a young person who had a very troubled relationship with his parents and a strong desire to develop a gratifying heterosexual relationship. In the same group, there was a new immigrant to Canada whose major goal was to become socially competent so that he could start a career in retail marketing. There was also a woman who was trying to reintegrate into the social world, including her husband's social circle, after a long period of illness and relative social isolation. These individuals had very different personalities, subscribed to different cultural orientations, and preferred different styles of interpersonal interaction, but they all went through similar learning procedures in terms of their self-presentation.

Physical Appearance

An obvious first step in self-presentation is physical appearance. Whereas there are already a few humongous industries devoted to this purpose, many of us are better at shopping for skincare products or items of clothing than assessing how effectively our appearance is managing to achieve the goals we desire. More than a few people erroneously believe that there is a linear relationship between the price of an item and its actual interpersonal or social impact. In a way, we spend inordinate amounts of energy and time on purchases and activities that may or may not be helpful, and we often neglect the possibility of a more effective strategy through systematic learning.

In various SSLD group settings, including the one mentioned above, I have asked members to do a simple exercise that surprisingly few people actually tried, despite its simplicity and *prima facie* relevance. The exercise was the simple act of obtaining honest feedback from other people. In a training program for front-desk receptionists, for example, I asked each of the participants to come up to the centre of the group and receive feedback on their physical appearance. Members of the group had been instructed to avoid negative comments such as "that sweater is too dull" or "I would not use the same mascara, ever"; instead, they were to provide feedback in a positively framed manner, such as "it would look better if you had a lighter-coloured one" or "I think a hint of purple could be more flattering."

In a fun-filled hour, my group of receptionists learned things that they truly needed, and learned to value the feedback in the process. I often let participants work in small groups to develop strategies for improving their self-presentation, and in these groups they can play with even the most minute details, such as how much teeth one should be showing when one smiles. Video recordings, and sometime mirrors, can also come in handy. Part of the secret is that people do not often have the privilege of a group of observers who can be trusted, a learning environment that is safe, a set-up that allows them to be open and take some risks, and the time to really focus on minute details of their appearance. In such exercises, what participants often found was that their physical appearance was not an isolated feature of their presentation of self. More often than not, participants noticed that their posture, facial expressions, and the simple way that they greeted people could often make a bigger difference than the make-up and the clothes they wore.

Positive Self-Statement

Once the review of physical appearance is complete, the process usually moves on to the next step of what we call self-statements, which include what we tell ourselves internally as well as what we tell others. Internal self-statements have been found by cognitive therapists (e.g., Beck, 1967, 1976; Capuzzi & Gross, 1995; Ellis, 1987; Meichenbaum, 1986) to be of critical importance for one's mental health and social functioning. Repeating positive self-statements internally can enhance our social and interpersonal performance. It also has the side effect of distracting us from social anxiety and repetitive cycles of worrying. Positive reframing is a helpful composite skill to be learned in this case. In the example of a young woman who believes that no one will be attracted to her, and that no one will ever discover the good qualities that she has, we try to help her articulate the good qualities that she wishes other people would discover. This may include "passive" qualities such as loyalty, or being a good listener, but we can turn them into more proactive qualities. The good listener, for example, can be positively reframed into someone who is genuinely interested in the other person and is not just self-absorbed. This quality can even be translated into actual performances at a later point; we can ask the question of how she might show her interest in another person in an appropriate and effective manner. With positive reframing, the loyal friend and good listener can transform herself into someone who shows an active interest in other people, is ready to engage in meaningful relationships, and has the courage to make a commitment.

Positive self-statements exercise a different part of the brain than anxiety and are able to distract us from it. They boost self-confidence and may sometimes form part of the effective statements that we can use in front of others. Instead of anxiety-provoking negative self-statements such as, "I am totally unqualified and I am going to blow this," the person can instead be thinking, "I am taking this so seriously that I can even see myself feeling a bit anxious." The use of these positive

> **Box 9.1. Ingredients for Interpersonal Attraction**
>
> 1. Perceived security is attractive:
>   - Individuals who are generally more secure are more attractive.
>   - One's perceptions of potential love objects, rather than their actual characteristics, may play a greater role in the attraction process (Klohnen & Luo, 2003).
> 2. Do you see what I see?
>   - People often assume that their romantic partner sees them as they see themselves (Murray et al., 2000).
> 3. Self-esteem at work:
>   - People with low self-esteem often incorrectly believe that their romantic partners perceive relatively few positive qualities in them. By contrast, people with high self-esteem correctly believe that their romantic partners perceive many valuable qualities in them (Murray et al., 2000).
>   - People with high self-esteem perceive themselves to be engaging in more positive relationship behaviour than their counterparts with lower self-esteem (Feeney & Collins, 2001; Strelan, 2007).
>   - Trust in one's partner's love and commitment is the key to intimate connection (Murray et al., 2006). To arrive at such a level of trust, two related inferences are required: one needs to (1) be (or feel) just as good a person as one's partner; and (2) feel that one's qualities measure up to alternative partners that the other party may have (Murray et al., 2005).

self-statements enhances our self-confidence, or what social cognitive theorists call self-efficacy. Research in social psychology suggests that people who feel better about themselves are usually perceived to be more attractive by others (Feeney & Collins, 2001; Klohnen & Luo, 2003; Murray, Holmes, & Collins, 2006; Murray, Holmes, & Griffin, 2000; Murray, Rose, Holmes, Derrick, Podchaski, Bellavia, & Griffin, 2005; Strelan, 2007). A summary of the key ingredients for interpersonal attraction is given in Box 9.1.

A positive attitude enhances both our interpersonal attractiveness as well as our sense of confidence and well-being. Most people can therefore benefit from learning to reframe their self-statements as well as their experiences in life. Box 9.2 provides a list of strategies for positive reframing, and these can be learned in both individual and group set-

Box 9.2. Positive Reframing

Positive reframing does not always come as a natural gift; most people actually need to learn to do it. One of the ways to learn positive reframing is to practise reframing negative statements through repeated exercises.

The following are some of the strategies that may be of help:

1. Looking for the Positive through the Other Side of the Coin
There is a structural duality to most human realities, meaning that there is always a positive and a negative side. To get to this, one can ask the questions: is there anything good about this? what could have been worse? The Friar Lawrence example in Box 9.3 illustrates this process.

2. Discovering Positive Elements by Thinking of the Conditions of Possibility
The conditions that make a negative experience possible are often positive in themselves.

For example, a high school student says that his math teacher always criticizes him. For this to happen, the following conditions are necessary: (1) the student attends his math class; (2) the teacher pays attention to him; (3) the teacher expects something of him; (4) the student can recognize criticisms; (5) the student can understand and remember the criticisms instead of blocking them out; and (6) the student is talking to someone about his problem. All of these conditions are actually positive.

3. Translation of Negative Experience/Emotion into Expression of Wish
Negative experiences are often the result of frustration or disappointment, which means that some important personal needs are not being met. For example, when someone says that he is a poor communicator, that statement can be reframed as his wish to be able to communicate more effectively. If someone complains about being lonely, it can be reframed into a wish for finding companionship or developing relationships.

4. Scaling the Negative Can Help to Establish the Opposite Pole
When a scale is used, the presence of two poles is implied, and one of the poles can be extended to take the individual into the positive. Instead

of asking a person how depressed he feels on a scale from zero to ten, we can say that zero means that you feel neutral, minus ten means that you are extremely unhappy, and ten means that you are extremely happy.

5. Taking a Different Perspective
Viewing the same thing from a different angle or taking the perspective of another person can often help us appreciate the positive side of our experience. A recent graduate from a prestigious law school who has to work in a small law firm may feel that she is a total failure, but someone from her hometown who could not get into law school may consider that an enviable accomplishment.

6. Humour
Humour almost always involves taking a different perspective and triggering an emotional response that is incompatible with the negative affect associated with the original event. For example, a man in a treatment group for insomnia and sleep-related issues jokes about another member's complaint of a snoring partner by saying, "That's annoying, okay, but I am sure you do not want another woman to take your place."

tings. Box 9.3 is an illustration of positive reframing taken from Shakespeare's *Romeo and Juliet*.

Self-Introduction

Positive self-statements usually make us better equipped to start engaging with other people. Whereas the specifics of what we do or say vary across social situations, a few things are helpful to consider. The first thing, of course, is to remember what our purpose is within that particular social context. In activities such as house-by-house campaigning for public office, or trying to raise money for a local charity, the best strategy is usually to be simple, direct, and to the point. People generally do not appreciate disguises. In other situations, our self-introduction may need to be a bit more elaborate or formal, such as when we are invited to give a speech or to perform some specific social ritual. For some people, it is helpful to have prepared scripts. These opening or self-introduction scripts can usually be better developed when there is honest and constructive feedback from one's peers. This can be ob-

Box 9.3. Friar Lawrence: The Natural Positive Reframer

Positive reframing is based on the belief that there is a structural duality to most human realities. Where there is a negative side, there is always a positive side. The character of Friar Lawrence from Shakespeare's *Romeo and Juliet*, who I think has the natural gift of positive reframing, said, "Nothing that lives on earth is so vile that it doesn't have some individual goodness that it can yield" (Act 2, Scene 3).

Whereas there are always two possible sides to things, it requires particular mental facility to perform a good act of positive reframing. The most brilliant piece of positive reframing by the Friar was performed at the lowest point of Romeo's life. He had just killed Juliet's cousin Tybalt in a duel and had been sentenced to exile by the Prince of Verona, meaning that he could not see his love again. Under such dreadful circumstances, Friar Lawrence had the following to say:

> O deadly sin! O rude unthankfulness!
> Thy fault our law calls death; but the kind prince,
> Taking thy part, hath rush'd aside the law,
> And turn'd that black word death to banishment:
> This is dear mercy, and thou seest it not.

And,

> What, rouse thee, man! Thy Juliet is alive,
> For whose dear sake thou wast but lately dead;
> There art thou happy: Tybalt would kill thee,
> But thou slew'st Tybalt; there art thou happy too:
> The law that threaten'd death becomes thy friend
> And turns it to exile; there art thou happy:
> A pack of blessings lights up upon thy back;
> Happiness courts thee in her best array;
> But, like a misbehaved and sullen wench,
> Thou pout'st upon thy fortune and thy love.
>
> (Act 3, Scene 3)

tained easily in an SSLD group setting, but the ultimate goal is always for people to be able to identify people they can work with in their everyday lives. In one-on-one counselling or consultation, the practitioner can sometimes offer the feedback, and the use of collaborators can be helpful as well.

Apart from what is spoken, the importance of non-verbal behaviour has been well established (Argyle, 1983, 1988; Knapp & Hall, 2007). Facial expression, posture, and demeanour can all play a role in producing a good performance. Specific behaviours such as eye-contact, gestures, handshakes, and hugging can also be learned and refined with helpful feedback in an SSLD context. A point that should be noted here is that in an increasingly globalized world, cultural diversity is becoming an ever greater part of our social reality. As different cultures have varying conventions regarding what is appropriate, the mastery of appropriate etiquette is often necessary for intercultural encounters. Particular cultural communities have specific conventions with regard to things like dress code, physical distance, eye contact, greeting gestures, formal addresses or salutations, bodily contact, gender-based segregation of social space, exchange of gifts, and even serving or not serving food or drink. Some communities are very tolerant of outsiders not knowing and following their rules, while there are others who can be more easily offended. When we are new to a cultural community, we may want to seek consultation from an insider or a knowledgeable informant with regard to appropriate self-presentation.

I can give as an example my own personal experience in various cultural contexts. In Toronto, for example, it is not uncommon for family and friends to give each other a hug when they see each other, but that is not practised among the Hong Kong Chinese community I come from. It took me a while to figure out the more subtle rules regarding when and whom to hug, and the additional conventions regarding kisses on the cheek. The actual set of rules can become quite complicated when I try to spell it all out. For example, there is the question of whether to initiate the hug or wait till you see the other party getting ready for it, such as by opening her or his arms; and the question of how to respond to other cues when you see a former graduate student dressed in her traditional ethnic costume. We have to learn that when we are dealing with the huge diversity of people coming from different ethnic, cultural, and religious backgrounds (Toronto claims over 160 language/dialect communities), one needs to be very sensitive and careful so as not to communicate the wrong message, be it lack of interest or impolite intrusion into personal space. I can give other examples such as learning the toasting conventions when attending a formal dinner or banquet in China, where there are significant regional differences. Another example is the use of formal salutations versus first names within academia; there are huge differences on this point when one travels internationally. Even if we only look within the one university where I work, differences can still be found across the various disciplines and departments. What I do need to add, however, is that such cultural diversity offers interesting and fascinating lessons to be learned and significantly enriches my social and cultural life.

Presentation of Facts

After initial contact has been established, we will move on to perform the interpersonal or social function that is intended. Presentation of facts or factual information is usually seen as a more straightforward interaction than the expression of complex emotions. Following the same comparison, factual presentation is also given more attention in our education system. Language and speech-arts courses in schools and colleges teach people how to put factual information together, organize it into a logical sequence, or use visual representation to express it. Computer software has been developed specifically to support such presentation. In SSLD practice, we often find that people do not need as much assistance in factual presentation compared to other forms of expression and communication, yet a key point that many people often miss is that such communication has to be purposeful, and that thinking about what we intend to accomplish is usually helpful in making a presentation more effective. A closely related point is the need to consider the audience or recipient. In teaching, for example – a context in which a lot of factual presentation has to be done – it is important to understand the learner's background, interests, and learning needs. Feeding the learner with what the teacher thinks is important is not always useful. Teaching and learning will be more effective when the presentation matches the needs and interests of the learner. In simple, practical terms, we should ask what the other party needs and wants to know, rather than what we want to tell.

The skill of focusing on what the other party wants to know is increasingly important in our current historical era of information overload. In theory, anyone with access to the Internet has billions of items of factual information within easy reach. The information we provide will be perceived as valuable when we offer it at a time when it is needed. Many of us may have already noticed how frequently we give out Internet links or keywords to be searched, rather than all of the relevant information on a topic. Just over the last week as I was writing this book, I came across several situations when friends and colleagues told me part of a book title – the author of which they did not remember – or only one of the features of a product they thought I would be interested in. Knowing how to get other people to access the information they need is often adequate in achieving our desired interpersonal or social goals.

As an academic, I am of course aware of the situations in which some research and organization of factual information are required. For example, when we are asked for specific information regarding prevalence rates, such as rates of depression in different countries or across different age groups or ethnic communities, we need to work on putting the information together. What I have found in these situations is that the two SSLD questions of (1) what the other party wants, and (2) what their underlying needs and interests are, often help me in coming up with a better presentation.

We have to note, however – in line with SSLD thinking – that being responsive to the needs of others is *instrumental* in attaining our own goals, such as effectively disseminating knowledge or realizing a certain outcome. The reciprocal consideration of our own goals and the needs of others is a key feature of the SSLD approach. Finding the right balance and aiming at a win-win outcome is always a preferred option.

Expression of Ideas

Compared to factual presentation, the expression of ideas requires more deliberation. The generation of ideas often requires creativity as well as independent or critical thinking. At the very least, it takes a certain responsiveness to our external environment, including the people we are interacting with. Many of us have experienced difficulty in coming up with an idea to express, as in, "I have no idea…" In social situations, the ability to express one's ideas effectively plays a pivotal role in shaping the outcome. For example, if we wish to sell a new product to someone, or convince another person that spending the rest of her or his life with us is a good idea, or persuade a person in authority to make a decision in our favour, we need the other person to "buy" our idea. Again, similar to what we do in the presentation of factual information, the key consideration is still what other people need and want, and how that relates to our desired outcome in any given encounter.

Recognition of the other party's needs and wants is often a good way to preface our own expression of ideas. Being able to connect our ideas to another person's needs or interests will increase the chance that our ideas get a positive reception. The emphasis on reciprocity reflects an important value regarding human interaction and connection. A good interpersonal or social encounter is not just about us getting our way and achieving our goals without regard for others. More often than not, being able to work towards mutual or reciprocal benefit is more gratifying. Presenting our ideas is even more effective when we do not only understand other people's needs but also have a sense of their perspective or mindset, including the language they are most familiar with. As I write this paragraph, for instance, a few philosophical ideas rooted in my Chinese cultural background come through my mind, and many of them will not be immediately relevant to the typical English reader. I have come up with the idea of mutuality and reciprocity without going into a lengthy discussion and critique of utilitarian individualism, for I do not assume that all my readers subscribe to this ideology. Some of you may be interested in learning more about my philosophical views while others may be happy to move on to the more pragmatic ideas. In a rapidly globalized environment where we get in touch with an increasingly diverse set of people in our everyday lives, ideas have to be packaged differently for different audiences. Flexibility and contingency thinking are usually helpful. The following are some of the principles to consider:

(1) Try to understand the other party's needs and goals in the encounter or interaction.
(2) Have a sense of how the idea you are presenting fits into the context of the other party's circumstances.
(3) Present the idea with reference to the other party's needs and circumstances.
(4) Use language, examples, and metaphors that are within the other party's scope of imagination; it is best to use what can be understood by most of the people when working with diverse or heterogeneous audiences.
(5) Explain the unfamiliar in terms of the familiar: when it is necessary to use new or unfamiliar concepts or examples, try to connect them to what the audience is familiar with, and provide background information and explanations.

(6) Stay attuned to the other party's responses; watch for signs of interest, attention, engagement, and resonance, or boredom, puzzlement, disagreement, and resentment.
(7) Whenever appropriate, seek direct feedback from the other party to see if your idea has been understood.

Expression of Emotions and Feelings

As mentioned before, most of us have not received systematic instruction with regard to the expression of feelings. We tend to learn through observation learning or modelling. Goleman's (1995) book on emotional intelligence has certainly drawn popular attention to the topic, and I believe we are all indebted to the empirical and theory-building work of Bandura (1977a, 1986). In a way, we all show our emotions one way or another – often when we are not even aware of it ourselves. Tone of voice, gestures, facial expression, and signs like clenched fists, sweating palms, pounding heart, or shivering legs are all expressions of emotional state or feelings.

Emotions and Feelings

In SSLD, our focus is more on conscious and goal-directed expression of emotions and feelings. First of all, we have to clarify what emotions and feelings may mean, for these words are often used to refer to different experiences; while they are sometimes interchangeable, they can also take on distinctly different meanings in other contexts. Without getting into a very technical inquiry, we can map out the domain of emotions and feelings into four major forms of experience: (1) emotional state; (2) emotional trait; (3) mood; and (4) relational feelings.

The first three forms are based on Rosenberg's (1998) conceptualization of emotion. What Rosenberg calls an affective trait, or what other authors (e.g., Burt, 2006) call an *emotional trait*, is a relatively stable predisposition towards certain types of emotional response. Affective traits, as components of personality, have some consistency over time and across life situations. For instance, we can talk about someone as having an angry or depressive personality, or someone who tends to be joyous and pleasant. More transient and situation-specific experiences are called emotions. In between the two are moods, which can fluctuate throughout or across days. Besides these three forms of emotional experience, I would like to add another way of looking at feelings or emotional experience that is often used by people: relational feelings.

Relational feelings refer to how we feel towards or about someone, as when someone in couple counselling says that "my feelings towards her have gone," or "I have intense and mixed feelings towards him."

When speaking of purposeful or goal-directed emotional experience, we have to recognize that people often experience their emotions and feelings as something natural or spontaneous, almost antithetical to the idea of deliberate or controlled expression. Sometimes emotional experiences occur without our anticipation or even awareness. People with a particular affective or emotional trait such as anxiety or anger may or may not be aware of its presence. Emotional states, being transient, do not always lend themselves easily to conscious or deliberate expression. Moods that linger on for hours or days are probably more noticeable to others, but we rarely talk about the expression of our moods. Relational feelings are probably more likely to be intentionally expressed in everyday life.

When we take a slightly different perspective, however, it is not too difficult for us to imagine how someone may need to learn to express emotions. People in their everyday lives often need to communicate to others what they are experiencing emotionally in order to obtain the responses they desire, be they understanding, sympathy, or tangible support or help. Many of us also need to express our emotions to maintain equilibrium, and we sometimes call that "ventilation." Under these circumstances, it is possible to talk about the expression of emotions that are more or less helpful. The unregulated expression of anger, for example, may have destructive consequences, which may be antithetical to the emotional needs that led to the anger in the first place. A good example of this is the emotional experience of people who abuse their partners. A person in this situation may have strong needs for esteem and emotional security. Whenever he feels that his chance to gratify these needs is threatened, for instance when his partner is acting independently and enjoying life without his participation, he feels fear, which then feeds into anger and aggression. The expression of such anger further undermines the very relationship that the person desperately needs to maintain.

Many people need to learn to express their feelings, for in everyday life this is usually left to chance. Our education system pays more attention to the development of our intellect, our bodies, and our artistic or musical skills than to our capacity to manage our emotional lives and relationships. Even after the hugely successful launch of Goleman's (1995) book on the topic, our educational and socialization agents are generally not pursuing systematic procedures to help children and adults learn to manage their emotions. In SSLD thinking, we believe that one can learn to manage and express one's emotions in a functional or effective manner in order to attain the personal goals that one desires.

As mentioned in the earlier section on how to receive or read emotional messages, human emotions are expressed in many forms, including verbal communication, non-verbal behaviours, and signifying acts. Some people learn emotional management and expression effectively through observation in everyday life, including symbolically mediated records of emotional interaction such as experiences recorded in an email or a home video. Some people, however, will need systematic training. In my own work with people experiencing psychological and relationship difficulties, learning to get in touch with their feelings, managing them, and expressing them appropriately is often a key part of the process.

The first step in learning to express emotions and feelings is awareness, for we cannot have effective emotional expression without being aware of the emotions we wish to express. Learning to be more aware of one's own emotional experience can be one of the most beneficial experiences in a person's life. People's awareness of their own emotions is often restricted as a result of social learning wherein certain emotions or feelings are socially discouraged or prohibited. Many cultures, for example, do not allow for free expression of sexual and erotic feelings. The control can be especially restrictive for specific social groups, such as women, the elderly, or people with physical developmental challenges. Some cultures also discourage the expression of fear, especially among men.

Apart from culture, regulation of emotional experience is most often enforced within the family. Most families have developed explicit and implicit rules regarding emotional experience and expression, and these are often internalized by family members. These rules then become natural checks on their emotional expression. Over time, people will learn to avoid connecting with emotions that they are not allowed to express or that they have been made ashamed of having. Dissociating from emotional experiences, and sometimes denying or avoiding them, can often become adaptive strategies in certain social contexts. Denying pain, fear, and anger in order to avoid dealing with them, for example, is a common strategy used by victims of family violence (Barnett, 2001).

In helping people to gain more awareness of their emotions, a few conditions have been found to be helpful by psychotherapists. Perhaps the most important is a trusting relationship (Iwakabe, Rogan, & Stalikas, 2000) between the client and the practitioner. It is important for the practitioner to communicate respect, acceptance, and a nonjudgmental stance. A key principle is to avoid applying undue pressure and to be respectful of the client's preferences, readiness, and pace. Another SSLD principle is that of incremental learning, allowing clients to take small steps towards increased emotional awareness instead of rushing them towards dramatic insight or cathartic expression.

Another important consideration is the question of how to identify the client's goal and get a sense of what the desired outcome is like – a consideration which is always emphasized in SSLD. Emotional expression can be a form of self-care when one intends to ventilate in order to feel peace and quiet afterwards. It can be part of a strategy to seek understanding, support, or help. It can be more instrumental, such as trying to assert a position, or to bring about a specifically desired response from the other party. It can also be an effective component of an intimacy development process.

As explained in the above discussion on the four forms of emotional experience, human emotions and feelings are of variable stability; we often have to deal with emotions that are not fixed, but are transient and contingent upon the person's external environment and internal state. Another important point about emotional expression is that emotions are not always simple and pure, but can be mixed or ambivalent. There are times when we feel both happy and apprehensive, as in the case of having a new job. There are times when we feel both sadness and relief, like when we finally lose a loved one after a long, painful struggle with a chronic illness. Learning to accept the contingent, transient, and ambivalent nature of our emotions is an important step in their management and expression.

Emotional Work in SSLD

Following the principles described above, procedures have been developed in SSLD practice to help clients manage emotional issues of various kinds (please see Box 9.4: Emotional Work in SSLD). When emotions are interfering with a person's actions, the person first needs to understand them. A necessary condition for this to happen is to have a safe space for people to explore and manage these feelings without

> **Box 9.4. Emotional Work in SSLD**
>
> **The process of working through emotions**
>
> (1) Create/maintain a safe space, allowing for the exploration of feelings.
> (2) Awareness, identification/recognition, getting the felt-sense, bodily sensation, and experiencing the emotion.
> (3) Articulation (includes: naming, labelling, describing, symbolization, and metaphors).
> (4) Ownership (can move through dis-identification).
> (5) Expression – private or interpersonal, verbal or nonverbal.
> (6) Channelling, ventilation, or catharsis – restoring homeostasis.
> (7) Self-acceptance – mastery and self-efficacy.
> (8) Transformation, reconstruction, and resolution (of conflict, ambivalence, or trauma) – often involves cognitive processing.

the fear of judgment or reprehension. Then, with some facilitation from the practitioner, clients should be able to get in touch with their feelings. For example, when someone reports emotional difficulty or outright disgust when she or he is asked to show appreciation for a partner in a couple counselling session, we can encourage the person to get in touch with her or his emotions instead of suppressing them. Procedures that help to focus attention on the person's immediate experience, including both bodily and emotional states, can often be employed. This includes sensing or body scanning as well as asking clients to locate the emotion in their bodies. Clients are usually able to say that they feel it in their stomach, shoulder, chest, or somewhere else. We can also adopt procedures such as spontaneous expression, which is encouraged by gestalt therapists and can include the well-known two-chair procedure; mindfulness practice; meditation; journal keeping; expressive arts such as drawing, dance, and body sculpture; and even free association. Once the client can access and connect with her or his emotions, we can usually get to the next step of articulation.

When an emotion can be named, the person is acknowledging or accepting the fact that they are experiencing this feeling – be it resentment, guilt, shame, or disgust – even though some people may spend some time struggling with it. Sometimes people may say something like, "I don't think I feel anger, although what she did was very hurtful." We can facilitate acceptance or ownership by saying something like, "When someone does something hurtful, the other party feels hurt. You are hurt, but you're not sure what you're experiencing is anger." Such verbalization does not put words into the client's mouth, but it opens up the narrative space, giving the client an opportunity to take a step forward. Some clients may feel safe enough to own the anger with this facilitation and say, "I guess I do feel some anger after all." More reserved clients may say something like, "Well, I guess it is easy to feel angry when one gets hurt." Although this statement is not indicating direct ownership of a feeling, the client is one step closer to it. We may actually just re-present the articulation by saying something like, "Yes, feeling angry is easy to understand," allowing the movement from "being hurt" to "feeling angry."

When clients come to own their feelings, it becomes possible for us to invite them to express them. The SSLD approach to emotional expression, again, is focused on options and choices. We will let the client know that expression can be done in private, in the consultation session with the practitioner, or, when the client is ready and the circumstances are appropriate, in front of the other party concerned. Clients can be made aware of the varied means of emotional expression, including verbal and non-verbal methods. In SSLD emotional work, we often help clients to understand the need for ventilation. Many people feel that it is socially inappropriate or a sign of personal weakness to let out their emotions. Some people may experience immense anxiety related to losing control. We can help them understand that such ventilation is actually helpful for restoring homeostasis, and that allowing one's emotions to be channelled in a safe and appropriate context is an agentive act.

The channelling, ventilation, and uninhibited expression of one's feelings, when done in a self-directed manner and with full awareness, usually reinforces one's sense of agency and self-efficacy. In a facilitated process of exploration and expression, most people get to understand their feelings better and become more accepting of them. This usually opens up a good opportunity for a new way to make sense of one's emotional experience, as well as the way that difficult feelings such as fear, conflict, ambivalence, or trauma can be managed. It is usually very empowering for people to find out that their feelings, which seemed dangerous and overwhelming in the beginning, can actually be accessed, understood, and managed.

The above procedures, though presented in a sequential manner to facilitate conceptualization, are not meant to be followed rigidly. We should recognize individual differences in emotional experience and learning, and understand that not everyone will go through exactly the same process. Learning to express emotions effectively through SSLD, therefore, entails learning multiple strategies and skills and using them with flexibility, with due consideration of the specific circumstances of the individuals concerned and the goals they wish to attain. A key idea in this process is expanding the person's repertoire of emotional expressions. This may involve learning words, symbols, or other ways of articulating and expressing emotions. Some people need to learn to associate words with experienced emotional states. Some individuals who are physically or intellectually challenged may have to learn to use symbols or colour-coded objects. Some people may need to learn to take an internal time-out, taking deep breaths and counting to ten before expressing themselves. Some people may learn to develop, design, and implement signifying acts. Some individuals may have to collectively develop group rituals to deal with certain emotions. One example comes from my work in Sichuan after the 12 May earthquake in 2008. Many people I encountered had lost their loved ones, and some had even watched them die. Many earthquake victims shared their experience of trauma, often associated with unspeakable grief, anguish, fear, guilt, and a host of other intense and overwhelming emotions. Whereas some of them preferred to deal with such experiences privately, many found it helpful to participate in group or community rituals specifically designed to assist people in their grieving process. Whereas it is difficult to imagine packaged programs that are universally effective, practitioners can follow SSLD principles to expand their own emotional response repertoires and those of their clients. A useful procedure here is the collaborative creation of new skills that was described in Chapter 6.

Expression of Needs

The expression of needs is often closely associated with the expression of emotions. A simple reason is that many of our needs can be seen as emotional in nature. As in the case of emotions, awareness and acceptance are important conditions for effective expression. With needs, however, expression is almost inevitable and very often is automatic, even when people are not aware or accepting of their own needs. Parents who are afraid of losing their children's love, for instance, may express their need for affection and intimacy through controlling and punitive behaviour. Some people who need to deal with the pain caused by traumatic experiences earlier in life, but who do not have a good understanding of this, may resort to the use of alcohol, chemical substances, or gambling.

In everyday life, being able to effectively communicate one's own needs clearly increases one's chance of having those needs met. Yet, as in the case of emotional expression, not all needs are considered legitimate or acceptable by society. The expression of sexual needs by seniors living in nursing homes, for example, is often met with negative responses (Bauer, McAuliffe, & Nay, 2007; Kamel, 2001). Unmet and conflicting needs are often found at the base of human suffering and tragedy, including in situations such as crimes and wars. Being able to express one's needs and negotiate their gratification is obviously a valuable skill to be mastered.

The problem translation procedure described in Chapter 4 provides a good basis for practitioners to identify needs that are sometimes not obvious to clients, and allows them to provide useful feedback. In situations where there is little conflict and adequate trust, the communication of needs can be more direct and explicit. In more challenging situations where there is risk of interpersonal incompatibility or conflict, more sophisticated strategies and skills have to be learned and developed. In SSLD practice, two principles are often helpful in the development of such strategies and skills. One is trying to help the other party to see things from your perspective and facilitating their empathic response. The other is to negotiate maximum common ground between two parties.

Trying to get people to see and experience things from your perspective is not always easy, for most people naturally stick with their own perspective. As was suggested earlier in the section on the expression of ideas, being attuned to the other party's position and experience can be very helpful. Using language that the other party is familiar and comfortable with is another strategy. Very often, a direct and explicit statement such as, "I need to have more personal space" can be effective. Connecting our needs with what the other person can do may be particularly helpful, such as, "If you could do that, it would make me feel much better." Whenever possible, we try to put the other person in the subject position of a sentence instead of placing them as an object. People usually feel better when they are in an agentive position and are capable of doing something that makes a difference.

What we may want to avoid in most situations are confrontational or accusatory statements such as, "You don't understand," or "I don't know why it is so difficult for you to get." Another problematic expression of needs or wishes is known as *guilt-tripping*, which is an attempt to get other people to do things we want by making them feel uncomfortable. As a strategy, guilt-tripping sometimes works, but the downside is that it tends to damage the relationship in the long run, leading to compromised gratification for both parties involved.

Now consider the following example: after the plane you are travelling in has taken off, you find out that your personal entertainment system is broken and the flight attendants are busy serving food and drinks. We can compare the following responses and see which might work better:

(1) I don't know why there is always something wrong with your flights. Now I am going to be without my TV for the next twelve hours.
(2) My system is broken; please see if you can fix it.
(3) I understand that you are busy right now, but when you have time later, would you mind taking a look at the system? It doesn't seem to be working.

Expressions of our own needs and wishes are usually more effective when they recognize the other party's needs and position, and when they express our needs without being accusatory.

Another helpful approach is to try to establish a common goal and create a win-win situation. When that is not really possible, we can at least try to negotiate compatibility or some compromise that the other person can live with. This is sometimes called an *assertive-responsive approach* – and this has to be distinguished from the kind of assertiveness advocated by practitioners of assertiveness training. In the traditional approach to assertiveness training (e.g., Smith, 1975), the emphasis is on "what I want" and "what I need," or "what my rights are." Assertive-responsiveness, by contrast, is about meeting our own needs (assertiveness) while at the same time having regard for other people's needs and rights (responsiveness).

Chapter Ten

Engagement

As Gergen (1991) observed over two decades ago, most people living in the developed world are living in a postmodern era, and we are experiencing a rapid increase in the number of individuals we meet in our lives. This increase in quantity is also associated with increased diversity in terms of geographical location, ethnicity, culture, profession, personal background, and so on; and must have been growing over the last twenty years. From a social psychological perspective, many people are overwhelmed with this increased quantity and complexity of contacts and interactions. People's overall life satisfaction and well-being are to a large extent conditioned by the quantity, nature, and quality of the relationships they have with others, ranging from brief encounters to longer-term relationships. Learning to effectively engage with others so that we can attain our desired goals in life is arguably central to our quest for well-being. In the last two chapters we have dealt with reception and expression, the two fundamental aspects of communication and interaction. In this chapter, we will explore the strategies and skills involved in interpersonal and social engagement, which is the first step in building relationships.

Engagement

In SSLD, engagement is conceptualized as the first step in any interpersonal or social encounter or interaction. Positive engagement will pave the way for the development of a mutually gratifying relationship. When two persons meet for the first time with the view of developing a relationship, such as on a first date, or when a client meets with a psychotherapist for a first session, engagement is of central significance. In general, engagement entails a few elements, which are similar to what I have mentioned in the section on problem translation and engagement. First, there should be compatibility between the goals, needs, expectations, and interaction styles of the participants. Then there is an emotional aspect; the participants need to feel at least some positive affect towards each other. This mutual positive affect is sometimes called *rapport*, and it includes an element of trust, some kind of attraction or liking, a general sense of comfort or pleasure, and a willingness to continue the interaction so that a relationship can be developed. Although the tasks of negotiating compatibility and creating a positive emotional environment are conceptually distinct, in actual interpersonal and social encounters they are usually accomplished simultaneously. Experiencing compatibility with another person in terms of agenda and interaction style is arguably a positive emotional experience in itself. The following section will explore the composite strategies and skills that can facilitate interpersonal engagement.

People engaging in interpersonal and social interactions or entering relationships are motivated by their personal needs. Some people are looking for company, some for emotional support, some for intimacy, some for approval, and some for help. When two or more persons meet for the first time to develop a relationship, their needs and goals may or may not be compatible. Compatibility, however, does not imply sameness. Whereas two persons both seeking company or intimacy have compatible needs, one person with strong dependency needs is compatible with someone who needs to dominate and control. Similarly, a person who seeks approval may have very compatible needs with someone who is looking for help and care.

An important fact about compatibility is that it is rarely perfect in any relationship. Although people often find gratification with regard to some of their needs in any given relationship, there are usually other needs that are not addressed. That is why people need multiple relationships in order to satisfy their needs. Being able to manage one's needs with reference to the various relationships in one's life-world is an important lesson to be learned, and something that the SSLD model supports. Many people, for instance, expect their partner or spouse to satisfy many aspects of their needs, ranging from security to affiliation, intimacy, pleasurable experience, intellectual stimulation, collaboration in parenting, sexual ecstasy, and so on. Such expectations are not always realistic, given that the needs profiles of their partners may or may not be compatible with theirs. In SSLD, while we seek maximum gratification in any given relationship, we are also open to reconfiguring our complex network of relationships in order to meet our diverse needs. A key principle here is that we do not take the set of needs that a person enters a relationship with as constant and fixed, but rather as contingent upon changing circumstances in the person's life-world. Needs do change and compatibility is negotiable in most relationships.

Another aspect of compatibility is the individual's interaction and communication style, which is conditioned by a number of factors, including personality predisposition, learning history, culture, and cognitive understanding of the relational context and the attending conventions, protocols, or rules. In cross-cultural psychotherapy, for example, a client expecting expert direction and guidance may be confused if the therapist prefers a non-directive approach, provides unrestricted narrative space for the client, and conducts the session in an unstructured manner. A person who was brought up in a more egalitarian social context may feel ill at ease when working within a hierarchical culture emphasizing power and status. Similarly, a person who prefers straight talk and direct communication does not always appreciate the emphasis on protocol and courtesy in some circles, and may have difficulty participating in an approach that involves extensive use of innuendos and euphemisms.

Compatibility between participants in a relationship, in terms of their needs and communication styles, has to be negotiated on an ongoing basis. This will be explored in more detail later in this book. In the engagement phase, a minimal level of compatibility is needed for the interaction to continue so that a relationship can subsequently develop. For example, an overworked person on a plane trying to catch some much-needed sleep has little compatibility with the needs of a child taking her first flight who is feeling excited. In situations where the incompatibility is very obvious, most people do not make serious attempts to engage. In most situations, however, a minimal level of compatibility can be achieved simply because people want to be seen as nice, or wish to avoid negative responses or consequences. Imagine, for example, the girl in the situation described above asking to change to the window seat taken by the tired passenger. There could be a fair chance of success.

Individuals with social phobia feel that they have the most difficulty in engaging with people, especially strangers. Their level of anxiety can be debilitating and they usually have a negative expectancy, fearing that the worst will happen. In a sense, they tend to have a pessimistic

> **Box 10.1. Strategies and Skills Facilitating Engagement**
>
> 1. Agenda management.
> 2. Positive responding: providing reinforcing feedback.
> 3. Finding commonalities and maximizing shared interest.
> 4. Strategic self-disclosure.

view of their potential compatibility, believing that people are not interested in them or are even potentially hostile. They do not think that they have something to offer with regard to the personal needs of the other party. In an SSLD program, we directly involve these individuals in role-playing situations that they dread and record them for subsequent playback and review. In the review process, we obviously pay attention to their performance, covering details such as posture, physical interpersonal distance, facial expression, eye contact, meshing, non-verbal behaviours, tone quality, content of their utterances, and so on. Review of these micro-processes focuses on how the client can present themselves as a more acceptable or pleasant participant in social interactions. The recorded role-play reviews also help them to assess the other party's experience more realistically. Whether it is a member of the group, a therapist, or a collaborator role-playing with them, they will have a chance to learn about the other person's needs and on-the-spot experience through direct questioning, if they want. This exercise often helps them to appreciate the room for compatibility.

Specific skills enhancing compatibility in the initial contact and engagement phase include topic management, positive responding, maximizing commonality and mutuality, and strategic self-presentation (Box 10.1). Assuming that the initial building blocks of reception and expression skills described in the preceding sections have already been established, an individual should now be capable of positive self-presentation, listening, expression, and so on. What is important now in the engagement process is to get the other party interested in continuing the interaction with us, and to create positive conditions for this interaction. Successful engagement enhances the chance of achieving whatever instrumental objectives we might have (e.g., trying to sell a financial product, requesting assistance, negotiating a deal), or it can improve the prospect of a rewarding relationship in the longer term.

1. Agenda Management

This is a very simple principle in interpersonal interaction – and it is probably applicable to almost all situations, but many people do not pay enough attention to it. The SSLD position on interpersonal interaction is that each party participates in such encounters with a purpose or is driven by specific needs. We need, therefore, to understand the purpose of the encounter, especially the other party's motivation and needs. Managing the compatibility of the participating parties' respective agendas is a key to successful engagement. Very often, people are preoccupied with their own agendas and do not pay enough attention to those of the other party or parties. What we learned in a previous chapter regarding reception skills – the ability to listen to the underlying needs and emotional messages – will be most helpful in this. When we know what the other party's agenda is, we can manage the interaction's agenda accordingly. Explicit reference to the other person's needs and emotional state is often helpful. In an SSLD training program for front-desk receptionists, participants learned that dealing with "difficult" customers or clients at the front desk can usually be helped significantly by recognizing their needs and emotions such as, "I know how hard it is for you to get here through the rush-hour downtown traffic, and I understand you expect your problem to be solved when you get here. It is definitely disappointing and frustrating for you to find out that our office actually does not provide the service you needed. What I am now trying to do is to find the best solution for you …"

Once we have figured out what the other party's agenda is, the engagement process needs to stay connected with that agenda while we weave in what we wish to accomplish. This can be a pretty straightforward process in some cases, but can become extremely complicated in others. The front-desk example above involves recognizing the customer's needs and feelings, and then referring the customer to the service they require. In my research on psychotherapy with individuals with borderline personality disorders, a group which is considered particularly difficult to engage with, I have learned a few helpful lessons about engagement (Chambon, Tsang, & Marziali, 2000; Tsang, 1995). A key point is to stay on the agenda. Changing the topic from what the other party is pursuing and interrupting the other party are both likely to work against successful engagement. If we need to change the topic, the general principle is not to interrupt the other person and change the topic abruptly but to do it through what I call *mediated shifts*, which usually recognize what the other party is currently talking about. For example, we can say something like, "I know you're eager to find a [nursing home] placement for your mother, and I can relate to the frustration you are experiencing, but we need to know a bit more about her health conditions in order to be able to assist you to make the best arrangement for her." In training programs, participants sometimes express the concern that if we are accommodating listeners, we will end up spending too much time listening to people, but testing this out in simulated exercises in-session usually shows that it actually takes less time to accomplish our agenda if we stay tuned in to the other person's. In contrast, in high-tension or high-conflict interactions, we see people trying to talk over each other, which can sometimes deteriorate into a shouting game and leave very little room for effective communication or engagement.

2. Positive Responding: Providing Reinforcing Feedback

People will engage better with us if they receive positive responses from us. Positive responding means producing responses that will be experienced as positive by the other party; this involves both cognitive-behavioural as well as emotional components. In the very beginning of an interaction, it can involve simple acts such as a warm and friendly smile, a courteous greeting, and being able to address the other party by name. In an indoor or office environment, offering a comfortable seat, something to drink, or anything that makes the other party feel physically comfortable usually helps. If a situation is intrinsically unpleasant, like when you are a nurse taking blood samples from a patient, it usually helps to anticipate the unpleasant and show some empathy. You could say something like, "I know it is going to hurt, but the good news is that it will be over very soon." There is a little trick related to expectation management that we often use in management training as well as in the training of service personnel. The idea is to overstate the unpleasant or inconvenient aspect a little bit so that the other party can feel that it is not as bad as they expected. Receptionists, for example, can predict the waiting time for the client by adding a few more minutes. Being overly optimistic and underestimating the unpleasant or inconvenient aspect can backfire by creating disappointment and resentment.

Paying attention and listening carefully to the other person, a set of skills covered earlier, usually works towards successful engagement.

Most people enjoy being valued and taken seriously. An easy way to indicate attention and careful listening is by repeating what the other party has expressed. It can be simple things like, "I know you don't drink coffee," or, "You said you hated trains," or it can be implied positions or needs such as, "You will have some problem with the fur she is wearing" (the other person has expressed views on animal rights). In training psychotherapists and counsellors, one thing we emphasize is to be respectful and nonjudgmental. Very often people express their opinions in a strong manner, which can come across as rigid, judgmental, or even offensive. Using derogatory labels such as addicts, losers, morons, and the like also has a high probability of conveying negative judgment. The use of phrases like "those people" is often a linguistic marker of distancing, exclusion, and judgment. Sometimes we may inadvertently make sweeping statements that apply to people we are interacting with, which can silence or alienate them. Something like, "No decent human being would leave her child unattended in the house," or, "I don't think any person with even minimal intelligence will buy into that crap," can turn some people off immediately. These statements can often be positively reframed, for example, "The child needs constant attention," or "There are people who will try whatever means imaginable to cheat us."

Another well-known strategy in positive responding is to say something positive about the other party. We may be paying a compliment to the other person's appearance or the positive implications of the person's actions. We want to do this with sincerity; challenging ourselves to find something we genuinely appreciate in the other party not only helps to facilitate interpersonal engagement but it may actually contribute to our own long-term well-being by reinforcing a positive outlook and mindset in our own lives. In SSLD workshops we have an exercise in which participants will take turns receiving positive feedback from the other members of the group. It is usually a fun-filled session that unleashes a lot of creativity. In a recent workshop on sleep and insomnia, one member said to another, "You're the most humorous and positive insomniac I have ever come across."

Positive responding can be more focused when there are behaviours we wish to reinforce in the other party. For instance, a baby-boomer parent can thank his daughter for helping her grandparents learn to use the Internet, pointing out that the action literally expands the lifeworld of the old folks and contributes to family solidarity, communication, and sharing. As another example, if we are meeting with another party and wish for them to see us again, it usually helps to point out something special about the meeting and what it does or means to us. We can, for example, talk about how a dollar spent on dining can generate six dollars' worth of economic activities (and therefore we need to do it more often to contribute to the economic well-being of society). What we say can often be helped by a little research into the history of the place (e.g., "this restaurant first started operating one hundred years ago"), the special circumstances of the day (e.g., "the coldest day in February in thirty years" or "since I was born"), or the other party's interests (e.g., "this place only serves organic and fair trade products" [a subject from the other person's Facebook account]). Another exercise we ask SSLD group participants to do is called "you are the first person." In this exercise, we have to think of something that the other party is the first person to say or do. Examples can range from, "You are the first person to tell me the difference between a latte and a cappuccino," or "to define for me what an overture is," to "this is the first time someone has really been able to explain the subprime meltdown to me," or "the connection between Heidegger's concept of time and Stephen Hawking's."

In interpersonal and social situations, some negativity is almost inevitable, and what we have learned in the earlier section on positive reframing should come in handy in these cases. The ability to reframe positively clearly enhances our capacity for successful engagement, but there are situations in which positive reframing may not be the best response. Imagine when someone is sharing an extremely unpleasant or even traumatic emotional experience; in this case, constant positive reframing may be experienced as emotional distancing, which can be counterproductive in our attempt to engage. What we have learned from studying psychotherapy and the counselling process is that when there is obvious emotional content, some form of empathic response is most conducive to the development of trust and emotional bonding. Positive reframing that is prefaced with an empathic response is more likely to be effective when we are dealing with emotionally charged situations. For example, when a friend has just found out that he has prostate cancer, our response can be something like, "It's awful news for anyone, it must be tough for you, but I guess it's better to find out sooner rather than later."

3. Finding Commonalities and Maximizing Shared Interest

An important condition for successful engagement is common interest or mutuality. Whereas every human being is unique, it is also true that we always have something in common with other people. Negotiating our similarities and differences while trying our best to expand what is shared is a key to the development of relationships. In one couple counselling training situation, I was asked how two partners coming from very different socio-economic class backgrounds could develop a sense of mutuality when they talked about their childhood experience. One of the partners came from a very privileged background whereas the other came from a relatively deprived environment. We did a few video-recorded sessions demonstrating how attention to emotional experience and meaning instead of materiality or physical property could help to foster mutuality. More specifically, when the couple talked about the toys they played with and the activities they enjoyed as children, these were very different and carried distinct class signatures. The couple was then encouraged to focus on emotion and meaning, such as their most memorable play moments and most valued childhood experiences, and to connect those with their needs, interests, and personality development.

In my experience working with people who have difficulty in developing relationships, I find many of them do not have much interest in others, nor do they believe people will be interested in them. They do not consider themselves interesting and likeable, but deep down they wish some people would get to like them and want to be with them. Whereas these people can learn to redesign their lives and make themselves more interesting in the long run, they can often start expanding their social lives in the short run by learning to show interest in other people. People have much variability in their scope of interest; those who have a wider range of interests have an obvious advantage. People who have a very narrow range of interests often find that they have little or nothing to contribute to a conversation, and feel that they have nothing interesting to offer to others. These people are likely to come across as lacking motivation to develop interpersonal relationships, although they may be desperately in need of affiliation and social life.

Almost regardless of the reason for such a lack of interest, gradually expanding the client's repertoire of activities can be helpful. Exploring activities that people find enjoyable is a good starting point. I once worked with a young person (see Box 10.2) with a long history of schizophrenic disorder, which had started when he was a teenager. He spent a good part of his teenage and early adult years in and out of mental health facilities. He had a general mistrust towards people and

Box 10.2. The Case of Eugene

Eugene was thirty years old when he was referred for psychotherapy. He had a major breakdown while he was in undergrad, reporting auditory hallucinations, and he shifted into a mode of extreme social withdrawal. In the eight years before the commencement of treatment he had been living at home with his parents, but maintained minimal contact with them. He reported pervasive fear of physical injury to his brain, which he valued as the organ essential for learning, understanding the meaning of life, and enjoying life. He lived in a neighbourhood with many high-rise buildings and was concerned with possible falling objects that might cause damage to his brain. He was also very concerned about food safety, worrying that microorganisms or toxic ingredients might damage his brain. The client did psychotherapy for thirteen weekly sessions and made significant progress, and then participated in a self-help group that met monthly. The following is a summary of my notes from this case.

Engagement
The engagement process emphasized empathic listening, focusing on the client's underlying unmet needs. I avoided an authoritative diagnostic stance, and was careful not to show any judgment of his expressed fears.

N3C Assessment
- Needs for security, safety, learning, achievement, enjoyment, and pleasure.
- Circumstances: under medication, good family support, lack of activity and occupation for over eight years.
- Characteristics: insecure, suspicious, motivated to improve his situation, believes in "scientific knowledge" and that knowledge is the key to happiness in life.
- Capacity: intelligent, good self-regulatory and executive functions.

Goal Setting
- Being able to do something he would enjoy, such as reading and going to the library, with due regard for physical safety.
- Explore more enjoyable activities in life.

Strategies and Skills Learning and Development
- Planned a safe trip to the library, avoiding passing by high-rise buildings.
- Researched how to acquire a library card.
- Performed a simulation role-play of how to talk to the front-desk staff to obtain a library card. Eugene did not have serious skills deficit, but the role-play reduced his anticipatory anxiety and he experienced a sense of achievement for learning simple skills such as eye contact and smiling.
- After a successful trip to the library and checking out books, joined a self-help group for adults with schizophrenic disorder. He felt valued by the other members, who found him knowledgeable and smart (meeting some of his achievement and esteem needs).
- Achieved a gradual increase in the range and frequency of activities: group activities, listening to music, writing.
- Performed a simulation role-play of calling old friends he had not seen in a long while.
- Published an article in a community newspaper: after submitting the article, practised preparation and expectation management (in case of rejection) and came up with alternate explanations other than "I am not good enough." The article was accepted.
- Performed a simulation role-play for a job interview for a part-time position in the library.

Outcome (Maintained over Many.Years)
- Increase in activities as well as self-efficacy and interest in interpersonal interaction.
- Experienced life to be more enjoyable, appeared to be more relaxed, and smiled more frequently.
- Decreased reports of hallucination and less preoccupation with brain injury.
- Found part-time job and continued with writing.

the world in general. He was constantly haunted by a sense of vulnerability and the feeling that he could easily be harmed by falling objects, toxic agents present in his food, or a variety of imaginable accidents. He showed no interest in interacting with people and considered himself socially clumsy. My work with him involved an incremental expansion of the activities he enjoyed, starting with solitary activities such as going to the library – that at least got him outside of his house. He gradually moved on to do more things, and he later agreed to join a self-help group for individuals with schizophrenic disorder. The expansion of his variety of activities paralleled his scope of interest, and he eventually became much more socially active. He started off as someone who had difficulty talking to friends on the phone, but after a couple of years in the group, he was hosting gatherings for other members at home. His interest in reading expanded into that of writing, and he eventually even contributed articles to newspapers. During that process, he participated in a much wider variety of social activities and led a much more interesting life. What I learned from this case was that expanding one's own range of interests and activities enhances our capacity for developing common or shared interests with others, and that showing interest in the other party's experience goes a long way in facilitating interpersonal engagement.

4. Strategic Self-Disclosure

Interpersonal and social relationships are pursued primarily to meet our own needs. Whereas we employ other-oriented strategies in engagement, we need not lose sight of our own needs. A relationship is never only about the other party. The role we play in it is of central significance. In interpersonal engagement, attention to the needs and circumstances of the other party is part of an effective strategy, but it is also important for us to make the desired impact and achieve our intended outcome. To the extent that we wish to be known, understood, accepted, liked, or even loved by the other, we need to manage how messages are sent to the other party. Strategic self-disclosure is done to control the communication of information about ourselves so as to bring about desired responses from the other party.

In the earlier section on expression skills, we learned to manage our physical appearance, self-introduction, and opening lines. Now we can think of other aspects of our social performance with regard to the image we want to project and the response we desire from others. We are sending coded messages to people whenever we interact with them. Physical appearance, though overrated by a lot people, does nonetheless convey some information about ourselves. Strategic disclosure is a result of deliberation. It is done with reciprocal consideration between our own agenda and those of the other parties we are interacting with. Strategic self-disclosure aims at reception and positive response by the other party. For instance, if someone is telling me about her unhappy childhood, it would be insensitive of me to talk about my own positive experiences or to express my view on how difficult it is for parents to raise children. If I could talk about some of my own unpleasant experiences of being misunderstood or unfairly treated as a child, it would probably facilitate our emotional engagement. This little example actually illustrates a few principles of strategic self-disclosure, namely: (1) staying attuned to the other party's experience, attitude, and emotional tone; (2) compatibility with the other party's needs or agenda; (3) maximizing commonality and minimizing psychological distance and power difference; (4) enhancing trust through selective disclosure of vulnerability or negative experiences; and (5) enhancing emotional bonding by sharing experiences and feelings that will likely create emotional resonance.

The four strategies for facilitating interpersonal engagement, agenda management, positive responding, maximizing commonalities, and strategic self-disclosure can be synthesized in our responses. Following contingency-based thinking, there is not a single set of procedures that work in all situations; and we need to understand the situation, address our purpose of engagement, and remain attentive to the other party in order to come up with the most appropriate response.

Chapter Eleven

Managing Relationships

When we are successful with our initial engagement with people, we can proceed with our interaction with them. What follows can be the accomplishment of specific instrumental tasks, such as selling a product or completing an interview, or it can be the development of a longer-term relationship, which will be the substance of this chapter.

All human beings need at least a few relationships in order to survive. The ability to make relationships work for us is one of the most important competencies we need to develop, although society does not always provide the best resources and support for it. Given the diversity of relationships that are central to our lives – ranging from parent-child to sibling, intimate partner, work and business, social, or friendship, and so on – it is not possible for us to cover all of them adequately in one chapter of a book. What we will be focusing on from an SSLD perspective is how strategies and skills can be learned to improve people's likelihood of building gratifying and rewarding relationships in a wide range of contexts.

Reciprocal Need Gratification

People enter relationships to meet aspects of their personal needs. Relationships are functional, and they are maintained as long as they can function. When a relationship can no longer perform its function, it becomes difficult to maintain. Over half a century ago, Homans (1958) proposed a social exchange analysis, maintaining that relationships are formed on the basis of a subjective cost-benefit analysis and the comparison of alternatives. People develop relationships only when they perceive a net benefit. When the perceived costs of a relationship outweigh the perceived benefits, the theory predicts that the people will choose to leave the relationship. This formulation was further developed by a number of scholars (e.g., Blau, 1964; Cook, 1986; Emerson, 1981), but it has also been criticized for being too rational, being too influenced by the dominant social values of its time, not taking into account the nonlinear quality of relationships, and being too entrenched in an individualist culture (Heath, 1976; Miller, 2005).

The SSLD model construes human experience in terms of the multiple domains of functioning as well as the role of the social environment, including dominant discourses, values, and cultural influences. We also recognize the fact that many people feel trapped in dysfunctional relationships even though they may be convinced that they should leave. The maintenance of dysfunctional relationships can be very painful and destructive to the parties involved, and is often regarded as pathological by some mental health professionals. In practice, psychotherapists and other mental health professionals find many of their clients deeply entrenched in relationships with negative cost-benefit balances.

According to social exchange thinking, when partners in a relationship have needs and goals that are incompatible, or when the gratification of needs is inequitable between partners, the relationship will become charged with tension or conflict, making it difficult to sustain. Many relationships in real life afford gratification of some needs even when there is tension and conflict. A good example can be found in marital relationships. Many couples experiencing high tension or conflict still stay in their relationships because certain needs are still being met. These needs can be shelter, company, social status, financial security, identity, familial support, social approval, and so on. A review of people's relationships will reveal that many of them are characterized by tension, frustration, or conflict, but very often they still choose to maintain those relationships. An SSLD analysis shares the view with social exchange analysis that these people are still motivated to carry on the relationship and that some of their needs are still being gratified even in these apparently negative or dysfunctional relationships.

One of the reasons is the survival value of relationships, mentioned above. Starting in childhood, we learn that our needs are mostly met within the context of interpersonal and social relationships. We get food, shelter, company, protection, emotional support, pleasurable experience, and so on from our parental figures, siblings, friends, and extended family. When we grow older, we obtain knowledge, recognition, employment, and other forms of social reward through an expanding network of relationships. The termination of relationships often makes people feel uneasy, especially when those relationships are of high personal significance. We therefore cannot assume that people can always make rational decisions about their relationships by objectively weighing the pros and cons. Moreover, society usually imposes a cost on people who wish to exit from relationships that are socially reinforced to support social stability or economic functions. When people want to leave a relationship such as marriage, they have to deal with the needs that the relationship still addresses, the negative reaction from others, financial costs, bureaucratic and legal hassle, and so on. Another reason why people stay in difficult or dysfunctional relationships is the lack of alternatives or substitutes. Yet another reason is that changing or terminating a relationship requires a certain level of self-efficacy and skills that people may not have had the opportunity to learn and develop.

SSLD procedures can be employed to help people manage their relationships in order to meet their needs more effectively. This includes relationship building, maintenance and improvement, transformation, and termination. The central principle in managing relationships is due regard for the needs of the participants. This implies reciprocity, mutuality, and fairness. The effective management of negativity, tension, and conflict in relationships often requires openness and flexibility in our imagination of those relationships, including the readiness to consider transforming or even terminating significant relationships. SSLD pursues a pragmatic direction and is open to innovation and creative possibilities. It also empowers clients by equipping them with the necessary strategies and skills for doing what is most beneficial to them with regard to relationships.

Relationship Building

People build relationships to address their needs. Sometimes the relationship itself provides direct gratification of needs such as intimacy and emotional support. Sometimes relationships are pursued because they are useful in meeting other needs. One example could be a salesperson joining a religious group with the purpose of looking for prospective customers. Another example could be a student in elementary school befriending an older and bigger student in order to gain protection from being bullied. In any case, people are looking for something when they start to build a relationship. The first step in assisting people to manage their relationships is, therefore, to gain a better understanding of the needs they are seeking to meet in any given relationship. The quality of a relationship is therefore assessed with reference to the needs profile of the participants. People in a relationship can achieve more effective communication and negotiation of common goals, and can learn new ways to enhance the relationship, by making it more effective in meeting the respective needs of the parties involved. This can be done by combining some of the composite sets of strategies and skills described earlier in this book. The problem translation procedure described in Chapter 4, for instance, can be very helpful in achieving a better understanding of a participant's needs. As well, reception skills can enhance people's ability to assess the needs of the other parties in a relationship, while expression skills increase the odds of one's needs being recognized and addressed.

Compatibility

Compatibility between the relationship participants' needs profiles, which is important in the interpersonal engagement process, remains a key factor in the long-term viability of a relationship. People with complementary needs profiles are likely to form lasting and functional relationships. Perfect complementarity, however, is relatively rare, and people need to negotiate relationship patterns that match their needs profiles as best they can. Having an open and honest discussion of each other's needs and goals in a relationship, unfortunately, is not as common as one would hope to see. Even in relationships that are supposed to be characterized by intimacy and trust, people often do not have a good understanding of each other's needs. One of the reasons is that the expression or disclosure of one's needs can sometimes put a person in a vulnerable position. People feel exposed and believe that they can be hurt if they allow others to know exactly what they need and what they want.

Specific procedures can be designed according to SSLD principles to assist individuals in assessing and increasing needs compatibility. In couple counselling, for example, we often try to get the couple to have a better understanding of their respective needs and how their relationship can be modified to address these needs. A frequently used procedure is the review of a video-recorded conversation focusing on direct exploration of the couple's needs and compatibility. The SSLD practitioner can offer them feedback, mainly following the principles of problem translation. The procedure typically includes: (1) establishing a safe space for open expression of the participants' needs, met or unmet; (2) applying problem translation analysis to the current situations of both partners; (3) examining and managing perceived incompatibility; (4) negotiating maximal compatibility through innovative reframing; and (5) developing strategies and skills that will improve need gratification for both parties.

From Engagement to Relationship Building

The factors that are conducive to positive engagement are usually helpful in further development of a relationship, and the skills related to reception, expression, and engagement are all relevant. When people move on from satisfactory engagement to develop a longer-term relationship, they usually pursue more activities together. In theory, increase in shared activities should also lead to increased exchange of information and deepened understanding between the participants. In real life, however, a lot of relationships can carry on with shared activities without significant deepening of understanding, and sometimes even without substantial exchange of information. One example of this is family members who live in the same house and spend a lot of time together, such as while having meals, watching TV, or doing chores, but seldom communicate much. Another example is members of a club based on a particular activity or hobby. People can go to the club for years and play chess or badminton with each other without much deepening of their mutual knowledge or understanding. Such a relationship can still be experienced as good or gratifying by the members concerned. When their expectations are met, and no one demands additional content, the equilibrium is maintained. People who pursue relationships like these sometimes find that they satisfy their other needs as well, such as the need for a sense of belonging or identity, or a sense of order, routine, or stability. The relationship experienced by the individual may be more oriented towards the collective, be it the family or the club, than towards individual members.

Some of us believe that most people want to develop relationships with more depth or intensity, yet we have to recognize that such depth and intensity can be threatening to some people, even when they actually desire them. Managing intense and intimate relationships requires a certain emotional capacity. Psychoanalytic wisdom has it that a solid sense of self, or identity, is a prerequisite for intimacy (Erikson, 1950, 1959). In SSLD language, we can say that a capacity for intimacy requires emotional self-efficacy, which may include the mastery of strategies and skills that enable a person to feel safe and in control even when experiencing immense emotions in a relational context.

There are people who do not really want anything beyond routine and functional relationships consisting mainly of activities they can manage with ease, even when these activities are not particularly exciting. Whereas there can be multiple reasons why people prefer relationships that are more or less emotionally intense, the SSLD position is that it is better for people to have the choice. In other words, if people have developed the capacity for such emotional engagement and have mastered the relevant skills for it, they have a real choice of whether they want to get involved or not. In contrast, if people are avoiding emotional intimacy and intensity because of the fear of rejection, being overwhelmed, getting hurt, or losing oneself, or because of a lack of interpersonal competence or social resources, they do not really have a choice. In my experience, many people who are socially withdrawn, either because they are not confident or not interested, will usually become more socially active if they are given the opportunity to master the relevant strategies and skills.

Another important point is that we need to distinguish between a lack of interest in a particular relationship and a lack of interest in general. People maintain different types of relationships simultaneously for different purposes, and they do not need to achieve the same depth or intensity with all of them. Whereas society assumes that certain relationships, such as marriage or family, need to be more significant and intense, we do not have to make the same assumption in SSLD practice. The key consideration is whether the needs of our clients are effectively being met within their current network of relationships. People can assign varying significance to different relationships in their lives, and the diversity of their relationship patterns can be a result of personal choice, personality structure, culture, social circumstances (e.g., war, political conflict), and so on.

Furthermore, people who are concurrently involved in multiple relationships do not have to maintain perfect equity in each of them, as social exchange theorists assume. It is possible for people to balance what they are missing in one relationship with what they can attain in another. For example, a person may effectively meet security and material needs within their marriage while seeking emotional intimacy and sexual pleasure elsewhere. Many people can maintain equilibrium with multiple relationships in this manner for a long period of time while others cannot. With such understanding in mind, we will move on to explore how we may develop relationships involving more in-depth exchange and sharing.

Deeper Sharing and Intimacy

In the above section, we mentioned that people in a relationship with each other usually pursue some activities together. These activities may or may not facilitate the deepening of their relationship. Usually a relationship grows in intensity and intimacy under a number of conditions. The first is the extent to which the other party is needed for gratifying one's needs. A good example is the relationship between a baby and a parent. When the baby is almost totally dependent on the parent for all its needs, including its very survival, the emotional significance of that relationship is likely to be very high. Attachment theorists (e.g., Ainsworth, Blehar, Waters, & Wall, 1978; Ainsworth & Bowlby, 1965) actually believe that this emotionally significant relationship during childhood plays a key role in shaping relationship patterns in later life. When a social other is of minimal or peripheral importance in terms of meeting an individual's needs, then the relationship is unlikely to be assigned much significance. Similarly, activities can vary in their significance according to what gratification people can derive from them.

Activities, Events, and Signifying Acts

The dynamic interplay between activity and relationship is an important topic in SSLD. A strong relationship usually consists of many shared activities that are of high emotional significance. Emotional significance can be positive, negative, or mixed. It can include a wide range of possibilities – from physical violence to ecstatic sex. It can also include intense experiences such as war, natural disaster, adventure, expedition, dedicated research leading to major discovery, and so on. Whereas the occurrence of some of these events and activities is not always within the control of the individuals concerned, much less so the SSLD practitioner, there are always things people can learn to do in response to them, which can help them manage the effects these events may have on people's lives. In my own work with natural disasters such as tsunamis and earthquakes, for instance, I have found the collaborative creation of mourning and grieving rituals with people who have lost their loved ones to be very powerful, both in helping the individual members and in developing a sense of community. Learning to design activities that can strengthen relationships is an important composite skill to be acquired.

Couples who are dating apparently understand the importance of designing emotionally significant experiences and trying to make them special and memorable. The creativity and enthusiasm, however, tend to decrease when the relationship becomes more stable and cycles and patterns set in. An activity that is repeated many times tends to lose its valence. Even highly ritualized activities supported by extremely powerful social and economic processes, such as Christmas consumption and Valentine's Day indulgence, cannot consistently generate high levels of excitement and joy. Expectation is a variable that mitigates the effect of anniversaries or routine activities. Many people wish to exceed their own expectations to make an experience special, while most people have difficulty going beyond what marketing professionals and advertisers prescribe for them. For instance, as the idea of romance has been appropriated by the consumerist machinery (Illouz, 1997), most people now imagine the romantic in terms of consumer behaviour.

In SSLD practice, we focus on emotional sensitivity to the other party's needs, and we encourage people to be creative and innovative. The idea of learning and developing new strategies and skills implies creativity and innovation. In SSLD couple counselling, for instance, one of the exercises we often employ is for couples to design and implement pleasurable activities together as well as surprise activities for each other. In such exercises, the composite skills of reception, expression, communication, and engagement that have been covered in previous chapters are often important building blocks. Clients are constantly expanding their repertoire of possible activities with their partners, family, or friends.

Signifying acts are another related concept that was introduced earlier. Action we take to signify positive affect, care, or love can be very powerful in strengthening relationships. A middle-aged woman, for example, took it as strong evidence of her husband's love for her when he took care of the physical needs and personal hygiene of her aging and ailing father. Whereas the consumer market teaches us to spend money on presents for designated days and perform ritualistic consumption to maintain relationships, it often takes only a little extra care and imagination to come up with creative ideas that will become truly memorable.

Sharing

Apart from activities and signifying acts, talking about things that matter is another key process in deepening and strengthening relationships. This includes the sharing of ideas that are central to one's life-world, which can be a religious faith, a spiritual commitment, a political position, a value, a commitment to a social or humanistic cause, devotion to music or art, or – in Paul Tillich's (1973) words – "matters of ultimate concern." Our life-world is structured by such ideas, which relate to each other in very complex and variable ways. For some people, there is a superordinate idea, belief, or principle, and all other ideas are subordinate to it. Some people do not have such a hierarchical organization of ideas, and they can have more fluid relations with each other. Moreover, some people hold on to ideas in a more stable, consistent manner, while others go through more transition and change. On top of all this, not everyone has a clear sense of the ideas, principles, and values that are conditioning their lives. Some people have difficulty understanding how they think and what they believe, let alone telling others.

Sharing is actually a form of communication that emphasizes mutuality. In SSLD, the composite reception skills of listening and deciphering factual, attitudinal, motivational, and emotional content in other people's utterances are often applied not only to enhance one's understanding of others but also to improve self-understanding. This is most effectively done in a group-learning context, including smaller groups such as families or couples. The feedback people obtain through interacting with others can often contribute to a better understanding of their own views, attitudes, feelings, needs, and goals. In a sense, most SSLD intervention programs involve interactional exercises through which the clients learn to communicate more effectively, while at the same time learning more about themselves through feedback. When people learn to develop stronger relationships through sharing, they combine the composite skills of reception, expression, and engagement while emphasizing content that is personally significant.

Such content can include ideas like the ones suggested above. It can also include needs and goals, feelings, and experiences. In general, the breadth and depth of sharing progresses with the development of a relationship. Content conducive to the deepening of a relationship can include experiences that have had a major impact on one's life or personality development (e.g., childhood trauma, life-transforming events such as war), aspects of self that are not easily understood or accepted (e.g., having been imprisoned, psychiatric history, invisible disability, being HIV-positive), or other forms of unusual experience or views. Under ordinary circumstances, interaction and exchange between people usually starts with conventions established in the common-sense world, which reflect the dominant discourses in any given society or community. Ideas, experiences, and feelings that are compatible with such conventions are easier to share. As trust develops, and when there is the desire to get closer, people will increasingly share aspects of their life and personality that may not be fully compatible with the dominant ideas or values in their social context. The idea of sexual minorities coming out, for instance, clearly illustrates this reality. Certain things are not supposed to be "out" in a society that is not accepting of people who are not heterosexual, and people are not expected to openly share this aspect of their sexuality in these environments. In a social environment when sexual minorities are fully accepted, by contrast, this coming-out process will not be necessary.

In general, when relationships grow in depth, intensity, and intimacy, sharing will progress from the conventional to the unconventional, from the open to the hidden. It can be wishes or fantasies that we think other people may consider crazy or inappropriate, which are thus held in secret. It can be things we are not proud of, such as having been imprisoned or in a drug withdrawal program. It can be painful or traumatic experiences such as childhood sexual abuse or being tortured during a war or political strife. It can be things we feel guilty about such as not having had the opportunity to care for a loved one before she or he died. The more that participants in a relationship can share their "dark sides," the more the likelihood of intimacy increases. This progression, however, does not occur naturally in all relationships, for people usually select the particular relational contexts within which to share what is personally significant. Safety, or more specifically freedom from judgment or negative consequences, is usually a necessary condition. This partially explains the legendary "stranger on the train" (or on the flight) phenomenon. Other conditions include the other party's capacity to understand and communicate acceptance, as well as situational factors that allow or facilitate sharing such as privacy, time together, or a triggering event.

Whereas such sharing is typically found in more intense and intimate relationships, we cannot assume that a relationship is necessarily sound once such sharing has occurred. In couple counselling and family therapy, we come across partners and family members who have shared many intimate details of their lives and yet have difficulty living with each other. In many of these cases, the parties concerned have gone through years of shared activities and sharing of personal experiences, including those they are not proud of or will not share with others because of their social implications, but the quality of their relationship is on a downward spiral. What is worse in some of these cases is that the partners or family members use what was shared in trust and confidence against each other, causing tremendous damage and resentment.

Nourishment and Maintenance: Pleasure and Growth

One way to look at this is to take intimate sharing as a necessary but insufficient condition for a strong relationship. In SSLD practice, we are often reminded that relationships need to be nourished and maintained. Through working with our clients, we have come to learn about ways to nourish and maintain relationships. Pleasure and growth are two key components of this. For a relationship to flourish, the partners involved have to derive satisfaction and pleasure from it. As mentioned above with regard to romantic relationships, designing and implementing pleasurable activities is an important ingredient. In an ideal situation, people in a relationship will keep learning and developing new strategies and skills to bring pleasure to each other. These principles have been outlined in the earlier section on activities, events, and signifying acts.

In order to bring more pleasure and growth to partners in a relationship, it is important to avoid taking things for granted and learn to adopt an appreciative stance. Such a stance entails discovering new and delightful aspects of the relationship on an ongoing basis. It may be in our psychology that when an experience is repeated, its power to stimulate or excite will diminish. In the psychology of learning, we talk about reactive inhibition. In everyday life, people talk about getting tired of something. It is, however, an oversimplification to think that all repeated events will automatically be devalued. Some people actually need certain events and experiences to be repeated in order to feel safe and secure. The balance between repetition and novelty is probably variable across situations and individuals, and may change over time with the same individual.

An appreciative stance involves paying attention, including paying attention to variation and change. In SSLD, a key idea is to maximize choice and expand people's repertoire of possible strategies and skills. In the development of an appreciative stance, we need to combine cognitive, emotional, motivational, and behavioural strategies. Cognitively, an appreciative review of life circumstances means counting one's blessings. The ordinary life that we take for granted in the West is actually out of reach for the majority of the people on this planet. Think of a stable shelter, freedom of movement, clean water, legal and political rights, access to banking and financial services, freedom from violence and persecution, access to the market, exposure to international culture and arts, and the like. In theory, we can always find something to be thankful about.

Within the context of a relationship, being appreciative of what the other person is doing, or has done, is a good start. When we find it difficult to appreciate the other person's behaviours, it is often helpful to try to understand how they are formed or developed. A stingy person might have experienced deprivation or financial insecurity as a child, while a person preoccupied with the opinions of others might have experienced harsh criticisms by parents and authority figures. In SSLD, we sometimes ask participants to go through exercises such as the 3-D Appreciation Exercise (discover, document, and display), which involves documenting positive qualities about a person in their life and showing appreciation for something the other person has done in a creative manner, such as staging a mini recognition event (e.g., making a point to say something positive about a person in a family get-together or a work meeting, presenting an award to the person in a small party). Such exercises very often reinforce the appreciative stance. In group programs, participants often enjoy sharing ideas of how to discover, document, and display appreciation.

While many people learn to develop an appreciative stance without much of a problem, sometimes we will come across individuals having certain emotional barriers. This is especially true for people having a history of emotional injury, such as people whose partners have had affairs behind their backs. It is important for us to acknowledge such emotional issues and assist clients to manage them. In some cases, it is possible that the exploration of such feelings may lead clients to conclude that they do not want to maintain the relationship with their partner. Then we may have to work on the transformation or termination of the relationship, which will be covered later in this chapter. If the client is still motivated to work on the relationship, collaborative management of such emotional barriers is usually feasible. The procedures

Worksheet 11.1. 3-D Appreciation Exercise

Name of member:_____
Subject (the person you want to appreciate more):_____
Date: From _____ to _____

Discover
Between now and the next session, you have to discover a few things that you genuinely appreciate about your chosen subject. Examples include:
- Positive responses towards you or other people: anything nice, such as compliments, help, service, assistance, gifts, kindness.
- Any positive quality of the subject: skills, experience, attitude, appearance, value.

Document
Keep a record of what you have discovered and the display methods that you think will be appropriate for these discoveries:

Date	What you appreciate	Display of appreciation

Display
- Direct feedback: telling the subject directly. Cards, emails, text messages, and so on are okay (caution: AVOID sarcasm or anything that can be construed as sarcasm).
- Open acknowledgment: choose an appropriate context to openly indicate your appreciation. It can be a family gathering, work-team meeting, party, or Facebook posting (caution: make sure that it is something that the subject would not mind others hearing about; do not proceed and resort to direct feedback when in doubt).
- Recognition event: stage a small recognition event for your subject (e.g., preparing a small award to be presented, making an address) with an appropriate audience (can be just the two of you, a close circle of friends, your family, or in front of the children).

described in Chapter 9 (in the section titled "Emotional Work in SSLD") will be relevant here.

The appreciative stance reinforces a generally positive approach to life, which is actually a key feature of SSLD. Further to the development of an appreciative stance, a relationship can be nourished by actions taken towards mutual self-enhancement. What this means is a proactive approach to making the relationship work in favour of the personal growth and development of the parties involved. This approach involves allowing space for the other person to grow and develop while strengthening and deepening the quality of communication through sharing. It also involves providing positive feedback and actual support to increase the other party's self-efficacy. The self-enhancement is mutual in that the capacity to allow space for the other person to grow, to maintain quality communication, and to provide support involves a high level of self-efficacy and interpersonal competence. Ideally, partners in a relationship will continue to grow and develop, deriving gratification and support from each other.

Strategies and skills for mutual self-enhancement can range from giving empowering feedback that recognizes the other person's strength to supporting that person through a professional training or a graduate program, a change in career, or an existential quest for meaning and fulfilment. It is always important to remember that we are talking about mutual self-enhancement instead of an unequal, one-sided arrangement with one party giving and the other party taking, without reciprocation. The key ingredients for mutual self-enhancement are (1) responsiveness to the other person's needs; (2) respecting the other's need for personal space to grow and develop; (3) maintaining power equity by saying and doing things that empower the other person; and (4) providing actual support. In relationships in which the growth and development of the other person is not valued, the risk of overdependence and the corresponding over-control and stifling can threaten the long-term well-being of both the relationship and the individual partners. Extreme examples include overprotective parenting and abusive couple relationships. In such relationships, the person with more power tries to keep or even expand the power difference by fostering dependence so as to maintain or tighten control. One common strategy is to restrict the other person's (child or spouse) life-world or range of activities and to issue disempowering messages, which usually imply that the other party is not capable of doing well without the person in power.

Some people may worry that encouraging the other person to grow and develop will decrease the other person's need for the current relationship, and therefore undermine the very relationship that they are trying to strengthen. Many people in a romantic relationship tend to do this, as do some parents. This leads to an important issue in how we view relationships. People are motivated by different needs and drives when they get involved in relationships. Abraham Maslow (1943, 1971) distinguished between two types of drives: one type he called D drives, referring to deficiency, and the other type he called B drives, referring to being. The D drives, based on the need for things such as food, shelter, and safety, can be satiated. B drives, which are based on the need for qualities such as truth, goodness, beauty, unity, perfection, and completion, can be fulfilled but not satiated. This view is echoed by Rogers's (1961) view on personal development.

The SSLD view, grounded in multiple contingencies analysis, is that people are differentially motivated. Many people develop relationships for the more instrumental reasons of satisfying their basic needs, and people who are seeking personal growth or mutual self-enhancement are likely to be in the minority. Even people who desire ongoing growth, development, or transcendence probably do not seek them in all relationships. The self-actualizing individual may still maintain relationships that are more mundane. Considering the network of relationships within a person's life-world, we will probably find that most relationships are more instrumental in nature and are not intended to be developed into a context for ongoing growth and self-actualization. Hopefully there will be some relationships within each person's life-world that have the potential to facilitate or support continual growth and being-oriented quests. A summary of relationship building strategies can be found in Box 11.1. As a learning system, SSLD supports clients in all kinds of relationship building, ranging from those instrumental in meeting ordinary needs to those associated with existential or transcendental quests. Based on this position, the principles of (1) staying attuned to each other's needs and aspirations, and therefore knowing what the relationship means and is expected to provide; (2) developing an appreciative stance; and (3) pursuing mutual self-enhancement, should be able to help enrich most relationships.

Personal Life Course and Relationship Life-Cycle

The related question of the life-cycle of a relationship, or the period

> **Box 11.1. Relationship Building**
>
> - Interaction through activities and events:
>   - Ordinary, everyday activities;
>   - Pleasurable activities;
>   - Personally significant events;
>   - Rituals;
>   - Signifying acts.
> - Sharing of:
>   - Ideas, views, and values;
>   - Hopes and aspirations;
>   - Experiences;
>   - The "dark side," what is socially unacceptable.
> - Nourishment and maintenance – pleasure and growth:
>   - Appreciative stance;
>   - Mutual self-enhancement.

of time over which a relationship is needed or wanted, has yet to be answered. As people go through different stages of their lives, they develop new relationships, and some of their earlier relationships simply fade away. While some of us may occasionally get sentimental over a childhood friend that we have not seen in decades, we usually just accept that certain relationships will naturally cease to be important in our current life-world. There are, however, relationships that people wish to maintain over a long duration. It is important for us to realize that the kinds of relationships we need do change over our life course, and that relationships all have their respective life-cycles. The nature and dynamics of a parent-child relationship, for example, have to change through different stages of life. While the relationship starts with the parents being the centre of the child's world and the child being almost totally dependent on them, the centrality of the parents' position usually diminishes as the child grows older. There are periods in the child's life when the child actively seeks freedom and independence from the parents.

A lack of shared understanding between two parties with regard to their respective needs and aspirations, which are conditioned by their respective life-stages, often contributes to tension or conflict in their relationship. In marital relationships, many people expect the relationship to stay strong over the course of a lifetime, but the needs and aspirations of two partners often cannot remain complementary. It is actually difficult for two individuals to have compatible needs and aspirations through a lifetime during which both parties are growing and changing. Recognizing the reality of individual growth and change over times, especially within a social context where people are exposed to an ever-increasing array of individuals with whom they can form significant relationships, the chance of an intimate relationship being maintained over a long time is not high. In SSLD, the priority is to develop and manage relationships so that they work for the participants in terms of meeting their needs. Relationships can sometimes be transformed to achieve this goal, but if the personal and emotional cost of staying in the relationship outweighs its benefits, the relationship can be adjusted in its significance and intensity – or even terminated if that turns out to be the best possible option for the client. This position brings us to the topics of transforming and terminating significant relationships.

Transformation and Termination

Actually, people experience the transformation and termination of relationships quite frequently in their lives; it is just that when the relationships are not significant we do not pay much attention to them. As pointed out above, our needs, aspirations, and circumstances change as we grow and move through different stages of life, and people will occupy different positions and play different roles in our life-world. Many of us have lost touch with people who were important in an earlier phase in our lives, or have become much less attached to them over time. Such growing apart and separation are not unexpected in the natural life-course of most relationships, such as childhood friends, teacher-student relationships, classmates, or colleagues. Usually, it is when people experience difficulties in making a relationship work before it is expected to expire, or when people do not know or accept that a relationship is going to expire, that they consider seeking professional help.

Whereas SSLD aspires to be an effective system for helping people learn and develop strategies and skills for managing various challenges in life, it has to be recognized that no matter how effective our intervention system is, it will not be able to save all relationships from major transformation or termination. Separation and divorce rates, for example, are not negatively correlated with the popularity or availability of couple or marital counselling. As mentioned above, the SSLD position is that relationships should work for people, and the choice of nourishing and maintaining, or transforming, or terminating a relationship is to be based on how it meets the need of the parties involved. This section will explore the processes of relationship transformation and termination, again with a clear emphasis on how people's needs are best met within various relational contexts.

Transformation

Relationships are constantly changing. Even when we are talking about stable relationships with interaction patterns that apparently do not change much, like couples who live in the same house, share certain routines, and do not pursue innovative activities nor bring new content into their shared life, something is changing. For one thing, people's experience of the same thing changes over time. The aging process itself is a process of change. Moreover, when other aspects of a person's life-world change, the meaning of an apparently unchanged relationship will change as well. The role and significance of a partner or spouse in a person's life, for example, will almost inevitably change over time. Many people experience this transformation as something that happens to them instead of something that they have caused to happen, at least in part. Actually, in SSLD, one of the common tasks in the intervention process is for the clients to understand their own role in making the relationship what it is. This is consistent with our belief in people's agency and the idea of mutual conditioning and transformation between the person and the environment.

As suggested earlier, transformation of an insignificant relationship usually does not cause much concern. We are, therefore, focusing our attention on transformation of more significant relationships. Such transformation can be associated with major transitions in human development, such as the separation-individuation process described by Mahler (Mahler, 1963, 1972; Mahler & Furer, 1968; Mahler, Pine, & Bergman, 1975), which involves the mother-child dyad moving through phases of transformation. This is a process that requires the child to develop cognitive representation of self and relationships, emotional regulation, and increasingly autonomous behaviour. Whereas developmental psychologists have different ideas regarding what is healthy or normal, the fact that the child's relationship with its parents has to go through major transformation is probably recognized by all of them. What creates a problem is when the transformation compromises optimum growth and development, or when desirable transformation cannot be made.

SSLD can be employed to assist individuals in different phases of their lives to transform relationships to their best advantage. For instance, when an older person needs the care and support of a nursing home while it is better for her or his partner to remain living in the community, the relationship will have to be transformed. In our increasingly globalized environment, we have more and more people in significant relationships relocating to distant cities or countries without the option of bringing their partner or family. Apart from changes in physical conditions or geographical location, major transformation of relationships can become necessary as a result of accident, illness, unemployment, or drastic changes in economic or social circumstances.

When transformation naturally brings improved circumstances for the parties concerned, and therefore more effective gratification of their needs, it is usually not regarded as a problem. It is when the transformation threatens some of the basic needs of at least one of the parties concerned that it becomes an issue. In SSLD, the focus is on need gratification and goal attainment for both parties. In general, if a relationship can be transformed to achieve such objectives, then we will work towards that by developing new strategies and skills. This may include proactive and open negotiation to work towards a collaborative transformation of the relationship. In certain situations, however, there is very limited room for negotiation, such as when an adult child finds a new job and moves to another town. If a relationship transformation will inevitably compromise the need gratification of one or both parties, people will need to find gratification of the same needs elsewhere, be it in other concurrent relationships or in new relationships. This principle, as will be shown later, can be applied to the management of relationship termination as well.

When the transformation of relationships is open to negotiation, people can be assisted to learn to do that more effectively. SSLD principles covered earlier in this book can be applied here to help people achieve better outcomes. Mutual understanding of each other's needs, together with each other's views and feelings regarding the relationship, is perhaps the most important first step. Learning and developing skills to effectively communicate one's needs, views, and feelings can be very helpful. In the negotiation of relationship transformation, like in the case of relationship nourishment and maintenance, reciprocal consideration of each other's needs is of critical significance in working towards the best possible arrangement for both parties. Negotiating how a relationship can be transformed can take anything from a good conversation to a lengthy process of dialogue and adjustment. Many of the composite skills regarding reception, expression, communication, and relationship nourishment and maintenance described in earlier sections can be applied in the process. In general, the following components are likely to be useful:

(1) Understanding the circumstances of the transformation (e.g., aging parent moving into nursing home, adult child leaving home, a significant other resettling to another city or country), as well as its implications;
(2) Recognition of the transition that both parties have to go through (e.g., adjusting to a new environment, losing certain opportunities or freedom, learning new skills, developing new relationships, increased or decreased responsibility/role);
(3) Awareness of the needs that will be affected, both for oneself and the other party (e.g., affiliation/company/intimacy, [in]dependence, autonomy, identity, financial security, achievement and self-actualization, etc.);
(4) Effective communication of the above, showing respect for the other person's position and needs while clearly articulating one's own;
(5) Collaborative exploration of options, keeping an open attitude towards innovative ideas;
(6) Knowing the limits of concession or compromise, including when to give up.

It is of course good when a win-win transformation can be negotiated, but in many cases the transformation will almost inevitably compromise the need gratification of at least one of the parties (e.g., when a significant other resettles in another city or country). In such cases, the unmet needs have to be addressed, likely through the development of new relationships or nourishing of some of the existing ones. The strategies and skills that are needed for the development of new relationships, or for getting other existing relationships to take over functions of the relationship to be transformed, have been discussed before. In

SSLD practice, we recognize that the shift from getting what we need from one relationship to another is not a simple, mechanical process of switching, for it involves emotional investment, and sometimes additional processing of emotions is necessary. The section on emotional work covered earlier in Chapter 9 will be relevant here. A parent whose child is growing and becoming increasingly independent may, for instance, feel unwanted. We can infer from this that the parent needs to feel needed, useful, or important. In this case, quite a few strategies may work, such as getting recognition from other caring relationships, volunteering in community service, getting more involved in work or career, starting a business, keeping a pet, and so on. Yet the transition process has to be managed appropriately. This usually involves managing the emotional significance of the relationship.

When relationships are transformed, people sometimes feel disappointed, abandoned, betrayed, rejected, or unfairly treated. Such emotions can feed into emotional processes that are connected to a wide range of possible feelings including resentment, anger, sadness, shame, or even a more existential sense of futility or emptiness. Such emotional experiences often have a cognitive underlay. Recognition of such emotional and cognitive processes is necessary in helping clients who are going through relationship transformation. A lesson learned through my years of working with people going through various kinds of relationship transformation or termination is that it is important to preserve the self, or the sense of self, of the client. Very often, even with people who are highly competent in interpersonal and social functioning, they need to feel that what they have invested in a relationship is being valued, acknowledged, and appreciated. Our help is likely to be more effective if we show recognition of such additional needs, which may sometimes go unmet, because the other person may never come to show such appreciation or positive regard – or it may not happen till much later.

Sometimes we also need to recognize that although the need can be met through an alternative arrangement, the particular mode or intensity of gratification cannot be readily substituted. To some people, being appreciated and valued by someone you help as a volunteer in a children's shelter brings similar satisfaction as caring for your own child, yet for some people the two are very different. It is the same way that some people have no problem with diet drinks and sweeteners, while for others the craving for the real thing cannot be completely quenched by substitutes. In such cases, recognition of the actual experience of the client is a good starting point. We have to recognize that some relationships have qualities that may never be reproduced or replaced, at least for the individual concerned. In such cases, instead of trying to find direct substitute relationships – which some people may regard as almost sacrilegious to the original relationship – we may want to explore alternative life designs. The general principle is to enhance self-efficacy while at the same time expanding the repertoire of strategies for pleasure and gratification, sometimes not of the exact same needs, but of other related needs.

For example, the experience of children growing up and leaving home, which is a common experience for millions of baby boomers all over the world, represents a significant transformation of relationships. Many parents go through this transition smoothly and learn to enjoy a new phase of freedom and growth. Some people experience loss, confusion, and even depression. Obviously, the parenting role means different things for different people, and is functionally related to different needs in different cases. For some people, parenting involves chores that they do not miss. Some find a sense of satisfaction in the completion of the most demanding phases of parenting. Some people, however, define their identity with their parenting role and use it to order or structure their life design. The varied needs profiles explain the different responses people have towards such transformation of their parent-child relationships.

When a significant relationship is transformed, the equilibrium in a person's life-world is inevitably disrupted. This disruption often is a blessing in disguise. If we can learn to take full advantage of the opportunity, the transition can often enrich our lives. Developmental psychologists and researchers on aging and the life course have in many ways helped people to anticipate these transitions. What SSLD attempts to do is to offer a systematic procedure to help us maximize our potential for gratifying our needs and realizing our goals and aspirations through managing relationship transformations. Similar principles and procedures can actually be applied to transitions through different life stages as well. It is easy to imagine how SSLD intervention can be of help to people going through transitions such as children beginning school, young people starting university and living away from home, new adoptive parents starting to raise their kids, new immigrants arriving at their host country, an older person moving into a retirement facility, and the like.

Termination

The management of relationship termination is in many ways similar to that of relationship transformation. In theory at least, termination can be construed as one kind of transformation. Whereas what was discussed in the above section is generally applicable to relationship termination, there are a couple of issues that are perhaps more often associated with termination than transformation, although they can probably be found in certain relationship transformation situations as well. These issues include irreversibility, be it real or perceived, as well as mourning and grief. Termination is such an emotionally charged process that many people are not comfortable with it. It is rarely covered in our education system and socialization process. Even in professional training programs for counsellors and psychotherapists, termination does not occupy an important position (Gelso & Woodhouse, 2002; Joyce, Piper, Ogrodniczuk, & Klein, 2007; Zuckerman & Mitchell, 2004). In this section, we will look at these issues through the specific examples of death, separation, and divorce, and describe how SSLD procedures may be employed to assist individuals in managing such challenging situations in life.

My colleague Howard Irving (Irving 2002a, 2002b; Irving & Benjamin, 2002) founded the system of therapeutic family mediation to assist couples going through divorce. He combines psychotherapeutic principles and mediation procedures to help couples manage the tension and conflict that arise out of the separation and divorce process and can often become extremely irrational and destructive. One of the positive outcomes of the procedure is a more rational process that will allow partners to negotiate the best possible arrangement with regard to their own interests and the well-being of the children involved. I have worked with him in training practitioners to apply his system cross-culturally. Readers who wish to learn more about the system are encouraged to consult his work directly. This section is more focused on the application of SSLD principles in such situations, especially when it is not possible to work with the couple – and it is not uncommon that couples going through separation and divorce do not want to receive counselling or therapy together.

As mentioned above, the management of relationship termination can be quite similar to that of relationship transformation. The termination of a marriage, for example, can be experienced as a transformation by some people, some of whom will actually continue to be friends with their ex. There are people who experience separation and divorce as more than just the transformation or termination of a relationship; it can be seen as a disruption of the entire order of their life-world, a threat to their sense of identity, a loss of social status, a financial crisis, a severe personal failure, trauma, and so on. When children are involved, it is important to note that the separation or divorce usually means significant transformation of the parent-child relationship as well as disruption of the children's lives.

Given the huge variation from case to case, the needs to be addressed and the strategies and skills to be learned and developed will vary accordingly. While we can follow similar steps to those described in relationship transformation, management of relationship termination can sometimes demand more intensive intervention. Using separation and divorce as an example, the termination of a spousal relationship has an impact on multiple areas of a person's life-world, often including the person's sense of self. While some people make the transition more easily and are soon able to find gratification and fulfilment in new relationships, some people have to almost totally reconfigure their life-world. The range of strategies and skills to be learned and developed will obviously be very different for these cases, and it is probably not possible for us to have a standard procedure for them. Following a contingency-based approach, SSLD intervention may include the following components:

(1) Assessment of the impact of the relationship's termination: this usually requires a scanning of the major areas of human needs, given the centrality of couple relationships in many people's lives. Couplehood, especially in the form of marriage, receives enormous support as a social arrangement and plays a role in people's access to all sorts of material, social, cultural, and personal resources essential for gratifying a wide spectrum of needs, from physical needs such as housing and food to companionship, financial security, emotional support, sexual gratification, social status, identity, and even personal growth and development. The more people are reliant on their couple or marital relationship for meeting their needs, the more difficult it is for them to manage the full impact of its termination. In cases where children are involved, it is important to assess the needs of the children, who are often very dependent on the parental system for meeting their needs and are too often neglected, misunderstood, or underestimated by the adults.

(2) Assessment of the emotional and personal impact: this, in theory, can be included under needs assessment. In the management of divorce, especially difficult cases, we often find that the emotional and personal impact takes centre stage in relation to material and instrumental needs. Experiences of rage, sadness, betrayal, resentment, guilt, fear, and many other intense emotions – which sometimes seem totally out of proportion – are often the most vivid reality for the individuals going through the process. Whereas these emotions have to be managed, as will be highlighted in the following paragraph, they often reflect damage and/or threat to people's sense of self, and sometimes to the very sense of order underlying their life-world. Trauma is often used to describe such experience. Whereas the word *trauma* is overused in everyday language, I use it to refer to a significant event that disrupts the fundamental order of a person's life-world. Separation and divorce can often be traumatic according to this definition, both for the partners and the children involved. Many people, be they adults or children, go through a chronic course of self-doubt together with a sense that their world has been shattered. The heightened sense of aloneness, vulnerability, and helplessness can be extremely debilitating. SSLD intervention, therefore, prioritizes the self and the ordering or design of the person's life-world. Gaining an understanding of what the relationship and its termination may mean emotionally and personally to the individual is an important task. In the initial phase of engagement and assessment, attention is paid to empathic understanding of the person's experience of the termination's impact. In later phases of actual learning and development of strategies and skills, we keep a clear focus on self-efficacy so that the client can maintain a strong sense of agency, mastery, and autonomy. Some of the key components of successful outcomes include being able to feel positively about oneself, and being able to maintain a sense of mastery over one's internal experiences such as feelings, thoughts, and behaviour as well as over one's external life-world, which includes design for daily living and the performance of social roles.
(3) Emotional work: following the SSLD procedure on emotional work described in Chapter 9, the first key task is to facilitate the client's exploration, awareness, and ownership of her or his feelings. Normalizing, which refers to the creation and maintenance of a safe space for the client to deal with emotional issues without

fear of judgment or prohibition, is usually helpful. Being able to connect with one's own internal emotional processes is a prerequisite for subsequent work on the articulation, expression, and resolution of emotional needs and emotional reactions.

(4) Review of current strategies: when people feel that their very being and their life-world is threatened, it is not unusual for them to pursue strategies that are not necessarily in their own best interest. People going through separation or divorce, or feeling the threat of losing their partner, often perform acts that are self-defeating or outright self-destructive, which in extreme cases can include violence, substance use, reckless behaviour, random sexual indulgence, criminal acts, suicide, and the like. Even people who do not pursue extreme and counterproductive strategies will often employ strategies that are ineffective with regard to the needs that they are trying to meet, such as binge eating, excessive spending, or social withdrawal. Helping clients to understand that they may want to act in their best interest through effective strategies that address their personal and emotional needs – as well as the well-being of their children, if that is on their agenda – is a pivotal step in setting the stage for effective SSLD intervention.

(5) Life-world redesign: given the pervasive impact of separation or divorce, and the strong influence of social discourse favouring marriage and couplehood, many people have difficulty imagining their life after termination of a couple or marital relationship. Enabling clients to imagine how their life can be reconfigured by considering their needs, current capacity, and resources can be a very empowering step towards redesigning a life that can be gratifying, enjoyable, or even growth enhancing.

(6) Specification of the strategies and skills to be learned and developed: following the assessment and review, and once we have figured out how life after the termination of a significant relationship can be imagined, we can come to specify the strategies and skills that the client needs to learn and develop. As repeatedly emphasized in this book, what each person needs to learn can be different, ranging from emotional management and cognitive reframing to finding new sources of pleasure and/or purpose; pursuing self-enhancement; establishing socio-economic independence; handling inappropriate or negative reactions from others such as judgment and guilt-tripping; adapting to single or shared parenting; managing the previous social network; and

so on. SSLD programs can be tailor-designed with regard to the client's specific needs, goals, coping style, personal capacity, and available resources.
(7) Systematic learning and development of strategies and skills: once a program for the client has been designed, systematic learning and development can take place. Clients can incrementally master strategies and skills that will allow them to pursue personal goals effectively, gradually building a new life that affords satisfaction, fulfilment, and even personal growth.

This procedure is applicable to children as well. As mentioned above, parental separation or divorce usually implies the transformation of relationships between children and both of their parents. It can also mean the termination of a child's relationship with one or both of their parents in some cases. The most difficult part for children is their lack of control over the process, and the fact that their well-being is largely at the mercy of the adults. Helping children to access information and preparing them cognitively, emotionally, and behaviourally for contingencies is a potentially valuable task. Adults often underestimate children's ability to comprehend divorce and the processes involved (Moxnes, 2003), and SSLD procedures can be applied either directly by working with children through an effective needs assessment and problem translation process, or indirectly through helping parents master the skills of talking to their children about divorce and supporting them through the process.

Death

Going through the death of a loved one shares some similar processes with that of terminating a significant relationship, such as the experience of loss and varying degrees of disruption to one's life-world. Death is the most absolute termination of a relationship, and a process over which we often do not have much control. Its inevitability and irreversibility make it one of the most difficult events in human life. Unlike the breaking up of intimate relationships, which can be a result of an interactive process that the client can participate in, death is usually experienced as something that happens to the other party beyond the client's control. The SSLD approach to helping people deal with the death of a significant person is characterized by a number of principles or features, which will be listed below.

(1) People experience death differently: the death of a significant person can mean very different things to different people. The survivor's relationship with the deceased is a key factor in conditioning their reaction. Other factors include age, both of the deceased and the survivor; cause of death, particularly whether the death was anticipated or abrupt; timing with regard to the life course of the survivor; previous experience with death and loss; self-efficacy; availability of support; culture and religion; and so on. For instance, we can imagine a victim of intimate partner violence whose perpetrator has just died, and contrast that with an older individual losing his adult child who has been his main source of care and support. SSLD practice, therefore, does not imagine a universal process of stages that everyone will go through, but recognizes that there will be diverse responses. Not taking a normative approach actually opens up space for clients to communicate their experience and express their feelings and thoughts freely and allows for creative response strategies that can address individual contingencies.

(2) Replacing the functions of the lost relationship: an important part of the assessment of the client's needs is to review the functions of the lost relationship. Like in the case of divorce, the relationship can be of central significance in many domains of the client's needs, including those that are material, financial, emotional, and social. In some cases, the relationship is only of limited function, meaning that the client is not very dependent on the relationship with the deceased in addressing her or his needs. The loss of a relationship in terms of means for need gratification can be managed by following similar principles and procedures suggested in earlier sections for relationship transformation and termination.

(3) Addressing personal significance: the implication of the death of a significant person often goes beyond that of meeting current needs. This is, for example, quite obvious in the case of adults who lose their parents after many years of living independently. In a way, these individuals do not depend on their relationship with the deceased to fulfil their needs, but they can still experience immense personal impact from its termination. In clinical practice, it is not uncommon to find these individuals going through grief, guilt, and a host of other intense emotions. The death can also trigger a life-review process for many of them, leading to various responses and outcomes. As mentioned above, SSLD practice re-

spects individual experience and does not superimpose a normative frame with regard to what is normal and healthy grieving. Instead, we want to understand what the relationship meant to the client and how the client wishes to deal with its loss, and then we will assist the client to achieve what she or he desires.

(4) Moving on with life: this is probably a common goal across different approaches to helping people deal with the death of a significant person. The SSLD approach is characterized by its incrementalism. Clients need to learn to imagine their lives in the next phase, but some people need more time to shift the temporal structures of their life-world. The death of a significant person tends to bring on a retrospective orientation, which includes the life-review process mentioned above. Other processes such as reminiscing, mourning, and grieving are also predicated on a retrospective orientation. Very often, the resolution of long-standing conflicts or emotional baggage entails reimagining the life of the deceased, and therefore understanding her or his circumstances, experiences, decisions, and actions. This process can bring about insight into the mind and the life-world of the deceased – and, in cases where the deceased has caused the client much harm and distress, can subsequently lead to reconciliation and forgiveness. While retrospection is probably a necessary process for most people, they will usually become increasingly engaged with the present and the future. In SSLD practice, emotional experience and cognitive processes are often understood as being motivated by, or functionally linked to, people's needs that are still to be met. These needs can even include the need to reconcile, to forgive, or to work through the resentment or ambivalence that one may have towards the deceased. These retrospectively oriented processes, however, can be temporally reframed by focusing on needs and goals, such as "you wish to resolve this guilt towards your father (retrospective) so that you can regain your peace of mind (present and future)."

(5) Learning and development: learning and development are intrinsically future-oriented. By suggesting that we can learn to do something, we are simultaneously pursuing several tasks. Take, for example, when we say to a client something like, "It's tough that you have suddenly found yourself having to deal with her death before you could resolve the emotional tension between the two of you, and you're not prepared for it. You may need to learn to deal

with this and its implications on your life now and in the future." First, we are recognizing what the client needs and wishes to accomplish. The learning paradigm implies the possibility of change and improvement, and thereby infuses hope. The explicit future orientation takes the client outside the confines of a retrospective frame. The SSLD approach almost always entails positive reframing. In this way, the need to learn something is less likely to be taken as inadequacy or pathology, which is sometimes implied in other clinical approaches. Once clients are engaged in a program of learning, they are already in a proactive mode instead of a passive mode that is more likely to feed into the experience of aloneness, vulnerability, and helplessness.

Transformation or Termination

In the above section, we have looked at death primarily as the termination of a relationship, but in actual practice many people still maintain a relationship with the deceased in that the deceased remains part of their life. Many clients go through processes that they will describe as reconciliation with the deceased, or a renewed bonding, or a sense of their presence, and the like. SSLD analysis takes these experiences to be functional and assesses their value with regard to how well they serve to meet the clients' needs. It is, therefore, possible for us to deal with death as a relationship transformation process, and not necessary as termination. In terms of our lived experience, whether we experience the process as transformation or termination is pretty much a result of how we construct reality. We have discussed these topics under different headings mainly to facilitate conceptualization by providing anchorage points or coordinates to map out the direction and process of our intervention. It is not surprising that in actual practice, we find clients moving through relationship building and maintenance, transformation, or termination in different sequences. Their needs and aspirations, the continual expansion of their repertoire of strategies and skills, and their growing self-efficacy are the key directions that keep us on track.

Summary

In this chapter, we have looked at the application of SSLD principles to one of the most important aspects of human life – that of relationships. As stated earlier, building and maintaining positive relationships are critical to our physical and social survival, as well as our personal growth and overall well-being. The SSLD approach recognizes the multiple challenges in contemporary life, the rapid pace of social change, the vicissitudes in our life course, and the contingent nature of relationships. What SSLD is committed to is helping people manage their relationships and their lives according to their own needs and aspirations. The illustrations provided in this chapter emphasize the flexible application of SSLD principles that embrace the contingent nature of human experience, advocating for individualized or contingency-based intervention design.

Chapter Twelve

Instrumental Tasks

Instrumental Tasks

Most of our life goals are accomplished within interpersonal and social contexts. We often find ourselves in situations in which we have goals that are more instrumental, meaning that we only wish to get things done and do not necessarily want to develop a relationship with the person after the goal has been accomplished. The relationship is only developed for a practical purpose, so it is either incidental or secondary to the instrumental goal. In everyday life, people try to attain instrumental goals in a huge range of possible scenarios. One can be trying to talk oneself out of a traffic ticket, searching for a job, looking for a trustworthy driver to hire a vehicle on an excursion to an unfamiliar destination, finding the best deal on a car, applying for an immigrant visa, or purchasing or selling a property. Given the diverse possibilities, this chapter obviously cannot cover them all. As a matter of fact, there is already a significant amount of literature on such topics in the form of self-help books, DIY (do-it-yourself) manuals, guides, and advice columns. The purpose of this chapter is to outline general SSLD principles that can be applied to most situations in which people wish to achieve their instrumental goals.

It's the Performance That Counts

Self-help guides are usually written by experts who know the area reasonably well. Much of the information they contain can be very useful. As will be discussed later, we believe that knowledge is power and these guides and manuals can therefore be very helpful if used appropriately. The major limitation of the use of such guides and manuals lies not in the content of the materials themselves but in the learning process. First of all, people's motivation to follow through with written instructions tends to waver. The amount of people who actually follow the instructions after purchasing these manuals is relatively small (Clark et al., 2004; Curry, 1993). The other key issue is the knowledge-action gap mentioned in the beginning of this book. The ability to translate written words into action varies across individuals. In SSLD practice, we realize that people often need to go through more experiential and interactive learning involving observation learning, coaching, simulation, feedback, rehearsal in real life, and so on. In most cases, the design of a program for learning and developing instrumental strategies and skills follows the same SSLD procedures of problem translation, goal setting, and the systematic learning of strategies and skills.

What SSLD programs do is ensure that the learner is actually performing the instrumental tasks effectively in real life. Based on multiple-contingencies thinking, SSLD is an open and flexible learning system, meaning that it can include the use of guides and manuals in parts of the program. Let us imagine, for example, the case of an individual reading a book on dieting and exercising to lose weight, and then compare this to the same individual learning to do it in a group-learning situation with an instructor or coach who will help to structure the learning process, group members to provide emotional support and offer useful feedback, schedules to be met with homework assignments, discussion to deal with obstacles or setbacks, the sharing of similar experiences and helpful tips such as how to refuse food offers or how to overcome inertia when it comes to exercising, and so on. It will not be difficult for us to see the potential advantages of a well-designed learning program. While there will always be individuals who prefer to go through a self-instruction program on their own, and who are successful with it, there are probably more people who need support and social facilitation in their learning. In the experience of monitoring one's diet, for instance, an important dimension that is not given enough attention and emphasis is the social facilitation factor in how people choose and prepare their food, and what they order when they eat out with other people. In SSLD-informed health education programs, specific attention will be given to helping people effectively explain their needs and practices to others, as well as helping them to manage the social pressure to take less healthy options.

Understanding that it is performance in real life that counts, SSLD intervention supports individuals in pursuing instrumental tasks through a well-designed program and a systematic learning process, either individually or in groups, to ensure that the task is actually carried out and the desired outcome is achieved. The intervention will address specific issues and challenges related to task performance, and will help the individual to manage them effectively.

It's Instrumental, So Don't Get Personal

In our attempt to accomplish instrumental tasks, maintaining our focus on the outcome is central to a good strategy. Instrumental tasks can often be derailed or disrupted by other issues and events that are not necessarily relevant to the task or the desired outcome. One example is when people take things personally and respond in a manner that probably meets more of their need to ventilate or express their feelings than that of getting things done. For instance, I have personally gone through many frustrating experiences in negotiating bureaucratic systems that have spent multimillion dollars on setting up automated answering services and training employees to protect company interests instead of responding to customers' needs. These employees are highly capable of irritating customers or service users like you and me, and very often we find ourselves responding to this emotionally, as most normal human beings would, and the task does not get accomplished. It can be us trying to claim insurance coverage or to correct an overcharge on our telephone bill. When we get emotional or take things too personally, it may help for us to understand that the interaction is not personal. The majority of the people we talk to within those systems have very limited discretion and have to follow standard procedures over which they do not necessarily have much control. They are actually trained to be instrumental instead of genuinely caring about our needs and emotional responses. I have worked with phone-enquiry and reception personnel, and these people have been yelled at, mocked, verbally abused, and have even received death threats for loyally following their instructions. I have also listened to clients who are on the other side, trying to access services or resources that they need, and many of them have felt disappointed, frustrated, bullied instead of served, or even abused.

I have developed a cynical view regarding junior corporate or government employees who enjoy being mean to the people they are supposed to serve. It is my speculation that people's tendency to do trivial things to upset others is inversely proportional to the status, overall power, and discretion that they have. The employees who are most likely to behave in a mean manner towards others are typically of low status and have circumscribed power. Experimental psychologists Fast, Halevy, and Galinsky (2011) have actually conducted research to demonstrate how people with low status are more likely to abuse the circumscribed power they are given. I imagine this understanding may be of some help when we are trying not to take such abuse too personally. Another postulate of my theory is that not all people in the same position of power and status have the same behaviour. There are always people who are nice and people who are mean. In my untested theory, one of the variables contributing to the tendency to be mean is a general lack of satisfaction in a person's life. A mean person is therefore more likely to be an unhappy person. If you follow this logic, the person whom you are mad at for insisting that you and your kids cannot be admitted to the museum because it is exactly sixty minutes before closing time – completely oblivious to the fact that you drove 153 kilometres to get there and that the museum parking lot had misleading signs – has already been punished by having the life that he or she has. You do not really have to do anything to get back at that person. If you are in a more charitable mood, you may be able to appreciate that being able to turn someone away is probably the only high point in that person's day.

There will be times when we are dealing with people who do have some substantial power or discretion that can affect our well-being. They can be the police officer about to give you a speeding ticket, an immigration officer who can prevent you from seeing your parents for three more years, or the magistrate who can either give you a fine or put you away for two weeks. In those cases, it is always in our best interest to stay instrumental. Some of us may need to learn to differentiate between instrumental operations and relationship-oriented operations. Government officers, people who try to sell us things that we do not actually need, advertisers, and public relations professionals often design their communication or even their business model to make us confuse the two, mostly to their advantage. If we are motivated to be on good terms with a salesperson or telemarketer and not make him or her feel bad, we are confusing relationship-orientation and instrumental thinking, and that will actually increase our chance of buying something we do not need (or at least wasting more time than we have to) while our need for affiliation or interpersonal cosiness may be temporarily met. A simple test we can perform on ourselves is to ask if we would immediately hang up when we are answering an unsolicited call that is obviously trying to get us to pay for something that we have not planned for. Hanging up immediately is actually the best response, short of protecting our number from such calls. When we find ourselves wanting to be nice, or not wanting to hurt the other person's feelings, we are misunderstanding the very nature of the interaction. It is instrumental, not personal.

One of the steps in this direction is to understand instrumental thinking and take the perspective of both parties. The person who is being paid a small salary to call us up is intruding on our privacy, and if we are using a number that is being billed by the minute, the person is inflicting unnecessary cost on us. To be hung up on is part of the work package, and that may well become a good reason for that person to want to quit her or his job and find something more pleasant to do. Telemarketing, like junk mail and junk email, is taking time away from more productive or meaningful activities that we may otherwise pursue and is a huge burden on the environment, considering the waste produced and the energy consumed. In SSLD, we understand that rational thinking alone often does not lead to corresponding action, for our responses are motivated by many other factors, and that is what advertisers, marketers, and sometimes government bureaucrats like to exploit. Many people do not want to say no to others; some people find it difficult to deny help (if called upon by a charity fundraiser); some people are afraid of tension and conflict; and some people need to keep a self-image of being nice. These responses reveal emotional needs that should be met elsewhere. We need to be clear of the needs we wish to meet within any given interpersonal or social context. This thinking can be applied to other situations that call for an instrumental approach. If we are applying for a bank loan or a mortgage, for instance, our key purpose is not to make the bank officer happy but to get the best deal for ourselves. This leads us on to another important point in instrumental thinking: knowledge is power.

Knowledge Is Power

It usually pays to be well informed about the situation we are getting into. Researching online is a good place to start. We can also speak to people who have had similar experience, and we can seek professional assistance if necessary. This applies to a wide range of situations, from the mortgage application example above to buying a car, job searching, or even online dating. Research empowers us by giving us knowledge and information which we can then utilize in accomplishing instrumental tasks. SSLD seeks to empower clients by assisting them to develop effective strategies for gaining information and knowledge, as well as teaching them how to apply such information and knowledge in accomplishing instrumental tasks. This principle has been applied to a wide spectrum of practice situations, including community organizing and helping marginalized and disadvantaged people to advocate for their rights. The knowledge they acquire can be statistics, policy analysis reports, how the issue of concern has been reported in the media, and so on. In working with clinical populations, knowledge about their diagnosis, available treatment and services, self-help practices, alternative treatment, legal rights, and the like can be empowering.

In SSLD programs, effective dissemination of information and knowledge is usually achieved by taking into account the clients' need for knowledge, their motivation level, their capacity for taking in and digesting the information, and their preferred learning style. Experiential learning and interactive learning in a group format tend to be more effective than conventional didactic approaches. The use of audio-visual material and online resources usually works well, especially among younger clients.

Stay Goal-Oriented

When pursuing instrumental tasks, we need to keep our eyes on the desired outcome and respond to contingencies as they arise. Getting emotional or getting personal, as mentioned above, are only two of the possible distractions. Other distractions can arise from needs that are unrelated to the original goal. This is how advertisers often try to get us; they try to sell us items by suggesting that our purchase can meet needs other than those that the product is supposed to address. We are sometimes shown images of a new car driving on terrain that we would like to visit, while in reality 80 per cent of our time in the car we would spend stuck in city traffic. It is well known that many commercials exploit people's longing for an intimate relationship to sell them products ranging from deodorants to chewing gums, beer, jewellery, travel packages, cosmetic surgery, instant coffee, and whatnot. Our vulnerability to distraction is functionally related to unmet needs. Discovering unmet needs while we are trying to pursue something instrumentally is not always a bad thing, if we can somehow manage to meet these needs effectively. What is less satisfactory is that our original plan to address a particular need or goal can be derailed by a vague promise of meeting other needs that eventually will not pan out.

Having clearly thought out and well-defined outcomes helps us stay goal-oriented. For instance, if we are planning to do some major home renovations, we need to know the purpose. If we are thinking of selling the house, the ultimate outcome is maximum financial benefit. Our decision should be guided by the marginal increase in sale value for every dollar we put in, and we need to be imagining the prospective buyer's perception. If we are renovating for our own use instead, we may want to focus on our subjective utility. Renovating a house to suit our tastes and preferences before putting it up for sale is not an effective goal-oriented strategy. Giving too much thought to what friends, family, and neighbours may like instead of what we would enjoy the most ourselves is similarly problematic, unless we have underlying needs for approval and acceptance that cannot be gratified through means other than renovating the house. Those needs can probably be more effectively and more economically met by consulting a counsellor or an SSLD practitioner than by renovating our homes.

Considering Multiple Contingencies: The Instrumental Tasks in a Complex Project

The home renovation project and the need to impress one's friends, family, and neighbours are actually good examples to illustrate the principles of multiple contingencies and how instrumental tasks fit into a bigger and more complex project. In a home renovation project, we need to coordinate a host of variables, and the outcome can be multifaceted. We may consider space utilization for different members of the household and their respective needs and circumstances, which can be functions of age, health status, work-related demands, and so on. We may also consider the prospective turnover of people living in the house such as the arrival of a baby, adult children leaving home, an older person moving to a senior's facility, and the like. The budget we are working with is often a key part of the formula. The availability of options and services in different geographical areas can also condition our plan. In Asia, for example, the availability of inexpensive labour and professional services and the lack of a do-it-yourself culture or tradition make contracting out more popular than in North America. The higher proportion of people living in high-rise condominiums instead of detached houses is another significant factor shaping home renovation as a form of social practice, as well as the industries associated with it. Gardening and yard work, for example, are less popular in Asian cities compared to their North American counterparts.

The home renovation project can serve as a good metaphor for other projects in life, especially those perceived to be a complex undertaking involving multiple components. Negotiating and defining the outcome can be an ongoing process, meaning that what people perceive to be the desired outcome in the beginning can be modified as we move on. This may read as contradictory with the principle of staying goal-oriented, as was mentioned in the section above. In practice, however, recognizing the fluidity of our articulated goals and defined outcomes is a necessary accompaniment of staying goal-oriented. In SSLD, we often start with well-defined objectives that are seen as related to people's needs. We are, however, prepared to accommodate a revised understanding of needs and articulation of goals, and usually we can see the connection or continuity between a previously set goal and a revised one. Staying attuned to people's current needs and circumstances, therefore, goes hand in hand with a goal-oriented emphasis.

Many projects in life are a product of multiple contingencies, and we often have to manage many variables at the same time. The home renovation analogy helps us to break a complex project down into discrete, manageable tasks that have to follow certain logical sequences. For example, we may need to look at spatial organization, plumbing, flooring, painting, and furniture one by one. Garden and yard work can be considered separately, although coordination in terms of style and taste is often implied. In the completion of specific tasks, there can be a logical sequence. For instance, we need to determine spatial organization such as where to put the kitchen and the washrooms before we can decide on the plumbing work to be done. Plumbing arguably goes before flooring, and in most cases, it is advisable to finish working on the flooring before painting the walls. The furniture is likely to be put in last because it is usually more flexible than the structural elements.

Each of these tasks involves due consideration of a host of variables, which often include subjective factors like preference and taste. Sometimes sentimental factors like attachment to certain elements of the house and more objective factors like budget and availability of material and/or services also play a role. Each of these tasks, however, will become more clearly instrumental when the decision is made, such as the kind of flooring to be put in. In SSLD practice, similar partialization of the problem or the project is often necessary to help to make an overwhelming task manageable for the client. We understand that instrumental tasks are rarely purely instrumental but can be tied to some other tasks of emotional significance, and partializing them and managing them systematically can often be helpful.

In a recent case that I came across, a woman with a heroin addiction had just been diagnosed with breast cancer, and her boyfriend at the time did not want to deal with it and showed signs of denial and rejection. She was in a state of crisis. She had to deal with multiple challenges at the same time and was overwhelmed and confused. Through the initial session of problem translation with this client, she was able to lay out a few instrumental steps for herself, which would not solve all her problems but gave her a sense of direction and mastery. She figured out that her immediate need was to find a temporary shelter to stay in and decided that she could probably go back to her stepmother's place. She also came to understand in the same session that her fear regarding the breast cancer was closely connected to her fear of losing her figure, and therefore her attractiveness, but in the process realized that she was also looking for someone who could accept her the way she was, and that her current partner was probably not the one she would stick it out with in the long run. She understood that she might have to go through an emotionally difficult process of separation, for there were needs that the relationship could still gratify. Yet she was able to see that finding another place to stay could be a good step in that direction. She realized that she would need a new home base to review her current relationships and to contemplate her future plan, including treatment for her cancer. She felt more relaxed and more in control after the problem translation and goal setting. Although the instrumental task of getting temporary shelter was only a small part of the overall solution that she needed, she had mapped out the big picture in some way and could see how this instrumental task was functionally related to the other issues.

Coming back to the home renovation analogy again, we mentioned earlier that many people imagine their renovation project with regard to other people's opinions instead of their own preferences and utility. This is akin to this woman's initial idea that her attractiveness and her value as a woman were contingent upon the physical integrity of her breasts, or her figure for that matter. This idea was examined in her review of other relationships in her life and the kind of love that she actually wanted, through which she realized that she actually valued love that was not conditional upon her physical attractiveness. She was able to cite her ex-boyfriend as an example, although that man had died several years ago.

During that session, the woman came to a revised understanding of what she needed, from the integrity of her body to a love that is more accepting and unconditional. This understanding would be useful in informing the treatment decision she would have to make later. This is a good illustration of how needs and goals can change while the position of staying goal-oriented remains. From this point onwards, we can imagine how making treatment decisions regarding this woman's breast cancer may be regarded as primarily instrumental tasks, but having an understanding of the multiple contingencies related to the client's needs and circumstances will probably be helpful.

Developing a Game Plan

Continuing with the home renovation analogy, instrumental tasks can be parts of a bigger overall game plan, yet each task may require its own planning. This hierarchical imagination of what we need to do can serve as a useful road map for action. As mentioned a few times in previous sections, SSLD procedures follow incremental steps, and when dealing with more complex situations, partialization, prioritization, and logical sequencing are necessary to make things manageable. The design of a game plan does not only take into account the objective or external factors, but also the client's current capacity, resources, and limitations. Intervention plans should always start with a task at which that the client is likely to succeed.

Instrumental tasks, in a way, are more likely to be manageable when they do not involve heavy emotional investment and are only indirectly linked to significant relationships. In many situations, the emotional and relational aspects are very peripheral or not really relevant. In many work settings, for example, tasks can be more purely instrumental, although issues related to self-esteem, achievement, need for approval by colleagues or supervisors, and so on can be in the background. The application of SSLD in management training or in organizational and human resource development, for example, usually involves game plans that are primarily instrumental.

Preparing for Action: Learning the Specific Skills

Following the SSLD principles outlined above, we can approach instrumental tasks systematically. Like in learning other tasks, we will always come back to the mastery of very specific skills. The major emphasis in the learning process, as pointed out in the beginning of this chapter, is to enable the learner to actually perform the instrumental task and attain the desired goals. Designing a learning program for instrumental tasks can take in composite skills in reception, expression, and communication, and more situation-specific components either designed by the SSLD practitioner or through collaborative creation. In-session practice, including simulation role-play and video-assisted review and feedback, is routinely used in SSLD programs. Take-home exercises and rehearsal in real life are also regularly employed procedures.

Assisting people in job-hunting, for instance, is an instrumental task that SSLD practitioners in different service settings can get involved with. It can be clinical practitioners helping individuals with severe mental health issues, community development workers helping women who have been full-time homemakers for a long time, corporate consultants working with middle-aged executives who have been laid off, settlement workers helping new immigrants, student counsellors working with university graduates, and so on. The process involves a set of instrumental tasks such as accessing employment information, strategic self-presentation through CV packaging, designing web pages and other web-based platforms, or preparation for interviewing and other forms of performance assessment.

I have been on both the recruitment side and the application side of this game. I have also trained head-hunters and helped job applicants for various positions in different industries. In my experience, the knowledge-action gap is bigger with the tasks that involve interpersonal interaction than with those that do not. Tasks such as interviewing for a job, speaking in public, or participating in a group usually cause more anxiety and self-doubt in people. With tasks not involving face-to-face interpersonal contact, such as doing research online, writing an application letter, or putting a CV together, people seem more capable of translating knowledge to action and following relevant instructions and guidelines. Related to this is the phenomenon that many people are better prepared for the non-interactional tasks and actually start preparing for them earlier than the interpersonal ones. Many people, for example, have their CV ready and update their Facebook or personal website regularly, but will only come to prepare for the interview, presentation, or group exercise pretty close to the actual day.

There are reasons for this, such as the socialization and the education we receive. Schools put a disproportionate emphasis on cognitive tasks, and we have been asked to perform tasks that are primarily based on reading and writing thousands of times since elementary school. By contrast, syllabi in formal education pay very little attention to the learning and development of interpersonal skills. Presentation skills are covered to some extent but systematic training on interpersonal skills is usually lacking or inadequate. SSLD relies heavily on experiential skills learning, which facilitates transfer to real-life performance situations. Covering the spectrum from strategy to skills and microprocesses provides comprehensive support to someone who wants to learn to perform better in those interactional situations.

Back to the job-hunting example, the spectrum can include an overall game plan for job searching, mobilization of social capital, the use of consultants, and strategic presentation of oneself, focusing on how to maximize one's advantage over prospective competitors. In terms of skills, learners need to combine good listening skills with receptive skills, such as in deciphering the position taken by the prospective employer. Effective presentation, expression, and communication skills can include formal presentation, strategic self-disclosure, or groupwork skills.

Within the academic job market, I have coached doctoral students with regard to their market-readiness, which is part of their overall game plan. The plan involves research on the job market, including current and prospective openings. Major national and international trends are taken into consideration. Another important factor is whether the student is planning to apply to research-oriented universities or more teaching-focused institutions. Knowing the kind of job one is interested in will have an impact on how the program of doctoral studies is managed. Students interested in faculty positions in world-class research-oriented universities, for instance, are encouraged to focus on building an impressive research and publication track record before they defend their doctoral thesis. Some students will have to consider if they are prepared to resettle to another city or not, weighing their needs and circumstances as well as those of their partners and families. Depending on the student's background and specific area of research interest, they will have to strategically build connections with researchers in their area through thesis committee membership, conference participation, correspondence, research collaboration, and so on.

Apart from having a good game plan, students have to be prepared for the actual job-search procedure. For instance, part of the ritual of academic hiring is a lunch or dinner attended by the search committee and the candidate, which is less constrained by the rules and conventions applicable to the formal interview procedure. Over a semi-formal meal, search committee members are trying to assess the suitability of the candidate with regard to multiple agendas. For instance, it may not be politically correct to enquire about a candidate's class background, specific religious or political views, social resourcefulness, or fundraising ability in an interview. Over lunch or dinner, people can talk more freely about leisure activities, vacations, and social lives. It is also a social skills assessment exercise in real life. Some candidates will use such opportunities to demonstrate their social grace and interpersonal engagement skills, or to strategically disclose information that can affect their chances favourably, such as personal connections with influential characters in the field. They can also establish a favourable connection with members of the search committee over a diverse range of possible topics – from wine to skiing, skin care, or art collection.

One of the principles I mentioned above can be integrated into this particular performance: the principle of empowering oneself with knowledge and information. I usually encourage students applying to academic jobs to research the profile of the academic department they are applying to, including the individual profiles of faculty members. People are usually pleased when their work is known and appreciated, even when they are aware that it is part of the homework that the candidate has done. Similarly, research into workload, compensation packages, and benefits at the target institutions and comparable institutions can empower the candidate in the negotiation of these aspects.

In corporate recruitment contexts, group interaction formats are used to assess many dimensions of personality and interpersonal skills. Most group process skills can be acquired through SSLD, including group dynamics analysis, careful listening, thematization and summary, timely and appropriate intervention, managing agenda development and topic shifts, negotiating multiple agendas, facilitation, use of free information and following leads, management of conflict and tension, and so on. These skills, however, are not supposed to be attained at the last minute, but take several learning and practice sessions involving simulated group processes, video recording and review, feedback, and progressive refinement. Some of these learning tasks require attention to micro-processes such as turn-taking, interruption of other people's utterances, self-referencing, assimilation of other participants' content, reframing, and a host of others. To date, only very few people realize the significance and the advantage of developing these group skills, and those who do are more likely to be ahead of the game.

Apart from the learning of strategies and skills, and inclusive of the related micro-processes, job hunting can usually be regarded as an instrumental task within a more complex project. There are often associated or parallel processes, such as balancing personal life, family obligations, and social demands. In a globalized job market, the need for resettlement is increasingly common and it can affect relationships, the growth and development of children (if they are part of the picture), adjustment to different sociocultural environments, health care arrangement, financial planning, and many other aspects of life. Managing the instrumental task of job hunting within the context of the complex project of maintaining quality of life for oneself and the significant others in one's life-world can all be integrated in an SSLD formulation. In practice, people who require SSLD service in job hunting very often benefit from related work on the clarification of personal goals, management of significant relationships, stress management, and overall emotional and interpersonal capacity building.

It is tempting for SSLD practitioners to think that our intervention can play a decisive role in our clients' successes with their job hunts, but we have to realize that there are environmental forces that can be more powerful. Major market shifts, economic downturns, changes in public or corporate policy, structural adjustments in a given industry, regional or seasonal fluctuations, changes in the administration, and many other factors beyond our control can have impacts on the outcome of our clients' job hunts. When people experience setbacks or do not get the jobs they desire, one of the principles we mentioned above should be reinforced – when it is instrumental, do not get personal. It is important to maintain the clients' sense of self-efficacy. In SSLD, the practitioner should always help people to believe that they are worthwhile, regardless of whether a particular employer decides to hire them or not. The practice of positive reframing, which was introduced in Chapter 9, can be helpful in such circumstances. When self-efficacy is not severely compromised, it is usually easier for people to be more flexible and creative with their overall game plan, opening themselves up to more options that can eventually address their needs.

Summary

Effective accomplishment of instrumental tasks and management of relationships are essential for attaining well-being and general satisfaction in life. The principles emphasized by SSLD, such as focusing on actual performance, goal-orientation, multiple contingencies thinking, flexible utilization of knowledge and information, and systematic experiential learning, can all be weaved into programs that are capable of addressing the particular needs and circumstances of individuals requiring help. The balance between instrumental tasks and personal needs is congruent with the basic tenets of SSLD values and practice. A more global or comprehensive view of human life is always helpful to keep things in perspective.

PART FOUR

SSLD Practice and Related Issues

The building blocks introduced in the last section can be combined flexibly to form SSLD intervention programs in response to specific client needs and circumstances. Over the last three decades or so, I have applied SSLD – either in its current form or in its earlier form as social skills training – to a wide variety of settings, be it through direct practice myself or through my role as program designer, consultant, supervisor, trainer, or coach. A network of colleagues and graduate students in North America and Asia has worked closely with me in the development of numerous programs for a wide spectrum of clients in many diverse settings. In terms of substantive areas, SSLD has addressed issues such as chronic schizophrenic disorder, infantile autism and autistic spectrum disorders, dating and intimacy, couple relationships, insomnia and sleep-related issues, social phobia, interpersonal relationships, substance abuse, Internet addiction, youth at risk, parenting, cross-cultural communication, front-desk reception, management training, human resources, community organization and development, leadership training, health promotion, weight management, immigrant settlement services, and caregiver training and support. SSLD programs have been delivered in community service organizations, hospitals and health care systems, university-based service units, private practices, and corporate contexts. Numerous training programs for practitioners in a wide range of disciplines have been conducted internationally. Over the last few years, SSLD's application has experienced steady growth both in terms of the scope and type of settings.

It is not possible to describe the entire range of SSLD applications, which is expanding even as this book is being written. Readers can browse the SSLD website (http://ssld.kttsang.com) for updates. In this section, we will explore issues pertaining to SSLD practice to provide readers with more specific information and guidelines in learning and applying SSLD methods and procedures.

Chapter Thirteen

Learning and Applying SSLD

This chapter addresses issues pertaining to the adoption of SSLD as a practice system. The first question for practitioners is the obvious one of why should one choose SSLD. When one has satisfied oneself that it is beneficial to include SSLD in one's professional toolbox, then comes the question of how one should go about learning and mastering the new system. Then there are the related issues of scope of application, logistics, support, and resources.

Why SSLD?

Practitioners have a rich array of choices with regard to possible practice systems that promise to be useful. When thinking of adopting a new system, practitioners may want to consider the five variables suggested by Rogers (1995). Key considerations include:

1. *Compatibility*: Is the new system consistent with existing values, goals, or norms?

SSLD is developed within the context of human service. It focuses on person-centred service, believes in the possibility of positive change, and values client agency and autonomy. It seeks to enhance clients' self-efficacy and empowers them through capacity building and by increasing their life chances. It follows an education and learning paradigm rather than a disease or pathology paradigm. It should be highly compatible with the values, goals, and professional norms of professions such as social work, counselling, clinical psychology, nursing, and most health and mental health disciplines.

2. *Relative Advantage*: How can it improve on existing practice and methods?
SSLD offers a versatile conceptual frame built on multiple contingencies thinking. It allows practitioners to gain a good understanding of the needs, circumstances, characteristics, and capacities of their clients. This comprehensive understanding facilitates engagement and strengthens the working alliance. It also informs the design and implementation of specific intervention procedures. The rich practice experience cumulated within the SSLD system provides practitioners with an extensive menu of procedures, enabling them to respond effectively to a wide range of practice situations.

3. *Complexity*: How easy or difficult is it to learn and use?
The SSLD system consists of the key procedures of engagement and problem translation, formulation and design of strategies and skills to be mastered, implementation or the actual learning and development of strategies and skills, and the final phase of review, evaluation and completion. Procedures in each component have been clearly spelled out, often with specific instructions. The extensive practice experience supplies a rich resource of case examples. All of the above should facilitate learning and mastery of the practice system. It should, however, be emphasized that proficiency in any skill requires extensive practice and self-monitoring; SSLD practitioners are expected to observe and review their own professional performance, preferably supported by electronic recording and feedback.

4. *Triability*: Can it be experimented on a limited basis?
Practitioners can take each case of application as an experiment. This is actually an attitude encouraged in SSLD practice. Given that the system targets specific and concrete outcomes, usually associated with observable or even measurable behavioural change, it will be easy for practitioners to see if it works. The carefully documented practice procedures can facilitate process review by practitioners to locate specific interventions requiring refinement or improvement.

5. *Observability*: How visible are the results?
As mentioned before, SSLD intervention procedures, as well as results, are mostly based on concrete, observable behaviour and outcomes. Many SSLD procedures involve documentation of measurable behaviour, such as the behavioural diary on page 109. Changes in human

action and experience, apart from those immediately observable by clients and practitioners, can sometimes be assessed by direct self report. Measurements such as goal attainment scaling (Kiresuk & Sherman, 1968; Kiresuk, Smith, & Cardillo, 1994), and the three key-issues evaluation (3-KIE) (Tsang, George, & Bogo, 1997) can be easily adopted into the SSLD practice.

Another process many practitioners go through in deciding to adopt a new practice is to consider how it compares with other existing systems. The question of how SSLD differs from other practice systems often comes up in professional training workshops and similar programs. The systems that are often raised in comparison include cognitive behavioural therapy, solution focused therapy, and motivational interviewing. This section will summarize the key features that distinguish SSLD from these systems, and hopefully this will help colleagues considering adoption of the SSLD system.

Cognitive Behavioural Therapies (CBT)

Cognitive behavioural therapy includes a cluster of intervention models, such as rational emotive therapy (Ellis, 1957), cognitive therapy (Beck, 1970; Beck, Rush, Shaw & Emery, 1979; Leahy, 1996), dialectical behaviour therapy (Dimeff & Linehan, 2001), social skills training (Argyle, 1967, 1972, 1983; Liberman, DeRisi, & Mueser, 1989), and cognitive behavioural therapy just by that name (Meichenbaum, 1986). This label covers a wide range of theoretical systems ranging from classical or respondent conditioning to social learning theory and social cognitive theory (Leahy, 1997). As the name implies, it combines cognitive and behavioural intervention procedures. As mentioned in Chapter 1, cognitive behavioural therapies have gone through three waves or stages of development (Hayes, 2004a, 2004b). In the first stage, psychologists following respondent and operant conditioning theories developed empirically-based treatment procedures that are focused on behavioural change. In the next stage, more attention is paid to cognitive processes and social learning. In the third wave, contextual and experiential dimensions become more salient and the intervention procedures are more inclusive and flexible, enabling the practitioner to address a wider range of issues. SSLD shares some of the characteristics of the Third Wave CBTs and can be considered compatible with their major emphasis and orientation. What distinguishes SSLD from the other CBT procedures is its adoption of multiple contingencies analysis, emphasis on understanding the needs of clients, and a more eclectic and pragmatic approach to practice research, which will be discussed in more detail below.

Solution Focused Therapy

SSLD is often compared with solution focused therapy (de Shazer & Berg, 1975; Miller, Hubble, & Duncan, 1996). Solution focused therapy (SFT) relies heavily on cognitive procedures such as focusing on the solution rather than the problem, the miracle question, exploring exceptions, and the like. The transfer of in-session cognitive understanding or reformulation to real life behaviour is often taken for granted. SSLD does not assume that cognition always determines action, nor that in-session cognitive change will automatically be transferred to behavioural change in everyday life. SSLD recognizes that the performance of certain actions, such as handling criticisms or mediating conflicting agendas among family members, often requires experiential learning efforts.

Another key emphasis of SSLD, which does not receive the same attention in SFT, is the notion of needs. In SFT, the client is encouraged to imagine a solution, or a problem-free situation. In SSLD, goals and desired outcomes are established on the basis of a more thorough understanding of one's needs. Goal setting in SSLD practice is often done in sequential steps. Care has to be taken to avoid simplistic problem-solution thinking. When people are asked to imagine solutions, it is easy for them to follow simple linear logic. Moving directly from problem to solution can create formulations that make sense on the surface but do not address the underlying needs. For example, a teenage girl who is doing sex work to make enough money to have cosmetic surgery performed on her nose may imagine that when all her problems are solved, she will find herself waking up with a fixed nose. While we do not rule out the possibility that having the nose fixed may be exactly what some people need, it is also possible that people who want to have their noses fixed do not really need the surgery. The underlying needs can be peer approval, sexual self-image, mastery over one's body, or expression of resentment and hostility. Similarly, someone with the problem of excessive credit card debt as a result of uncontrolled spending may imagine a solution of having all his debts cleared and not having the same impulse to spend. Understanding the underlying needs such as gaining social approval, psychological stimulation, pleasure derived from a sense of potency, or emotional discharge can inform the goal setting process.

SSLD practice requires careful listening to clients, facilitating the task of translating their presenting problems or issues into statements of needs and goals. A good understanding of needs instead of imagining a single concrete solution has the advantage of not being tied to a particular outcome. The fact is that what we want is not always what we need. Following the principle of equifinality, we can achieve the same goal of meeting important needs through a variety of different means. For clients struggling with insomnia and sleep-related issues, for example, sleeping eight hours every night is one of the ways, not the only way, for the body to have sufficient rest and regeneration of energy. Being fixated on getting eight hours of sleep is not necessarily the best solution, and in some cases can become part of the problem. Working towards getting enough rest and generation of energy, on the other hand, allow us to adopt multiple alternative strategies, such as relaxation exercises, meditation, taking power naps, working out, healthy eating, improving our social life, and so on. The eight-hour sleep can certainly be included in the list but should by no means be the only designated solution.

Motivation Interviewing

SSLD shares a number of positions assumed by motivation interviewing (MI). According to Miller and Rollnick (2002), MI is *"a client-centered, directive method for enhancing intrinsic motivation to change by exploring and resolving ambivalence"* (p. 25). MI focuses on the client's needs and aspirations, and is careful to avoid confrontation or adversarial forms of interaction with the client. MI focuses on the beginning phase of intervention, aiming at mobilizing positive motivational forces within the client. It takes a non-judgmental and empathic approach to engagement, and understands client reluctance or resistance to change as natural rather than pathological. These principles are fully compatible with SSLD. Like SSLD, MI emphasizes client motivation, agency, and self-efficacy.

MI and the associated motivational enhancement therapy (Miller, 2000; Miller, Zweben, DiClemente, & Rychtarik, 1995) do not emphasize systematic learning and development of skills. It is asserted that the responsibility for developing change methods should be left with the client, and they do not utilize skills training, modelling, or practice procedures. Motivational enhancement therapy "assumes that the key element for lasting change is a motivational shift that instigates a decision and commitment to change" (Miller, Zweben, DiClemente, & Rychtarik, 1995, p. 10). The systematic learning and development of skills is seen as premature if such a decision or commitment has not been established yet and is considered unnecessary when it has been achieved. The assumption is that clients will be able to obtain what they need from their natural environment and resources. From the SSLD perspective, we do not rule out the possibility that some strongly motivated clients who are committed to change can actually acquire the skills necessary for addressing their needs and attaining their goals. We do believe, however, that many clients can benefit from systematic learning and development of strategies and skills. Following multiple contingencies thinking, we do not believe that every client will have to go through exactly the same change trajectories. While many of the strategies and skills clients learn and develop in SSLD are behavioural, they can learn cognitive and emotional ones as well. SSLD, emphasizing learning instead of training, is prepared to let clients take an active role in designing the strategies and skills they need to acquire, if they are prepared to do so, as illustrated by the collaborative creation procedure in Chapter 6.

SSLD: Interfacing with Other Systems

SSLD can be seen as a practice system sharing some features with other systems, while it distinguishes itself with other features. The most important characteristic of the SSLD system is perhaps multiple contingencies thinking, which frees the practitioner from thinking in terms of fixed categories, avoiding simple linear formulations assumed to be applicable to all clients in all situations. Cognition does not always determine emotion, nor the other way around. Skills learning is beneficial to many clients, but some clients may be able to learn in their natural environment. Some clients need more guidance and support from their practitioner, some of them collaborate with their practitioner to generate the skills, and some may even teach their practitioners new strategies and skills. The multiple contingencies model allows much flexibility in practice, while at the same time it provides a conceptual framework that allows practitioners to locate what they are doing and where they are heading with their clients. The six domains of the life world – environment, body, motivation, cognition, emotion, and action – can be used to map out where the issues and intervention tasks are at any given stage of SSLD practice. Practitioners and clients can collaboratively determine which domain should be the focus of the next intervention step.

Following multiple contingencies thinking and the principle of equifinality, SSLD has the flexibility and capacity to interface with other practice systems. It can be used as an independent practice model, and it can be used in combination with other intervention procedures as well. For example, when working in the healthcare field, SSLD programs developed for establishing better health practice, or what is called Proactive Health Strategies (PHS), are often combined with other health service programs including medication, nutritional counselling, kinesiology, and alternative healing practices. Programs have been developed for management of chronic conditions such as diabetes or kidney problems, caregiver education and support, insomnia and sleep-related issues, weight management, cancer care, palliative care, and so on. As SSLD is framed within an educational paradigm, it can be introduced and delivered easily as an adjunct psycho-educational or health education initiative, while its capacity for dealing with complex issues and challenges can also be realized.

Specific SSLD procedures have been used in conjunction with other therapeutic approaches in the CBT cluster. As mentioned above, procedures such as motivational interviewing can be quite compatible with SSLD principles. Practitioners can employ MI procedures in the beginning phase of engagement and bring in systematic learning procedures when a shared understanding of clinical goals and tasks has been established with the client within a positive therapeutic alliance. Within a multiple contingencies framework, such combinations are not arbitrary but pursued in a purposeful manner. Guiding principles for adopting procedures taken from different practice systems include: (1) the chosen procedure achieves a specifiable clinical or learning task, which is appropriate at the current point of the clinical change process; (2) the practitioner is competent in carrying out the intended procedure; (3) the practitioner is able to articulate the logical sequential connection between each step and the next; (4) the chosen intervention matches the specific needs, circumstances, characteristics, and capacity (N3C) of the client; and (5) the client is ready to take this on, and does not experience this as incompatible with intervention objectives or as something confusing or irrelevant.

Scope of SSLD Practice: Potential and Limitation

SSLD has been applied to an extensive range of situations, and it interfaces easily with other intervention models. In theory, it can be used whenever there are unmet needs and when learning and developing new strategies and skills seem relevant to the pursuit of goals in life, individually or collectively. It is probably the only practice system that is applicable as therapeutic intervention to people with severe mental illness, as empowerment and capacity building for disadvantaged communities, as supplementary education in social skills and personal development, and as management training for executives. With a growing number of practitioners trying to bring it to different areas of practice, we are cumulating valuable experience and feedback. While the scope of SSLD application continues to expand, it is perhaps helpful to have some sense of its potential and possible limitation.

The first point I want to highlight is a reality that SSLD shares with all other systems of intervention. Meta-analysis of psychotherapy has consistently demonstrated that the system of intervention only accounts for a small percentage of variance in terms of positive client change. The more powerful factors are the relationship or working alliance between client and practitioner, and the characteristics of the practitioner and the client (Duncan, Miller, Wampold, & Hubble, 2010; Hubble, Duncan, & Miller, 1999). Despite the fact that proponents of particular practice systems or intervention programs like to emphasize how effective their intervention is, and offer research evidence they interpret as supportive of such claim, the fact remains that effective intervention is only partially explained by the system of intervention. There are many problems associated with this kind of claim, often marketed as evidence-based practice. The underlying conceptual and research issues will be explored in more detail below in the section entitled "SSLD Practice and Research."

My own assessment of the value of SSLD follows multiple contingencies thinking. First, I believe in equifinality, meaning that there are multiple pathways to the same goal. What can be achieved through SSLD, despite my own wish and preference, can also be achieved with other methods or procedures. When SSLD is found to be successful in various situations, we cannot attribute all the credit to the system alone. For instance, we have to recognize that some practitioners are effective with a variety of methods and have generally good outcomes with their clients, and that there are practitioners who are generally less effective regardless of what system they practice, even if they are using SSLD.

Following this line of reasoning, it is important for practitioners to pay attention to the factors and processes associated with positive client change. A system is valuable when it can be used to support effective engagement with the client, enabling the development and maintenance of a functional working alliance. The system should support the practitioner's work by offering a framework for making sense of the case in hand, providing direction for professional action. The guidelines and instructions for specific procedures should empower the practitioner by enhancing a sense of professional efficacy. Practitioners are likely to benefit from an attitude of openness and active learning, instead of religious adherence to any given system. With regard to the client, a good practice system is one that empowers the client in a similar manner. Clients can learn to make sense of their own situation or circumstances, and pursue alternative constructions of reality, including new options for thinking and taking action. Whereas SSLD strives to do these, we are mindful of the fact that positive change can take place through other pathways as well. What we are offering is a procedure explicitly designed with due regard for such reality, and a clear understanding that it is the collaborative as well as the agentive decisions and actions taken by practitioners and clients that ultimately produce the positive change and desired outcome.

Another dimension relevant to the evaluation of a practice system is its role in the intended agenda of change. Wolberg (1986) classified psychotherapy into three types: supportive, reeducative, and reconstructive. SSLD is developed primarily within an educational paradigm and is perhaps not the treatment of choice when reconstructive psychotherapy is indicated or desired. SSLD is not insight-oriented, although it does help clients to gain a better understanding of their needs, circumstances, characteristics, and capacity. The educational paradigm translates clinical issues into an understanding of needs and corresponding strategies and skills, and in the process it blurs the boundary between clinical and non-clinical issues, thus taking the system beyond the therapeutic space and frame. This feature of SSLD can be seen either as a limitation or strength, contingent upon the goal to be pursued and preferences regarding approach and process.

Practitioners in various areas of health, mental health, social work, and human services can find SSLD relevant to their work. In a sense, all these professional colleagues are working with clients with needs that have not been effectively met. Most forms of professional intervention require the client to learn new information and adopt new action. SSLD explicates the process of gaining a better understanding of the client's needs, circumstances, characteristics, and capacity, and facilitates the design and implementation of procedures for learning and developing strategies and skills to address them. The following section will cover issues related to the learning and mastery of SSLD principles and practice methods.

Learning to Become an SSLD Practitioner

Practitioners interested in SSLD typically enrol in specific professional education programs. Given our emphasis on the knowledge-action gap and how knowledge can be transferred to everyday life, readers may question whether people can just read a book on strategies and skills and then go ahead and apply what is learned. Based on SSLD thinking and experience, I have to say that not too many people will be able to do that. Readers who are experienced practitioners, especially those who have established proficiency in self-learning, are more likely to start applying contents covered in this book on their own. Many readers may want to participate in formal SSLD programs designed for practitioners and receive further coaching, consultation, or supervision in order to apply the methods and procedures effectively. This book is largely intended as a text for SSLD practice courses.

In this section, we will explore a number of components that contribute towards a good preparation for SSLD practice: personal qualities, professional preparation, previous learning experience and current learning style, and specific training in SSLD.

The aptitude for interpersonal sensitivity, assessment of social situations, strategic thinking, management of multiple contingencies, and so on varies significantly across individuals. As in the case of general intelligence, genetic predisposition may have a role to play (Rushton, Bons, & Hur, 2008; Vernon, Petrides, Bratko, & Schermer, 2008). Some people are particularly challenged in terms of their interpersonal sensitivity and skills, such as individuals with autistic spectrum disorder or Asperger's syndrome. Some of these individuals may have amazing abilities in other domains of life. I, for example, worked with a calendar savant about twenty years ago (Ho, Tsang, & Ho, 1991). Recognizing that people are differently abled or differently endowed is an important position in SSLD, for we are committed to assisting people in learning the appropriate strategies and skills so as to attain their goals in life, regardless of their initial endowment. Colleagues who wish to become SSLD practitioners, similarly, come with very different aptitudes, abilities, experiences, as well as personal and professional goals.

Hundreds of colleagues and graduate students have learned SSLD practice with me or my students, and many have learned the earlier version of social skills training. Based on over three decades of experience in practice, training, consultation, coaching, supervision, and program design, I have come across practitioners with a diverse range of talents, professional training, personal aptitude, and background. What I have noticed in my work is that people's general social and interpersonal competence is usually an asset in their SSLD practice. Basic competence in receptive skills such as listening and understanding other people's feelings and needs and engagement and presentation skills, for example, are critical in any kind of professional work involving interpersonal interaction, SSLD practice included.

Practitioners who are aware of their individual strengths and limitations can benefit maximally from an SSLD practice course by focusing on areas in which they need more improvement or support. What I have noticed in actual SSLD programs is that participants learn from each other and the talents and strengths that people bring in are often the most valuable resources in the program. Given its focus on skills learning and emphasis on performance, SSLD programs can help practitioners improve on their personal, interpersonal, social, and professional competencies simultaneously. There are, however, situations when colleagues discover specific areas that are particularly challenging for them, such as emotional sensitivity, and they may require more time and space than what is available in a professional training or development program to acquire the relevant skills. In this case, colleagues are encouraged to pursue additional learning and development to complement the professional practice program.

Besides aptitude and competence, another personal quality that is important in preparing for SSLD practice is interest in and openness to new learning and development. This factor is to be distinguished from personal qualities, which are more a matter of endowment. A person with relatively limited endowment, for instance, can be strongly motivated to improve on her or his interpersonal and social competence, whereas a better endowed individual may not be open to more learning and development. In my experience, people who are motivated to learn and improve, and keep making an effort, are likely to achieve significant advancement in their competence level. One key factor that is of particular importance is the readiness to adopt something new or different, whether in terms of thought or action. Cognitive or behavioural rigidity is often something to be overcome in expanding our repertoire of strategies and skills, for SSLD often requires openness, creativity, and flexibility in order to generate and implement new ways of thinking about and doing things.

The creation of a safe and open space for learning and exploration, therefore, is always an important feature of SSLD practice programs. Given the busy schedules of colleagues, and the limited contact hours we typically have for formal educational or professional development programs, we are unlikely to cover all the specific content we want to. In preparing professional colleagues for practice, we focus on two major learning outcomes on top of the mastery of specific content. One is strengthening motivation for continual learning and development. The other is learning how to learn. My belief is that a practitioner who is motivated to continue self-directed learning and knowing how to do it is likely to make significant progress in the long run. Learning how to learn is more important than learning specific strategies and skills, as we will continue to face new circumstances and new challenges. No matter how rich our current repertoire is, it will prove inadequate at some point unless we keep updating it. SSLD learning principles always emphasize self-directed learning and empowering the learner. We encourage and support colleagues, as well as clients, to become active learners and producers of knowledge instead of passive recipients of knowledge. To support such ongoing development, the availability of consultation, case-conference, supervision, or coaching opportunities is very important. Peer work teams and learning or study groups can also be extremely valuable. A group of my graduate students, for example, has kept a study group running for over twenty years after graduation, and members of the group are now key SSLD practitioners.

Apart from personal qualities, I am often asked what kind of professional or academic preparation is needed for enrolment in an SSLD practice course or program. In my opinion, an open attitude, motivation to learn and develop, and aptitude and competence in interpersonal and social functioning are probably more important than formal education in becoming an SSLD practitioner. People who have received training in SSLD practice include social workers, psychologists, psychiatrists, medical practitioners in other specialties, counsellors, nurses, occupational therapists, various mental health professionals, dieticians and nutritional counsellors, managers, human resource professionals, immigration and settlement counsellors, volunteers in community organizations, group leaders, parents, and so on. Although I think some post-secondary education in the social sciences, especially social work, psychology, and counselling, can be helpful, I have seen people without such background learning the SSLD procedure effectively. Another kind of preparation that I have found valuable is the experience of working in groups. As many SSLD programs are designed for delivery in small group contexts, having extensive experience in group work, either as a participant or a facilitator/leader, is likely to be an asset.

A related issue is the level of sophistication one wishes to attain. In general, it is less demanding to learn to practice SSLD according to a well-established program, such as in the areas of insomnia or social phobia, where manuals and specific guidelines are available. Learning to be able to work in a more unstructured context or addressing a new practice problem or client population, where there is no established program or manual, the practitioner needs to be better prepared for contingencies and more proficient in applying the appropriate SSLD principles creatively and flexibly. The most complex and challenging practice of SSLD is perhaps in program design. It involves the accumulation of practice experience and extracting practice wisdom to articulate a program systematically, including the writing up of a practice manual, complete with exercises, assignments, worksheets, and handouts. The knowledge and skills required in these activities are not confined to a particular profession. Actually, most academic and formal education programs in the human service professions do not target these knowledge and skills.

In a way, the SSLD system prepares practitioners for what I have come to call the post-professional era. Traditional professional disciplines try to divide human experience and our life-world into discrete domains such as body, mind, relationships, and so on, and claim expert knowledge over them. Increasingly we are finding that most solutions we need in life involve multiple domains instead of a single one. Multi-disciplinary collaboration is often called for, but the efficiency of actual multi-disciplinary work is compromised by inter-discipline competition for power, resources, and status, on top of sometime incompatible epistemology, value commitment, and preferred methods. My observation is that individuals, organizations, and communities are increasingly adopting a pragmatic orientation when they are seeking professional help, and the ability to provide a convenient and comprehensive solution to the client's concerns and issues is going to carry more weight than the profession we belong to. Of the things we learn in universities and professional training programs, quite a few of them can be helpful. They include the ability to assess and conceptualize problems or issues in multiple frameworks and make meaningful connections among them, interpersonal and emotional sensitivity, strategic thinking, and a pragmatic orientation that translates abstract conceptualization into design for action. Logical reasoning, analytic thinking, research skills, critical appraisal of information and knowledge claims, and synthesizing or integrating knowledge from diverse sources are all helpful intellectual facilities. SSLD professional programs seek to build on the talents, experience, knowledge, and skills that learners or participants bring, and to assist them in acquiring the knowledge and skills they need to deal with challenges in their work. As mentioned earlier, we try to enhance their motivation for continual learning and development, and help them to learn how to learn by equipping them with self-directed learning strategies and resources.

Apart from personal qualities and professional or academic preparation, an individual's experience in learning and developing strategies and skills in life is another important factor in preparing for SSLD practice. In a way, all of us have learned and developed strategies and skills in order to manage our lives up to this point. If what we have acquired is adequate for managing the demands and challenges in life and satisfactorily meeting our goals, we probably do not need SSLD. SSLD can be conceived as supplementary or specifically enhanced learning processes to assist individuals or collectives to become better able to attain their desired goals in life. In theory, observation learning occurs naturally in everyday life (Bandura, 1977a, 1986). People's ability to selectively assimilate elements of interpersonal and social performances of people who serve as models, however, varies tremendously. Apparently, people with similar exposure to opportunities for observation learning do end up learning different things, depending on motivational factors, the nature of the model's performance, their relationship with the models, and so on. In SSLD, we focus not only on what people have learned but also on how they have been learning, and try to help people to develop more effective learning strategies and methods.

In our review of people's previous learning, we often find that people sometimes missed valuable opportunities to model other people's behaviour for a host of reasons. Some people, for example, are not aware that what they need, such as a gratifying intimate relationship, requires the mastery of certain skills, like self-presentation, initiation of contact, engagement, relationship nourishment, and so on. They may attribute their lack of success in that area of life, be it love or career, to their personal qualities, such as "I am not attractive physically" or "I am not smart enough," instead of the fact that they have not mastered the appropriate skills for it. In some cases, people know what they need and have good models, but are prevented by emotional factors to benefit from those opportunities. For instance, someone who has a highly competent friend in high school who is very successful socially and otherwise may experience immense jealousy and resentment. The internalized articulation of "I do not want to be like her (or him)" can prevent people from modelling that person's performance, which could have been extremely helpful. Such internalized articulations, unfortunately, are often unexpressed and reinforced by the need to preserve one's self-esteem, in that people often wish to maintain an internal representation that compares them favourably with others. Very often, people who are not getting what they desire in life tend to maintain an explanatory framework such as "I am not as crazy about money and material achievement as he (or she) is" or "I have my values," which are not working in the direction of goal attainment but just help to ease the pain of deprivation and frustration.

In learning to practice SSLD, it is usually helpful to review our own learning history and look at how we used to learn to manage the demands and challenges in life. If we notice patterns that do not facilitate goal-oriented strategies, or a tendency to overlook opportunities for learning and development, we may need to adjust our overall orientation and approach to life. Shifting from a passive attitude that channels energy into remorse, complaints, guilt, or shame into a positive and proactive one that enhances our sense of purpose, agency, and autonomy is a key feature of SSLD thinking and action.

In addition to a proactive orientation or attitude, a review of the way we learned in the past can be instructive. Many of us can observe an interpersonal or social performance and reproduce it with high fidelity afterwards in a similar context. Some of us have difficulty understanding how things work or have trouble with specific elements, such as non-verbal communication, emotional expression, or appropriate verbal articulation. Some on us are better at observing and analysing than copying and reproducing. Some of us are good at translating more abstract practice principles directly into action. Some of us need more video recording and playback, coaching, and rehearsal. A good understanding of our learning styles will prepare us to benefit maximally from an SSLD program. Being able to communicate our learning needs and preferences with the instructor is an excellent first step towards self-directed learning and development. Correspondingly, a good SSLD program should respond to the varied learning needs and learning styles of the participants. That is why multiple contingencies thinking is always at the heart of SSLD program design, and rigid adherence to pre-designed programs is not encouraged.

After considering personal qualities, professional preparation, learning experience, and learning style, we have to look at the specific SSLD training for which a person is looking. As suggested before, colleagues may have different needs with regard to the knowledge and skills they have to utilize in their practice. Some colleagues come to learn SSLD for very specific issues, such as training caregivers of seniors struggling with Alzheimer's, helping people to manage insomnia and sleep-related problems, assisting parents to develop better relationships with their children, and so on. Some colleagues wish to understand the basic principles and procedures so that they can adopt and apply them to a range of service situations. Some colleagues plan to develop a more advanced level of competence in SSLD so that they can become supervisors, coaches, or instructors in the method. There are also colleagues who are in professional training or academic positions who wish to adopt SSLD as part of their professional education or academic syllabi. Obviously, different kinds of SSLD study programs have to be designed to address their respective learning needs.

Recognizing individual differences in personal endowment and qualities, professional or academic preparation, previous learning experience and current learning styles, as well as the specific SSLD learning to be pursued, the design and delivery of professional courses in SSLD have to address multiple contingencies, and allow different pathways of learning. Most SSLD practice courses are, therefore, characterized by a certain level of openness and flexibility, grounded on an ongoing interactive process with the participants, and trying to respond to their needs and learning styles in a dynamic manner. In more recent programs, emphasis is put on follow-up and continual learning and development through activities such as case-conference, peer support or study groups, and periodic consultation and/or supervision, supplemented by personalized coaching, booster sessions, and support for self-directed program of learning.

Applying SSLD

As mentioned above, SSLD, in its current and earlier versions, has been applied to a very extensive range of settings. This range of application is sometimes difficult for some colleagues to imagine, but it actually reflects the system's capacity for responding to diverse demands and multiple contingencies. It is expected that SSLD application will continue to grow, and part of the purpose of this book is to articulate a common ground for communication, sharing of experience, and accumulation of experience, knowledge, and skills. In this section, I will suggest a number of coordinates to help colleagues locate their work within the extensive terrain of SSLD, and in relation to the work of others. The first dimension is the substantive area of practice or intervention. The second dimension is the mode of intervention. An additional dimension is the service setting.

Substantive Areas

To state that SSLD can be applied to almost any area of human service may sound like an exaggerated claim, but three decades of practice experience attest to its robust applicability. I started using social skills procedure in psychotherapy and counselling for individuals with mental health concerns in the late 1970s. My own personal history as a student activist led me to experiment with a methodical application of social learning principles in community organization and activism at around the same time. We used systematic training to help disenfranchised community members learn to talk to other members and motivate them to participate, organize, analyse issues, articulate their agenda, convene meetings, talk to the press, negotiate with government officials, and so on. When I was first asked to work with children with autism in 1980, I found that the major intervention models, which have been dominated by operant conditioning formulations, very limiting. I started to target the building of imitative learning capacities in these children, while at the same time running parallel programs for parents to learn to apply social skills training techniques at home. We experienced extremely encouraging results. Within a few years, the social skills training model was applied to address a wide spectrum of mental health and social issues.

The application continued to grow in the next few decades, with colleagues and students accumulating valuable experience and providing extremely helpful feedback. The open and flexible approach to learning and change allowed us to make ongoing modifications to the system, refine practice principles and specific procedures, and add to the ever-growing repertoire of techniques. What is most exciting is the readiness to take on new requests for service, which challenges us to respond to diverse needs and circumstances. In each of these situations, we have come up with programs of intervention that address the needs of colleagues and clients, bringing new solutions that entail positive changes in how we imagine the issues and how we work.

At this point, I am optimistic that the SSLD system can be applied to most situations involving interpersonal interaction, either as the key intervention model or as an adjunct or complementary procedure. In the area of health and mental health, SSLD has been applied to psychotherapy, counselling, self-help groups, community rehabilitation, caregiver education, and preventative intervention. Clients served include children, young people, adults, seniors, parents, couples, families, and caregivers. It has been used in working with severe mental illnesses such as schizophrenic disorder, conditions such as depression, anxiety disorder, and social phobia, specific problems such as insomnia, and the like. More recently, we are developing programs that target prevention and/or management of chronic health conditions such as fibromyalgia, kidney disease, obesity, stroke, and diabetes. A new set of programs to promote Proactive Health Strategies, or PHS, is currently being developed and tested.

Immigrant settlement service is another recent development in SSLD application. New immigrants have to learn and master a wide repertoire of social and cultural skills in the process of settlement and integration into the host society. They need specific coaching and systematic skills learning in cross-cultural communication, job hunting, negotiating cultural identity and cultural practices inter-generationally, or simply interpersonal and social skills for everyday interaction with people in the mainstream. Some members of immigrant communities can also learn leadership skills and take on organization and advocacy roles.

Apart from health, mental health, and social issues, SSLD has been applied to support people working in human resource management, organizational development, team building, and international cross-cultural work. In an increasingly globalized environment, SSLD, as a system initially developed in Asia under strong Western influence and subsequently in an international and multi-cultural context, is well suited for working with individuals and groups with diverse backgrounds. The application of SSLD in the workplace outside of the conventional human service context is a welcome development, as it can contribute to a humanistic approach to combine effective performance and goal attainment, caring for personal needs, and the development of healthy interpersonal relationships within companies and organizations.

Mode of Application

The mode of application covers a few different dimensions. First, it is the format of delivery. SSLD can be used in one-on-one individual consultation, including psychotherapy, counselling, coaching, and life design. It has also been used in working with couples, parent-child dyads, families, and groups. Group program is probably the most popular format of SSLD intervention, and it is very cost-effective. Many SSLD practitioners' first exposure to SSLD is in a group work context. As a matter of fact, SSLD interventions in organizational and community contexts often start with working in groups, be they managers, employees, community members, or leaders.

Another dimension in the mode of application is the role of SSLD in the overall service delivery or intervention program. Although SSLD is a very robust system with extensive applicability, it does not claim to be a panacea for all problems. It is possible that in many situations, SSLD is only a constituent component of the overall program. For example, in the recent development of a program for individuals with fibromyalgia, we find that while SSLD analysis such as problem translation and practice principles like incrementalism and self-empowerment are extremely valuable, the actual program has to incorporate body awareness and body work procedures, such as yoga and yoga-inspired techniques, as well as Feldenkrais methods. In the broader area of pain management, SSLD can contribute to stress management, mobilization of interpersonal and social support, and design for proactive health strategies in life. Other interventions, including body work, medication, alternative medicine, or even surgery can well be part of the overall treatment package. Depending on the circumstances of specific cases, the role of SSLD can be central or subsidiary. The important point is that the SSLD approach seeks to obtain maximum benefit for the client and is solidly grounded in the client's specific needs and circumstances. Unlike in forms of practice where practitioners make an *a priori* commitment to an intervention method almost regardless of the client's needs and circumstances, SSLD practice is always driven by the client's needs and goals in life.

Service Settings

Following the discussion above, it is clear that SSLD can be used in a wide variety of service settings. It can be used in traditional social service units, hospitals and health care centres, residential service units, community and outreaching teams, companies, schools, and religious or faith-based organizations. Service programs based on SSLD principles can be offered for a fee, or they can be free. The programs can be offered by highly trained professional practitioners, volunteers trained in the method, members of self-help groups, or leaders of communities. Reframing challenges and issues in human life as learning needs and opportunities, SSLD can be seen as a practical orientation to managing different aspects of life. Its flexibility supports its extensive application. There are now a growing number of service settings that have adopted SSLD as a key practice model for their practitioners, associated with growing interest in custom designing in-house SSLD programs to address specific service needs. The accumulation of SSLD practice experience in service settings within different sociocultural contexts will hopefully lead to further innovations and refinement, offering more options to people working in various areas of human service.

Special Application: Working with Communities

Community work represents a very special application of SSLD and it highlights the specific features of the practice system in a number of ways. Earlier work in social skills training was mainly done in clinical contexts, assisting people with health, mental health, or developmental challenges (e.g., Gresham, 1997, 1998; Heinssen, Liberman, & Kopelowicz, 2000; Kopelowicz, Liberman, & Zarate, 2006; Mathur & Rutherford, 1996; Smith & Travis, 2001; Strain, 2001). Working with communities who do not necessarily represent clinical populations highlights the non-medical character of SSLD. Taking SSLD beyond individuals, families, and small groups demonstrates a scope of application that exceeds most forms of psychological or behavioural intervention. Community work requires more attention to systemic and organizational realities than individual, group, or family work. Power, for instance, is a more salient aspect. A community orientation challenges the practitioner to reflect on professional values and ethics outside of a medico-clinical framework. The practice context is typically not within a consultation room where most aspects are within the control of the practitioner. The professional relationship between community members and the practitioner can also be quite different from that of a clinical or therapeutic relationship.

Given all these special features of community work, it is interesting to see how similar SSLD principles and procedures can be applied. As mentioned above, SSLD is applicable whenever there are unmet needs, and when there are strategies and skills that people can learn to address these needs. Communities are collections of people sharing similar circumstances and/or characteristics. These can be geographical location, history, culture, sexual orientation, income level, housing condition, medical condition, special talent in music, age, immigration experience, and so on. People sharing similar circumstances and/or characteristics are likely to have shared needs. When these shared needs are not met, the community will have motivation to work collectively to address them. This is the basis of community work within the SSLD model.

Following this understanding, the first step of community work is actually not fundamentally different than SSLD practice with individuals, families, groups, or organizations. The practitioner will first have to engage with the community and develop a collaborative relationship or working alliance with it. In this process, the SSLD emphasis on needs, especially needs that are unmet, will become very salient. Similar to individual work, a problem translation will take place, reframing the presenting problems into unmet needs and then goals to be attained. When the goals are set, specific strategies and skills are to be formulated and mastered by members of the community in order to address the needs and achieve the goals.

Figure 13.1 summarizes how a low-income community in Asia responded to the lack of water supply. There was only one communal water tap for the community of over 100 households. In order to obtain water for the family, most residents had to line up in front of the water tap with their buckets and containers throughout most of the day. Some residents would rearrange their sleeping hours and got up at 3 a.m. in the morning to get water when there were very few people there. Some of them employed other strategies, such as sending their elderly parents to the communal tap with their water buckets. Given the cultural respect for senior citizens, they could often jump the queue, although

256   SSLD Practice

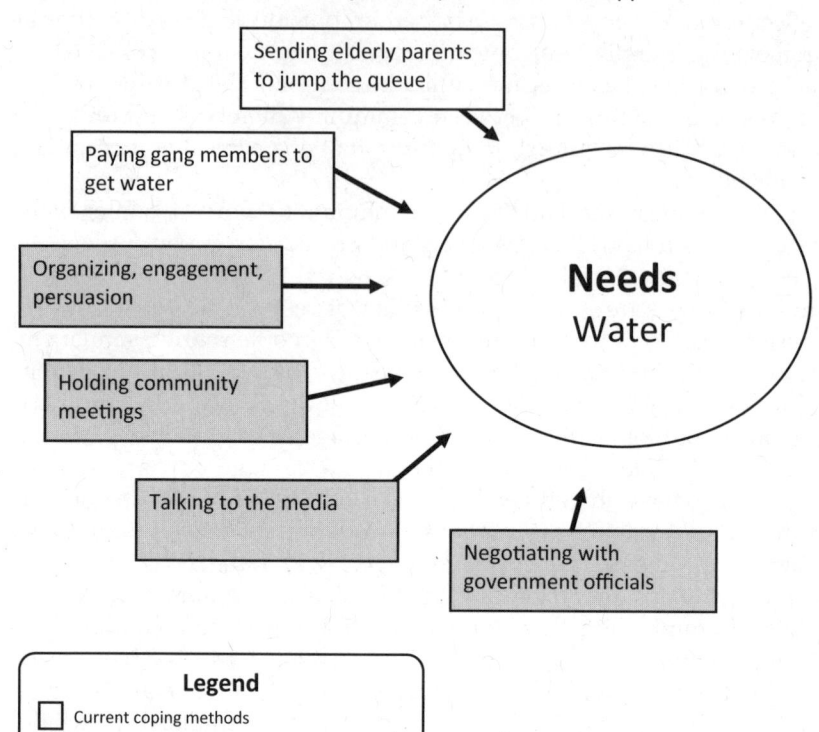

Figure 13.1. SSLD in Community Development and Anti-oppressive Practice

```
                    ┌──────────────────────┐
                    │ Sending elderly parents│
                    │ to jump the queue     │
                    └──────────────────────┘
                              ↘
     ┌──────────────────────┐
     │ Paying gang members to│
     │ get water            │
     └──────────────────────┘
                              ↘              ╭─────────╮
     ┌──────────────────────┐                │         │
     │ Organizing, engagement,│   →          │  Needs  │
     │ persuasion           │                │  Water  │
     └──────────────────────┘                │         │
                                             ╰─────────╯
     ┌──────────────────────┐                  ↗    ↑
     │ Holding community    │   →
     │ meetings             │
     └──────────────────────┘
            ┌──────────────────────┐
            │ Talking to the media │
            └──────────────────────┘
                          ┌──────────────────────┐
                          │ Negotiating with     │
                          │ government officials │
                          └──────────────────────┘
```

Legend
☐ Current coping methods
▨ Strategies and skills

conflicts and arguments did occur on some occasions. The task was also too much of a demanding chore for some of the old folks. Another strategy was to pay a local gangster who practically ran a water supply service, but this was something that only a few families were able to afford.

In this particular case, the community change process basically involved the learning and development of new strategies and skills by some community members. With the help of the community development worker, members learned to get organized. Some of them mastered specific skills in engaging and persuading their neighbours to join a campaign. Other skills learned by the leaders include holding community meetings, talking to the press, and negotiating with local government officials. With the successful completion of the campaign, the government agreed to put in a network of pipes that would bring water to each family.

This example illustrates how SSLD can be practiced in a community context in a manner comparable to individual work, going through similar steps of engagement, assessment and problem translation, and designing and mastering new strategies and skills, leading to the attainment of desired goals and therefore meeting the previously unmet needs. Some of the specific practice issues, principles, and procedures will be briefly described below.

1. Engagement

Engagement is the first step of establishing a working relationship. When the community worker is not a member of the community, a trusting relationship has to be built to enable future collaboration. The components of a working alliance (Bordin, 1979) – namely, a shared understanding of goals, a shared understanding of the tasks and processes required to attain such goals, and a positive interpersonal relationship – are arguably equally important in community work as in individual work. The community worker has to communicate understanding, care, and respect to the community in order to establish the alliance. Acceptance and a non-judgmental attitude, empathy, careful listening, and similar skills in individual work are all relevant to community practice.

2. Problem Translation

Problems experienced by community members or presenting issues or requests are to be understood within the SSLD framework. A N3C (needs, circumstances, characteristics, and capacity) assessment will reframe the community problems and issues into needs to be addressed (e.g., shelter, financial security, food safety, transportation, healthcare, or citizenship), giving due consideration to the specific circumstances of the community (e.g., natural disaster, war, or cut-back in public funding), their characteristics (e.g., being very old, immigrants, or people with chronic conditions), and capacity (e.g., resources, awareness, knowledge of the issues, readiness to speak up, existing networks, talents, knowledge, or experience and skills). Such an assessment avoids disease, deficiency, or deviance perspectives and focuses on setting realistic goals to be attained, with attention to needs, agency, autonomy, and capacity building. It is important to emphasize at this point that the assessment process is not something that the worker carries out in a transitive manner on the community. The assessment has to be done collaboratively with the community, and it has to be shared with the community. As mentioned above, a good working alliance specifically requires such shared understanding.

A key component in the problem translation process in SSLD practice with communities is the integration of a systemic and structural perspective. The N3C of a community has to be understood within the context of social structures and processes, including discourses, policies, political economy of resources, and life-chances. A critical analysis is often involved. A key emphasis in SSLD practice is that we do not perform the analysis from an expert position, but try to involve community members in the process. The ultimate goal is to let community members develop the capacity to perform their own analysis in the future. The problem translation and goal setting procedure is to be completed through a collaborative process.

3. Design and Implementation of Strategies and Skills Learning and Development

After the problem translation is done, the community and the SSLD practitioner will have established a shared understanding of the community's N3C and agreed-upon goals towards which to work. The N3C assessment includes a survey of community capacity, including resources, knowledge, and skills. The community will then have to figure out what actions are likely to be strategic, in the sense that they are more likely to lead to the achievement of community goals. The next step is to identify what strategies and skills are needed, compared to what is currently available from within the membership. This community capacity audit will indicate the strategies and skills that have to be acquired by the community. Such capacity, knowledge, and skills are usually unevenly distributed in a community, with some members being better endowed or equipped with certain skills and knowledge. A key condition for successful community work is the development of indigenous leadership that is capable of building, mobilizing, and coordinating community capacity.

Box 13.1 provides a scale for assessing community capacity by measuring the level of participation and leadership behaviour of the mem-

Box 13.1. Community Participation Scale (Tsang, 1979, 2011a)

Level	Name	Description
Level −1	Negative Respondent	Respond to program negatively, including hostility and aggression towards worker, program, or organization
Level 0	Non-respondent	Does not respond to worker's input, refuses to engage
Level 1	Passive Respondent	Passively responding to invitation or input: willing to receive information about community activities, answers questions
Level 2	Active Respondent	More active response such as showing interest in the group or its activities, asking question regarding the community or other members
Level 3	Passive Participant	Participation may include attendance of meetings or events, willing to contribute occasionally when asked, such as sharing information and resources
Level 4	Active Participant	Active participation includes regular attendance of meetings and events, willingness to contribute, frequently volunteering to help out
Level 5	Task Leader	Taking on some form of leadership function, assumption of responsibility for specific tasks such as distributing flyers, preparing food, teaching a specific skill to members, calling up members to come to events, etc.
Level 6	Organizational Leader	Providing vision, sense of direction, building a leadership team, delegation and division of labour, coaching, mentoring, managing crisis and conflicts

bers. The scale allows community workers and community leaders to locate where members are on the scale and have a sense of the current level of participation and leadership. SSLD practice procedures facilitate the transition of community members from lower levels of participation to higher levels of participation. The scale indicates what the next step is for any member of a group, allowing the practitioner or community leader to design and implement specific procedures targeting such transition.

In the water supply example given above, community members initially did not have the knowledge and skills required to bring about change in government policy and action. When the community worker first entered the community and tried to engage, most members were at levels −1 (Negative Respondent) or 0 (Non-respondent). Some members were more ready to talk to the worker (Level 1, Passive Respondent), and there were a few others who actively indicated a willingness to get involved (Level 2, Active Respondent). The worker invited every community member contacted to come to a meeting to discuss possible action. Anyone who came was at least a Passive Participant (Level 3); and at the meeting, Level 4 (Active Participant) behaviour was evident in a small number of members. These active participants were then recruited to take on various leadership tasks (Level 5), including talking to less involved members and getting them to show support or agree to come to future events. Systematic training of specific leadership tasks started at this stage. The key learning procedure was simulation role-play of various situations, complemented by careful observation and feedback. These learning sessions were usually conducted in a fun-filled atmosphere, emphasizing sharing and mutual support.

Through the process, members learned leadership skills and became leaders. They learned to analyse the situation, and they reported their analysis to their community. They learned about social action possibilities and had meetings to discuss strategies, roles, and division of labour. Members with organizational leadership (Level 6) potential were quite noticeable at that stage. The community worker focused on working with the small but growing leadership group to help them master the necessary skills, both in task leadership and organizational leadership.

Leadership

In most community development situations, the number of organizational leaders tends to be small. It is, however, important to have a group of leaders to share the power and the roles, instead of only having one leader who would become dominating. It is not unusual for someone with charisma to emerge as a leader, attracting willing followers while at the same time marginalizing other members with good leadership potential. Without becoming unduly formal, it is advisable to introduce democratic power sharing and leadership arrangements that will prevent the newly formed community organization from the negative processes of power play and interpersonal rivalry or conflict.

The emergence of indigenous leadership from within means that the community is increasingly capable of taking care of its own affairs, and therefore needs less direct input from the community worker. It is very probable that the community, as a collective, actually possesses more knowledge and skills than what the worker has. The development of leadership in a community is associated with an ongoing re-negotiation of the roles of the community worker, with a careful transfer of knowledge, skills, power, responsibility, resources, roles, and so on to the community leadership.

Organizational Development

The kind of leadership developed is contingent upon the nature of the community initiative. In my own experience, community initiatives can be ad hoc or they can be long term. The one-time ad hoc initiatives typically mobilize the community to get organized and take action, but the organization may no longer be needed when the goals are accomplished. For example, a rat-infested immigrant squatter community advocated for relocation to public housing projects. When everyone was rehoused according to the members' preference, they might be distributed all over town, and the need to get together would no longer be there. In other cases, the community initiative may lead to the establishment of lasting organizations that continue to serve their constituencies.

When there is longer-term development of a community organization, such as the formation of a people's council on housing policy, a mutual aid group for people with schizophrenic disorder, a community economy co-operative, or a women's collective for survivors of domestic violence, organizational development becomes a salient concern. Issues of vision, direction, leadership, growth, succession, sustainability, organizational structure, and so on have to be managed effectively. The community worker, therefore, has to take on the role of an organizational consultant. There are coaching and training functions as well. A key feature of SSLD intervention is empowerment through capacity building. The community as a whole should eventually come to acquire the knowledge and skills they need for their ongoing development, including growth and transformation. Ideally, a community can become fully autonomous and independent, and the worker is no longer needed.

This learning and development process almost always takes the community beyond the repertoire of knowledge and skills of the worker. The collaborative creation procedure described in Chapter 6 is a useful tool in this process. When organizations continue to grow, they may need to bring in other consultants and resource persons. It is important for community workers to understand their own role, capacity, and limit. In order to provide the best service, we may need to transform our relationship with the community or community organization, including our possible exit from the situation, especially when it is evident that they have developed the capacity to manage their own affairs. The reluctance to let go, or the worker's need to remain important and needed by the community, can often impede the otherwise natural growth of the community group or organization. In SSLD, we explicitly identify community capacity development, autonomy, and self-sufficiency as criteria of successful intervention. The final transformation of the role of the worker, including possible exit, is built into the intervention design.

Summary

The SSLD approach to community work is inherently empowering. The key intervention is enabling communities to gain better understandings of their own needs, circumstances, characteristics, and capacity. This understanding is then translated into specific goals to be attained. Members of the community will be encouraged to become more actively involved, as measured by the Community Participation Scale. Indigenous leadership is developed methodically to encourage autonomy and independence. This action-oriented approach privileges the needs and the autonomy of the community. It does not allow itself to slip into a NATO (no action, talk only) position of spending the majority of the energy on analysing and criticizing existing conditions and problems. Some practitioners claiming to be pursuing AOP (anti-oppressive practice) have kept their constituencies from developing effective strategies of change by focusing on ideological criticisms of oppressive realities instead of actions that would result in changes to those oppressive conditions. SSLD intervention is guided by the community's autonomous assessment of its own needs and circumstances, as well as the goals it sets for itself. It empowers the communities by assisting their members and leaders to acquire the necessary knowledge, strategies, and skills to bring about the real changes they desire. The explicit target of community independence and the eventual exit of the worker complement this approach.

SSLD Practice and Research

SSLD is a system developed out of practice. Concepts, formulations, frameworks, methods, procedures, and so on mostly come from the review of actual practice cases and situations. In a significant way, it is the product of practice experience, guided by ongoing learning, reflection, and review. It is also the product of collaborative efforts by many practitioner colleagues who generously contributed to the process. The research question in SSLD, therefore, is raised with the practitioner in mind. Our question is how research can help to refine the system, so as to make it more useful to the practitioner. This interest obviously takes us beyond the narrow scope of outcome research focusing on the efficacy of the system, although that is recognized as an essential component of our research program. Our key focus is on the intervention process and how specific changes to these processes are connected to our desired outcomes.

Given the extensive application of SSLD, and the fact that clients participate actively in defining intervention goals and objectives, what constitutes desired outcome is not fixed or standardized but contingent upon a host of factors. In some cases, the desired outcome can be the elimination or significant reduction of problems such as depression, addiction, pain, or insomnia. In other cases, people desire to be more independent, or capable of enjoying intimacy, or to acquire leadership or management skills. Our grounding in direct practice has led to a number of positions that we take with regard to how professional practice is understood, and consequently how practice research should be conducted.

Evidence-Based Practice and the Drug Metaphor

Evidence-based practice (EBP) is a concept increasingly used in health, mental health, and human service to establish the value of chosen interventions. The idea is that competent and ethical professional practice requires the practitioner to use methods that have evidence of efficacy. This usually means that the method has to be empirically validated as effective, preferably through randomized clinical trials or randomized controlled trials (RCT). RCT is the standard procedure for establishing the clinical effectiveness of medications. It is developed within the paradigm of physical sciences in the West and its basic rationale includes: (1) knowledge of causal principles enables prediction; (2) establishing these causal principles requires standardized experimental methods to avoid the possibility of confounding influences; and (3) mathematical or statistical techniques are used to measure the inferences that can be made from empirical observation and to determine their level of probability (Bolton, 2002). The procedure allows the researchers to establish that a drug, with its particular therapeutic ingredients, is the cause of therapeutic change, and not any other random variables such as placebo, chance, patient characteristics, and so on.

Much of practice research in the health, mental health, and human services has been influenced by this conceptual framework, which is sometimes mistaken as *the* medical model. Medicine encompasses more than prescribing drugs. In surgery, for example, standardized procedures form the foundation upon which more expert clinicians demonstrate their individual skills. It is unfortunate that the pharmacology framework is taken as the primary metaphor for mental health and human services. The drug metaphor is based on a number of assumptions, most of them untenable or not substantiated by clinical and research evidence in the area of mental health and human service. The following section will explore some of problems of the drug metaphor and the assumptions it makes.

The CAIRO Assumption

We can start with the CAIRO assumption, which is an acronym I use to refer to the formulation that the clinician (C) applies or administers (A) an intervention or ingredient (I) to a recipient (R), causing the desired outcome (O). This line of thinking is linear, categorical, and transitive. It assumes that the clinician is the subject in the formula and the client is the object. It assumes that the clinician is an active agent and the client is a passive patient or recipient. It assumes that change is caused by some active ingredient contained in the intervention or treatment administered. Moreover, in most cases, the desired outcome is determined by the clinician. The CAIRO assumption ignores major facts in the reality of therapeutic change, including the interaction of multiple factors and processes such as the active role of the client, the role of the therapeutic relationship, that the cherished intervention or therapy program explains only a small percentage of the variance, or that standardized measures do not always make the most sense to the clients who are active users of a service, just to name a few.

The Active Ingredient as Cause of Therapeutic Change

A core concept in the drug metaphor is the active ingredient. The metaphoric imagination is based on the idea that there is some active ingredient in the treatment that causes the positive therapeutic change to happen. In the history of psychotherapy, many systems have claimed to contain more effective ingredients than other competing systems, be they rational cognition, psychodynamic insight, or emotional work. Such claims are, however, not supported by empirical evidence. Meta-analyses of psychotherapy outcome research have shown that there is actually no evidence that any form of psychological treatment is systematically more effective than others (Robinson, Berman, & Neimeyer, 1990; Shapiro & Shapiro, 1982; Wampold, Minami, Baskin, & Callen Tierney, 2002). Review of the research evidence has highlighted a number of important issues in conceiving the actual process of therapeutic change, which will not allow us to adopt a simple linear model assuming that faithful application of an intervention by a clinician will consistently cause the desired outcome to happen. It appears that a number of interacting factors and processes are involved in determining the outcome of psychological intervention.

Linear Causal Thinking and Multiple Contingencies Modelling

Moving away from a simple linear imagination of therapeutic change, we can attempt to build a more comprehensive model that takes into account the key factors and processes. As described earlier in this book, Multiple Contingencies thinking recognizes the complexity of human life, and supports a conceptual modelling that can accommodate multiple factors and processes. Review of the psychotherapy literature has led to the recognition of many factors and processes that play important roles in therapeutic change (Duncan, Miller, Wampold, & Hubble, 2010; Hubble, Duncan, & Miller, 1999). It is perhaps more realistic to conceive of positive client change as a complex process contingent upon multiple factors and processes, which can be configured differently in individual cases, rather than a uniform process that everyone goes through, responding to the same standardized input administered by the practitioner.

The Relationship

The therapeutic relationship, sometimes called the *therapeutic alliance* or *working alliance,* has consistently been found to be a central factor in successful psychological intervention (Grencavage & Norcross, 1990; Lambert & Barley, 2002; Norcross, 2010) and explains more variance than the system of therapy employed (Lambert, 1992). The salient role of the therapeutic relationship highlights the non-transitive nature of therapeutic change. Change is not caused by the practitioner to the client. Instead, client and practitioner collaborate to bring about the changes. In SSLD, we emphasize that the desired outcome itself has to be a result of collaborative process.

The Client Is an Agent, Not a Patient

In a collaborative process, the client is an active participant, an agent. I learned English as a second language. When I was small, we were drilled in antonyms and synonyms. I remember that the opposite of patient is agent. This set of antonyms is very inspiring when I consider my many years of work in the human service sector. In the drug metaphor, a patient is a passive object, who is literally expected to demonstrate patience when receiving diagnosis, prescription, or treatment. When the treatment works, the patient cannot take much credit other than for following or complying with what the physician prescribed. This view ignores clinical experience and research evidence. Research has shown that clients play an important role in determining outcome (Bohart & Tallman, 2010). In psychotherapy, counselling, education, and professional training and development, the client or the learner is an active partner. Things clients do include making sense of the therapeutic process (Busseri & Tyler, 2004; Philips, Werbart, Wennberg, & Schubert, 2007), planning (Levitt & Rennie, 2004; Rennie, 2000); actively managing the therapy agenda (Greaves, 2006), and transferring in-session learning to their everyday life (Dreier, 2000). Positioning them as passive recipients of treatment and denying them credit in accounting for therapeutic success are both scientifically and ethically unacceptable.

RCT: The Gold Standard?

As mentioned above, RCT (randomized controlled trials, or sometimes called randomized clinical trials) is the key procedures for establishing evidence-based practice (EBP), and it is mainly drawn from a pharmacological metaphor, which is probably most relevant for internal medicine. Psychological interventions, as argued in the preceding section, do not work in the same manner as drug treatment. The evidence we need in psychological and human service interventions does not lie in establishing a particular treatment, assumed to contain the therapeutic ingredients, as the cause of positive changes in the client's life. We need better information on how multiple factors and processes, which are contingent upon each other, work to make positive client change possible.

Even with the medical field, there is now growing concern over the reliance on the empirical methods such as RCT and systematic review (e.g., Burns & Catty, 2002; Cooper 2003; Marshall, 2002). Gould (2006), for instance, has summarized some common critiques of RCT: (1) RCT can offer measures of probability across populations but never certainty about the effects of an intervention with a particular service user; (2) RCT assumes that all people with the same diagnosis are similar to each other; (3) rigid exclusion criteria are often applied to avoid complexity in research; (4) RCT are much less externally valid; (5) RCT inaccurately assumes that the same intervention can be provided by different clinicians in different settings with the same quality; (6) RCT also does not value the expertise of those with experience that can contribute to the knowledge base; and (7) RCT rarely recognizes power and inequality that determines whose voice is included in the research.

Conventional systematic reviews, which combine published reports on outcome studies to support evidence-based practice, suffer from a number of methodological problems as well. They include: (1) over-reliance on electronic databases and under-representation of research not included in such databases; (2) publication bias towards positive findings; (3) bias towards English-language publications; and (4) inappropriate pooling of different studies to increase statistical power of the research (Burns & Catty, 2002; Cooper 2003; Marshall, 2002). Again, both RCTs and systematic reviews focus on the type of intervention, and do not question the drug metaphor. The selective attribution of therapeutic causative factors to the intervention studied instead of engaging with the reality that therapeutic change is co-produced through a collaborative relationship between client and practitioner remains a key conceptual bias.

What Are the Practitioners Doing with Research Evidence?

When researchers try to reduce the complexity of the clinical situation to a simplified understanding of what I characterized above as the CAIRO sequence, it is not surprising that practitioners are not enthusiastic about research. Clinical practitioners generally do not read or utilize clinical research in their practice (Hardcastle & Bisman, 2003; Morrow-Bradley & Elliott, 1986; Rosen, 1994) and seldom participate in research (Bednar & Shapiro, 1970; Lynch, Zhang, & Korr, 2009; Norcross, Prochaska, & Gallagher, 1989; Orme & Powell, 2008; Vachon et al., 1995; Wakefield & Kirk, 1996). The gap between research and practice, especially the neglect of research findings by practitioners, has been documented by many authors (e.g., Green, 2001; Haines & Jones, 1994; Tanenbaum, 2003; Tsang, 2000). Adhering to their narrow view of research and knowledge production, many researchers are incapable of accommodating the complex reality of the practitioners. Holding on to their cherished standards of scientific rigor, which they adopted quite uncritically from the physical sciences, some researchers reject practice knowledge they brand as anecdotal or opinion-based (Tanenbaum, 2003). Practice-based knowledge is considered inferior, and is only tolerated as a last resort when other sources of knowledge are unavailable.

As Haines and Jones (1994) observe, research and practice can be seen as differing but perhaps complementary world views on the same subject matter: researchers see data while practitioners see people and situations. Research data need to be translated to the real-life situations before they can be recognized as relevant by practitioners. Shaugnessy, Slanson, and Bennett (1994) suggest that practitioners' perception of the utility of evidence depends on its relevance to a specific setting and its validity for that setting.

The call for researchers and practitioners to work together to close this gap has been made by many authors (e.g., Fox, 2003; Grimshaw & Russell, 1993; Haines & Jones, 1994). The arguments range from accommodating different versions of knowledge or truth to paying attention to the relevance of research to practice. Over a decade ago, I made a similar observation and proposed an integrated practice-oriented approach to research that may bridge the gap (Tsang, 2000). There is little evidence that my suggestion has been taken up by many colleagues. The reality remains that researchers and practitioners, though sharing a common interest in improving our interventions, inhabit two different worlds, where the modes of operation and the mechanisms of rewards are quite different. When research funding and the quantity of refereed publications are the key structures of the economics of academic research, and the relevance to practice is determined by people who control the research agenda and resources, it would be naïve for us to assume that a good proposal for addressing the gap between practice and research will automatically lead to corresponding action by researchers and practitioners.

In the following section, I will continue to trace the development of what I believe to be a sensible approach to practice research, with full awareness that good ideas have to find their niche in the political economy of research and practice.

Evidence-Based Practice: From the First to the Second Generation

As mentioned above, I proposed an integrated approach to practice-oriented research (Tsang, 2000) and since then colleagues have talked about practice-based research (e.g., Fox, 2003) and practice-based evidence (e.g., Barkham et al., 2001; Hubble, Duncan, Miller, & Wampold, 2010). We have all found the narrowly defined understanding of evidence-based practice inadequate and tried to propose an alternative that is more relevant to the lived experiences of practitioners and clients (Anker, Duncan, & Sparks, 2009; Duncan, Miller, & Sparks, 2004; Miller, Duncan, & Hubble, 2005). The quest for a better research approach usually requires us to engage with epistemological (pertaining to the nature of knowledge), substantive, and methodological issues. More specifically, we have to reflect on our assumptions regarding what knowledge is, and how knowledge is produced or acquired. We have different understandings regarding the substance of psychological and social interventions, such as whether we think that the theory and the method applied by the practitioner cause the desired outcome, or that the process and results are co-produced through a collaborative relationship. These diverse understandings are usually reflected in the method we choose, such as experiments that are supposed to give objective data or discovery-oriented methods for learning practical lessons from the interactive process between client and practitioner.

Trying to address these issues, Otto, Polutta, and Ziegler (2009) proposed a second generation version of EBP. Informed by phenomenological insights, they observed that the original or first-generation EBP model had been framed within a technology paradigm with clear cause-effect formulations guiding standardized action. They suggest that we should move beyond this technology paradigm and affirm the humanistic foundation of social work, which I believe is similar to what is shared by most mental health and human service professions. Their proposed model combines causal explanation (German: *Erklären*) and empathic or interpretive understanding (German: *Verstehen*) as complementary approaches to knowledge. The model recognizes the complexity of human conditions and emphasizes the subjectivity of the client. Attention is also paid to the unique characteristics of the clients and the enveloping contexts. They are in favour of a more eclectic approach that combines research methods based on different epistemological positions.

This second generation version of evidence-based practice, or what I will call EBP 2.0, is quite compatible with the integrated practice-oriented approach to research I proposed over a decade ago (Tsang, 2000). Both approaches do not rigidly follow a single epistemological position. Epistemological eclecticism is embraced as a pragmatic approach to engaging with the complexity of human situations. Given the emphasis on discovering valuable lessons for practitioners, a lot of attention is paid to the change process. Methodological pluralism is adopted to enable varied but complementary access to different aspects of the practice reality. In my own research program, I have brought in a developmental perspective that could guide our methodological decisions through different stages of investigation with reference to the pragmatic objectives to be achieved during that phase of research (Tsang, Bogo, & George, 2003).

EBP 3.0

I first came up with the idea of a third-generation version of evidence-based practice when I was asked to make a keynote presentation at a conference on the topic (Tsang, 2009). This version, which I call EBP 3.0, is my attempt to address the various issues pertaining to practice research, including epistemology, conceptualization of the change process, methodology, value and ideological issues, and the political economy of knowledge production. I am currently developing a fuller version of the model (Tsang, 2011b), which will be beyond the scope of this book. In the following section, I am going to give a brief description of the key features of EBP 3.0.

1. Epistemological Eclecticism

EBP 3.0 recognizes the complexity of human reality. While many aspects of human reality are socially constructed, not all aspects are equally malleable or plastic. There are aspects of human reality that are better understood in terms of formulations similar to physical laws, such as the mechanical realities involved in a car accident leading to broken bones. There are aspects that are more heavily conditioned by social discourses or practices, such as what constitutes an accident, or impaired driving. There are aspects of reality that are contingent upon personal constructions, which can be idiosyncratic, such as whether an automobile accident is experienced as a traumatic event or not. To insist that a singular epistemology can apply equally well to all human situations is more an article of faith than a pragmatic engagement with human reality. In EBP 3.0, we do not assume a fixed epistemological position but adopt positions in a contingent manner, considering the specific circumstances, the key aspects of reality to be dealt with, and the pragmatic objectives to be accomplished.

2. Pragmatism: Grounded in Real Life

Epistemological pluralism implies that we do not make absolute claims on the certainty or truthfulness of our representation of reality. Empiricism in the physical sciences recognizes fallibility and probability. Our quest for knowledge is constantly accompanied by uncertainty and doubt. In real life, many of our significant decisions are made without the benefit of all the information we need. EBP 1.0 typically furnishes us with grouped data, allowing actuarial estimates of probabilities. Unfortunately, such probabilistic formulations are sometimes translated by over-zealous advocates into hegemonic claims of facticity, truthfulness, and effectiveness, without due regard for individual circumstances.

If we consider the idea of RCT again, we will notice that for it to work well, the experiment has to be careful with who is included and excluded in the sample. Among people who are often excluded from such experimental trials are individuals with co-morbidity or multiple diagnoses, those with additional health risks, people who do not speak the language used by the researchers, or people who are not familiar with the cultural practice or research participation. The low external validity of RCT has been well documented (Epstein, 1993; Howard, Krause, & Orlinsky, 1986; Roth & Fonagy, 1996; Rothwell, 2005). When the tested or established treatment is later applied in real life, it is no longer limited to a similarly limited sample. The research design systematically biases the researchers to look at the common phenomenon when the treatment works, and relatively less attention is paid to the minority of cases who do not respond favourably. In real life, it is not unusual to see clients receiving the same "treatment of choice" repeatedly without benefiting from it.

EBP 1.0 further assumes that reliable knowledge is available for responsible professional decision-making in most cases. In EBP 3.0, we humbly acknowledge the limitations and the contingent nature of our best knowledge. Practitioners in health, mental health, and human services are often called to situations that are new, unfamiliar, and challenging, with little previous experience or established protocol. In situations like this, we rely more on the knowing process than the claims of what is known. Research, therefore, is a key attitude and activity in EBP 3.0.

In real life, practitioners in the human service professionals are called upon for a pragmatic purpose. Our conduct as practitioners is therefore purposeful, and how we make sense of any given professional situation is conditioned by our role and function in it. What we wish to accomplish, such as trying to discharge most patients as soon as possible or not going over the allowable insurance coverage for a given client, often conditions the reality we construct. When health care and social service resources are limited and when the people in charge of those resources prefer particular outcomes and processes, the political economy of knowledge production has a strong influence on professional discourse and practice (Singer, 2007; Warner, 2004).

3. Professional Practice as Inter-Subjective

As argued above, psychological and social interventions involving clients are better understood as interactive and collaborative processes instead of a transitive subject-to-object sequence, in which the cause is the intervention administered by the practitioner, and client change is regarded as effect, or what I called the CAIRO assumption. EBP 3.0 recognizes the interactive and collaborative relationship as a key factor and key process. Moving away from a transitive view, change is believed to be brought about through an inter-subjective process – both the client and the practitioner are conceived of as subjects. There is growing evidence that recognition of the client's agentive input, and allowing the client to participate in directing and monitoring the treatment process, can significantly improve the outcome of intervention (Anker, Duncan, & Sparks, 2009; Duncan, Miller, & Sparks, 2004; Miller, Duncan, & Hubble, 2005).

4. Collaborative Knowledge Production

In EBP 3.0, we do not only emphasize the client's agency in the collaborative process of therapeutic change but also recognize their potential role in knowledge production. The assumption of an authoritative voice by professional practitioners and researchers effectively excludes clients or service users from the knowledge production process. Such exclusion increases the risk of professional hegemony and deprives us of potentially valuable information, perspectives, and insights. Back in the early 1980s, Reason and Rowan (1981) advocated for a collaborative approach to research. Researchers in the social sciences and humanities have become increasingly aware of the diverse possibilities in knowledge production. Attempts to involve people we work with or serve in the knowledge production process are gaining acceptance in the research community (e.g., Bray, Lee, Smith, & Yorks, 2000; Duncan, Miller, & Sparks, 2004; Israel, Eng, Schulz, & Parker, 2005).

5. Methodological Pluralism

The adoption of epistemological eclecticism, the grounding in real life, the recognition of psychological and social interventions as collaborative, and the recognition of the client's role in knowledge production all feed into the methodological pluralism supported by EBP 3.0. We recognize that research methods are purposeful, and their function and value are contingent upon the research question to be answered. Many researchers identify themselves as primarily quantitative or qualitative but that amounts to making an *a priori* decision on the research method without regard for the question to be answered.

One of the methods that deserves more research attention is practice-based procedures. There is a wealth of knowledge and experience shared by clients and practitioners that has not been incorporated into mainstream practice research. Unusual cases, specific experience with critical moments, counter-intuitive or unconventional procedures, carefully reasoned deviations from prescribed or standardized practice, and the like are often excluded in our research and knowledge production process. What has been called *practice wisdom* (Goldstein, 1990; Klein & Bloom, 1995) probably deserves more research attention. Many practitioners are interested in how more experienced colleagues make moment-by-moment decisions when they face similar situations and how they actually perform in-session. Clients can be invited to observe and comment on the procedures that we believe are beneficial, and offer their input with regard to what might work better. As mentioned above, the involvement of clients in monitoring the intervention process has already generated some encouraging results (Anker, Duncan, & Sparks, 2009; Duncan, Miller, & Sparks, 2004; Miller, Duncan, & Hubble, 2005). Procedures such as interpersonal process recall (Clarke, 1997; Crews et al., 2005; Kagan, Schauble, Resnikoff, Danish, & Krathwohl, 1969; Wiseman, 1992) can be used with both practitioners and clients to extract their observations, reflections, and insights.

EBP 3.0 recommends situation and phase specific methods, each chosen with a clear understanding of research objectives and the kind of information needed. Experimental and quasi-experimental designs are likely to be helpful in establishing the effectiveness of an intervention, especially when contributing variables are adequately covered or measured. Discovery-oriented narrative procedures are probably necessary if we wish to answer process questions such as what kinds of practitioner utterances can best facilitate self-disclosure among clients. RCTs may have better internal validity, but naturalistic designs can have better external validity. Practitioners, clients, and third-party observers can all observe the same phenomenon, but they have both convergence and differences. Depending on the purpose of our study, we may pay more attention to their similarity (e.g., establishing the validity of a construct to be measured) or difference (e.g., contrasting client and practitioner perception of power and control over therapy agenda).

6. *Equifinality*

Equifinality is a concept taken from systems theory (Bertalanffy, 1968). It refers to the fact that the same end can be achieved through different pathways. In EBP 3.0, the concept is applied both to practice and knowledge production. In practice, the concept of equifinality allows us to imagine that the same desired outcome can be achieved through different methods and procedures. We now have considerable evidence that different systems of psychotherapy can often lead to similar positive outcomes (Duncan, Miller, Wampold, & Hubble, 2010). In research, the idea is that the same research question can often be pursued through different means. For example, the question of whether SSLD is an effective intervention can be addressed by using objective standardized measures, subjective client-directed measures, third party observation of electronically recorded sessions, or practitioner assessment of outcome. We can imagine the use of naturalistic designs, retrospective interviews with clients, and experimental or quasi-experimental designs. What is the best method is contingent upon a host of considerations, including the specific information sought, the intended utilization of research findings (e.g., to refine the system or to apply for funding), the context (resources, facilities, or constraints), the interest of the constituencies (funders, clients, practitioners, service unit/organization, or researchers), timeline, problem or issue (e.g., suicide prevention, parenting skills, disaster relief, or community health education), and so on.

7. From Linear Categorical Thinking to Multiple Contingencies Modelling

As a concept, equifinality is very compatible with the multiple contingencies thinking that characterizes SSLD. The simultaneous consideration of multiple factors and processes not only enhances our capacity to deal with complex realities, but it also frees us from the linear categorical thinking that still dominates many areas of practice and research. A good example is the idea that CT (cognitive therapy), or SSRI (selective serotonin reuptake inhibitor) for that matter, is the treatment of choice for depression. This idea is only meaningful, either in practice or research, when we believe that there is a phenomenon we can categorize as depression, and that it is distinguishable from non-depression or the absence of depression. CT, or SSRI, is an imaginable category of treatment. These categorical entities are then fit into a linear formulation that runs something like the following: if a person is determined to be falling within the category of depression, then a treatment that matches the categorical definition of CT or SSRI will cause positive therapeutic change in the patient.

Multiple contingencies thinking or modelling does not preclude categories but recognizes them as conceptual constructs. What is conceptualized as categorical can sometimes be construed non-categorically, such as on a continuum. The relationship between two phenomena assumed to be categorical is very often not fixed and linear, but can be contingent upon many other factors and processes that interact with each other. Going back to the example of depression, there are obviously people who do not benefit from either CT or SSRI, or both. Following multiple contingencies modelling (MCM), we would want to understand how people are actually doing during treatment. For instance, we may look carefully at how their in-session behaviours are different than those of clients who get better (e.g., Tsang, Bogo, & Lee, 2010). EBP 3.0 encourages the complementary consideration of grouped and individual data, the engagement with multiple factors and processes through both quantitative and qualitative analyses.

MCM challenges the researcher who selectively investigates a selected aspect of the picture to locate the investigation within a broader context. Research resources and opportunities often restrict how much of the phenomenon we can cover, and selective focusing is inevitable. When doing research on the complex phenomenon of professional practice, however, we need to be mindful of the temptation to adopt simple linear formulations such as "if depression, administer CT or SSRI." More pertinent questions may have to be asked, such as who is more likely to benefit from what, during which phase of the intervention, under what circumstances, and so on. SSLD is a practice system built on similar multiple contingencies thinking and lends itself readily to practice-oriented research following EBP 3.0 principles.

8. Engaging with Intersecting Diversities

Another advantage of MCM is its smooth interface with diversity issues in practice research. Over the last couple of decades, increasing research attention has been given to diversity issues in professional practice. The intersecting diversities related to gender, sexuality, age, ethnicity, culture, religion, socio-economic status, difference in ability, and so on have been asserted as significant research agendas. MCM supports a more sophisticated engagement with such complex realities. When working cross-culturally, for instance, we may not want to fall into the trap of linear categorical thinking, which sometimes appears in the form of cultural literacy (Dyche & Zayas 1995; Tsang & George,

1998). Cultural literacy thinking makes the homogeneity assumption that all people belonging to a given cultural category will share common characteristics. For example, practitioners may assume that if a client is Asian, then family solidarity will be valued more than individual autonomy. This if-then linear categorical thinking ignores the multiple contingencies such as personal history, family dynamics, age, gender, education level, extent of multicultural exposure, internalized culture, class, regional difference (e.g., rural or urban), the issue at stake (e.g., making financial, medical, or educational decisions), and so on.

Both the SSLD practice system and the EBP 3.0 approach to research are built upon MCM. The conceptualization is capable of simultaneous engagement with multiple factors and processes that interact with each other. Diversity issues are not confined to simple categories but are conceptualized through the flexible application of conceptual tools that will allow us to make sense of the key issues to be explored. Such an open and flexible approach enables us to move beyond the taken-for-granted notions within a world view based on Euro-American precepts and categories. Diversity is not just an additional substantive dimension in research. It is an aspect of our social reality that conditions how we view the world, including our understanding of what knowledge is, how knowledge is produced through research, and how knowledge is to be used in practice.

Research and Practice

At its current phase of development, SSLD is mainly built upon practice experience and findings of research studies conducted on other intervention or practice approaches, including earlier work on social skills training. A significant amount of research effort is probably needed to support further development of SSLD as a practice system. Research on SSLD is likely to follow the principles of EBP 3.0, with a distinct focus on practice. We do not subscribe to the CAIRO assumption, and do not assert that when clients experience positive change, it is SSLD that causes such change as an effective practice system. We duly recognize the significant roles of the collaborative relationship, the input of the client, and other extra-therapeutic factors and processes. An ideal research program should allow us to explore all these relevant factors and processes, involving SSLD practitioners and clients as well as researchers who have no allegiance to the SSLD systems.

Following multiple contingencies thinking, SSLD intervention takes current research findings into account but recognizes the limitation of group-based data when applied to individual cases. Contingency-based intervention is built on practice-based evidence, meaning that we pay careful attention to the responses and performances of clients and accommodate such variations with a clear goal-oriented direction. Contingency-based intervention does not rely on religious compliance with standardized manuals. In SSLD, manuals are used as guidelines and helpful references, and practitioners are not required to follow them rigidly. Instead, they are encouraged to stay attuned to client responses and changing realities in the actual practice situation.

Practitioners move through different phases of learning when trying to master SSLD. Again, we do not believe that everyone necessarily moves through the exact same phases or within the same amount of time. Some practitioners find it helpful to have practice manuals and guidelines; some require more intensive coaching or supervision in the early phase of learning. Some practitioners prefer to have more openness and flexibility. We do emphasize to those colleagues that SSLD is a disciplined practice, and we have to be able to account for what we do, and justify the moment-by-moment decisions we make in the process of working with our clients. As mentioned above, we try to address individual differences in personal qualities, professional background, learning history and learning style, and the specific SSLD knowledge and skills they want to acquire.

When it comes to actual practice, there are SSLD programs that are more established and supported by more documentation, practice guidelines and manuals, practice experience, and program material. These programs are usually designed for known issues or conditions such as relationship problems, insomnia, social phobia, or schizophrenic disorder. I also recognize that SSLD practitioners are often called upon to work with situations that are not well known, let alone well researched or well understood. Such situations obviously call for a more contingency-based rather than manual-based intervention, and I believe that the disciplined and methodical application of SSLD principles and procedures can be helpful in those cases. While there are individual differences, an SSLD practitioner's capacity for contingency-based instead of manual-based practice tends to increase with experience and professional self-efficacy. Continual learning and professional development are emphasized in SSLD, and special programs can be designed for such purpose.

To illustrate the contingent nature of SSLD practice, I am including a case with multiple issues and challenges, and a summary of the intervention and outcome (Box 13.2).

Logistics: Some Suggestions

Finally, we wish to outline a few points regarding logistics in SSLD intervention. The first point relates to client preparation. Since SSLD is committed to client empowerment, we wish to support clients who want to be informed about SSLD practice. The SSLD official website offers useful information for clients who wish to gain a basic understanding of the system. In line with SSLD principles, clients can learn to use SSLD services more effectively by being better informed and by gaining proficiency in self-directed learning. Practitioners are encouraged to prepare program material for this purpose, and we hope that the SSLD website can be further developed to support practitioners in this regard.

Given the increasing utilization of web-based resources, especially with younger clients, it is anticipated that SSLD programs will increasingly incorporate web-based components, and with advances in web-based communication technology, design and delivery of web-based SSLD programs is already imaginable. In the future development of SSLD programs, we expect to post more program materials online. In the recently developed program for insomnia and sleep-related issues, for instance, we are planning to put the information provision components, such as basic information on insomnia, the neurophysiology of sleep, and basic principles of SSLD intervention, online. This can save in-session time and allows participants to stay connected with the program and continue their own learning outside of the scheduled sessions.

In more conventional face-to-face practice, a couple of logistical suggestions can be made. One is the preparation of a program package or binder in which participants can keep related program materials such as handouts, assessment forms, worksheets, exercise and assignment instructions, DVDs, or CDs. It can also be used by clients to take notes and to record their activities, performance, and progress. Most participants of SSLD programs find such packages or binders helpful. Related to this point is the preparation of program materials to be distributed in each session. It is a good idea to have the relevant worksheets or handouts ready before each session. In more contingency-based programs, it is good for relevant materials to be easily available in digital format, so that they can be printed out easily when needed.

Box 13.2. The Case of Suna

Suna was in her early forties, though she looked much older. She came from a very poor village in Asia and immigrated to Canada twelve years ago, sponsored by her husband. Her husband's physical and sexual abuse of her had started in her home village even before they got married. He hit her and forced her to have sex whenever he visited. Her family was aware of that but still encouraged her to get married and move to a new country as they wanted to have the substantial financial gift her husband had offered. Her elder brother, in particular, indicated to her that she had been a financial burden to the family, and he wanted her to leave home as soon as possible. The abuse continued after immigration, including sexual violation and physical assault, and she gave birth to three children, who were 4, 6, and 9 at the time of intake. The eldest and the youngest were girls. She suspected that her husband was doing something "unusual" with the girls. She had limited English ability and had few friends. She had little understanding of the legal system and almost no knowledge of available services. She did not understand the roles of the professionals she had come across. She left home and lived on the streets for two weeks but found it difficult to survive on her own. She had been to the emergency room on a couple of occasions but she was careful not to attract law enforcement attention. She felt powerless and believed that her husband would eventually get her regardless. She went to see a family service social worker after an emergency room social worker and a police officer suspected family violence and suggested she seek help. She was then referred to a women's shelter.

Intake and Engagement

Suna appeared traumatized when she showed up for intake. She looked scared, her body was all tensed up, and she made no eye contact with people, including the receptionist and the social worker. The social worker created a safe space for her to tell her story, in a very soft and inhibited voice. She emphasized her helplessness and powerlessness in her narrative. She also reported on how her previous contact with the referring social worker had been stressful because she always asked her what she planned to do and what her imagined solution would look like. She also felt judged by the family service worker who seemed to have a problem with her plan to take care of herself first, instead of taking her children with her. The only positive aspect of her story was how she found some satisfaction in a part-time caretaker job. The worker was sensitive to her need for security, personal space, and a sense of agency, and was careful not to communicate judgment or expectations that might be perceived as overwhelming demands. Suna experienced a gradual narrative shift from helplessness and passivity to an awareness of her needs and desired changes. She enjoyed talking about her experience, particularly when she felt understood and supported. Towards the end of the session, Suna was working collaboratively with the worker on immediate physical safety.

N3C Assessment
- Needs: Security, safety, self-esteem, affiliation, independence.
- Circumstances: Victim of intimate partner violence, immigrant, limited English, no family support, no social network, limited financial resources, culturally reinforced shame about intimate partner violence and strong sanction against involving law-enforcement.
- Characteristics: Extremely low self-image, deep sense of powerlessness, difficult to establish trust.
- Capacity: Resilience, strong executive function, excellent emotional regulation ability, ability to articulate her own experience and her needs and wants.

Goal Setting
- Her own safety.
- Personal space, including freedom from socially enforced maternal role.
- Independence – she wanted to be financially self-sufficient through working.

Strategies and Skills Learning and Development
- Cognitive reframing of her experience, emphasizing her agency and efficacy.
- Address specific concerns of the client, regardless of how "realistic" they might be, such as in-session simulation of strategies and skills required if harassed by husband in the street or at work (which never happened in real life, but the client feared that it would).
- Learning about her legal rights and how to exercise them, including simulation of how to make an emergency call in her own language.
- Learning how to use relevant social services effectively, including ethno-specific organizations that provided services in her language.

282 SSLD Practice

- Learning technical skills to communicate with children through in-session simulation.
- Simulation of talking assertively to husband over the phone without disclosing information about herself, and managing her own emotional responses of fear, resentment, and the tendency to be submissive.
- Learning to establish relationships with acquaintances (e.g., co-workers at part-time employment), mobilizing them to form a support network.
- Developing a trusting alliance with another woman at the shelter, which she later considered the most helpful relationship in her life.

Outcome (After eleven individual sessions over three months)
- Discarded the self-defeating belief of her own helplessness and the exaggerated power and control her husband had over her.
- Started to consider the options of separation and divorce, including a de facto separation to buy herself time.
- Moved out of the house, sharing an apartment with a woman she met at the shelter, whom she considered her comrade.
- Children came under the attention of a child protection agency.

The use of video recording and playback is another important point. Since the procedure is used extensively in SSLD, it is advisable to have the equipment ready and tested for proper performance before use. A general guideline is that such recording is mainly for the purpose of providing feedback; we do not wish to pay inordinate attention to finesses such as lighting and visual effect, as long as we have clear images and good sound quality. Before electronic recording of any form, it is necessary to have signed consent from clients specifying their willingness to participate, and the limits they wish to set with regard to how the recordings are kept and used. If we wish to use the recordings for research or professional education, explicit consent has to be obtained for such specific purposes.

In some practice situations, we will engage the help of collaborators in simulation role-plays with clients. Again, informed consent has to be obtained from clients. The consent document should clearly state our commitment to protecting the client's confidentiality. As a general principle, we discourage outside of session contact between the collaborators and clients, unless it is part of a designed in-vivo exercise. Similar precaution has to be taken with activities and relationships between participants of a program or members of an SSLD group. It is understood that these principles and procedures are usually applied in clinical practice situations, and are not as seriously enforced in community development or educational and training settings, but the protection of participant privacy and rights should always be considered.

Summary

This book is intended as a useful resource for colleagues interested in becoming SSLD practitioners. It is expected that many readers will also enrol in an SSLD professional practice course or program. SSLD is not just a set of conceptual formulations and practice principles, but includes direct practice skills, which have to be acquired and mastered through repeated practice, likely requiring coaching, consultation, or supervision by a more experienced SSLD practitioner. We have described different SSLD practice levels in this chapter and individual colleagues may aim at developing their own desired level of competence, as well as their preferred scope and mode of practice. I have emphasized the advantage of contingency-based practice but it should be noted that SSLD remains a disciplined practice, and practitioners are expected to be accountable for their professional activities and practice decisions.

In line with SSLD principles and values, we encourage and expect colleagues to pursue continual learning and professional development. SSLD itself is not a closed system but is continually being developed and refined. Colleagues are welcome to stay in touch and share their experience, insights, observations, comments, critiques, suggestions, innovations, and so on. The SSLD website can serve as a platform for feedback, exchange, mutual support, and collaboration.

Chapter Fourteen

Issues Related to SSLD: A Personal Note

I have introduced SSLD practice to hundreds of colleagues, and in a wide variety of contexts, including universities, social service organizations, community organizations, health care establishments, companies, professional associations, volunteer groups, and direct practice settings. I have come across many questions, comments, feedback, suggestions, and critiques. Once an experienced psychologist in private practice commented that I tended to introduce SSLD in a manner that was probably too theoretical for practitioners. He suspected that it was due to my long-term employment in an academic position. I can actually think of many incidents that support his observation, mostly involving colleagues asking for very specific technical information or practical answers. While I am personally very interested in the theoretical issues related to SSLD, I have noticed that the majority of colleagues tend to be more interested in the practical issues. I have therefore chosen to write this book in a practice-oriented way and have tried to introduce conceptual formulations in relation to practice as much as possible.

In this chapter, however, I am going to indulge in more conceptual explorations, some of which may even sound like personal musings. Readers who do not find the topics helpful can feel free to skip any of them, or even the entire chapter. First, I wish to locate SSLD intellectually in relation to my other projects. Second, I will look at the value base of SSLD practice. This discussion will then lead us on to the issue of diversity. Finally, I will address the issue of research and knowledge building.

SSLD and My Other Projects

I have been working in academia since 1984, but I am not a typical academic, at least not according to North American convention. I am interested in too many things, ranging from psychotherapy practice and research to epistemology, discourse analysis, identity politics, cross-cultural work, globalization, and immigration. I have done work in sexuality, the health and well-being of seniors, and reproductive technology. I also have been actively promoting the development of social work, psychotherapy, health and mental health practice in China. Such diverse and apparently scattered interests can often cause suspicion in colleagues and students. Well-intentioned colleagues have suggested that I get more focused so that I can establish a program of scholarship and research that will look more discrete and solid. I am, however, passionate about the things that I do, and do not want to be confined by the narrow scope of knowledge production and dissemination supported by the prevailing academic convention.

When I first took on an academic job, I thought I would be able to combine my interests in practice, teaching, and research. The circumstances have changed dramatically over the last quarter-century of my career. Now, working in a research-oriented university, the emphasis is on competitive research funding and refereed publications, which I do enjoy and have been moderately successful with, but the teaching and the practice that I enjoy as well have been pushed to the margins, or outside my job description altogether. What is known but often unacknowledged among my colleagues is that teaching actually does not count for much. In a social work school, maintaining direct practice in the same area that we teach is not even on the list for appraising performance and academic "productivity."

I think in an integrative manner, and I see threads that run through my apparently diverse and divergent interests. When asked, I will tell my colleagues and graduate students that my program of scholarship and research aims at developing a multidisciplinary knowledge base for human service in a globalized context. In practice and in professional and academic education, unlike in competitive research program development, we need to engage with diverse bodies of knowledge. As someone who cares and wants to do something about the well-being of other human beings, many systems of knowledge are relevant. We can be talking about the genetic and neurophysiological correlates of depression, or how shifts in the global economy are impacting employment and health care in India or China. I believe that when we have armies of specialists who are focused on narrow spectrums of the overall picture and often do not or cannot communicate effectively with each other, taking on a more inclusive and holistic perspective may have its value.

When I get immersed in a specific inquiry, I sometimes shift into the narrow-focus mode as well. For instance, my doctoral thesis is on the development of a psychotherapy process coding system to detect clinical processes that may be associated with early drop out from psychotherapy among clients with borderline personality disorder. I did very careful and focused analysis of how psychotherapists and clients negotiate the therapy agenda. One of my current projects involves analysing how cross-cultural client–therapist dyads engage with each other in the first session (Tsang, Bogo, & Lee, 2010). At the same time, I am conducting research on how women who donate and receive oocyte in assisted reproduction experience the process and how they make their decisions about their reproductive choices. In another project, I am looking at the relationship between social capital and employment among immigrant youth. As a practitioner, I see all of these as relevant to the work I am doing, and the expanding scope of SSLD application over the last three decades reflects a parallel openness or responsiveness that I would like to maintain.

Multiple-contingencies thinking probably represents a central theme in my diverse explorations into different ways to work with people, through psychotherapy or otherwise. My taken-for-granted approach to knowledge and reality was upset once and for all when I attended my first lecture in psychology as an undergraduate in 1973. The late Erik Kvan, my teacher at the University of Hong Kong, showed us how we still talked about the sun rising in the east more than 400 years after Copernicus had proposed a heliocentric cosmology. Today, we are still using a geocentric language system. I continue to use Kvan's brilliant illustration in my master's class on social theories and my doctoral class on epistemology. The classic work by Berger and Luckmann (1966) on the social construction of reality opened the door to the phenomenological tradition, which transformed my understanding of psychotherapy. Recognizing the role of language, professional and scientific language included, in the construction of reality helped me appreciate the contingent nature of knowledge. This appreciation of contingency has, over time, taken me beyond the debate between positivist-empiricist and constructivist-epistemological positions. It occurs to me that our lived reality is so complex and polythetic that it is unlikely that a single epistemological position can get it all right. As knowledge is contingent, so is epistemological positioning. As a practitioner, I follow a more pragmatic approach, and I think we may benefit from different epistemological orientations under different circumstances. When working with people who are HIV positive, for instance, I appreciate that the idea of reality they use when they are looking at CD4 T cell count (more likely to be positivist) is very different than the one they use when they discuss the influence of organized religion on the politics of funding or safe-sex campaigns (more likely to be constructivist). This pragmatic approach to epistemology is not new, Polkinghorne (1992), who recognizes the contingent nature of reality and knowledge, has suggested a pragmatic orientation. Appreciating the complexity and plurality we have to deal with in psychotherapy and psychotherapy research, Rennie and Toukmanian (1992) proposed an eclectic approach to epistemology and research methodology.

In the actual practice of psychotherapy, we need to move beyond recognizing the contingent nature of reality and the knowledge we produced about it, and appreciate how contingencies operate along multiple dimensions so we can interact with each other in a dynamic manner. What is contingent is not fixed, but variable. Contingency also refers to dependence on other variables and processes. For example, a client's reaction to the practitioner is contingent upon how professional relationships are construed within the client's culture and social group. Contingency is sometimes captured in a simple linear "if a, then b" structure, but in real life, people are often dealing with the dynamic interaction of multiple factors and variables. To imagine that everything is contingent and constantly changing may seem reasonable in theory, but in practice, we are limited by our capacity to process multiple chunks of information simultaneously and by our attention span. I have, therefore, developed a conceptual framework for managing multiple contingencies in clinical practice (Tsang, 2008) to help colleagues make sense of the overwhelming array of interconnected factors and processes by conceptualizing clinical events according to (1) domains of human experience, covering biology, motivation, cognition, emotion, action, and environment, (2) how clinical change processes develop or unfold over time, (3) client variables, (4) therapist variables, and (5) setting and situational factors.

As mentioned a few times earlier in this book, SSLD practice tries to incorporate multiple-contingencies thinking in order to maximize its openness, flexibility, and relevance to particular client needs and circumstances. Reflecting on my own learning and development, however, has reminded me that I have gone through different phases myself. I did not start my practice with a contingency-based method but instead followed a more structured approach that I learned from others. Having a more structured system, complete with manuals, guidelines, and relevant program materials can make a beginning learner more comfortable and relaxed, therefore facilitating further learning and development. Colleagues who are more experienced are more likely to appreciate the flexibility and versatility of the system, and they can infuse their own knowledge and experience into the practice. This pragmatic orientation embodies a number of principles:

(1) We need to draw from diverse sources of information, knowledge and experience in order to help clients develop effective strategies and skills to deal with the demands and challenges of life, while trying to meet their needs and attain their goals in life.
(2) What we practice is not a mechanical application of a fixed and stable system, but involves an organic synthesis of professional knowledge, practice experience, and our own personal characteristics.
(3) Whereas we seek to articulate a shared body of knowledge, principles, and procedures, each one of us is going through a process of learning and development, which means that our practice is evolving and changing instead of staying the same over time. Hopefully, our practice continues to improve over time.
(4) The SSLD system remains open to new input, modification and refinement, and there is a limit to what we can standardize across practitioners, clients, and practice situations.
(5) Standardized manuals can provide valuable guidelines, principles, and specific procedures but their ultimate value is realized in helping the clients achieve positive outcome, given their specific needs and circumstances.
(6) A rigorous and disciplined approach to practice requires us to pay careful attention to process so that we know where the client is going. We need to be able to account for what we do in practice, and justify the decisions and choices we make.

(7) Multiple contingencies thinking is used to enhance our responsiveness to the particular needs and circumstances of our clients.

These principles can actually be found connected to my other projects as well. Abstract principles such as holistic understanding complemented by differentiation, epistemological and methodological eclecticism, integration and transcendence, dynamic structural analysis, and so on, can be found in more than one area of my work, although they may be operationalized differently.

The Value Base of SSLD

In this section we will explore the value base of SSLD. When we say that knowledge is contingent, one of the contingencies is value. Values are associated with the positions we take and the perspectives we use. Values are therefore intimately tied to knowledge, both in terms of how it is produced and how it is mobilized or used. Pragmatism, for instance, is a value-laden orientation. Whereas professions in the human services share certain core values such as respect for the person, individual rights, and professional accountability, there are values that are more emphasized in some professions. Equity and social justice, for example, are accorded central significance in contemporary social work in the West, at least in academic and professional discourse.

Pragmatism, Knowledge, and Values

SSLD is an explicitly pragmatic system. In a way, being pragmatic is a value position in itself. For instance, pragmatism conditions the way we look at knowledge and how we produce and mobilize knowledge. Some social scientists seek knowledge for its own sake, and do not think that knowledge production has to be related to any pragmatic aim. There are academics and scholars who make a distinction between pure and applied knowledge, some even consider applied knowledge, including applied social science, as less than pure and therefore of inferior value. I personally believe that practice in the human service professions creates a privileged site for knowledge production as well as knowledge mobilization. When challenged to come up with a solution or to bring about change, the professional practitioner needs to develop a practical understanding, which has to be commensurate with the complexity of the given human situation. Very often we need to take action before complete or adequate knowledge can be obtained, and our weighing of the odds or assessment of risks and benefits will be subject to test. Regardless of the outcome, we will gain further knowledge about the situation. One example that I often use is how social workers had to deal with complex situations involving domestic violence before systematic research knowledge and formal theories could be made available. Psychotherapy is another good example of how knowledge developed out of practice, starting with practitioners taking on the challenge of dealing with complex human phenomena that we had little knowledge about. This willingness to take on demanding and challenging tasks without the assurance of complete or adequate knowledge is often underrated in the current climate of evidence-based practice. The fact that we often have to respond to human situations without sufficient information or knowledge that meets the evidence-based criteria is too easily neglected. In cases like this, we utilize the best available information and knowledge, integrating them with relevant experience, and a readiness for active inquiry.

While a well-established evidence-based practice is not yet available, we may need to start developing practice-based evidence. My involvement in the relief efforts after the earthquake in Sichuan, China, on 12 May 2008 can serve as an example. With regard to trauma therapy or counselling, the evidence that any particular approach or procedure would have worked for the earthquake victims in Sichuan was clearly inadequate if we assume that randomized clinical trials based on a manualized intervention tested on samples equivalent to the diverse population groups to be treated should be the standard. Psychiatrists, psychotherapists, and other mental health workers had to respond to the request for help without being equipped with evidence-based knowledge and skills. There were reports of inappropriate interventions but we had witnessed a steady accumulation of valuable knowledge and experience long before more formal and systematic research studies could be designed and conducted. If we were talking about community redevelopment initiatives, the unique circumstances – including geographic, social, cultural, political, and economic realities – called for extreme caution as well as ingenuity in the transfer of knowledge, practice experience, or whatever we claimed to be evidence from other contexts.

In human services, the production of knowledge and the transfer of knowledge are not mechanical processes following a linear logical sequence from evidence to practice, but involve the negotiation of multiple contingencies. SSLD practice emphasizes needs and goal setting and we have to be aware that the translation of needs into goals usually involves the application of values. Maintaining the integrity of the family and protecting individual rights and safety, for example, are values that are not always compatible in cases of family violence and they do impact on how personal goals are set by the clients as well as practitioners. Negotiating competing or even conflicting values and aims is a task that human service professionals often come across, and strategies and skills can be learned and developed to deal with it.

Human Agency and Change

One of the fundamental values of SSLD is the belief in change, or that positive change is possible in most human situations. Human beings are construed as active agents pursuing goals and human action is conceived as purposeful and functional. SSLD recognizes and supports human agency. Whenever possible, we try to help people learn to take actions to bring about desired change instead of trying to change things for people. This emphasis on human agency and the possibility of change protects us from pathologizing people. The procedures we use to translate problems reconstruct those problems into goals to be accomplished as well as strategies and skills to be learned and developed. This position reflects a fundamentally optimistic view of human nature, emphasizing potential and positive tendencies instead of negative ones. While we recognize that negative events and processes in life cannot be avoided, the way we approach and manage these challenges will make a significant difference in our experience. Associated with this positive orientation is the idea of hope and the insistence on exploring what can be done to help clients move away from states of despair and inaction.

Empowerment, Power, and Equity

SSLD practice empowers people by enabling them to expand their repertoire of strategies and skills, and thus making more options available to them. People facing the vicissitudes of life can often feel defeated, helpless, and vulnerable. Very often people are left immobilized and trapped in feelings of passivity, self-doubt, or even self-blame and shame. Using the operational concept of self-efficacy, SSLD helps people to develop a sense of mastery and control and a positive expectancy that they can do better. In the face of unfair treatment – which can include a wide range of interpersonal and social responses such as criticism, putdowns, rejections, exploitation, exclusion, abuse, or oppression – SSLD intervention seeks to help people in a disadvantaged position maximize their capacity to redress the power imbalance by learning to take effective action, individually or collectively, to defend and assert their rights. The consistent emphasis on goal attainment, and the flexible but persistent pursuit of effective action, can usually help people take incremental steps towards empowerment.

Contemporary analyses of power tend to emphasize structural inequities related to social positions and resources. Factors such as poverty or minority status are taken as stable personal characteristics with fixed effects. Predicated on multiple contingencies thinking, SSLD resists simple deterministic thinking and believes that there is always something that people in disadvantaged positions can do. Power is not completely determined by social location, identity, or demographic characteristics, and individual agency and action can always make a difference. To the extent that power is construed as the ability to bring about results or changes that one desires, SSLD is always about power. SSLD analysis of power recognizes the difference between potential and actualized power, and the dynamics between performance and perception. People with less power often do not realize their full potential, meaning that they have more power than they know or believe they have. Potential power refers to untapped or unrealized capacity to bring about desired results or changes. Learning and developing effective strategies and skills transform potential power into actualized power.

The dynamics between performance and perception is another dimension neglected by structural analyses of power. Much of socially constructed power is based on performance and perception. Fear is the best example. Oppressive and abusive forms of power are more often than not built on fear. Fear is a socially constructed perception of power that can turn into a strong motivation that keeps people in silence and inaction. SSLD mobilizes basic human needs and channels them into action or into actual social performance that brings about change, thus disrupting the status quo that people using oppressive forms of power desire to maintain. This value can be realized in a wide range of situations, from empowering individuals abused by their spouse or intimate partners, to employees who are unfairly treated by the employers, to communities subject to inequality and disadvantage. Power comes from three major sources. The first is institution, organization, or position, including the associated social capital and sociocultural resources. The second is property and material and financial resources. The third is personal capacity, which includes knowledge, strategies, and skills, and can be pooled together in groups and communities. Analyses of power that only emphasize the first two sources of power are potentially disempowering because they discount or discard the personal source of power. In my own practice of SSLD, this never falls out of focus.

Diversity

SSLD practice explicitly embraces bio-psycho-social diversity as a positive dimension of human reality. This diversity enriches human life and offers the opportunity for us to develop diverse actions and responses that add to our collective repertoire of strategies and skills as a species. Interpersonal differences and our shared humanity are like two sides of a coin and we cannot have one without the other. This diversity-positive orientation prepares us for practice or service in an increasingly globalized context, in which colleagues of human service professions often have to work with clients coming from backgrounds very different from our own. The massive transnational movement of people has transformed the demographic structure of many of the Western countries, which still dominate academic and professional discourses globally. Diversity in terms of ethnicity, country of origin, culture, and religion is only part of the extensive spectrum of bio-psycho-social diversity. Differences with regard to gender, age or life-stage, socio-economic status, sexuality, ability, aptitude, and so on can be found even in apparently homogenous societies.

Research and development of psychological and social interventions have been dominated by the idea of standardization, which hopes to find the best treatment for a given group of people. Individual differences, atypical or unique experiences are often excluded in statistical analysis. In the early phases of development of cross-cultural psychotherapy, for instance, most authors still relied on broad categories with dubious validity such as Asians, Hispanics or Latinos, Natives, Africans or Blacks, and Whites or Caucasians. The simple but obvious facts that people are exposed to multiple sources of cultural influence and that they selectively internalized aspects of different cultural systems are often ignored (Ho, 1995). With other dimensions of diversity, most people still prefer to think of them in terms of discrete categories such as men or women, straight, gay, or lesbian, children or adult, able-bodied or disabled.

Multiple-contingencies thinking facilitates non-categorical imagination, with enhanced capacity to deal with fine differentiation. This mode of thinking does not require us to project difference or diversity onto others, but helps us to appreciate that both difference and commonality co-exist between any two human beings. What aspects of difference or commonality are important in any given interpersonal context, again, is not fixed but contingent. For instance, when a lesbian woman of mixed cultural heritage interacts with a straight heterosexual man of African descent, we cannot assume that ethnicity, gender, sexual orientation, a combination of these or none of them will be an important difference between them. It is contingent upon the situation, the purpose of engagement, the subject being pursued, and a host of other factors. In SSLD practice, we probably pay more attention to the performance of identity than socially defined identity categories. People perform their identities through multiple actions they take, ranging from appearance, clothing, language, demeanour, social display of identity markers, strategic self-presentation, and so on. Analyses assuming that difference is the key issue to be dealt with when someone is of a different ethno-cultural background or sexual orientation are obviously inadequate to deal with the complex and contingent nature of reality.

The inability to engage with differences in an open and flexible nature is often related to some form of self-centredness blended with a lack of comfort or self-efficacy when faced with realities that we are not familiar with. As such, it can be overcome through learning strategies and skills for managing interpersonal and social situations involving dimensions of difference. I believe that diversity education that equips people with the ability to work with others who are different on multiple dimensions will be increasingly in demand, and SSLD can be a useful tool.

Research and Knowledge-Building

Professional practice is supposedly based on a set of well-established knowledge and skills. Social sanction of professional practice often refers to a body of legitimated knowledge. In the human service professions, however, the relationship between practice and academic knowledge-building reveals some very interesting dynamics. The academics in professions such as social work and clinical psychology claim to be producing knowledge for their respective professions, but practitioners in those fields are not ready consumers of the knowledge they produce (e.g., Gonzales, Ringeisen, & Chambers, 2002; Rosen, 2003; Rosen, Proctor, Morrow-Howell, & Staudt, 1995). From my own observation over the last thirty years of professional practice, the popularity of treatment or intervention models used by practitioners is not always a function of the amount or quality of the evidence. Academics and researchers have been urging practitioners to build their practice on the basis of empirical research since the 1970s (Bergin & Lambert, 1978; Fischer, 1973, 1981; Hanrahan & Reid, 1984; Lambert, Shapiro, & Bergin, 1986) and, more recently, they are advocating for evidence-based practice (Addis, 2002; Drake et al. 2001; Duncan, Miller, Wampold, & Hubble, 2010; Gambrill, 1999; Gibbs & Gambrill, 2002). Whereas evidence of efficacy of what we are doing is always desirable, there are a few critical questions. The first question is what constitutes good evidence. Another question is how evidence is most effectively gathered. The third question is a more practical one and is concerned with how practitioners utilize evidence.

Some colleagues understand evidence-based practice more narrowly in terms of only applying methods that have been tested experimentally, typically through a randomized controlled trial (RCT). Others have a more flexible understanding that focuses on the dynamic process of decision-making in practice. This approach tries to bring together available research information and practice experience, giving due consideration to specific client characteristics, including client needs and circumstances, as well as the situational factors, including the environmental and the practice context. This approach has room for client input, including goal setting and preference with regard to the practice procedure, instead of taking a more authoritative and directive stance. Such an approach is probably more compatible with SSLD practice and the underlying multiple-contingencies thinking.

As mentioned above, when we use evidence gathered among people who are different from the clients we serve and in contexts that do not resemble our actual practice context, we need to exercise caution. In most cases, it is usually helpful that we have process research data that complements outcome data. In-depth analysis of the actual interactive processes between client and practitioner can provide very helpful practice guidelines and information for making decisions about our practices (Tsang, 2000). Taking a more flexible and dynamic approach to evidence-based practice, we may want to pay attention to the gathering and accumulation of practice-based evidence as well. Given the preference for reports on RCTs and similar experimental studies, careful narrative analysis of cases, segments, and episodes in everyday or naturalistic practice is not well supported by the academic and professional publication mechanisms. It is therefore not surprising to find practitioners relying more on modes of learning and consultation that are better grounded in day-to-day practice, such as practice workshops, case conferences, and supervision. I believe that accumulation of practice experience, articulation and documentation of practice wisdom, production of professional education material based on actual cases, and opportunity for sharing and exchange among colleagues should receive more support in terms of professional time, resources, and recognition.

Developing SSLD Practice

Along this line, colleagues interested in SSLD practice are encouraged to develop a habit of reviewing their practice, which should include tracking outcomes both through objective measures and client self-report. The opportunity to review electronic recordings of actual practice sessions has been found to be extremely helpful by me, my immediate colleagues, my supervisees, and my students. More systematic research studies, especially when they can adopt a process-outcome design and include naturalistic practice samples, can be extremely valuable (e.g., Tsang, Bogo, & George, 2003; Tsang, Bogo, & Lee, 2010). Careful articulation and documentation of experience and practice wisdom are probably more user-friendly, and I hope they can be disseminated more extensively.

I am planning to use the SSLD website as a platform to facilitate connection, sharing, exchange, and collaboration among colleagues interested in SSLD practice. As indicated before, I want SSLD to remain an open system that will assimilate and accommodate input and feedback from clients and professional colleagues on an ongoing basis, so that it can stay responsive to the ever-expanding and changing needs and demands presented by clients. Some readers will be using this book as part of a professional program in SSLD, and we will facilitate professional connection and exchange through the setting up of case conferences, study groups, and other platforms for exchange and sharing. Some readers may be using this book more independently and I encourage you to connect to our website and use the resources we have made available online.

The SSLD website: http://ssld.kttsang.com

References

Addis, M.E. (2002). Methods of disseminating research products and increasing evidence-based practice: Promises, obstacles, and future directions. *Clinical Psychology: Science and Practice*, 9(4), 367–78. http://dx.doi.org/10.1093/clipsy.9.4.367

Ainsworth, M.D.S. (1982). Attachment: Retrospect and prospect. In C.M. Parkes & J. Stevenson-Hinde (Eds.), *The place of attachment in human behaviour* (pp. 3–30). New York: Basic Books.

Ainsworth, M.D.S., Blehar, M.C., Waters, E., & Wall, S. (1978). *Patterns of attachment: A psychological study of the Strange Situation*. Hillsdale, NJ: Erlbau.

Ainsworth, M.D.S., & Bowlby, J. (1965). *Child care and the growth of love*. London: Penguin Books.

Alford, B.A., & Beck, A.T. (1997). *The integrative power of cognitive therapy*. New York: Guilford.

Allaz, A.F., Bernstein, M., Rouget, P., Archinard, M., & Morabia, A. (1998, Apr). Body weight preoccupation in middle-age and ageing women: A general population survey. *International Journal of Eating Disorders*, 23(3), 287–94. http://dx.doi.org/10.1002/(SICI)1098-108X(199804)23:3<287::AID-EAT6>3.0.CO;2-F Medline:9547663

Anker, M.G., Duncan, B.L., & Sparks, J.A. (2009, Aug). Using client feedback to improve couple therapy outcomes: A randomized clinical trial in a naturalistic setting. *Journal of Consulting and Clinical Psychology*, 77(4), 693–704. http://dx.doi.org/10.1037/a0016062 Medline:19634962

American Psychiatric Association. (2004). *Practice guideline for the treatment of patients with schizophrenia* (2nd ed.). Retrieved 9 June 2011, from http://psychiatryonline.org/content.aspx?bookid=28&sectionid=1665359

Applegate, J.S. (1989). The transitional object reconsidered: Some sociocultural variations and their implications. *Child and Adolescent Social Work*, 6(1), 38–51. http://dx.doi.org/10.1007/BF00755709

Argyle, M. (1967). *The psychology of interpersonal behaviour*. Middlesex, UK: Penguin.
Argyle, M. (1972). *The psychology of interpersonal behaviour* (2nd ed.). Middlesex, UK: Penguin.
Argyle, M. (1983). *The psychology of interpersonal behaviour* (4th ed.). Middlesex, UK: Penguin.
Argyle, M. (1988). *Bodily Communication* (2nd ed.). Madison: International Universities Press.
Ayllon, T., Haughton, E., & Hughes, H.B. (1965, Aug). Interpretation of symptoms: Fact or fiction. *Behaviour Research and Therapy, 3*(1), 1–7. http://dx.doi.org/10.1016/0005-7967(65)90037-9 Medline:14340593
Bandura, A. (1969). *Principles of behavior modification*. Oxford: Holt, Rinehart, & Winston.
Bandura, A. (1977a). *Social learning theory*. Englewood Cliffs, NJ: Prentice-Hall.
Bandura, A. (1977b, Mar). Self-efficacy: Toward a unifying theory of behavioral change. *Psychological Review, 84*(2), 191–215. http://dx.doi.org/10.1037/0033-295X.84.2.191 Medline:847061
Bandura, A. (1986). *Social foundations of thought and action: A social cognitive theory*. Englewood Cliffs, NJ: Prentice Hall.
Bandura, A. (1989). Social cognitive theory. In R. Vasta (Ed.), *Annals of child development* (Vol. 6, pp. 1–60). Greenwich, CT: Jai Press.
Bandura, A. (1991). Social cognitive theory of moral thought and action. In W.M. Kurtines & J.L. Gerwitz (Eds.), *Handbook of moral behaviour and development* (Vol. 1, pp. 45–103). Hillsdale, NJ: Erlbaum.
Bandura, A. (1997). *Self-efficacy in changing societies*. New York: Cambridge University Press.
Bandura, A. (2001). Social cognitive theory: An agentive perspective. *Annual Review of Psychology, 52*(1), 1–26. http://dx.doi.org/10.1146/annurev.psych.52.1.1
Barkham, M., Margison, F., Leach, C., Lucock, M., Mellor-Clark, J., Evans, C., Benson, L., Connell, J., McGrath, G., & Clinical Outcomes in Routine Evaluation-Outcome Measures. (2001, Apr). Service profiling and outcomes benchmarking using the CORE-OM: Toward practice-based evidence in the psychological therapies. *Journal of Consulting and Clinical Psychology, 69*(2), 184–96. http://dx.doi.org/10.1037/0022-006X.69.2.184 Medline:11393596
Barnett, O.W. (2001). Why battered women do not leave. Part 2: External inhibiting factors social support and internal inhibiting factors. *Trauma, Violence & Abuse, 2*(1), 3–35. http://dx.doi.org/10.1177/1524838001002001001
Barrett-Lennard, G.T. (1962). Dimensions of therapist response as causal factors in therapeutic change. *Psychological Monographs, 76*(43), 1–36. http://dx.doi.org/10.1037/h0093918

Bauer, M., McAuliffe, L., & Nay, R. (2007, Mar). Sexuality, health care and the older person: An overview of the literature. *International Journal of Older People Nursing*, 2(1), 63–8. http://dx.doi.org/10.1111/j.1748-3743.2007.00051.x Medline:20925834

Beck, A.T. (1967). *Depression: Clinical, experimental and theoretical aspects*. New York: Harper & Row.

Beck, A.T. (1970). Cognitive therapy: Nature and relation to behavior therapy. *Behavior Therapy*, 1(2), 184–200. http://dx.doi.org/10.1016/S0005-7894(70)80030-2

Beck, A.T. (1976). *Cognitive therapy and the emotional disorders*. New York: International Universities Press.

Beck, A.T. (1999). *Prisoners of hate: The cognitive basis of anger, hostility, and violence*. New York: Harper Collins Publishers.

Beck, A.T., Rush, A.J., Shaw, B.F., & Emery, G. (1979). *Cognitive therapy of depression*. New York: Guilford.

Beck, J.S. (1995). *Cognitive therapy: Basics and beyond*. New York: Guilford.

Bednar, R.L., & Shapiro, J.G. (1970, Jun). Professional research commitment: A symptom or a syndrome. *Journal of Consulting and Clinical Psychology*, 34(3), 323–26. http://dx.doi.org/10.1037/h0029339Medline:5523437

Berg, F.M. (1995). *Health Risks of Weight Loss* (3rd ed.). Hettinger, ND: Healthy Living Institute.

Berger, P., & Luckmann, T. (1966). *The social construction of reality: A treatise in the sociology of knowledge*. New York: Random House.

Bergin, A.E., & Lambert, M.J. (1978). The evaluation of therapeutic outcomes. In S.L. Garfield & A.E. Bergin (Eds.), *Handbook of psychotherapy and behaviour change* (2nd ed., pp. 143–89). New York: Wiley.

Berlin, S.B., Mann, K.B., & Grossman, S.F. (1991). Task analysis of cognitive therapy for depression. *Social Work Research & Abstracts*, 27(2), 3–11.

Bertalanffy, L.V. (1968). *General system theory: Foundations, development, applications*. New York: George Braziller.

Blau, P.M. (1964). *Exchange and power in social life*. New York: Wiley.

Bogo, M. (2006). *Social work practice: Concepts, processes, and interviewing*. New York: Columbia University Press.

Bohart, A.C., & Tallman, K. (2010). Clients: The neglected common factor in psychotherapy. In B.L. Duncan, S.D. Miller, B.E. Wampold, & M.A. Hubble (Eds.), *The heart & soul of change: Delivering what works in therapy* (2nd ed., pp. 83–111). Washington, DC: American Psychological Association. http://dx.doi.org/10.1037/12075-003

Bolton, D. (2002). Knowledge in the human sciences. In S. Priebe & M. Slade (Eds.), *Evidence in mental health care* (pp. 3–10). Hove: Brunner-Routledge.

Bordin, E.S. (1979). The generalizability of the psychoanalytic concept of the working alliance. *Psychotherapy (Chicago, Ill.), 16*(3), 252–60. http://dx.doi.org/10.1037/h0085885

Bowlby, J. (1958, Sep-Oct). The nature of the child's tie to his mother. *International Journal of Psycho-Analysis, 39*(5), 350–73. Medline:13610508

Bowlby, J. (1969). *Attachment and loss: Vol. 1. Attachment.* New York: Basic Books.

Bowlby, J. (1988). *A secure base: Parent-child attachment and healthy human development.* London: Routledge.

Bowlby, J. (1999). *Attachment and loss: Vol. 1. Attachment.* (2nd ed.). New York: Basic Books.

Bray, J.N., Lee, J., Smith, L.L., & Yorks, L. (2000). *Collaborative inquiry in practice: Action, reflection, and making meaning.* Thousand Oaks, CA: Sage.

Buck, R. (1991). Temperament, social skills, and the communication of emotion: A developmental-interactionist perspective. In D. Gilbert & J.J. Conley (Eds.), *Personality, social skills, and psychopathology: An individual differences approach* (pp. 85–106). New York: Plenum.

Burns, T., & Catty, J. (2002). Mental health policy and evidence: Potentials and pitfalls. *Psychiatric Bulletin, 26*(9), 324–7. http://dx.doi.org/10.1192/pb.26.9.324

Burt, C. (1939). The factorial analysis of emotional traits. Part II. *Journal of Personality, 7*(4), 285–99. http://dx.doi.org/10.1111/j.1467-6494.1939.tb02151.x

Busseri, M.A., & Tyler, J.D. (2004, Mar). Client-therapist agreement on target problems, working alliance, and counseling outcome. *Psychotherapy Research, 14*(1), 77–88. http://www.ncbi.nlm.nih.gov/entrez/query.fcgi?cmd=Retrieve&db=PubMed&list_uids=22011118&dopt=AbstractMedline:22011118

Capuzzi, D., & Gross, D.R. (1995). *Counselling and psychotherapy: Theories and interventions.* Englewood Cliffs, NJ: Merrill.

Cash, T.F., & Henry, P.E. (1995). Women's body images: The results of a national survey in the USA. *Sex Roles, 33*(1-2), 19–28. http://dx.doi.org/10.1007/BF01547933

Cassidy, J. & Shaver, P. (Eds.). (1999). *Handbook of attachment: Theory, research, and clinical applications.* New York: Guilford.

Chambless, D.L., & Ollendick, T.H. (2001). Empirically supported psychological interventions: Controversies and evidence. *Annual Review of Psychology* (pp. 685–716). Retrieved 28 Sep 2009, from http://doi:10.1146/annurev.psych.52.1.685.

Chambon, A.S., Tsang, A.K.T., & Marziali, E. (2000). Three complementary coding systems for coding the process of therapeutic dialogue. In A.P. Beck

& C.M. Lewis (Eds.), *The process of group psychotherapy: Systems for analyzing change* (pp. 311–56). Washington, DC: American Psychological Association. http://dx.doi.org/10.1037/10378-012

Chee, M., & Conger, J.C. (1989). The relationship between hetersocial and homosocial competence. *Journal of Clinical Psychology, 45*(2), 214–22. http://dx.doi.org/10.1002/1097-4679(198903)45:2<214::AID-JCLP2270450207>3.0.CO;2-Z

Chu, S.H. (1999). Multicultural counselling: An Asian American perspective. In D.S. Sandhu (Ed.), *Asian and Pacific Islander Americans: Issues and concerns for counselling and psychotherapy* (pp. 21–30). New York: Nova Science.

Clark, M.M., Cox, L.S., Jett, J.R., Patten, C.A., Schroeder, D.R., Nirelli, L.M., Vickers, K., Hurt, R.D., & Swensen, S.J. (2004, Apr). Effectiveness of smoking cessation self-help materials in a lung cancer screening population. *Lung Cancer (Amsterdam, Netherlands), 44*(1), 13–21. http://dx.doi.org/10.1016/j.lungcan.2003.10.001 Medline:15013579

Clarke, P. (1997). Interpersonal process recall in supervision. In G. Shipton (Ed.), *Supervision of psychotherapy and counseling: Making a place to think* (pp. 93–104). Buckingham, UK: Open University Press.

Colvin, G. (2008). *Talent is overrated: What really separates world class performers from everybody else.* New York: Penguin.

Cook, K.S. (Ed.). (1986). *Social exchange theory.* Beverly Hills, CA: Sage.

Cooper, B. (2003, Aug). Evidence-based mental health policy: A critical appraisal. *British Journal of Psychiatry, 183*(2), 105–13. http://dx.doi.org/10.1192/bjp.183.2.105 Medline:12893663

Cooper, M. (2008). *Essential research findings in counselling and psychotherapy: The facts are friendly.* London, UK: Sage Publications Ltd.

Correctional Services Canada. (2008, Aug). Aboriginal offenders and incarceration. Aborignal sex offenders: Melding spiritual healing with cognitive-behavioural therapy. Retrieved 10 Apr 2009, from http://www.csc-scc.gc.ca/text/pblct/so/aboriginal/toce-eng.shtml.

Crews, J., Smith, M.R., Smaby, M.H., Maddux, C.D., Torres-Rivera, E., Casey, J.A., & Urbani, S. (2005). Self-monitoring and counseling skills: Skills-based versus interpersonal recall training. *Journal of Counseling and Development, 83*(1), 78–85. http://dx.doi.org/10.1002/j.1556-6678.2005.tb00582.x

Curran, J.P. & Monti, P.M. (Eds.). (1982). *Social skills training: A practical handbook for assessment and treatment.* New York: Guilford.

Curry, S. (1993, Oct). Self-help interventions for smoking cessation. *Journal of Consulting and Clinical Psychology, 61*(5), 790–804. http://dx.doi.org/10.1037/0022-006X.59.2.318 Medline:2030194

Datamonitor. (2008, 31 Jan). Anti-aging and beauty attitudes and behaviours.

Retrieved 10 Apr 2009, from http://www.marketresearch.com/map/prod/1684374.html
de Shazer, S., & Berg, I.K. (1995). The brief therapy tradition. In J. Weakland & W. Ray (Eds.), *Propagations: Thirty years of influence from the mental research institute* (pp. 249–52). Binghamton, NY: The Haworth Press.
Deffenbacher, J.L., Dahlen, E.R., Lynch, R.S., Morris, C.D., & Gowensmith, W.N. (2000). An application of Becks cognitive therapy to general anger reduction. *Cognitive Therapy and Research, 24*(6), 689–97. http://dx.doi.org/10.1023/A:1005539428336
Derrida, J. (1973). *Speech and phenomena* (D.B. Allison, Trans.). Evanston: Northwestern University Press.
Derrida, J. (1978). *Of grammatology* (G.C. Spivak, Trans.). Baltimore: Johns Hopkins University Press.
DiGennaro Reed, F.D., Hyman, S.R., & Hirst, J.M. (2011). Applications of technology to each social skills to children with autism. *Research in Autism Spectrum Disorders, 5*(3), 1003–10. http://dx.doi.org/10.1016/j.rasd.2011.01.022
Dimeff, L., & Linehan, M.M. (2001). Dialectical behavior therapy in a nutshell. *California Psychologist, 34*(3), 10–13.
Drake, R.E., Goldman, H.H., Leff, H.S., Lehman, A.F., Dixon, L., Mueser, K.T., & Torrey, W.C. (2001, Feb). Implementing evidence-based practices in routine mental health service settings. *Psychiatric Services, 52*(2), 179–82. http://dx.doi.org/10.1176/appi.ps.52.2.179 Medline:11157115
Dreier, O. (2000). Psychotherapy in clients' trajectories across contexts. In C. Mattingly & L. Garro (Eds.), *Narrative and the cultural construction of illness and healing* (pp. 237–58). Berkeley: University of California Press.
Duncan, B.L., Miller, S.D., & Sparks, J. (2004). *The heroic client: A revolutionary way to improve effectiveness through client directed outcome informed therapy* (Rev. ed.). San Francisco: Jossey-Bass.
Duncan, B.L., Miller, S.D., Wampold, B.E., & Hubble, M.A. (Eds.). (2010). *The heart & soul of change: Delivering what works in therapy* (2nd ed.). Washington, DC: American Psychological Association. http://dx.doi.org/10.1037/12075-000
Dutton, D.G., & Aron, A.P. (1974, Oct). Some evidence for heightened sexual attraction under conditions of high anxiety. *Journal of Personality and Social Psychology, 30*(4), 510–17. http://dx.doi.org/10.1037/h0037031 Medline:4455773
Dyche, L., & Zayas, L.H. (1995, Dec). The value of curiosity and naiveté for the cross-cultural psychotherapist. *Family Process, 34*(4), 389–99. http://dx.doi.org/10.1111/j.1545-5300.1995.00389.x Medline:8674520

Ellis, A. (1957). Rational psychotherapy and individual psychology. *Journal of Individual Psychology, 13*(1), 38–44.

Ellis, A. (1987). The evolution of rational-emotive therapy (RET) and cognitive behaviour therapy(CBT). In J. K. Zeig (Ed.), *The evolution of psychotherapy* (pp. 107–32). New York: Brunner/hazel.

Epstein, W.M. (1993). Randomized controlled trials in the human services. *Social Work Research and Abstracts, 29*(3), 3–10.

Erikson, E.H. (1950). *Childhood and society.* New York: Norton.

Erikson, E.H. (1959). *Identity and the life cycle.* New York: International Universities Press.

Emerson, R.M. (1981). Social exchange theory. In M. Rosenberg & R.H. Turner (Eds.), *Social psychology: Sociological perspectives* (pp. 30–65). New York: Basic Books.

Exum, H.A., & Lau, E.Y. (1988). Counseling style preference of Chinese college students. *Journal of Multicultural Counseling and Development, 16*(2), 84–92. http://dx.doi.org/10.1002/j.2161-1912.1988.tb00644.x

Farmer, T.W., Van Acker, R.M., Pearl, R., & Rodkin, P.C. (1999). Social networks and peer-assessed problem behaviour in elementary classrooms: Students with and without disabilities. *Remedial and Special Education, 20*(4), 244–56. http://dx.doi.org/10.1177/074193259902000408

Fast, N.J., Halevy, N., & Galinsky, A.D. (2011). The destructive nature of power without status. *Journal of Experimental Social Psychology.* doi:10.1016/j.jesp.2011.07.013. Retrieved 13 Dec 2011, from http://www-bcf.usc.edu/~nathanaf/power_without_status.pdf

Feeney, B.C., & Collins, N.L. (2001, Jun). Predictors of caregiving in adult intimate relationships: An attachment theoretical perspective. *Journal of Personality and Social Psychology, 80*(6), 972–94. http://dx.doi.org/10.1037/0022-3514.80.6.972 Medline:11414378

Field, A.E., Cheung, L., Wolf, A.M., Herzog, D.B., Gortmaker, S.L., & Colditz, G.A. (1999, Mar). Exposure to the mass media and weight concerns among girls. *Pediatrics, 103*(3), E36–E40. http://dx.doi.org/10.1542/peds.103.3.e36 Medline:10049992

Fischer, J. (1973). Is social work effective: A review. *Social Work, 18*(1), 5–20.

Fischer, J. (1981). The social work revolution. *Social Work, 26*(3), 199–207.

Forness, S., Kavale, K., Blum, I., & Lloyd, J. (1997). A mega-analysis of meta-analyese: What works in special education and related services. *Teaching Exceptional Children, 13*(1), 4–9.

Foucault, M. (1990). *The history of sexuality: Vol. 1. An introduction* (R. Hurley, Trans.). New York: Vintage Books.

Fox, N.J. (2003). Practice-based evidence: Towards collaborative and transgressive research. *Sociology, 37*(1), 81–102. http://dx.doi.org/10.1177/0038038503037001388

Freud, S. (1936). *The ego and the mechanisms of defense*. New York: International University Press. (Original work published 1936)

Freud, S. (1966). The neuro-psychoses of defence. In Strachey, J. (Ed. & Trans.) *The standard edition of the complete works of Sigmund Freud* (Vol. 3, pp. 45–61). London: Hogarth Press. (Original work published 1894).

Frueh, J. (2003). *Political identity and social change: The remaking of the South African social order*. Albany, NY: SUNY Press.

Gambrill, E. (1999). Evidence-based practice: An alternative to authority-based practice. *Families in Society, 80*(4), 341–50.

Geller, J. (2001). *Here comes the bride: Women, weddings, and the marriage mystique*. New York: Four Walls Eight Windows.

Gelso, C.J., & Woodhouse, S.S. (2002). The termination of psychotherapy: What research tells us about the process of ending treatment. In G.S. Tryon (Ed.), *Counseling based on process research: Applying what we know* (pp. 344–69). Boston, MA: Allyn & Bacon.

Gergen, K. (1991). *The saturated self: Dilemmas of identity in contemporary life*. New York: Basic Books.

Gergen, K.J. (1999). *An invitation to social construction*. London: Sage.

Gergen, K.J. (2001). *Social construction in context*. Thousand Oaks, CA: Sage.

Gibbs, L., & Gambrill, E. (2002). Evidence-based practice: Counterarguments to objections. *Research on Social Practice, 12*(3), 452–76. http://dx.doi.org/10.1177/1049731502012003007

Gladwell, M. (2008). *Outliers: The story of success*. New York: Little, Brown & Co.

Goffman, I. (1959). *The presentation of self in everyday life*. Garden City, NY: Doubleday.

Goldstein, A.P. (1981). *Psychological skill training: The structured learning technique*. Oxford: Pergamon Press.

Goldstein, H. (1990). The knowledge base of social work practice: Theory, wisdom, analogue, or art? *Families in Society, 71*(1), 32–43.

Goleman, D. (1995). *Emotional intelligence: Why it can matter more than IQ*. New York: Bantam.

Gomes-Schwartz, B. (1978, Oct). Effective ingredients in psychotherapy: Prediction of outcome from process variables. *Journal of Consulting and Clinical Psychology, 46*(5), 1023–35. http://dx.doi.org/10.1037/0022-006X.46.5.1023 Medline:701541

Gonzales, J.J., Ringeisen, H.L., & Chambers, D.A. (2002). The tangled and thorny path of science to practice: Tensions in interpreting and applying "evidence." *Clinical Psychology: Science and Practice, 9*(2), 204–9. http://dx.doi.org/10.1093/clipsy/9.2.204

Goode, E. (2000, 11 Jan). A pragmatic man and his no-nonsense therapy. *The New York Times.* Retrieved 21 Nov 2008, from http://partners.nytimes.com/library/national/science/health/011100hth-behavior-beck.html.

Gould, N. (2006). An inclusive approach to knowledge for mental health social work practice and policy. *British Journal of Social Work, 36*(1), 109–25. http://dx.doi.org/10.1093/bjsw/bch243

Greaves, A.L. (2006). *The active client: A qualitative analysis of thirteen clients' contribution to the psychotherapeutic process.* Unpublished doctoral dissertation, University of Southern California, Los Angeles.

Green, L.W. (2001, May-Jun). From research to "best practices" in other settings and populations. *American Journal of Health Behavior, 25*(3), 165–78. http://dx.doi.org/10.5993/AJHB.25.3.2 Medline:11322614

Greenacre, P. (1969). The fetish and the transitional object. *Psychoanalytic Study of the Child, 24,* 144–64. Medline:5353361

Greenberg, L.S. (2002). *Emotion-focused therapy: Coaching clients to work through feelings.* Washington, DC: American Psychological Association Press. http://dx.doi.org/10.1037/10447-000

Greenberg, L.S. (2007). A guide to conducting a task analysis of psychotherapeutic change. *Psychotherapy Research, 17*(1), 15–30. http://dx.doi.org/10.1080/10503300600720390

Greenberg, L.S., & Paivio, S.C. (1997). *Working with emotions in psychotherapy.* New York: Guilford.

Greenberg, L.S., & Safran, J. (1987). *Emotion in psychotherapy: Affect, cognition and the process of change.* New York: Guilford.

Grencavage, L.M., & Norcross, J.C. (1990). Where are the commonalities among the therapeutic common factors? *Professional Psychology, Research and Practice, 21*(5), 372–78. http://dx.doi.org/10.1037/0735-7028.21.5.372

Gresham, F.M. (1997). Social competence and students with behavior disorders: Where we've been, where we are, and where we should go. *Education & Treatment of Children, 20*(3), 233–50.

Gresham, F.M. (1998). Social skill training: Should we raze, remodel, or rebuild? *Behavioral Disorders, 24*(1), 19–25.

Gresham, F.M., Cook, C.R., Crews, S.D., & Kern, L. (2004). Social skills training for children and youth with emotional and behavioral disorders: Validity considerations and future directions. *Behavioral Disorders, Special Issue: Elucidating Precision and Rigor in EBD Research, 30*(1), 32–46.

Gresham, F.M., & Elliott, S.N. (1984). Assessment and classification of children's social skills: A review of methods and issues. *School Psychology Review, 13*(3), 292–301.

Gresham, F.M., & Lopez, M.F. (1996). Social validation: A unifying concept for school-based consultation research and practice. *School Psychology Quarterly, 11*(3), 204–27. http://dx.doi.org/10.1037/h0088930

Grimshaw, J.M., & Russell, I.T. (1993, 27 Nov). Effect of clinical guidelines on medical practice: A systematic review of rigorous evaluations. *Lancet, 342*(8883), 1317–22. http://dx.doi.org/10.1016/0140-6736(93)92244-N Medline:7901634

Grogan, S. (1999). *Body image: Understanding body dissatisfaction in men, women and children*. London: Routledge.

Gurman, A.S., & Jacobson, N.S. (1986). *Clinical handbook of marital therapy*. New York: Guilford.

Hagermoser Sanetti, L.M., & DiGennaro Reed, F.D. (2011, May). Barriers to implementing treatment integrity procedures in school psychology research: Survey of treatment outcome researchers. In C. St. Peter Pipkin (Chair), *Current Issues in Caregiver Training and Treatment Integrity*. Symposium conducted at the annual meeting of the Association for Behavior Analysis International, Denver, CO.

Haines, A., & Jones, R. (1994, 4 Jun). Implementing findings of research. *British Medical Journal, 308*(6942), 1488–92. http://dx.doi.org/10.1136/bmj.308.6942.1488 Medline:8019284

Hanrahan, P., & Reid, W.J. (1984). Choosing effective interventions. *Social Service Review, 58*(2), 244–58. http://dx.doi.org/10.1086/644190

Hardcastle, D.A., & Bisman, C.D. (2003). Innovations in teaching social work. *Social Work Education, 22*(1), 31–43. http://dx.doi.org/10.1080/02615470309131

Hartley, D., & Strupp, H.H. (1983). The therapeutic alliance: It's relationship to outcome in brief psychotherapy. In J. Masling (Ed.), *Empirical studies of psychoanalytic theories* (Vol. 1, p. 138). Hillsdale, NJ: Lawrence Erlbaum.

Hayes, S.C. (2004a). Acceptance and commitment therapy and the new behaviour therapies. In S.C. Hayes, V.M. Follette, & M.M. Linehan (Eds.), *Mindfulness and acceptance: Expanding the cognitive-behavioral tradition* (pp. 1–29). New York: Guilford.

Hayes, S.C. (2004b). Acceptance and commitment therapy, relational frame theory, and the third wave behavioral and cognitive therapies. *Behavior Therapy, 35*(4), 639–65. http://dx.doi.org/10.1016/S0005-7894(04)80013-3

Hayes, S.C., Strosahl, K.D., & Wilson, K.G. (1999). *Acceptance and commitment therapy: An experiential approach to behavior change*. New York: Guilford.

Health Canada. (2002). *A statistical profile on the health of first nations in Canada*. Ottawa: Health Canada.

Heath, A. (1976). *Rational choice & social exchange: A critique of exchange theory.* Cambridge: Cambridge University Press.

Heinssen, R.K., Liberman, R.P., & Kopelowicz, A. (2000). Psychosocial skills training for schizophrenia: lessons from the laboratory. *Schizophrenia Bulletin, 26*(1), 21–46. http://dx.doi.org/10.1093/oxfordjournals.schbul.a033441 Medline:10755668

Henretty, J.R., Levitt, H.M., & Mathews, S.S. (2008, May). Clients' experiences of moments of sadness in psychotherapy: A grounded theory analysis. *Psychotherapy Research, 18*(3), 243–55. http://dx.doi.org/10.1080/10503300701765831 Medline:18815977

Ho, D.Y.F. (1995). Internalized culture, culturocentrism, and transcendence. *Counseling Psychologist, 23*(1), 4–24. http://dx.doi.org/10.1177/0011000095231002

Hollin, C.R. & Trower, P. (Eds.). (1986). *Handbook of social skills training* (2 vols.) Oxford: Pergamon.

Homans, G.C. (1958). Social behaviour as exchange. *American Journal of Sociology, 63*(6), 597–606. http://dx.doi.org/10.1086/222355

Horyn, C. (2007, 7 May). Fashion industry rallies to aid designer in trouble. *New York Times.* Retrieved 10 Apr 2009, from http://www.nytimes.com/2007/05/07/nyregion/07narciso.html?pagewanted+all.

Howard, K.I., Krause, M.S., & Orlinsky, D.E. (1986, Feb). The attrition dilemma: Toward a new strategy for psychotherapy research. *Journal of Consulting and Clinical Psychology, 54*(1), 106–10. http://dx.doi.org/10.1037/0022-006X.54.1.106 Medline:3958294

Hsu, F.L.K. (1971). Psychosocial homeostasis and *jen*: Conceptual tools for advancing psychological anthropology. *American Anthropologist, 73*(1), 23–44. http://dx.doi.org/10.1525/aa.1971.73.1.02a00030

Hubble, M.A., Duncan, B.L., & Miller, S.D. (Eds.) (1999). *The heart & soul of change: What works in psychotherapy.* Washington, DC: American Psychological Association. http://dx.doi.org/10.1037/11132-000

Hubble, M.A., Duncan, B.L., Miller, S.D., & Wampold, B.E. (2010). Introduction. In B.L. Duncan, S.D. Miller, B.E. Wampold, & M.A. Hubble (Eds.), *The heart & soul of change: Delivering what works in therapy* (2nd ed., pp. 23–46). Washington, DC: American Psychological Association. http://dx.doi.org/10.1037/12075-001

Hughes, J.N., & Hall, R.J. (1987). Proposed model for the assessment of children's social competence. *Professional School Psychology, 2*(4), 247–60. http://dx.doi.org/10.1037/h0090544

Hughes, J.N., & Sullivan, K.A. (1988). Outcomes assessment in social skills training with children. *Journal of School Psychology, 26*(2), 167–83. http://dx.doi.org/10.1016/0022-4405(88)90018-0

Human Resources Development Canada. (2003, Mar). Evaluation of the national homelessness initiative: Implementation and early outcomes of the HRDC-based components. Retrieved 10 Apr 2009, from http://publications.gc.ca/collections/Collection/RH63-2-203-03-03E.pdf.

Hurd Clarke, L. (2002). Older women's perceptions of ideal body weights: The tensions between health and appearance motivations for weight loss. *Ageing and Society*, 22(6), 751–73. http://dx.doi.org/10.1017/S0144686X02008905

Illouz, E. (1997). *Consuming the romantic utopia: Love and cultural contradictions of capitalism*. Berkeley: University of California Press.

Ilsley, P.J. (1992). The undeniable link: Adult and continuing education and social change. *New Directions for Adult and Continuing Education*, 54, 25–34. http://dx.doi.org/10.1002/ace.36719925405

Irving, H. (2002a). *Family mediation: Theory and practice with Chinese families*. Hong Kong: Hong Kong University Press.

Irving, H. (2002b). *Therapeutic family mediation*. Boston, MA: Sage Publications.

Irving, H., & Benjamin, M. (1995). *Family mediation: Contemporary issues*. Boston, MA: Sage Publications.

Irving, H., & Benjamin, M. (2002). *Therapeutic family mediation: Helping families resolve conflict*. Thousand Oaks, CA: Sage.

Israel, B.A., Eng, E., Schulz, A.J., & Parker, E.A. (Eds.). (2005). *Methods in community-based participatory research for health*. San Francisco: Jossey-Bass.

Iwakabe, S., Rogan, K., & Stalikas, A. (2000). The relationship between client emotional expressions, therapist interventions, and the working alliance: An exploration of eight emotional expression events. *Journal of Psychotherapy Integration*, 10(4), 375–401. http://dx.doi.org/10.1023/A:1009479100305

Jacobson, N.S., & Margolin, G. (1979). *Marital therapy strategies based on social learning and behavior exchange principles*. New York: Brunner/Mazel.

Jakubowski, S.F., Milne, E.P., Brunner, H., & Miller, R.B. (2004). A review of empirically supported marital enrichment programs. *Family Relations*, 53(5), 528–36. http://dx.doi.org/10.1111/j.0197-6664.2004.00062.x

Joyce, A., Piper, W.E., Ogrodniczuk, J.S., & Klein, R.H. (2007). *Termination in psychotherapy: A psychodynamic model of processes and outcomes*. Washington, DC: American Psychological Association. http://dx.doi.org/10.1037/11545-000

Kagan, N., Schauble, P., Resnikoff, A., Danish, S.J., & Krathwohl, D.R. (1969, Apr). Interpersonal process recall. *Journal of Nervous and Mental Disease*, 148(4), 365–74. http://dx.doi.org/10.1097/00005053-196904000-00004 Medline:5768914

Kamel, H.K. (2001). Sexuality in aging: Focus on institutionalized elderly. *Annals of Long-Term Care*, 9(5), 64–72.

Katzenstein, P.J. (Ed.). (1996). *The culture of national security: Norms and identity in world politics*. New York: Columbia University Press.

Kauffman, J.M. (2005). *Characteristics of emotional and behavioral disorders of children and youth* (8th ed.). Columbus, OH: Merrill Prentice Hall.

Kazantzis, N., Deane, F.P., Ronan, K.R., & L'Abate, L. (Eds.). (2005). *Using homework assignments in cognitive behavior therapy*. New York: Routledge.

Kazdin, A.E. (1977). Assessing the clinical or applied significance of behavior change through social validation. *Behavior Modification, 1*(4), 427–52. http://dx.doi.org/10.1177/014544557714001

Kiresuk, T., & Sherman, R. (1968). Goal attainment scaling: A general method for evaluating comprehensive community mental health programmes. *Community Mental Health Journal, 4*(6), 443–53. http://dx.doi.org/10.1007/BF01530764

Kiresuk, T., Smith, A., & Cardillo, J. (1994). *Goal attainment scaling: Applications, theory, and measurement*. London: Erlbaum.

Klein, W.C., & Bloom, M. (1995). Practice wisdom. *Social Work, 40*(6), 799–807.

Kleinman, A. (1982, Jun). Neurasthenia and depression: A study of somatization and culture in China. *Culture, Medicine and Psychiatry, 6*(2), 117–90. http://dx.doi.org/10.1007/BF00051427 Medline:7116909

Kleinman, A. (1986). *Social origins of distress and disease: Depression, neurasthenia, and pain in modern China*. New Haven, CT: Yale University Press.

Klohnen, E.C., & Luo, S. (2003, Oct). Interpersonal attraction and personality: What is attractive – self similarity, ideal similarity, complementarity or attachment security? *Journal of Personality and Social Psychology, 85*(4), 709–22. http://dx.doi.org/10.1037/0022-3514.85.4.709 Medline:14561124

Knapp, M.L., & Hall, J.A. (2007). *Nonverbal communication in human interaction* (5th ed.). Wadsworth: Thomas Learning.

Koester, L.S., Brooks, L., & Traci, M.A. (2000, Spring). Tactile contact by deaf and hearing mothers during face-to-face interactions with their infants. *Journal of Deaf Studies and Deaf Education, 5*(2), 127–39. http://dx.doi.org/10.1093/deafed/5.2.127 Medline:15454508

Kopelowicz, A., Liberman, R.P., & Zarate, R. (2006, Oct). Recent advances in social skills training for schizophrenia. *Schizophrenia Bulletin, 32*(Suppl 1), S12–S23. http://dx.doi.org/10.1093/schbul/sbl023 Medline:16885207

L'Abate, L. & Milan, M.A. (Eds.). (1985). *Handbook of social skills training and research*. New York: Wiley.

Lambert, M.J. (1992). Implications of outcome research for psychotherapy integration. In J.C. Norcross & M.R. Goldfried (Eds.), *Handbook of psychotherapy integration* (pp. 94–129). New York: Basic Books.

Lambert, M.J., & Barley, D.E. (2002). Research summary on the therapeutic relationship and psychotherapy outcome. In J.C. Norcross (Ed.), *Psychotherapy relationships that work* (pp. 17–32). New York: Oxford University Press. http://dx.doi.org/10.1037//0033-3204.38.4.357

Lambert, M.J., Shapiro, D.A., & Bergin, A.E. (1986). The effectiveness of psychotherapy. In S.L. Garfield & A.E. Bergin (Eds.), *Handbook of psychotherapy and behavior change* (3rd ed., pp. 157–212). New York: Wiley.

Landrum, T.J., & Lloyd, J.W. (1992, Oct). Generalization in social behavior research with children and youth who have emotional or behavioral disorders. *Behavior Modification*, 16(4), 593–616. http://dx.doi.org/10.1177/01454455920164009 Medline:1417716

Larsen, D., Flesaker, K., & Stege, R. (2008). Qualitative interviewing using interpersonal process recall: Investigating internal experiences during professional-client conversations. *International Journal of Qualitative Methods*, 7(1), 18–37.

Leahy, R.L. (1996). *Cognitive therapy: Basic principles and applications*. Northvale, NJ: Jason Aronson.

Leahy, R.L. (Ed.). (1997). *Practicing cognitive therapy: A guide to interventions*. Northvale, NJ: Jason Aronson.

Leiman, M. (1992, Sep). The concept of sign in the work of Vygotsky, Winnicott and Bakhtin: Further integration of object relations theory and activity theory. *British Journal of Medical Psychology*, 65(3), 209–221. http://dx.doi.org/10.1111/j.2044-8341.1992.tb01701.x Medline:1390355

Lee, J.A. (1990). Can we talk? Can we *really* talk? Communication as a key factor in the maturing homosexual couple. *Journal of Homosexuality*, 20(3-4), 143–68. http://dx.doi.org/10.1300/J082v20n03_10 Medline:2086645

Levitt, H.M., & Rennie, D.L. (2004). Narrative activity: Clients' and therapists' intentions in the process of narration. In L.E. Angus & J. McLeod (Eds.), *The handbook of narrative and therapy* (pp. 298–314). Thousand Oaks, CA: Sage. http://dx.doi.org/10.4135/9781412973496.d23

Liberman, R.P., DeRisi, W.J., & Mueser, K.T. (1989). *Social skills training for psychiatric patients*. Boston, MA: Allyn & Bacon.

Lin, Y.N. (2002). The application of cognitive-behavioral therapy to counseling Chinese. *American Journal of Psychotherapy*, 56(1), 46–58. http://csrp1.hku.hk/files/970_3880_1003.pdf Medline:11977783

Linehan, M.M. (1993). *Cognitive-behavioral treatment of borderline personality disorder*. New York: Guilford.

Luborsky, L., & Crits-Christoph, P. (1988). Measures of psychoanalytic concepts – the last decade of research from "the Penn studies." *International Journal of Psycho-Analysis*, 69(Pt 1), 75–86. Medline:3403154

Lynch, M.T., Zhang, L., & Korr, W.S. (2009). Research training, institutional support, and self-efficacy: Their impact on research activity of social workers. *Administration in Social Work, 10*(2), 193–210.

Maddux, J.E. (1995). *Self-efficacy, adaptation, and adjustment: Theory, research, and application.* New York, NY: Plenum Press.

Maag, J.W. (2006). Social skills training for students with emotional and behavioral disorders: A review of reviews. *Behavioral Disorders, 32*(1), 5–17.

Mahler, M.S. (1963). Thoughts about development and individuation. *Psychoanalytic Study of the Child, 18*, 307–24. Medline:14147283

Mahler, M.S. (1972). On the first three subphases of the separation-individuation process. *International Journal of Psycho-Analysis, 53*(Pt 3), 333–8. Medline:4499978

Mahler, M.S., & Furer, M. (1968). *On human symbiosis and the vicissitudes of individuation.* New York: International Universities Press.

Mahler, M.S., Pine, F., & Bergman, A. (1975). *The psychological birth of the human infant.* New York: Basic Books.

Mahoney, M.J. (1974). *Cognition and behavior modification.* Cambridge, MA: Ballinger.

Marshall, M. (2002). Randomised controlled trials: Misunderstanding, fraud and spin. In S. Priebe & M. Slade (Eds.), *Evidence in mental health care* (pp. 59–71). Hove: Brunner-Routledge.

Martin, D.J., Garske, J.P., & Davis, M.K. (2000, Jun). Relation of the therapeutic alliance with outcome and other variables: A meta-analytic review. *Journal of Consulting and Clinical Psychology, 68*(3), 438–50. http://dx.doi.org/10.1037/0022-006X.68.3.438 Medline:10883561

Maslow, A.H. (1943). A theory of human motivation. *Psychological Review, 50*(4), 370–96. http://dx.doi.org/10.1037/h0054346

Maslow, A.H. (1971). *The farther reaches of human nature.* New York: Penguin.

Mathur, S.R., & Rutherford, R.B., Jr. (1996). Is social skills training effective for students with emotional or behavioural disorders? *Behavioral Disorders, 22*(1), 21–8.

Meichenbaum, D.H. (1977). *Cognitive-behavior modification: An integrative approach.* New York: Plenum.

Meichenbaum, D. (1986). Cognitive behaviour modification. In F.H. Kanter & A.P. Goldstein (Eds.), *Helping people change* (pp. 346–81). New York: Pergamon Press.

Merriam, S.B., & Brockett, R.G. (1997). *The profession and practice of adult education.* San Francisco: Jossey-Bass.

Merrell, K.W. (2001). Assessment of children's social skills: Recent developments, best practices, and new directions. *Exceptionality, 9*(1&2), 3–18.

Miller, G., Yang, J., & Chen, M. (1997). Counseling Taiwan Chinese in America:

Training issues for counselors. *Counselor Education and Supervision, 37*(1), 22–34. http://dx.doi.org/10.1002/j.1556-6978.1997.tb00528.x

Miller, K. (2005). *Communication theories*. New York: McGraw-Hill.

Miller, S.D., Duncan, B.L., & Hubble, M.A. (2005). Outcome informed clinical work. In J. Norcross & M. Goldfried (Eds.), *Handbook of psychotherapy integration* (2nd ed., pp. 84–102). New York: Norton.

Miller, S.D., Hubble, M.A., & Duncan, B.L. (Eds.). (1996). *Handbook of solution-focused brief therapy*. San Francisco: Jossey-Bass.

Miller, W.R. (2000). Motivational Enhancement Therapy: Description of counseling approach. In J.J. Boren, L.S. Onken, & K.M. Carroll (Eds.), *Approaches to drug abuse counseling* (pp. 89–93). Washington, DC: National Institute on Drug Abuse.

Miller, W.R., & Rollnick, S. (2002). *Motivation interviewing: Preparing people for change* (2nd ed.). New York: Guilford.

Miller, W.R., Zweben, A., DiClemente, C.C., & Rychtarik, R.G. (1995). *Motivational enhancement therapy manual* (Project MATCH Monograph Series, Vol. 2). Washington, DC: National Institute on Alcohol Abuse and Alcoholism.

Morrow-Bradley, C., & Elliott, R. (1986, Feb). Utilization of psychotherapy research by practicing psychotherapists. *American Psychologist, 41*(2), 188–97. http://dx.doi.org/10.1037/0003-066X.41.2.188 Medline:3963612

Moxnes, K. (2003). Risk factors in divorce: Perceptions by the children involved. *Childhood, 10*(2), 131–46. http://dx.doi.org/10.1177/0907568203010002002

Murray, S.L., Holmes, J.G., & Collins, N.L. (2006, Sep). Optimizing assurance: The risk regulation system in relationships. *Psychological Bulletin, 132*(5), 641–66. http://dx.doi.org/10.1037/0033-2909.132.5.641 Medline:16910746

Murray, S.L., Holmes, J.G., & Griffin, D.W. (2000, Mar). Self-esteem and the quest for felt security: How perceived regard regulates attachment processes. *Journal of Personality and Social Psychology, 78*(3), 478–98. http://dx.doi.org/10.1037/0022-3514.78.3.478 Medline:10743875

Murray, S.L., Rose, P., Holmes, J.G., Derrick, J., Podchaski, E.J., Bellavia, G., & Griffin, D.W. (2005, Feb). Putting the partner within reach: A dyadic perspective on felt security in close relationships. *Journal of Personality and Social Psychology, 88*(2), 327–47. http://dx.doi.org/10.1037/0022-3514.88.2.327 Medline:15841862

Nanyang, R.P., & Hughes, J.N. (2002). Differential benefits of skills training with antisocial youth based on group composition: A meta-analytic investigation. *School Psychology Review, 31*, 164–85.

Norcross, J.C. (2010). The therapeutic relationship. In B.L. Duncan, S.D. Miller, B.E. Wampold, & M.A. Hubble (Eds.), *The heart & soul of change: Delivering what works in therapy* (2nd ed., pp. 113–41). Washington, DC: American Psychological Association. http://dx.doi.org/10.1037/12075-004

Norcross, J.C., Prochaska, J.O., & Gallagher, K.M. (1989). Clinical psychologists in the 1980s: II. Theory, research and practice. *Clinical Psychologist*, 42(3), 45–53.

O'Gorman, R., Wilson, D.S., & Miller, R.R. (2008). An evolved cognitive bias for social norms. *Evolution and Human Behavior*, 29(2), 71–78. http://dx.doi.org/10.1016/j.evolhumbehav.2007.07.002

Ontario Aboriginal Health Advocacy Initiative. (2003). *Aboriginal access to health care systems*. Toronto: Ontario Aboriginal Health Advocacy Initiative.

Orme, J., & Powell, J. (2008). Building research capacity in social work: Process and issues. *British Journal of Social Work*, 38(5), 988–1008. http://dx.doi.org/10.1093/bjsw/bcm122

Otnes, C.C., & Pleck, E.H. (2002). *Cinderella dreams: The allure of the lavish wedding*. Berkeley: University of California Press.

Otto, H., Polutta, A., & Ziegler, H. (2009). Reflexive professionalism as a second generation of evidence-based practice: Some considerations on the special issue "What works? Modernizing the knowledge-base of social work." *Research on Social Work Practice*, 19(4), 472–8. http://dx.doi.org/10.1177/1049731509333200

Pajares, F. (1997). Current directions in self-efficacy research. In M. Maehr & P.R. Pintrich (Eds.), *Advances in motivation and achievement* (Vol. 10, pp. 1–49). Greenwich, CT: JAI Press.

Palincsar, A.S. (1998). Social constructivist perspectives on teaching and learning. *Annual Review of Psychology*, 49(1), 345–75. http://dx.doi.org/10.1146/annurev.psych.49.1.345 Medline:15012472

Parker, J.G., & Asher, S.R. (1987, Nov). Peer relations and later personal adjustment: Are low-accepted children at risk? *Psychological Bulletin*, 102(3), 357–89. http://dx.doi.org/10.1037/0033-2909.102.3.357 Medline:3317467

Pavlov, I. (1927). *Conditioned reflexes*. Oxford: Oxford University Press.

Perepletchikova, F., Hilt, L.M., Chereji, E., & Kazdin, A.E. (2009, Apr). Barriers to implementing treatment integrity procedures: Survey of treatment outcome researchers. *Journal of Consulting and Clinical Psychology*, 77(2), 212–18. http://dx.doi.org/10.1037/a0015232 Medline:19309181

Perez, P.J. (1996). Tailoring a collaborative, constructionist approach for the treatment of same sex couples. *Family Journal*, 4(1), 73–81. http://dx.doi.org/10.1177/1066480796041016

Pfeiffer, J.W. & Jones, J.E. (Eds.). (1974). *A handbook of structured experiences for human relations training* (Vol. 1). San Diego, CA: University Associates Publishers and Consultants.

Philips, B., Werbart, A., Wennberg, P., & Schubert, J. (2007, Mar). Young adults' ideas of cure prior to psychoanalytic psychotherapy. *Journal of Clinical Psychology, 63*(3), 213–32. http://dx.doi.org/10.1002/jclp.20342 Medline:17211871

Polkinghorne, D.E. (1992). Postmodern epistemology of practice. In S. Kvale (Ed.), *Psychology and postmodernism* (pp. 146–65). London: Sage.

Pope, B. (1986). *Social skills training for psychiatric nurses*. London: Harper & Row.

Potter, J. (1996). *Representing reality: Discourse, rhetoric and social construction*. Thousand Oaks, CA: Sage.

Potter, S.H. (1988). The cultural construction of emotion in rural Chinese social life. *Ethos, 16*(2), 181–208. http://dx.doi.org/10.1525/eth.1988.16.2.02a00050

Quinn, M.M., Kavale, K.A., Mathur, S.R., Rutherford, R.B., & Forness, S.R. (1999). A meta-analysis of social skill interventions for students with emotional and behavioral disorders. *Journal of Emotional and Behavioral Disorders, 7*(1), 54–64. http://dx.doi.org/10.1177/106342669900700106

Reardon-Anderson, J., Stagner, M., Macomber, J.E., & Murray, J. (2005). Systematic review of the impact of marriage and relationship programs. (U.S. Department of Health and Human Services, Administration for Children and Families). Retrieved 11 Feb 2009, from http://www.acf.hhs.gov/programs/opre/strengthen/serv_delivery/reports/systematic_rev/sys_title.html.

Reason, P., & Rowan, J. (Eds.). (1981). *Human inquiry: A sourcebook of new paradigm research*. London: Wiley.

Rennie, D.L. (2000). Aspects of the client's conscious control of the psychotherapeutic process. *Journal of Psychotherapy Integration, 10*(2), 151–67. http://dx.doi.org/10.1023/A:1009496116174

Rennie, D.L., & Toukmanian, S.G. (1992). Explanation in psychotherapy process research. In S.G. Toukmanian & D.L. Rennie (Eds.), *Psychotherapy process research: Paradigmatic and narrative approaches* (pp. 234–51). Newbury Park, CA: Sage.

Richerson, P.J., & Boyd, R. (2005). *Not by genes alone: How culture transformed human evolution*. Chicago: University of Chicago Press.

Robinson, L.A., Berman, J.S., & Neimeyer, R.A. (1990, Jul). Psychotherapy for the treatment of depression: a comprehensive review of controlled outcome research. *Psychological Bulletin, 108*(1), 30–49. http://dx.doi.org/10.1037/0033-2909.108.1.30 Medline:2200072

Rogers, C. (1961). *On becoming a person: A therapist's view of psychotherapy*. London: Constable.

Rogers, E. (1995). *Diffusion of innovations* (4th ed.). New York: The Free Press.

Rosen, A. (1994). Knowledge use in direct practice. *Social Service Review, 68*(4), 561–77. http://dx.doi.org/10.1086/604084

Rosen, A. (2003). Evidence-based social work practice: Challenges and promise. *Social Work Research, 27*(4), 197–256. http://dx.doi.org/10.1093/swr/27.4.197

Rosen, A., Proctor, E.K., Morrow-Howell, N., & Staudt, M. (1995). Rationales for practice decisions: Variations in knowledge use by decision task and social work service. *Research on Social Work Practice, 5*(4), 501–23. http://dx.doi.org/10.1177/104973159500500408

Rosenberg, E.L. (1998). Levels of analysis and the organization of affect. *Review of General Psychology, 2*(3), 247–70.

Roth, A. & Fonagy, P. (Eds.). (1996). *What works for whom? A critical review of psychotherapy research.* New York: Guilford.

Rothwell, P.M. (2005, Jan 1–7). External validity of randomised controlled trials: "To whom do the results of this trial apply?" *Lancet, 365*(9453), 82–93. http://dx.doi.org/10.1016/S0140-6736(04)17670-8 Medline:15639683

Rushton, J.P., Bons, T.A., & Hur, Y.M. (2008). The genetics and evolution of the general factor of personality. *Journal of Research in Personality, 42*(5), 1173–85. http://dx.doi.org/10.1016/j.jrp.2008.03.002

Rutherford, R.B., Jr., & Nelson, C.M. (1988). Generalization and maintenance of treatment effects. In J.C. Witt, S.W. Elliott, & F.M. Gresham (Eds.), *Handbook of behavior therapy in education* (pp. 277–324). New York: Plenum Press.

Salter, A. (1949). *Conditioned reflex therapy: The direct approach to the reconstruction of personality.* Oxford: Creative Age Press.

Scarr, S., & McCartney, K. (1983, Apr). How people make their own environments: A theory of genotype → environment effects. *Child Development, 54*(2), 424–35. Medline:6683622

Schachter, S., & Singer, J.E. (1962, Sep). Cognitive, social, and physiological determinants of emotional state. *Psychological Review, 69*(5), 379–99. http://dx.doi.org/10.1037/h0046234 Medline:14497895

Schofield, W. (1964). *Psychotherapy: The purchase of friendship.* Englewood Cliffs, NJ: Prentice-Hall.

Schwartz, R.M., & Gottman, J.M. (1976, Dec). Toward a task analysis of assertive behavior. *Journal of Consulting and Clinical Psychology, 44*(6), 910–20. http://dx.doi.org/10.1037/0022-006X.44.6.910 Medline:993429

Segal, L. (1994). *Straight sex: The politics of pleasure.* London: Virago.

Segal, Z.V., Williams, J.M.G., & Teasdale, J.D. (2002). *Mindfulness-based cognitive therapy for depression: A new approach to preventing relapse.* New York: Guilford.

Seligman, M.E.P. (1974). Depression and learned helplessness. In R.J. Friedman & M.M. Katz (Eds.), *The Psychology of depression: Contemporary theory and research* (pp. 83–113). Washington, DC: Winston-Wiley.

Seligman, M.E.P. (1991). *Helplessness: On depression, development, and death* (2nd ed.). New York: W.H. Freeman.

Shapiro, D.A., & Shapiro, D. (1982, Nov). Meta-analysis of comparative therapy outcome studies: A replication and refinement. *Psychological Bulletin, 92*(3), 581–604. http://dx.doi.org/10.1037/0033-2909.92.3.581 Medline:7156259

Shaugnessy, A.F., Slanson, D.C., & Bennett, J.H. (1994). Becoming an information master: A guidebook to the medical information jungle. *Journal of Family Practice, 39*(5), 489–99.

Singer, D. (2007). The political economy of psychotherapy. *New Politics, XI*(2). Retrieved 6 Aug 2011, from http://newpolitics.mayfirst.org/node/195

Singleton, W.T., Spurgeon, P., & Stammers, R.B. (Eds.). (1979). *The analysis of social skills*. New York: Plenum.

Skinner, B.F. (1938). *The behaviour of organisms*. New York: Appleton-Century-Crofts.

Skinner, B.F. (1953). *Science and human behavior*. New York: Free Press.

Smith, M.J. (1975). *When I say no, I feel guilty*. New York: Bantam Books.

Smith, S.W., & Travis, P.C. (2001). Conducting social competence research: Considering conceptual frameworks. *Behavioral Disorders, 26*(4), 360–9.

Stajkovic, A.D., & Luthans, F. (1998). Self-efficacy and work-related performance: A meta-analysis. *Psychological Bulletin, 124*(2), 240–61. http://dx.doi.org/10.1037/0033-2909.124.2.240

Stokes, T.F., & Baer, D.M. (1977, Summer). An implicit technology of generalization. *Journal of Applied Behavior Analysis, 10*(2), 349–67. http://dx.doi.org/10.1901/jaba.1977.10-349 Medline:16795561

Strain, P.S. (2001). Empirically based social skills intervention: A case for quality-of-life improvement. *Behavioral Disorders, 27*(1), 30–6.

Strelan, P. (2007). The prosocial, adaptive qualities of just world beliefs: Implications for the relationship between justice and forgiveness. *Personality and Individual Differences, 43*(4), 881–90. http://dx.doi.org/10.1016/j.paid.2007.02.015

Taleb, T.N. (2005). *The black swan: the impact of the highly improbable*. New York: Random House.

Tanenbaum, S. (2003, May). Evidence-based practice in mental health: Practical weaknesses meet political strengths. *Journal of Evaluation in Clinical Practice, 9*(2), 287–301. http://dx.doi.org/10.1046/j.1365-2753.2003.00409.x Medline:12787192

Tillich, P. (1973). *Systematic theology* (Vol. 1). Chicago: University of Chicago Press.

Trower, P., Bryant, B., & Argyle, M. (1978). *Social skills and mental health*. London: Methuen.

Truan, F. (1993, Sep). Addiction as a social construction: A postempirical view. *Journal of Psychology, 127*(5), 489–99. http://dx.doi.org/10.1080/00223980.1993.9914886 Medline:8271227

Tsang, A.K.T. (1979). *Community participation scale*. Unpublished manuscript.

Tsang, A.K.T. (1995). *Negotiation of therapy agenda: Development of a process coding system* (Unpublished doctoral dissertation). University of Toronto.

Tsang, A.K.T. (2000). Bridging the gap between clinical practice and research: An integrated practice-oriented model. *Journal of Social Service Research, 26*(4), 69–90. http://dx.doi.org/10.1080/01488370009511337

Tsang, A.K.T. (2008). *Psychotherapy integration and beyond: The MCM model*. Retrieved 29 Mar 2009, from http://kttsang.com/about/mcm/Brief_Intro_to_MCM.pdf

Tsang, A.K.T. (2009, Dec). *Evidence-based practice in social work*. Keynote lecture at the International Conference on Globalization and Family Changes: Policy Implications, Service Initiatives and Evidence based Practice. Chinese University of Hong Kong.

Tsang, A.K.T. (2011a). *Community Participation Scale (revised)*. Unpublished manuscript.

Tsang, A.K.T. (2011b). *EBP 3.0 for practice research*. Unpublished manuscript.

Tsang, A.K.T., & Bogo, M. (1997). Engaging with clients cross-culturally: Towards developing research-based practice. *Journal of Multicultural Social Work, 6*(3/4), 73–91.

Tsang, A.K.T., Bogo, M., & George, U. (2003). Critical issues in cross-cultural counseling research: Case example of an ongoing project. *Journal of Multicultural Counseling and Development, 31*(1), 63–78. http://dx.doi.org/10.1002/j.2161-1912.2003.tb00532.x

Tsang, A.K.T., Bogo, M., & Lee, E. (2010). Engagement in cross-cultural clinical practice: Narrative analysis of first sessions. *Clinical Social Work Journal, 39*(1), 77–90.

Tsang, A.K.T., George, U., & Bogo, M. (1997). *Three key issues evaluation (3-KIE)*. Toronto: Faculty of Social Work, University of Toronto.

Tsang, A.K.T., & George, U. (1998). Towards an integrated framework for cross-cultural social work practice. *Canadian Social Work Review, 15*(1), 73–93.

Tsang, A.K.T., Irving, H., Alaggia, R., Chau, S.B.Y., & Benjamin, M. (2003). Negotiating ethnic identity in Canada: The case of the "satellite children." *Youth & Society, 34*(3), 359–84. http://dx.doi.org/10.1177/0044118X02250124

Vachon, D.O., Susman, M., Wynne, M.E., Birringer, J., Olshefsky, L., & Cox, K. (1995). Reasons therapists give for refusing to participate in psychotherapy process research. *Journal of Counseling Psychology, 42*(3), 380–2. http://dx.doi.org/10.1037/0022-0167.42.3.380

Vernon, P.A., Petrides, K.V., Bratko, D., & Schermer, J.A. (2008, Oct). A behavioral genetic study of trait emotional intelligence. *Emotion, 8*(5), 635–42. http://dx.doi.org/10.1037/a0013439 Medline:18837613

Wakefield, J.C., & Kirk, S.A. (1996). Unscientific thinking about scientific practice: Evaluating the scientist-practitioner model. *Social Work Research, 20*(2), 83–95.

Wampold, B.E., Minami, T., Baskin, T.W., & Callen Tierney, S. (2002, Apr). A meta-(re)analysis of the effects of cognitive therapy versus "other therapies" for depression. *Journal of Affective Disorders, 68*(2-3), 159–65. http://dx.doi.org/10.1016/S0165-0327(00)00287-1 Medline:12063144

Warner, R. (2004). *Recovering from schizophrenia: Psychiatry and political economy* (3rd ed.). New York: Brunner-Routledge.

Watson, J.B. (1925). *Behaviorism*. New York: Norton.

Williams White, S., Keonig, K., & Scahill, L. (2007, Nov). Social skills development in children with autism spectrum disorders: A review of the intervention research. *Journal of Autism and Developmental Disorders, 37*(10), 1858–68. http://dx.doi.org/10.1007/s10803-006-0320-x Medline:17195104

Winnicott, D.W. (1971). *Playing and reality*. London: Tavistock.

Wiseman, H. (1992). Conceptually-based interpersonal process recall (IPR) of change events: What clients tell us about our micro theory of change. In S.G. Toukmanian & D.L. Rennie (Eds.), *Psychotherapy process research: Paradigmatic and narrative approaches* (pp. 51–76). Newbury Park, CA: Sage.

Wolberg, L.R. (1986). *The technique of psychotherapy* (4th ed.). Philadelphia: Grune & Stratton.

Wolf, M.M. (1978, Summer). Social validity: the case for subjective measurement or how applied behavior analysis is finding its heart. *Journal of Applied Behavior Analysis, 11*(2), 203–14. http://dx.doi.org/10.1901/jaba.1978.11-203 Medline:16795590

Wolpe, J. (1958). *Psychotherapy by reciprocal inhibition*. Stanford: Stanford University Press.

Wolpe, J., & Rachman, S. (1960, Aug). Psychoanalytic "evidence": A critique based on Freud's case of Little Hans. *Journal of Nervous and Mental Disease, 131*(2), 135–48. http://dx.doi.org/10.1097/00005053-196008000-00007 Medline:13786442

Yeates, K.O., Bigler, E.D., Dennis, M., Gerhardt, C.A., Rubin, K.H., Stancin, T., Taylor, H.G., & Vannatta, K. (2007, May). Social outcomes in childhood brain disorder: A heuristic integration of social neuroscience and developmental psychology. *Psychological Bulletin, 133*(3), 535–56. http://dx.doi.org/10.1037/0033-2909.133.3.535 Medline:17469991

Yontef, G., & Simkin, J. (1993). *An introduction to gestalt therapy*. Behaviour on Line. Retrieved 29 March 2009, from http://www.behavior.net/gestalt.html

Zigler, E., & Phillips, L. (1961). Social competence and outcome in psychiatric disorder. *Journal of Abnormal and Social Psychology, 63*(2), 264–71. http://dx.doi.org/10.1037/h0046232

Zuckerman, A., & Mitchell, C.L. (2004). Psychology interns' perspectives on the forced termination of psychotherapy. *Clinical Supervisor, 23*(1), 55–70. http://dx.doi.org/10.1300/J001v23n01_04

Index

3-D appreciation exercise, 198–9
3-KIE (three key issues evaluation), 237
4Rs, 56, 57, 128, 131–2
10,000-hour rule, 48

abuse: and abuser, 166; experience of, 51, 52, 96, 220; physical, 83; sexual, 98, 196, 280, 292; substance, 47, 233
acceptance and commitment therapy (ACT), 7
acceptance, of emotions, 170, 171
accountability, 57, 299
achievement, 84, 183, 184, 206, 227, 249, 258; and need for, 71, 73, 75, 77
advocacy, 252
affect, 23, 105, 159, 175, 194
affiliation, 64, 72, 73, 75–6, 96, 119, 149, 175, 182, 206, 221, 281
agency, 74, 133, 170, 204, 221, 235, 239, 249, 258, 273, 281, 282, 291, 292
agenda management, 177, 178–9
alliance, working or therapeutic, 61–3, 266
anti-oppressive practice (AOP), 256, 262

anxiety disorder, 47, 252
Argyle, Michael, 6, 47, 70–1
art of the possible, the, 120–1
articulation: of emotional needs, 212, 169, 170, 212; of goals, 85–7, 225
Asia, Asian, 74, 152, 224, 225, 233, 252, 255, 277, 280, 293
assertiveness, 50, 173; training, 6, 44, 46, 173
assessment, 100, 101; individualized, personalized, 11; N3C, 183, 258, 281–2; of effectiveness, 10, 11, 101; and social skills training, 9; SSLD, 107, 116; tool, 100. *See also* needs assessment
asset, 245, 247
attachment, 13, 75, 193, 225
attraction: same-sex, 28
autism: children with, 34, 53, 109, 233, 251
autonomy, 74, 79, 82, 96, 133, 134, 135, 149, 206, 211, 235, 249, 258, 262, 277
awareness: of emotion and feelings, 169, 170, 171, 206, 211

B drives and D drives (Maslow), 201
Bandura, Albert, 6, 30, 33, 36, 81, 165
behaviour markers, 63–9, 85, 86, 88, 90, 91
behavioural diary, 92–4
behavioural disorder, 7, 8
behaviour-oriented functional analysis (BOFA), 63–9, 87
biology, 21, 22, 23, 25, 120, 287
body awareness, 253
body work, 253
brainstorming, 122, 123, 124

CAIRO assumption, 264–5, 268, 273, 277
capacity, 9, 13, 14, 15, 24, 49, 53, 56, 57, 82, 84, 92, 108, 111, 113, 116, 118, 120, 128, 132, 142, 143, 166, 181, 183, 185, 191, 192, 196, 200, 212, 213, 223, 227, 241, 243, 244, 251, 257, 258, 262, 275, 278, 281, 287, 292, 293, 294. *See also* N3C
capacity building, 231, 235, 242, 262
caregiver support: training and education of, 233, 241, 250, 252
case example, 19, 236
causal explanation. See *Erklären*
channelling: 169, 170
characteristic. *See* N3C
child protection, 33, 82, 83, 84
children leaving home, 208
China, 147, 162, 285, 286, 290
chronic health conditions, 252
circumstance. *See* N3C
client: as an agent, 266–7; empowerment of, 279; and needs profile, 72–3, 85-87; preparation, 279; strength and potential of, 107–8; system, 72, 79, 83, 120; variable, 287

client-centred orientation, 65–6
coaching, 6, 16, 33, 48, 53, 125, 141, 219, 244, 245, 246, 250, 252, 253, 259, 262, 278, 283
cognition, 16, 21, 22, 23, 26–9
cognitive behavioural therapy (CBT), 7, 26, 237
cognitive representation, 27, 81, 128, 204
collaboration, 18, 21, 35, 38, 61, 62, 63, 175, 229, 247, 257, 283, 296; client–practitioner, 18, 63; multidisciplinary, 247
collaborative creation: of new strategies and skills, 16, 18, 49, 117, 122–5, 133, 171, 228, 240, 262
collaborative creator, 16, 122–5
collaborative knowledge production, 273
collaborator, 97, 99, 100, 141, 161, 282
community: capacity audit, 258; cultural, 83, 161; leadership, 260–1; organization, 233, 247, 251, 261, 262, 284; work, 18, 254–63, 283
Community Participation Scale, 259, 262
compatibility, 17, 175, 176, 177, 178, 186, 190–1
competence, 5, 7, 13, 52, 53, 102, 142, 192, 200, 245, 246, 250, 283; interpersonal, 53, 142, 245, 246
composite skills, 102
confidentiality, 282
confrontation, 239
consultant, 20, 153, 228, 229, 233, 262
counselling, 247, 251, 253, 266, 290
counsellor, 15, 20, 29, 36, 54, 141, 153, 180, 209, 224, 246

couple, 15, 42, 66, 82, 83, 107, 110, 113, 115, 120, 153, 188, 195, 204, 252, 253, 276; abusive relationship, 200; counselling, 93, 105, 106, 117, 119, 120, 130 ,139, 141, 145, 147, 166, 169, 182, 190, 194, 196; dating, 194; divorce, 209; relationship, 210, 212, 233; same-sex, 138
creativity in relationships, 194
crisis management, 84
critical awareness, 82
critical thinking, 163
cross-cultural communication, 252

dark side, 196
death, 213–16
dementia, 110
demonstration, 6, 48, 50, 52, 53, 54, 129
depression, 29, 34, 45, 47, 190, 122–3, 126, 163, 208, 252, 263, 275, 276, 286
desire, 23, 25, 38, 72, 74, 79, 80, 81, 82, 83, 86, 89, 91, 146, 151; politics of, 69, 78
developmental challenges, 42, 45, 110, 167, 254
diabetes, 241, 252
dialectical behaviour therapy, 7, 237
diary, behavioural, 92–3, 94, 96, 131, 236
direct observation, 11, 52, 96, 97
disciplinary practices, 81
diversity, 9, 13, 15, 19, 136–9, 161–2, 164–5, 276–7, 293–4; cultural, 161, 162; sexual, 276, 293; working with intersecting diversities, 14, 19, 276–7
drive, 23, 25, 75, 76, 77
drug metaphor, 263, 264, 265, 266, 268

earthquake, 171, 193, 230; in Sichuan, 171, 290
eclecticism: epistemological, 270, 271, 273
emotion-focused therapy, 77
emotion work, 77, 168, 169, 170, 207, 211, 265
emotional significance, 193–4
emotions and feelings, 165–8
empathic and interpretive understanding. See *Verstehen*
empathy, 118, 179, 257
empowerment, 33, 35, 36, 40, 54, 79, 242, 262, 279, 291, 292
enactment, 54–6, 100
engagement, 61–3, 174
environment, 8, 14, 19, 21, 22, 23, 30, 31, 33, 37, 38, 54, 55, 68, 74, 79, 81, 101, 120, 130, 133, 155, 163, 164, 168, 175, 179, 182, 188, 196, 204, 205, 206, 220, 231, 240, 252, 287, 295; social, 79, 101, 188, 196
epistemological eclecticism, 271
equifinality, 47, 239, 241, 242, 274–5
equilibrium and homeostasis, 77
equity, 291–3
Erklären (causal explanation), 270
ethics, 255
evaluation, 29, 41, 57, 236, 237, 243
evidence-based practice (EBP), 8, 242, 263, 267, 269, 270, 290, 294, 295, 296; first generation (1.0), 271, 272; second generation (2.0), 270; third generation (3.0), 270–7
evocation, 122, 123
expectation management, 56, 179, 184
expert trainer model, 6
expression, 151–73; of emotions and feelings, 76–7, 146–7, 165–71; of

facts, 162–3; of ideas, 163–5; need for, 74–5; of needs, 81, 171–4; skills for, 138, 190; social realities, context and, 24, 25

family violence, 67, 84, 167, 280, 291
fear, 292
feedback, 13, 16, 23, 27, 31, 32, 46, 48, 54–6, 97, 99, 130–1, 155, 177, 179–81, 199, 260, 282, 283
fibromyalgia, 252, 253
Fiddler on the Roof (Joseph Stein), 148
finding commonalities and shared interests, 181–2
forgiveness, 215
free information, 90, 130, 230
front-desk, 153, 155, 178, 184, 233
frustration, 23, 24, 85, 158, 188, 249
functional analysis, 10, 61, 63, 64, 65, 83, 87

gender-analysis, 144
goal attainment scaling (GAS), 237
goals: articulation of, 61, 85–7, 225; setting of, 85
grief, 214–15
guilt-tripping, 173

homework exercise, 56, 131
hope, 216
human resource management, 252
humour, 159

identification, of emotion, 169
imitation, 48, 54
immigrant, immigration, 11, 42, 83, 84, 95, 103, 107, 142, 154, 208, 228, 252, 281; communities, 252, 261; settlement services, 233, 252; youth, 33, 286

incentive, 23
incremental learning, 41, 56, 120–1, 124, 132–3, 168
incrementalism, 56, 85–7, 112, 120–1, 122, 123, 132–3
inference, 68, 69, 71, 80, 85, 148, 157, 264
informed consent, 97, 98, 99, 282
insomnia, 92, 159, 180, 234, 239, 241, 247, 250, 252, 263, 278, 279
integration, 6, 258, 289
integration, social, 110, 111, 114, 252
internalized articulation, 249
international cross-cultural work, 252
international development agency, 70
Internet addiction, 233
interpersonal attraction, 157
interpersonal skills, 5, 38, 39, 50, 52, 53, 97, 147, 229, 230
interview: behaviour-focused, 87–91, 92; with client, 275; for a job, 38, 50, 99, 103, 184, 228; semi-structured, 10
intimacy, 18, 31, 36, 38, 42, 53, 75, 76, 105, 126, 137, 140, 150, 168, 171, 175, 189, 190, 191, 192, 193, 196, 206, 233

justice, social, 289

knowledge-action gap, 20, 26, 48, 53, 219, 228, 244
knowledge and power, 218, 222–3
knowledge base, multidisciplinary, 285
Korea, 19
Kvan, Eric, 286

leadership, 259; learning skills and tasks, 260
learning: cognitive, 48, 128; experiential, 48, 55, 113, 128, 130, 133, 223, 232, 238; group, 54, 98, 195, 219; module, 110, 111–12, 113, 114, 115, 116–19; objective, 48–9, 61, 97, 109–10, 111, 113, 114, 115, 116, 117, 118; paradigm, 38, 216, 235; skills, specific, 227–31; of strategies and skills, 32, 48–57, 291; style, 13, 17, 48, 53, 106, 116, 117, 223, 244, 250, 278; system, 201, 219
life course, personal, 201–3
life cycle, relationship, 201–3
life skills, 5, 6, 33, 38, 44, 64
life-world, 20–2, 201; redesign of, 212
linear categorical thinking, 46, 275–6, 277
listening triad exercise, 119, 145

maintaining positive outcome, 134
manageability, 85, 86, 121–2
mastery, 17, 21, 24, 37, 38, 39, 45, 46, 47, 48, 63, 68, 69, 74, 75, 100, 102, 133, 161, 169, 192, 211, 226, 228, 236, 238, 244, 246, 249, 292
matters of ultimate concern (Tillich), 195
maximizing shared interest, maximizing commonalities, 177, 181–5, 186
medical model, 38, 39, 264
mental illness, 7, 56, 86, 92, 107, 121, 242, 252
methodological pluralism, 270, 273–4
micro-processes, 23, 104, 105, 108, 109, 111, 112, 120, 130, 131, 137, 138, 139, 177, 229, 230, 231

mindfulness-based cognitive therapy, 7
modelling, 27, 33, 51, 52–4, 81, 121, 128, 165, 249. *See also* observation learning
modification, 14, 119, 123, 124, 252, 288
money, 23, 25, 77, 101, 150, 152, 159, 194
motivation, human, 18, 22–5
motivation interviewing, 239–40
motor-skill metaphor, 47–8
multiple contingencies modelling (MCM), 276
multiple contingencies thinking, 14, 15, 16, 17, 19, 21, 46–7, 231, 236, 240, 241, 242, 250, 264–6, 276, 277, 286, 288, 289, 292, 294, 295
mutual conditioning and transformation, 23, 29–32, 33, 37, 204
mutual self-enhancement, 200

N3C (needs, characteristics, circumstances, capacities), 15, 108, 116, 183, 241, 257–8, 281–2
narrative space, 62, 89, 91, 137, 139, 170, 176
needs: achievement, mastery, control, fulfilment, 75; actualization, transcendence, spiritual quest, 75; assessment of, 61, 63, 69–72, 83–4, 87; biological, survival, subsistence, 73; cognitive, meaning, order 76; connection, affiliation, community, intimacy, belonging, identity, 75–6; emotional, 76–7; hierarchy of (Maslow), 70, 201; and physical comfort, 74; physical safety, sense of security, stability, predictability, control, 74; pleasure, desire, 74;

politics of desire, 78, 79; profile, 61, 73, 83, 85, 86, 87, 190, 208; self-identity, self-esteem, agency, 74; socialization and internalization, 80–3; reference list, 72–7; token, 77; unconscious, 79–83
normalizing, 211–12
nourishment and maintenance: of relationships, 197–201

obesity, 22, 252
observation learning, 13, 27, 33, 46, 51, 53, 121, 124, 128, 165, 219, 248. *See also* modelling
operant conditioning, 7, 15, 30, 33, 237, 251
opportunity and marginalization, 84–5
oppression, 28, 84, 292
organizational development, 15, 252, 261–2

pain, 22, 38, 39, 126, 167, 172, 249, 263; emotional, 34, 37; management of, 253; psychological, 96
parenting, 13, 175, 200, 208, 212, 233, 275
peer support, 250
performance, 51, 67, 94, 99, 101, 102, 104, 105, 106, 125, 129, 130, 131, 133, 135, 138, 146, 154, 156, 161, 177, 218, 220, 228, 230, 231, 236, 238, 245, 253, 278, 279, 282, 285; real-life, 55, 132, 229; social, 97, 100, 185, 211, 248, 249, 292, 294
pervasive developmental disorders, 42, 107
physical appearance, 152, 155–6, 183
playback: of video, 6, 54, 55, 97, 143, 145, 177, 250, 282

pleasure, 23, 24, 34, 35, 38, 39, 45, 68, 72, 73, 74, 175, 183, 192, 197, 202, 208, 212, 238
pluralism, methodological, 270, 273–4
political economy, 25, 78, 258, 269, 271, 272
positive: expectancy, 85; reframing, 156, 157, 158, 159, 160, 181, 216, 231; responding, 177, 179–81, 186; self-statement, 156–60
post-professional era, 247
power, 33, 77, 254, 291–3
practice: professional, inter-subjective, 272–3; real-life, 46, 56, 112, 123, 125, 131, 132
practice-based evidence, 278
pragmatism, 271–80, 289–91
preplanned program, prepackaged program, 44–6, 49, 53, 65, 113, 115, 125
proactive health strategies (PHS), 241, 252, 253
problem translation, 37, 45, 46, 48–9, 61–94
production, knowledge, 268, 271, 272, 273, 274, 275, 285, 289
psychoanalytic theory, 74
psychological immunization, 121, 125
psychotherapy, types of (Wolberg), 243
public policy and social programs, 78

randomized controlled trials (RCT), 264, 267–8, 295, 296
rapport, 175
rational emotive therapy, 237
reactivity effect, 94

reciprocal determination, 22, 30; need gratification, 187–9
reciprocity, 164, 189
reconsideration, 215
reconstruction, cognitive, 42, 95; of emotion, 169
recording, audio, 98, 99; video, 6, 54, 55, 97, 98, 99, 130, 132, 155, 230, 250, 282
refinement, 13, 14, 27, 54, 55, 56, 123, 124, 131, 132, 230, 236, 254, 288
reflection, 105, 263, 274
rehearsal, 13, 46, 55, 123, 124, 125, 219, 228, 250
relationship: building of, 114, 138, 189–90, 191–3, 202; dysfunctional, 188, 189; functional, 190, 192; transformation of, 203–8
repertoire: of skills, 49, 115; of strategies and skills, 12, 15, 49, 108, 216, 246, 291, 293
report back, 56–7, 131–2
research: and knowledge building, 294–6; practice and, 268–9, 277–9; SSLD and, 263
resolution, of emotion, 169, 212, 215
respondent conditioning, 30, 33, 237
retrospective orientation, 215
review, 56–7
risk, risk taking, 56, 121, 125
role-play, 55, 97, 98, 99, 100, 105, 106, 112, 124, 133, 141, 142, 145, 149, 177, 184, 228, 282; in-session, 97–101, 129–31; reverse, 99–100
Romeo and Juliet (Shakespeare), 159, 160

schizophrenic disorder, 8, 63, 92, 102, 103, 143, 182, 184, 185, 233, 252, 261, 278
self-acceptance, 169
self-disclosure, strategic, 111, 177, 185–6
self-efficacy, 36, 45, 55, 57, 82, 100, 110, 124, 131, 157, 169
self-empowerment, 253
self-esteem, 45, 52, 157, 227, 249, 281
self-image, 22, 26, 27, 96, 126, 149, 222, 238, 281
self-introduction, 159–62, 185
self-presentation, 102, 103, 111, 153, 154–9, 161, 177, 228, 249, 294
self-report, 96, 97, 237, 296
seniors, 110, 250, 252, 285
separation-individualization (Mahler), 204
settlement counsellors, 228
settlement workers, 247
sexuality, 96, 196, 276, 285, 293
sharing, 138, 195–7
signifying acts, 146–8, 167, 171, 193–4, 195, 197, 202
simulation, 54–6, 97, 99, 123, 124, 133
skill, definition of, 49
social change, 78–9
social class bias, 6
social cognitive theory, 6, 22, 26, 28, 30, 41, 51, 80, 237
social exchange analysis, or social exchange thinking, 187, 188
social exchange theory, 187–8
social facilitation, 219
social learning theory, 6, 7, 15, 30, 237
social phobia, 31, 42, 47, 110, 111, 121, 153, 176, 247, 252, 278

social regulation, 78–9
social service, 281
social skills therapy, 6
social skills training (SST): addressing the challenges of, 10–12; application of, 7–8; brief review, 6–7; critique, 8–10; effectiveness, 8
social work, 18, 33, 235, 243, 247, 270, 285, 289, 294
social worker, 84, 246, 280, 290
socialization and internalization, 80–3
socio-economic development, 73
solution-focused therapy, 237, 238–9
South Asian, 84, 138
spirituality, 70
SSLD: basic premises and tenets, 32–8; compatability, 235; complexity, 236; conceptual advantage, theory, values, 39–40; features, 15; learning to become a practitioner, 244; logistics, 279; observability, 236–7; potential and limitation, 242–4; practical advantage, 41–3; practice, 79, 80, 82, 83, 87, 101, 110, 120, 121, 122, 129, 131, 132, 134, 135, 137, 148, 162, 168, 172, 192, 194, 197, 207, 214, 215, 219, 233–96; practitioner, practitioners, 16, 18, 20, 51, 62, 66, 78, 95, 117, 122, 127, 133, 134, 190, 193, 224, 228, 231, 236, 244–50, 253, 258, 277, 278, 283; relative advantage, 236; research and, 263; technical advantage of, 40–1; triability, 236; values, 232, 235, 289–94
standardization, the limits of, 11–12
stigmatization, 40, 41

stimulation, 23, 25, 27, 34, 175, 238; auto-, 13; sensory, 23, 34, 72, 73
stimuli, 30
strategy, definition of, 50
stress management, 39, 231, 253
stroke, 252
study group, 246, 250, 296
subjective experience and meaning, 64–5
suicide, 212, 275
supervision, 117, 244, 245, 246, 250, 278, 283, 296
symbolic mediation, 52–4, 129
systems theory, 274

team building, 252
temporal structures, 215
termination, of relationship, 203, 204, 205, 207, 209–13; of SSLD interview, 134–5
therapeutic family mediation (Irving), 209
therapeutic relationship, 255, 265, 266
Third Wave CBTs, 237
trainer, 6, 15, 17, 20, 40, 49, 51, 53, 57, 69, 101, 122, 129, 141, 153, 233
transfer of learning, 51
transformation, 138, 169, 203, 204–8, 209, 210, 213, 214, 216
transitional object, 77
trauma, 211
two-chair method, 100

unconscious needs, 79–83

Verstehen (empathic and interpretive understanding), 270

video recording and review, 97, 98, 130
volunteer, 67, 76, 104, 207

wants, 22, 25
web-based SSLD program, programs, 279

weight management, 219, 233, 241
well-being, 5, 29, 45, 76, 77, 157, 174, 180, 200, 221, 231

Yellow Earth (Chen Kaige), 147
youth, 233, 286